Statistics in Plain English

This introductory textbook provides an inexpensive, brief overview of statistics to help readers gain a better understanding of how statistics work and how to interpret them correctly. Each chapter describes a different statistical technique, ranging from basic concepts like central tendency and describing distributions to more advanced concepts such as *t* tests, regression, repeated-measures ANOVA, and factor analysis. Each chapter begins with a short description of the statistic and when it should be used. This is followed by a more in-depth explanation of how the statistic works. Finally, each chapter ends with an example of the statistic in use, and a sample of how the results of analyses using the statistic might be written up for publication. A glossary of statistical terms and symbols is also included. Using the author's own data and examples from published research and the popular media, the book is a straightforward and accessible guide to statistics.

New features in the fourth edition include:

- sets of work problems in each chapter with detailed solutions and additional problems online to help students test their understanding of the material;
- new "Worked Examples" to walk students through how to calculate and interpret the statistics featured in each chapter;
- new examples from the author's own data, published research, and the popular media to help students see how statistics are applied and written about in professional publications;
- many more examples, tables, and charts to help students visualize key concepts, clarify concepts, and demonstrate how statistics are used in the real world;
- a more logical flow, with correlation directly preceding regression, and a combined glossary appearing at the end of the book;
- a "Quick Guide to Statistics, Formulas, and Degrees of Freedom" at the start of the book, plainly outlining each statistic and when students should use them;
- greater emphasis on (and description of) effect size and confidence interval reporting, reflecting their growing importance in research across the social science disciplines;
- an expanded website at www.routledge.com/cw/urdan with PowerPoint presentations, chapter summaries, a new test bank, interactive problems and detailed solutions to the text's work problems, SPSS datasets for practice, links to useful tools and resources, and videos showing how to calculate statistics, how to calculate and interpret the appendices, and how to understand some of the more confusing tables of output produced by SPSS.

Statistics in Plain English, Fourth Edition is an ideal guide to statistics and research methods, for courses that use statistics taught at the undergraduate or graduate level, or as a reference tool for anyone interested in refreshing their memory on key statistical concepts. The research examples are from psychology, education, and other social and behavioral sciences.

Timothy C. Urdan is Professor of Psychology at Santa Clara University.

"Urdan's text provides exactly the right depth of information needed to understand statistical concepts from both a theoretical and practical perspective. His style of writing is extremely engaging and helpful as he balances his explanations of theory and analyses with many real world examples that help situate the practical application of the concepts and analyses."

—Robyn Cooper, Drake University, USA

"The book explains clearly many concepts in statistics and is written in an unintimidating and readable style. Both undergraduate and graduate students will find it helpful as an introduction to statistics."

—Bridget Sheng, Western Illinois University, USA

"This is a straight-forward and yet comprehensive treatment, providing students with a basic understanding of statistics in the social sciences without bogging them down with too many equations and complex examples."

—Robert M. Bernard, Concordia University, USA

"I know of no textbook on the market that even comes close to satisfying breadth of coverage/content readability/value for price point as does the Urdan text. ... My students continually tell me it is very helpful and easy to understand. ... The Website is a very useful tool ... Urdan writes very clearly and explains concepts at a level that is appropriate for multiple audiences, including undergraduate, graduate, and even academic audiences ... I like that Urdan uses a variety of examples as opposed to competing texts that limit their examples to specific disciplines."

—Catherine A. Roster, University of New Mexico, USA

"It is very clear and wherever possible uses normal, plain English. ... Simple terms are preferred to jargon and where key terms are introduced they are done so clearly. ... The online support materials ... provide useful additional tools for both students and lecturers. ... From the examples used it seems to be aimed at a variety of social science students ... Psychology, Childhood and Youth and Crime Studies. ... I would like to use the book and would encourage students to do so. It contains a lot they need to know in order to understand ... statistical tests."

—Nick Lund, Manchester Metropolitan University, UK

"Problem sets ... [are] a welcome addition. ... The interactive analyses, podcasts, PowerPoints and test questions are all a positive. ... The author understands the material quite well and does a good job explaining terms and concepts. ... The pedagogical aids ... trump ... what exists currently for adoption."

—Nicholas Corsaro, University of Cincinnati, USA

"I really like the 'writing it up section'. I think that adds a lot to what my students need in regards to statistics. ... This ... text will be purchased by people needing a baseline level of statistical knowledge. ... I enjoyed the text and writing style. ... The book would be beneficial to the students. ... Mr. Urdan does not attempt to take it too deep and keeps the book succinct enough to make it usable in a beginner stats class."

—Andrew Tinsley, Eastern Kentucky University, USA

"I am highly impressed with the latest edition (4th) of Tim Urdan's wonderful text. This author continues to deliver a highly readable yet nuanced text on research methods and fundamental statistics. I use this book in a number of graduate courses for clinical psychology students. It would also serve advanced undergraduates. In addition to clear writing and covering all the basics, I believe another essential strength is the author's commitment to training minds for critical thinking."

—Jamie K. Lilie, Argosy University, USA

Statistics in Plain English
Fourth Edition

Timothy C. Urdan

Routledge
Taylor & Francis Group

NEW YORK AND LONDON

Fourth edition published 2017
by Routledge
711 Third Avenue, New York, NY 10017, USA

and by Routledge
2 Park Square, Milton Park, Abingdon, Oxon, OX14 4RN, UK

Routledge is an imprint of the Taylor & Francis Group, an Informa business

Third edition published 2010 by Routledge

Library of Congress Cataloging in Publication Data
Names: Urdan, Timothy C.
Title: Statistics in plain English / Timothy C. Urdan, Santa Clara University.
Description: 4th edition. | New York, NY : Routledge, 2016. |
Includes bibliographical references and index.
Identifiers: LCCN 2016001650 (print) | LCCN 2016005945 (ebook) | ISBN
9781138838338 (hardback) | ISBN 9781138838345 (pbk.) | ISBN 9781315723112 ()
Subjects: LCSH: Statistics–Textbooks. | Mathematical statistics–Textbooks.
Classification: LCC QA276.12.U75 2016 (print) | LCC QA276.12 (ebook) |
DDC 519.5–dc23 LC record available at http://lccn.loc.gov/2016001650

ISBN: 978-1-13883-833-8 (hbk)
ISBN: 978-1-13883-834-5 (pbk)
ISBN: 978-1-31572-311-2 (ebk)

Typeset in ACaslon
by Out of House Publishing

Brief Contents

Contents

Preface

Why Use Statistics?

As a researcher who uses statistics frequently, and as an avid listener of talk radio, I find myself yelling at my radio daily. Although I realize that my cries go unheard, I cannot help myself. As radio talk show hosts, politicians making political speeches, and the general public all know, there is nothing more powerful and persuasive than the personal story, or what statisticians call anecdotal evidence. When a parent of an autistic child appears on television, crying and proclaiming that vaccinations caused the child to develop autism, one cannot help but be moved. Similarly, when a politician claims that public schools are failing and the solution is to break up teacher unions and create more charter schools, the argument can be compelling. But as researchers, we must go beyond the personal story or impassioned argument and look for broader evidence. How can we tell whether vaccines cause autism? How do we decide whether public schools are failing, whether teacher unions help or hinder valuable reform, and whether charter schools do a better job of educating students? To answer these questions, we need good data, and then we need to analyze the data using the appropriate statistics.

Many people have a general distrust of statistics, believing that crafty statisticians can "make statistics say whatever they want" or "lie with statistics." In fact, if a researcher calculates the statistics correctly, he or she cannot make them say anything other than what they say, and statistics never lie. Rather, crafty researchers can interpret what the statistics *mean* in a variety of ways, and those who do not understand statistics are forced to either accept the interpretations that statisticians and researchers offer or reject statistics completely. I believe a better option is to gain an understanding of how statistics work and then use that understanding to interpret the statistics one sees and hears for oneself. The purpose of this book is to make it a little easier to understand statistics.

Uses of Statistics

One of the potential shortfalls of anecdotal data is that they are idiosyncratic. One of our cognitive shortcomings, as people, is that we tend to believe that if something is true for us, it must be fact. "I eat a multivitamin every day and I haven't been sick for 20 years!" "My grandmother smoked a pack a day for 50 years and she lived until she was 96!" "My parents spanked me and I turned out fine!" Although these statements may (or may not!) be true for the individuals who uttered them, that does not mean they are true for everyone, or even for most people. Statistics allow researchers to collect information, or data, from a large number of people and then summarize their typical experience. Do *most* people who take multivitamins live healthier lives? Do most people who smoke a pack a day live shorter lives than people who do not smoke? Is there any association between whether one is spanked and how one "turns out," however that is defined? Statistics allow researchers to take a large batch of data and *summarize* it into a couple of numbers, such as an average. Of course, when many data are summarized into a single number, a lot of information is lost, including the fact that different people have very different experiences. So it is important to remember that, for the most part, statistics do not provide useful information about each individual's experience. Rather, researchers generally use statistics to make *general* statements about a population. Although personal stories are often moving or interesting, it is also important to understand what the *typical* or *average* experience is. For this, we need statistics.

Statistics are also used to reach conclusions about general differences between groups. For example, suppose that in my family, there are four children, two men and two women. Suppose that the women in my family are taller than the men. This personal experience may lead me to the conclusion that women are generally taller than men. Of course, we know that, on average, men are taller than women. The reason we know this is because researchers have taken large, random samples of men and women and compared their average heights. Researchers are often interested in making such comparisons: Do cancer patients survive longer using one drug than another? Is one method of teaching children to read more effective than another? Do men and women differ in their enjoyment of a certain movie? To answer these questions, we need to collect data from randomly selected samples and compare these data using statistics. The results we get from such comparisons are often more trustworthy than the simple observations people make from nonrandom samples, such as the different heights of men and women in my family.

Statistics can also be used to see if scores on two variables are related and to make predictions. For example, statistics can be used to see whether smoking cigarettes is related to the likelihood of developing lung cancer. For years, tobacco companies argued that there was no relationship between smoking and cancer. Sure, some people who smoked developed cancer. But the tobacco companies argued that (a) many people who smoke never develop cancer, and (b) many people who smoke tend to do other things that may lead to cancer development, such as eating unhealthy foods and not exercising. With the help of statistics in a number of studies, researchers were finally able to produce a preponderance of evidence indicating that, in fact, there is a relationship between cigarette smoking and cancer. Because statistics tend to focus on overall patterns rather than individual cases, this research did not suggest that *everyone* who smokes will develop cancer. Rather, the research demonstrated that, on average, people have a greater chance of developing cancer if they smoke cigarettes than if they do not.

With a moment's thought, you can imagine a large number of interesting and important questions that statistics about relationships can help you to answer. Is there a relationship between self-esteem and academic achievement? Is there a relationship between the physical appearance of criminal defendants and their likelihood of being convicted? Is it possible to predict the violent crime rate of a state from the amount of money the state spends on drug treatment programs? If we know the father's height, how accurately can we predict the son's height? These and thousands of other questions have been examined by researchers using statistics designed to determine the relationship between variables in a population. With the rise of the internet, data is now being collected constantly. For example, most casual users of the internet and social media provide information about their age, gender, where they live, how much money they make, how much they spend, what they like to buy, who their friends are, which websites they visit, what they like, whether they are married or single, etc. With the help of statistics, data analysts determine what advertisements you should see when you visit a website, how to attract you to certain websites, and how to get you to encourage your friends (without your knowledge) to like or buy various products. More than ever before, statistics and data are deeply affecting many aspects of your life. With this in mind, wouldn't it be nice to understand a bit more about how these statistics work?

How to Use this Book

If you are new to statistics, this book can provide an easy introduction to many of the basic, and most commonly used, statistics. Or, if you have already taken a course or two in statistics, this book may be useful as a reference book to refresh your memory on statistical concepts you have encountered in the past. It is important to remember that this book is much less detailed than a traditional statistics textbook. It was designed to provide a relatively short and inexpensive introduction to statistics, with a greater focus on the conceptual part of statistics than the computational, mathematical part. Each of the concepts discussed in this book is more complex than the presentation in this book might suggest, and a thorough understanding of these concepts may be acquired only with the use of a more traditional, more detailed textbook.

With that warning firmly in mind, let me describe the potential benefits of this book, and how to make the most of them. As a researcher and a teacher of statistics, I have found that statistics textbooks often contain a lot of technical information that can be intimidating to nonstatisticians. Although, as I said previously, this information is important, sometimes it is useful to have a short, simple description of a statistic, when it should be used, and how to make sense of it. This is particularly true for students taking only their first or second statistics course, those who do not consider themselves to be "mathematically inclined," and those who may have taken statistics years ago and now find themselves in need of a little refresher. My purpose in writing this book is to provide short, simple descriptions and explanations of a number of statistics that are easy to read and understand.

To help you use this book in a manner that best suits your needs, I have organized each chapter into sections. In the first section, a brief (1 to 2 pages) description of the statistic is given, including what the statistic is used for and what information it provides. The second section of each chapter contains a slightly longer (3 to 12 pages) discussion of the statistic. In this section, I provide a bit more information about how the statistic works, an explanation of how the formula for calculating the statistic works, the strengths and weaknesses of the statistic, and the conditions that must exist to use the statistic. Each chapter includes an example or two in which the statistic is calculated and interpreted. The chapters conclude with illustrations of how to write up the statistical information for publication and a set of work problems.

Before reading the book, it may be helpful to note three of its features. First, some of the chapters discuss more than one statistic. For example, in Chapter 2, three measures of central tendency are described: the mean, median, and mode. Second, some of the chapters cover statistical concepts rather than specific statistical techniques. For example, in Chapter 4, the normal distribution is discussed. There is also a chapter on statistical significance, effect size, and confidence intervals. Finally, you should remember that the chapters in this book are not necessarily designed to be read in order. The book is organized such that the more basic statistics and statistical concepts are in the earlier chapters, whereas the more complex concepts appear later in the book. However, each chapter in the book was written to stand on its own. This was done to enable you to use each chapter as needed. If, for example, you had no problem understanding *t* tests when you learned about them in your statistics class, but find yourself struggling to understand one-way analysis of variance, you may want to skip the *t* test chapter (Chapter 8) and go directly to the analysis of variance chapter (Chapter 9). If you are brand new to statistics, however, keep in mind that some statistical concepts (e.g., *t* tests, ANOVA) are easier to understand if you first learn about the mean, variance, and hypothesis testing.

New Features in this Edition

This fourth edition of *Statistics in Plain English* includes a number of features not available in the previous editions. Each of the 15 chapters now includes a set of work problems, with solutions and additional work problems provided on the website that accompanies this book. In addition, a section called "Worked Examples" has been added to most of the chapters in the book. In this section, I work through all of the steps to calculate and interpret the statistic featured in the chapter. There is also a link to a video of me calculating each statistic at the end of each Worked Examples section. These videos are available on the website that accompanies this book. Each chapter has also been revised to clarify confusing concepts, add or revise graphs and tables, and provide more examples of how the statistics are used in the real world. Throughout the book, there is a greater emphasis on, and description of, effect size. The supporting materials provided on the website at www.routledge.com/cw/urdan have also been updated, including many new and improved videos showing how to calculate statistics, how to read and interpret the appendices, and how to understand some of the more confusing tables of output produced by SPSS. PowerPoint summaries of each chapter, answers to the work problems, and a set of interactive work problems are also provided on the website. Finally, I have included a "Quick Guide to Statistics, Formulas, and Degrees of Freedom" at the beginning of the book, plainly outlining each statistic and when students should use them.

Acknowledgments

I would like to sincerely thank the reviewers who provided their time and expertise reading previous drafts of this book and offered very helpful feedback, including but not limited to:

Jason Abbitt, Miami University
Stephen M. Barkan, University of Maine
Robert M. Bernard, Concordia University
Danny R. Bowen, The Southern Baptist Theological Seminary
Nicholas Corsaro, University of Cincinnati
Heather Chapman, Weber State University
Seo-eun Choi, Arkansas State University
Robyn Cooper, Drake University
Margaret Cousins, University of Chester
Robert Crosby, California Baptist University
Clare Davies, University of Winchester
James Green, University of North Alabama
Henriette Hogh, University of Chichester
Matthew Jerram, Suffolk University
Jacyln Kelly, City University of New York, Graduate Center
Jo Ann Kelly, Walsh University
Yeonsoo Kim, University of Nevada, Las Vegas
Jennifer M. Kitchens, Lebanon Valley College
Franz Kronthaler, University of Applied Science HTW Chur
Jamie K. Lilie, Argosy University
Nick Lund, Manchester Metropolitan University
Gay McAlister, Southern Methodist University
Catherine A. Roster, University of New Mexico
Bridget Sheng, Western Illinois University
Joshua Stephens, Cleveland State University
Nathaniel Straight, Loyola University New Orleans
James Swartz, University of Illinois at Chicago
Christine Tartaro, Richard Stockton College of NJ
Andrew Tinsley, Eastern Kentucky University
Jon Yearsley, University College Dublin
Akane Zusho, Fordham University

I could not fit all of your suggestions into this new edition, but I incorporated many of them and the book is better as a result of your hard work. Thanks to Debra Riegert and Fred Coppersmith at Routledge/Taylor & Francis for your patience, help, and guidance. As always, students and colleagues at Santa Clara University made valuable contributions to this book, so thank you to Caitlin Courshon, Bhaumik Dedhia, and Elwood Mills. Thanks, again, to Ella, Nathaniel, and Jeannine for your patience while I worked through your vacation time to finish this book. Finally, thanks to you readers for using this book. We are in this statistics struggle together.

About the Author

Timothy C. Urdan is a professor in the Department of Psychology at Santa Clara University. He received his Ph.D. in Education and Psychology from the University of Michigan, where he received several honors including the School of Education Merit Award, the Horace H. Rackham Predoctoral Fellowship, and the Burke Aaron Hinsdale Scholar Award. He is an associate editor of the *Merrill-Palmer Quarterly* and serves on the editorial board for *Contemporary Educational Psychology*, the *Journal of Educational Psychology*, and the *American Educational Research Journal*. Dr. Urdan is the co-editor of two book series, *Adolescence and Education* and *Advances in Motivation and Achievement*, and also co-edited the *APA Educational Psychology Handbook*. He is a fellow of the American Psychological Association.

Quick Guide to Statistics, Formulas, and Degrees of Freedom

Statistic	Symbol	When you use it	Formula	Degrees of freedom (df)
Mean	$\bar{X}$, μ	To find the average of a distribution.	$\bar{X} = \dfrac{\Sigma X}{n}$, $\mu = \dfrac{\Sigma X}{N}$	
Standard deviation (sample)	s	To use sample data to estimate the average deviation in a distribution. It is a measure of variability.	$s = \sqrt{\dfrac{\Sigma(X - \bar{X})^2}{n - 1}}$	
Standard deviation (population)	σ	To find the average deviation in a distribution. It is a measure of variability.	$\sigma = \sqrt{\dfrac{\Sigma(X - \mu)^2}{N}}$	
Standard score for individual (z score)	z	To find the difference between an individual score and the mean in standard deviation units.	$z = \dfrac{X - \mu}{\sigma}$ or $z = \dfrac{X - \bar{X}}{s}$	
Standard score for mean (z score)	z	To find the difference between a sample mean and a population mean in standard error units.	$z = \dfrac{\bar{X} - \mu}{\sigma_{\bar{x}}}$	
Standard error of the mean	$s_{\bar{x}}$, $\sigma_{\bar{x}}$	To find the average difference between the population mean and the sample means when samples are of a given size and randomly selected.	$\sigma_{\bar{x}} = \dfrac{\sigma}{\sqrt{n}}$ or $s_{\bar{x}} = \dfrac{s}{\sqrt{n}}$	
One-sample t test	t	To determine whether the difference between a sample mean and the population mean is statistically significant.	$t = \dfrac{\bar{X} - \mu}{s_{\bar{x}}}$	$n - 1$
Independent samples t test	t	To determine whether the difference between two independent sample means is statistically significant.	$t = \dfrac{\bar{X}_1 - \bar{X}_2}{s_{\bar{x}1 - \bar{x}2}}$	$n_1 + n_2 - 2$
Dependent (paired) samples t test	t	To determine whether the difference between two dependent (i.e., paired) sample means is statistically significant.	$t = \dfrac{\bar{X} - \bar{Y}}{s_{\bar{D}}}$	$N - 1$, where N is the number of pairs of scores.
One-way ANOVA	F	To determine whether the difference between two or more independent sample means is statistically significant.	$F = \dfrac{MS_b}{MS_e}$	$k - 1$, $n - k$, where k is the number of groups and n is the number of cases across all samples.

Statistic	Symbol	When you use it	Formula	Degrees of freedom (*df*)
Cohen's *d* (effect size)	*d*	To determine the size of an effect (e.g., difference between sample means) in standard deviation units.	$d = \dfrac{\bar{X}_1 - \bar{X}_2}{\hat{s}}$	
Confidence interval for sample mean	CI	To create an interval within which one is 95% or 99% certain the population parameter (i.e., the population mean) is contained.	$CI_{95} = \bar{X} \pm (t_{95})(s_{\bar{x}})$	
Correlation coefficient (Pearson)	*r*	To calculate a measure of association between two intervally scaled variables.	$r = \dfrac{\Sigma(z_x z_y)}{N}$	
Coefficient of determination	r^2	To determine the percentage of variance in one variable that is explained by the other variable in a correlational analysis. It is a measure of effect size.	r^2	
t test for correlation coefficient	*t*	To determine whether a sample correlation coefficient is statistically significant.	$t = (r)\sqrt{\dfrac{N-2}{1-r^2}}$	$N-2$, where *N* is the number of cases in the sample.
Regression coefficient	*b*	To determine the amount of change in the *Y* variable for every change of one unit in the *X* variable in a regression analysis.	$b = r \times \dfrac{s_y}{s_x}$	
Regression intercept	*a*	To determine the predicted value of *Y* when *X* equals zero in a regression analysis.	$a = \bar{Y} - b\bar{X}$	
Predicted value of *Y*	$\hat{Y}$	To determine the predicted value of *Y* for a given value of *X* in a regression analysis.	$\hat{Y} = bX + a$	
Chi-square	χ^2	To examine whether the frequency of scores in various categories of two categorical variables are different from what would be expected.	$\chi^2 = \Sigma\left(\dfrac{(O-E)^2}{E}\right)$	$R-1, C-1$

CHAPTER 1

Introduction to Social Science Research Principles and Terminology

When I was in graduate school, one of my statistics professors often repeated what passes, in statistics, for a joke: "If this is all Greek to you, well that's good." Unfortunately, most of the class was so lost we didn't even get the joke. The world of statistics and research in the social sciences, like any specialized field, has its own terminology, language, and conventions. In this chapter, I review some of the fundamental research principles and terminology, including the distinction between samples and populations, methods of sampling, types of variables, the distinction between inferential and descriptive statistics, and a brief word about different types of research designs.

Populations, Samples, Parameters, and Statistics

A **population** is an individual or group that represents *all* the members of a certain group or category of interest. A sample is a subset drawn from the larger population (see Figure 1.1). For example, suppose that I wanted to know the average income of the current full-time employees at Google. There are two ways that I could find this average. First, I could get a list of every full-time employee at Google and find out the annual income of each member on this list. Because this list contains every member of the group that I am interested in, it can be considered a population. If I were to collect these data and calculate the **mean**, I would have generated a **parameter**, because a parameter is a value generated from, or applied to, a population. Another way to generate the mean income of the full-time employees at Google would be to randomly select a subset of employee names from my list and calculate the average income of this subset. The subset is known as a **sample** (in this case it is a **random sample**), and the mean that I generate from this sample is a type of **statistic**. Statistics are values derived from sample data, whereas parameters are values that are either derived from, or applied to, population data.

It is important to keep a couple of things in mind about samples and populations. First, a population does not need to be large to count as a population. For example, if I wanted to know the average height of the students in my statistics class this term, then all of the members of the class (collectively) would comprise the population. If my class only has five students in it, then my population only has five cases. Second, populations (and samples) do not have to include people. For example, suppose I want to know the average age of the dogs that visited a veterinary clinic in the last year. The population in this study is made up of dogs, not people. Similarly, I may want to know the total amount of carbon monoxide produced by Ford vehicles that were assembled in the United States during 2005. In this example, my population is cars, but not all cars—it is limited to Ford cars, and only those actually assembled in a single country during a single calendar year.

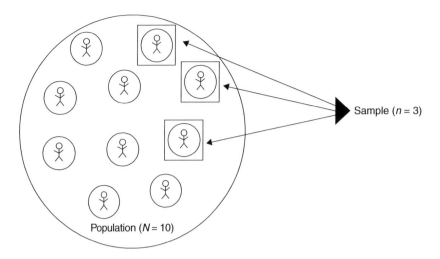

FIGURE 1.1 A population and a sample drawn from the population.

Third, the researcher generally defines the population, either explicitly or implicitly. In the examples above, I defined my populations (of dogs and cars) explicitly. Often, however, researchers define their populations less clearly. For example, a researcher may conduct a study with the aim of examining the frequency of depression among adolescents. The researcher's sample, however, may include only a group of 15-year-olds who visited a mental health service provider in Connecticut in a given year. This presents a potential problem, and leads directly into the fourth and final little thing to keep in mind about samples and populations: Samples are not necessarily good representations of the populations from which they were selected. In the example about the rates of depression among adolescents, notice that there are two potential populations. First, there is the population identified by the researcher and implied in the research question: adolescents. But notice that adolescents is a very large group, including all human beings, in all countries, between the ages of, say, 13 and 20. Second, there is the much more specific population that was defined by the sample that was selected: 15-year-olds who visited a mental health service provider in Connecticut during a given year. In Figure 1.1, I offer a graphic that illustrates the concept of a sample of 3 individuals being selected from a population of 10 individuals.

Inferential and Descriptive Statistics

Why is it important to determine which of these two populations is of interest in this study? Because the consumer of this research must be able to determine how well the results from the sample **generalize** to the larger population. Clearly, depression rates among 15-year-olds who visit mental health service providers in Connecticut may be different from other adolescents. For example, adolescents who visit mental health service providers may, on average, be more depressed than those who do not seek the services of a psychologist. Similarly, adolescents in Connecticut may be more depressed, as a group, than adolescents in California, where the sun shines and Mickey Mouse keeps everyone smiling. Perhaps 15-year-olds, who have to suffer the indignities of beginning high school without yet being able to legally drive, are more depressed than their 16-year-old, driving peers. In short, there are many reasons to suspect that the adolescents who were *not* included in the study may differ in their depression rates from adolescents who were included in the study. When such differences exist, it is difficult to apply the results garnered from a sample to the larger population. In research terminology, the results may not generalize from the sample to the population, particularly if the population is not clearly defined.

So why is generalizability important? To answer this question, I need to introduce the distinction between **descriptive** and **inferential** statistics. Descriptive statistics apply only to the members of a sample or population from which data have been collected. In contrast, inferential statistics refer to the use of sample data to reach some conclusions (i.e., make some inferences) about the characteristics of the larger population that the sample is supposed to represent. Although researchers are sometimes interested in simply describing the characteristics of a sample, for the most part we are much more concerned with what our sample tells us about the population from which the sample was drawn. In the depression study, the researcher does not care so much about the depression levels of the sample *per se*. Rather, the data from the sample is used to reach some conclusions about the depression levels of adolescents *in general*. But to make the leap from sample data to inferences about a population, one must be very clear about whether the sample accurately represents the population. If the sample accurately represents the population, then observations in the sample data should hold true for the population. But if the sample is not truly representative of the population, we cannot be confident that conclusions based on our sample data will apply to the larger population. An important first step in this process is to clearly define the population that the sample is alleged to represent.

Sampling Issues

There are a number of ways researchers can select samples. One of the most useful, but also the most difficult, is **random sampling.** In statistics, the term *random* has a much more specific meaning than the common usage of the term. It does not mean haphazard. In statistical jargon, *random* means that every member of a defined population has an equal chance of being selected into a sample. The major benefit of random sampling is that any differences between the sample and the population from which the sample was selected will not be systematic. Notice that in the depression study example, the sample differed from the population in important, *systematic* (i.e., nonrandom) ways. For example, the researcher most likely systematically selected adolescents who were more likely to be depressed than the average adolescent because she selected those who had visited mental health service providers. Although randomly selected samples may differ from the larger population in important ways (especially if the sample is small), these differences are due to chance rather than to a systematic bias in the selection process.

Representative sampling is another way of selecting cases for a study. With this method, the researcher purposely selects cases so that they will match the larger population on specific characteristics. For example, if I want to conduct a study examining the average annual income of adults in San Francisco, by definition my population is "adults in San Francisco." This population includes a number of subgroups (e.g., different ethnic and racial groups, men and women, retired adults, disabled adults, parents, single adults, etc.). These different subgroups may be expected to have different incomes. To get an accurate picture of the incomes of the adult population in San Francisco, I may want to select a sample that represents the population well. Therefore, I would try to match the percentages of each group in my sample with those in my population. For example, if 15 percent of the adult population in San Francisco is retired, I would select my sample in a manner that included 15 percent retired adults. Similarly, if 55 percent of the adult population in San Francisco is male, 55 percent of my sample should be male. With random sampling, I may get a sample that looks like my population or I may not. But with representative sampling, I can ensure that my sample looks similar to my population on some important variables. This type of sampling procedure can be costly and time-consuming, but it increases my chances of being able to generalize the results from my sample to the population.

Another common method of selecting samples is called **convenience sampling**. In convenience sampling, the researcher generally selects participants on the basis of proximity, ease of access, and willingness to participate (i.e., convenience). For example, if I want to do a study on the achievement levels of eighth-grade students, I may select a sample of 200 students from the nearest middle school to my office. I might ask the parents of 300 of the eighth-grade students in the school to participate, receive permission from the parents of 220 of the students, and then collect data from the 200 students that show up at school on the day I hand out my survey. This is a convenience sample. Although this method of selecting a sample is clearly less labor-intensive than selecting a random or representative sample, that does not necessarily make it a bad way to select a sample. If my convenience sample does not differ from my population of interest *in ways that influence the outcome of the study*, then it is a perfectly acceptable method of selecting a sample.

To illustrate the importance of the sampling method in research, I offer two examples of problematic sampling methods that have led to faulty conclusions. First, a report by the American Chemical Society (2002) noted that several beach closures in southern California were caused by faulty sampling methods. To test for pollution levels in the ocean, researchers often take a single sample of water and test it. If the pollution levels are too high in the sample, the beach is declared unsafe and is closed. But water conditions change very quickly, and a single sample may not accurately represent the overall pollution levels of water at the beach. More samples, taken at different times during the day and from different areas along the beach, would have produced results that more accurately represented the true pollution levels of the larger area of the beach, and there would have been fewer beach closures.

The second example involves the diagnosis of heart disease in women. For decades, doctors and medical researchers considered heart disease to be a problem only for men. As a result, the largest and most influential studies included only male samples (Doshi, 2015). Two consequences of this failure to include women in the samples that were researched were that doctors were less likely to order testing for heart disease for their female patients than their male patients, and the symptoms of heart disease and cardiac failure among women, which are often different from those of men, were not understood. Many women who could have had their heart disease treated early or their symptoms of cardiac arrest quickly diagnosed died because women were not included in the samples for research on heart disease and heart attacks. The population of people with heart disease clearly includes women, so the samples that included only men were not representative of the population.

Types of Variables and Scales of Measurement

In social science research, a number of terms are used to describe different types of variables. A **variable** is pretty much anything that can be codified and have more than a single value (e.g., income, gender, age, height, attitudes about school, score on a measure of depression, etc.). A **constant**, in contrast, has only a single score. For example, if every member of a sample is male, the "gender" category is a constant. Types of variables include **quantitative** (or **continuous**) and **qualitative** (or **categorical**). A quantitative variable is one that is scored in such a way that the numbers, or values, indicate some sort of amount. For example, height is a quantitative (or continuous) variable because higher scores on this variable indicate a greater amount of height. In contrast, qualitative variables are those for which the assigned values do not indicate more or less of a certain quality. If I conduct a study to compare the eating habits of people from Maine, New Mexico, and Wyoming, my "state" variable has three values (e.g., 1 = Maine, 2 = New Mexico, 3 = Wyoming). Notice that a value of 3 on this variable is not *more* than a value of 1 or 2—it is simply *different*. The labels represent qualitative differences in location, not quantitative differences. A commonly used qualitative variable in social science research is the **dichotomous variable**. This is a variable that has two different categories (e.g., male and female).

In social science research, there are four different scales of measurement for variables: nominal, ordinal, interval, and ratio. A **nominally scaled variable** has different categories (e.g., male and female, Experimental Group 1, Experimental Group 2, Control Group, etc.). **Ordinal variables** are those whose values are placed in meaningful order, but the distances between the values are not equal. For example, if I wanted to know the 10 richest people in America, in order from the wealthiest to the 10th richest, the wealthiest American would receive a score of 1, the next

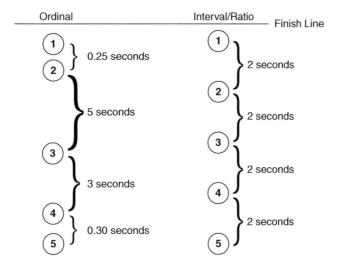

FIGURE 1.2 Difference between ordinal and interval/ratio scales of measurement.

richest a score of 2, and so on through 10. Notice that while this scoring system tells me where each of the wealthiest 10 Americans stands in relation to the others (e.g., Bill Gates is 1, Michael Bloomberg is 8, etc.), it does not tell me how much *distance* there is between each score. So while I know that the wealthiest American is richer than the second wealthiest, I do not know if he has one dollar more or one billion dollars more. Variables measured with an **interval** scale have values that have order, but they also have equal distances between each unit on the scale. For example, businesses often survey their customers to gain information about how satisfied they are with the service they received. They may be asked to rate the service on a scale from 1 to 10, and this kind of rating scale is an interval scale of measurement. On such surveys, the distance between each number is presumed to be equal, such that a score of 10 would indicate twice as much satisfaction than a score of 5.[1] Variables measured using a **ratio** scale of measurement have the same properties as intervally scaled variables, but they have one additional property: Ratio scales can have a value of zero, while interval scales do not. A great deal of social science research employs measures with no zero value, such as attitude and beliefs surveys (e.g., "On a scale from 1 to 5, how much do you like orange soda?"). Examples of ratio scaled variables include temperatures (e.g., Celsius, Farenheit), income measured in dollars, measures of weight and distance, and many others. Figure 1.2 illustrates a critical difference between ordinal and interval or ratio scales of measurement: Ordinal scales don't provide information about the distance between the units of measurement, but interval and ratio scales do.

One useful way to think about these different kinds variables is in terms of how much information they provide. While nominal variables only provide labels for the different categories of the variable, ordinal variables offer a bit more information by telling us the order of the values. Variables measured using interval scales provide even more information, telling us both the order of the values and the distance between the values. Finally, variables measured with ratio scales add just a little bit more information by including the value of zero in its range of possible values. Figure 1.3 provides a graphic to help you think about the information provided by each of these four types of variables.

Research Designs

There are a variety of research methods and designs employed by social scientists. Sometimes researchers use an **experimental design**. In this type of research, the experimenter divides the cases in the sample into different groups and then compares the groups on one or more variables of interest. For example, I may want to know whether my newly developed mathematics

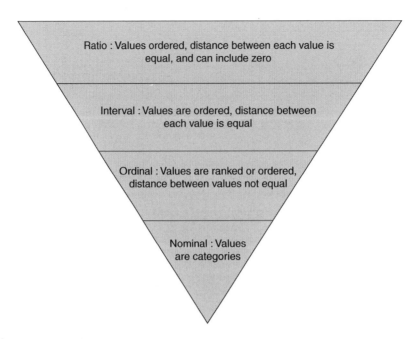

FIGURE 1.3 Hierarchical arrangement of scales of measurement.

curriculum is better than the old one. I select a sample of 40 students and, using **random assignment**, teach 20 students a lesson using the old curriculum and the other 20 using the new curriculum. Then I test each group to see which group learned more mathematical concepts. This method of random assignment to groups and testing the effects of a particular treatment is known as a **randomized control trial (RCT)** experiment. It has been used for years in medical and laboratory research in the physical and social sciences, and in recent years has been used to great effect in the social sciences outside of laboratory settings. For example, Walton and Cohen (2011) used an RCT design to examine whether a brief intervention could increase first-year college students' feeling of belonging and decrease their feelings of isolation at university. They randomly assigned about half of their participants to receive their intervention while the other half did not, then they compared the two groups and found that those who received the intervention had better psychological and academic outcomes. By assigning students to the two groups using random assignment, it is hoped that any important differences between the two groups will be distributed evenly between the two groups, and that any differences in test scores between the two groups is due to differences in the effectiveness of the two curricula used to teach them. Of course, this may not be true.

A **quasi-experimental research design** is quite similar to an experimental design. Both of these designs typically involve manipulating some variable to see if that variable has an effect on some outcome. In addition, both research designs include some sort of random assignment. The major difference is that in a quasi-experimental design, the research usually occurs outside of the lab, in a naturally occurring setting. In the earlier example used to illustrate the experimental design, I could have had the students come to my research lab and conducted my study in a controlled setting so that I could tightly control all of the conditions and make them identical between the two groups, except for the math curriculum that I used. In a quasi-experimental study, I might find two existing classrooms with 20 students each and ask the teacher in one classroom to use the old math curriculum and the teacher in another classroom to use the new curriculum. Instead of randomly assigning students to these two classrooms (which is difficult to do in a real school), I might randomly select which classroom gets the new curriculum and which one uses the old. I could take steps to try to minimize the differences between the two classrooms (e.g., conduct the study in two different classes of students that are taught by the same teacher, try to find two classrooms that are similar in terms of the gender composition of the students, etc.), but generally speaking it is more difficult to control the conditions in a quasi-experimental design than an experimental design. The benefit of a quasi-experimental design, however, is that it allows the researcher to test the effects of experimental manipulations in more natural, real-world conditions than those found in a research laboratory.

Correlational research designs are also a common method of conducting research in the social sciences. In this type of research, participants are not usually randomly assigned to groups. In addition, the researcher typically does not actually manipulate anything. Rather, the researcher simply collects data on several variables and then conducts some statistical analyses to determine how strongly different variables are related to each other. For example, I may be interested in whether employee productivity is related to how much employees sleep (at home, not on the job!). So I select a sample of 100 adult workers, measure their productivity at work, and measure how long each employee sleeps on an average night in a given week. I may find that there is a strong relationship between sleep and productivity. Now, logically, I may want to argue that this makes sense, because a more rested employee will be able to work harder and more efficiently. Although this conclusion makes sense, it is too strong a conclusion to reach based on my correlational data alone. Correlational studies can only tell us whether variables are related to each other—they cannot lead to conclusions about *causality*. After all, it is possible that being more productive at work *causes* longer sleep at home. Getting one's work done may relieve stress and perhaps even allows the worker to sleep in a little longer in the morning, both of which create longer sleep.

Experimental research designs are good because they allow the researcher to isolate specific **independent variables** that may cause variation, or changes, in **dependent variables.** In the example above, I manipulated the independent variable of the mathematics curriculum and was able to reasonably conclude that the type of math curriculum used affected students' scores on the dependent variable, the test scores. The primary drawbacks of experimental designs are that they are often difficult to accomplish in a clean way and they often do not generalize to real-world situations. For example, in my study above, I cannot be sure whether it was the math curricula that influenced the test scores or some other factor, such as a pre-existing difference in the mathematical abilities of my two groups of students, or differences in the teacher styles that had nothing to do with the curricula, but could have influenced the test scores (e.g., the clarity or enthusiasm of the teacher). The strengths of correlational research designs are that they are often easier to conduct than experimental research, they allow for the relatively easy inclusion of many variables, and they allow the researcher to examine many variables simultaneously. The principle drawback of correlational research is that such research does not allow for the careful controls necessary for drawing conclusions about causal associations between variables.

Making Sense of Distributions and Graphs

Statisticians spend a lot of time talking about **distributions**. A distribution is simply a collection of data, or scores, on a variable. Usually, these scores are arranged in order from smallest to largest and then they can be presented graphically. Because distributions are so important in statistics, I want to give them some attention early on in the book, and show you several examples of different types of distributions and how they are depicted in **graphs**. Note that later in this book there are whole chapters devoted to several of the most commonly used distributions in statistics, including the **normal distribution** (Chapters 4 and 5), *t* **distributions** (Chapter 8 and parts of Chapter 7), *F* **distributions** (Chapters 9, 10, and 11), and **chi-square** distributions (Chapter 14).

Let's begin with a simple example. Suppose that I am conducting a study of voters' attitudes and I select a random sample of 500 voters for my study. One piece of information I might want to know is the political affiliation of the members of my sample. So I ask them if they are Republicans, Democrats, or Independents. I find that 45 percent of my sample list

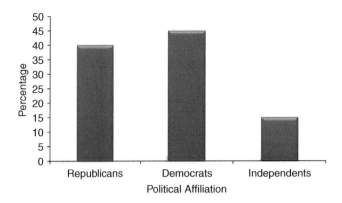

FIGURE 1.4 Column graph showing the distribution of Republicans, Democrats, and Independents.

themselves as Democrats, 40 percent report being Republicans, and 15 percent identify themselves as Independents. Notice that political affiliation is a nominal, or categorical, variable. Because nominal variables are variables with categories that have no numerical weight, I cannot arrange my scores in this distribution from highest to lowest. The value of being a Republican is not more or less than the value of being a Democrat or an Independent—they are simply different categories. So rather than trying to arrange my data from the lowest to the highest value, I simply leave them as separate categories and report the percentage of the sample that falls into each category.

There are many different ways that I could graph this distribution, including a pie chart, bar graph, column graph, different sized bubbles, and so on. The key to selecting the appropriate graphic is to keep in mind that the purpose of the graph is to make the data easy to understand. For my distribution of political affiliation, I have created two different graphs. Both are fine choices because both of them offer very clear and concise summaries of the distribution and are easy to understand. Figure 1.4 depicts the distribution as a column graph, and Figure 1.5 presents the data in a pie chart. Which graphic is best for these data is a matter of personal preference. As you look at Figure 1.4, notice that the *X* axis (the horizontal one) shows the party affiliations: Democrats, Republicans, and Independents. The *Y* axis (the vertical one) shows the percentage of the sample. You can see the percentages in each group and, just by quickly glancing at the columns, you can see which political affiliation has the highest percentage of this sample and get a quick sense of the differences between the party affiliations in terms of the percentage of the sample. The pie chart in Figure 1.5 shows the same information, but in a slightly more striking and simple manner, I think.

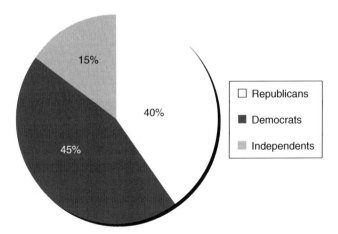

FIGURE 1.5 Pie chart showing the distribution of Republicans, Democrats, and Independents.

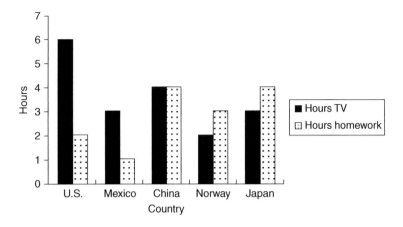

FIGURE 1.6   Average hours of television viewed and time spent on homework in five countries.

Sometimes, researchers are interested in examining the distributions of more than one variable at a time. For example, suppose I wanted to know about the association between hours spent watching television and hours spent doing homework. I am particularly interested in how this association looks across different countries. So I collect data from samples of high school students in several different countries. Now I have distributions on two different variables across five different countries (the U.S., Mexico, China, Norway, and Japan). To compare these different countries, I decide to calculate the average, or **mean** (see Chapter 2) for each country on each variable. Then I graph these means using a column graph, as shown in Figure 1.6 (note that these data are fictional—I made them up). As this graph clearly shows, the disparity between the average amount of television watched and the average hours of homework completed per day is widest in the U.S. and Mexico and virtually non-existent in China. In Norway and Japan, high school students actually spend more time on homework than they do watching TV, according to my fake data. Notice how easily this complex set of data is summarized in a single graph.

Another common method of graphing a distribution of scores is the line graph, as shown in Figure 1.7. Suppose that I select a random sample of 100 first-year college students who have just completed their first term. I ask them to each tell me the final grades they received in each of their classes and then I calculate a grade point average (GPA) for each of them. Finally, I divide the GPAs into six groups: 1 to 1.4, 1.5 to 1.9, 2.0 to 2.4, 2.5 to 2.9, 3.0 to 3.4, and 3.5 to 4.0. When I count up the number of students in each of these GPA groups and graph these data using a line graph, I get the results presented in Figure 1.7. Notice that along the X axis I have displayed the six different GPA groups. On the Y axis I have the **frequency**, typically denoted by the symbol f. So in this graph, the Y axis shows how many students are in each GPA group.

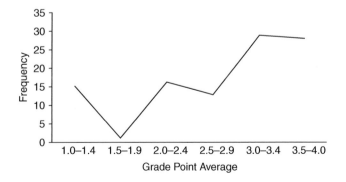

FIGURE 1.7   Line graph showing frequency of students in different GPA groups.

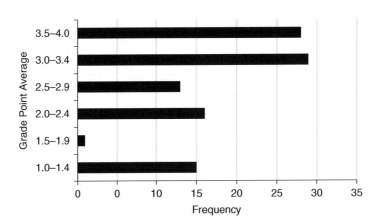

FIGURE 1.8 Bar graph showing frequency of students in different GPA groups.

A quick glance at Figure 1.7 reveals that there were quite a few students (13) who really struggled in their first term in college, accumulating GPAs between 1.0 and 1.4. Only 1 student was in the next group from 1.5–1.9. From there, the number of students in each GPA group generally goes up, with roughly 30 students in the 2.0–2.9 GPA categories and about 55 students in the 3.0 to 4.0 GPA categories. A line graph like this offers a quick way to see trends in data, either over time or across categories. In this example with GPA, we can see that the general trend is to find more students in the higher GPA categories, plus a fairly substantial group that is really struggling. In Figure 1.8, the same data is presented in a bar graph. Which graph gives you a clearer picture of the data?

Column graphs are another clear way to show trends in data. In Figure 1.9, I present a stacked column graph. This graph allows me to show several pieces of information in a single graph. For example, in this graph I am illustrating the occurrence of two different kinds of crime, property and violent, across the period from 1990 to 2007. On the *X* axis I have placed the years, moving from earlier (1990) to later (2007) as we look from the left to the right. On the *Y* axis I present the number of crimes committed per 100,000 people in the U.S. When presented in this way, several interesting facts jump out. First, the overall trend from 1990 to 2007 is a pretty dramatic drop in crime. From a high of nearly 6,000 crimes per 100,000 people in 1991, the crime rate dropped to well under 4,000 per 100,000 people in 2007. That is a drop of

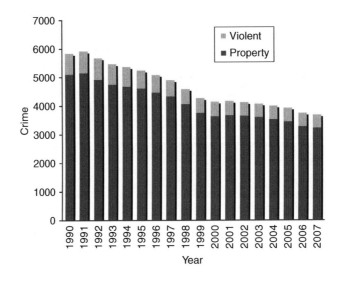

FIGURE 1.9 Stacked column graph showing crime rates from 1990 to 2007.

nearly 40 percent. The second noteworthy piece of information that is obvious from the graph is that violent crimes (e.g., murder, rape, assault) occur much less frequently than crimes against property (e.g., burglary, vandalism, arson) in each year of the study.

Notice that the graph presented in Figure 1.9 makes it easy to see that there has been a drop in crime *overall* from 1990 to 2007, but it is not so easy to tell whether there has been much of a drop in the violent crime rate. That is because violent crime makes up a much smaller percentage of the overall crime rate than property crimes, so the scale used in the *Y* axis is pretty large. This makes the tops of the columns, the parts representing violent crimes, look quite small. To get a better idea of the trend for violent crimes over time, I created a new graph, which is presented in Figure 1.10.

In this new figure, I have presented the exact same data that were presented in Figure 1.9, this time as a line graph. The line graph separates violent crimes from property crimes completely, making it easier to see the difference in the frequency of the two types of crimes. Again, this graph clearly shows the drop in property crime over the years. But notice that it is still difficult to tell whether there was much of a drop in violent crime over time. If you look very closely, you can see that the rate of violent crime dropped from about 800 per 100,000 people in 1990 to about 500 per 100,000 people in 2007. This is an impressive drop in the crime rate, but we have had to work too hard to see it. Remember: The purpose of a graph is to make the interesting facts in the data easy to see. If you have to work hard to see it, the graph is not that great.

The problem with Figure 1.10, just as with Figure 1.9, is that the scale on the *Y* axis is too large to clearly show the trends for violent crime rates over time. To fix this problem, we need a scale that is more appropriate for the violent crime rate data. So I created one more graph that includes the data for violent crimes only, without the property crime data (Figure 1.11). Instead of using a scale from 0 to 6,000 or 7,000 on the *Y* axis, my new graph has a scale from 0 to 800 on the *Y* axis. In this new graph, a column graph, it is clear that the drop in violent crimes from 1990 to 2007 was also quite dramatic.

Any collection of scores on a variable, regardless of the type of variable, forms a distribution, and this distribution can be graphed. In this section of the chapter, several different types of graphs have been presented, and all of them have their strengths. The key, when creating graphs, is to select the graph that most clearly illustrates the data. When reading graphs, it is important to pay attention to the details. Try to look beyond the most striking features of the graph to the less obvious features, like the scales used on the *X* and *Y* axes. As I discuss later (Chapter 11), graphs can be quite misleading if the details are ignored.

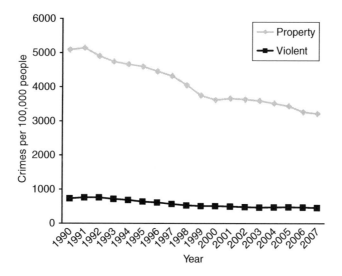

FIGURE 1.10   Line graph showing crime rates from 1990 to 2007.

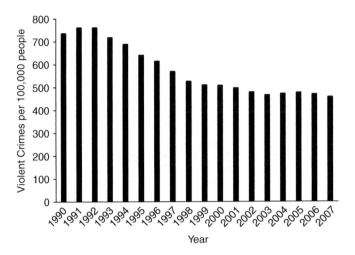

FIGURE 1.11 Column graph showing violent crime rate from 1990 to 2007.

Wrapping Up and Looking Forward

The purpose of this chapter was to provide a quick overview of many of the basic principles and terminology employed in social science research. With a foundation in the types of variables, experimental designs, and sampling methods used in social science research, it will be easier to understand the uses of the statistics described in the remaining chapters of this book. Now we are ready to talk statistics. It may still all be Greek to you, but that's not necessarily a bad thing.

Work Problems

Suppose that Starbucks wanted to conduct a study to determine whether men and women differ in the amount of money they spend when they visit one of their stores. They hired a researcher to collect these data from the first 100 customers to visit one of their stores in New York City one day. Forty of the customers were men and sixty were women. Please answer the following questions based on this information.

1. What kind of sampling method did the researcher use?
2. What is/are the sample(s) in this study?
3. What is/are the population(s) in this study?
4. Do you think the results of this study will generalize to the population(s)? Why or why not?
5. What are the independent and dependent variables in this study?
6. What type of measurement does each of these variables use (i.e., nominal, ordinal, interval, ratio)?
7. What kind of study is this (i.e., experimental, quasi-experimental, correlational)?
8. What are the statistic(s) and parameter(s) of interest in this study?
9. How could you re-design this study to get results from the sample data that would be more generalizable to the population(s)?

 For answers to these work problems, and for additional work problems, please refer to the website that accompanies this book.

Note

1 There has actually been quite a bit of debate about whether it is accurate to treat these kinds of attitudinal scales as ratio variables. It is not clear whether people really think of the intervals between the numbers as being equal in size. Nonetheless, researchers typically treat these kinds of attitudinal measures as intervally scaled when calculating statistics that require variables using either interval or ratio scales.

CHAPTER 2

Measures of Central Tendency

Whenever you collect data, you end up with a group of scores on one or more variables. If you take the scores on one variable and arrange them in order from lowest to highest, what you get is a **distribution** of scores. Researchers often want to know about the characteristics of these distributions of scores, such as the shape of the distribution, how spread out the scores are, what the most common score is, and so on. One set of distribution characteristics that researchers are usually interested in is central tendency. This set consists of the mean, median, and mode.

The **mean** is probably the most commonly used statistic in all social science research. The mean is simply the arithmetic average of a distribution of scores, and researchers like it because it provides a single, simple number that gives a rough summary of the distribution. It is important to remember that although the mean provides a useful piece of information, it does not tell you anything about how spread out the scores are (i.e., variance) or how many scores in the distribution are close to the mean. It is possible for a distribution to have very few scores at or near the mean.

The **median** is the score in the distribution that marks the 50th percentile. That is, 50 percent of the scores in the distribution fall above the median and 50 percent fall below it. Researchers often use the median when they want to divide their distribution scores into two equal groups (called a **median split**). The median is also a useful statistic to examine when the scores in a distribution are skewed or when there are a few extreme scores at the high end or the low end of the distribution. This is discussed in more detail in the following pages.

The **mode** is the least used of the measures of central tendency because it provides the least amount of information. The mode simply indicates which score in the distribution occurs most often, or has the highest frequency.

A WORD ABOUT POPULATIONS AND SAMPLES

You will notice in Table 2.1 that there are two different symbols used for the mean, $\bar{X}$ and μ. Two different symbols are needed because it is important to distinguish between a **statistic** that applies to a **sample** and a **parameter** that applies to a **population**. The symbol used to represent the population mean is μ. Statistics are values derived from sample data, whereas parameters are values that are either derived from, or applied to, population data. It is important to note that all samples are representative of some population and that all sample statistics can be used as estimates of population parameters. In the case of the mean, the sample statistic is represented with the symbol $\bar{X}$. The distinction between sample statistics and population parameters appears in several chapters (e.g., Chapters 1, 3, 5, and 7).

TABLE 2.1 Formula for calculating the mean of a distribution

$$\mu = \frac{\Sigma X}{N}$$

or

$$\overline{X} = \frac{\Sigma X}{n}$$

where $\overline{X}$ is the sample mean,
 μ is the population mean,
 Σ means "the sum of,"
 X is an individual score in the distribution,
 n is the number of scores in the sample,
 N is the number of scores in the population.

Measures of Central Tendency in Depth

The calculations for each measure of central tendency are mercifully straightforward. With the aid of a calculator or a statistics software program, you will probably never need to calculate any of these statistics by hand. But for the sake of knowledge, and in the event that you find yourself without a calculator and in need of these statistics, here is the information you will need.

Because the mean is an average, calculating the mean involves adding, or summing, all of the scores in a distribution and dividing by the number of scores. So, if you have 10 scores in a distribution, you would add all of the scores together to find the sum and then divide the sum by 10, which is the number of scores in the distribution. The formula for calculating the mean is presented in Table 2.1.

The calculation of the median (P_{50} and ***Mdn*** are commonly used symbols for the 50th percentile) for a simple distribution of scores[1] is even simpler than the calculation of the mean. To find the median of a distribution, you need to first arrange all of the scores in the distribution in order, from smallest to largest. Once this is done, you simply need to find the middle score in the distribution. If there is an odd number of scores in the distribution, there will be a single score that marks the middle of the distribution. For example, if there are 11 scores in the distribution arranged in ascending order from smallest to largest, the 6th score will be the median because there will be 5 scores below it and 5 scores above it. However, if there is an even number of scores in the distribution, there is no single middle score. In this case, the median is the average of the *two* scores in the middle of the distribution (as long as the scores are arranged in order, from smallest to largest). For example, if there are 10 scores in a distribution, to find the median you will need to find the average of the 5th and 6th scores. To find this average, add the two scores together and divide by two.

To find the mode, there is no need to calculate anything. The mode is simply the category in the distribution that has the highest number of scores, or the highest frequency.

To demonstrate how to calculate the mean, median, and mode, let's suppose you have the following distribution of IQ test scores from 10 students:

86 90 95 100   100 100 110 110 115 120

To calculate the mean, simply add all of the scores in the distribution together and divide by 10, which is the number of scores in the distribution:

86 + 90 + 95 + 100 + 100 + 100 + 110 + 110 + 115 + 120 = 1026

1026/10 = 102.6

So the mean of this distribution is 102.6. Because this distribution has an equal number of scores, to find the median we find the two scores in the middle (i.e., the 5th and 6th scores), add them together, and divide by two:

$$(100 + 100)/2 = 100.$$

Now we know that the median of this distribution is 100 and the mean is 102.6. Finally, we can determine the mode by looking for the score that occurs most frequently in the distribution. We can see that the number 100 occurs three times, and that is more than any other score in the distribution. So the mode of this distribution is 100.

If a distribution has more than one category with the most common score, the distribution has multiple modes and is called **multimodal**. One common example of a multimodal distribution is the **bimodal** distribution. Researchers often get bimodal distributions when they ask people to respond to controversial questions that tend to polarize the public. For example, if I were to ask a sample of 100 people how they felt about capital punishment, I might get the results presented in Table 2.2. In this example, because most people either strongly oppose or strongly support capital punishment, I end up with a bimodal distribution of scores.

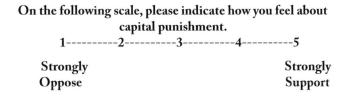

On the following scale, please indicate how you feel about capital punishment.

1----------2----------3----------4---------5

Strongly	**Strongly**
Oppose	**Support**

TABLE 2.2   Frequency of responses to "How do you feel about capital punishment?"

	Category of Responses on the Scale				
	1	**2**	**3**	**4**	**5**
	Strongly oppose				Strongly support
Frequency of Responses in Each Category	45	3	4	3	45

Example: The Mean, Median, and Mode of Skewed Distributions

As you will see in Chapter 4, when scores in a distribution are normally distributed, the distribution forms a bell-shaped curve with the mean, median, and mode all at the same point: the center of the distribution. In the messy world of social science, however, the scores from a sample on a given variable are often not normally distributed. When most of the members in a sample have scores that are bunched up at one end of the distribution and there are a few scores at the other end, the distribution is said to be **skewed**. When working with a skewed distribution, the mean, median, and mode are usually all at different points.

It is important to note that the procedures used to calculate the mean, median, and mode are the same whether you are dealing with a skewed or a normal distribution. All that changes are where these three measures of central tendency are in relation to each other. To illustrate, I created a fictional distribution of scores based on a sample size of 30. These scores represent the number of children born to women who were born in 1950 or earlier. (Note that these fictional data are based on actual data collected in the General Social Survey conducted at the University of California, Berkeley.) I have arranged my fictitious scores in order from smallest to largest and get the following distribution:

0	0	0	1	1	1	1	2	2	2
2	2	2	2	2	2	3	3	3	3
3	3	3	4	4	4	5	5	6	7

As you can see, there are only a few scores near the high end of the distribution (6 and 7 children) and more at the lower-middle part of the distribution (1, 2, and 3 children). To get a clear picture of what this skewed distribution looks like, I have created the graph in Figure 2.1.

This graph provides a picture of what one positively skewed distribution looks like. This graph is called a **histogram** and was produced using the SPSS statistical software. The histogram is a graph of frequency distribution, and it includes a line showing the normal distribution (see Chapter 4) so that it is easy to see how the distribution of these data compares to a normal distribution. Notice how most of the scores are clustered at the lower end and middle of the distribution, and there are a few scores creating a tail toward the higher end. This is known as a **positively skewed** distribution, because the tail goes toward the higher end. These few scores at the higher end of the distribution pull the mean up toward that end, so the mean of this distribution (2.60) is a bit higher than the median (2.00). You can also see that the mode, which is the most frequently occurring value in the distribution, is 2.00.

To calculate the mean, we apply the formula mentioned earlier. That is, we add up all of the scores (ΣX) and then divide this sum by the number of scores in the distribution (n). This gives us a fraction of 78/30, which reduces to 2.60. To find the median of this distribution, we arrange the scores in order from smallest to largest and find the middle score. In this distribution, there are 30 scores, so there will be two in the middle. When arranged in order, the two scores in the middle (the 15th and 16th scores) are both 2. When we add these two scores together and divide by two, we end up with 2, making our median 2.

As I mentioned earlier, the mean of a distribution can be affected by scores that are unusually large or small for a distribution, whereas the median is not affected by such scores. In the case

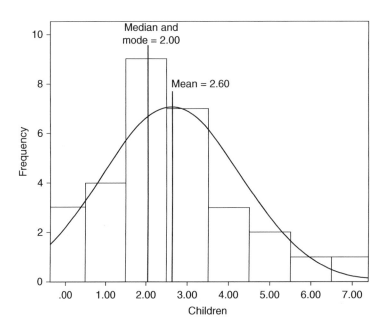

FIGURE 2.1 A histogram for a positively skewed variable, the number of children born per woman born in 1950 or earlier.

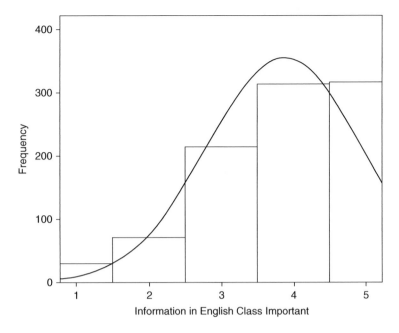

FIGURE 2.2 A histogram for a negatively skewed variable, "The information we are learning in English class is important."

of a skewed distribution, the mean is usually pulled in the direction of the tail, because the tail is where the unusually high or low scores are. In a positively skewed distribution, such as the one presented previously, the mean was pulled in the direction of the skew (i.e., positive), producing a mean that was larger than the median. In a **negatively skewed** distribution, we would expect the mean to be smaller than the median, because the mean is pulled toward the tail whereas the median is not. For example, when I asked a sample of high school students to answer a survey question that read "The information we learn in English class is important" (rated on a scale from 1 = *Not at all true* to 5 = *Very true*), I got the distribution produced in Figure 2.2 and Table 2.3. You will notice that the vast majority of students in this sample answered this question with a 4 or a 5, indicating that they thought the information was quite important. Almost everybody is told, from an early age, that education is important. Even students that pay little attention in class usually say they believe education is important. So on survey questions like this, most people strongly agree with the statement (note that the mode is 5), and only a minority of students are willing to disagree. The relatively few students who answered this item with a 1 or a 2 pulled the mean down toward the lower end of the distribution, below the median. In this example, the mean (3.87) is somewhat lower than the median (4.00).

Sometimes, distributions have a few scores that are very far away from the mean. These are called **outliers,** and because outliers are, by definition, extreme scores, they can have a dramatic effect on the mean of the distribution. When most of the outliers are at one side of a distribution (e.g., the

TABLE 2.3 Frequency of responses to the statement "The information we are learning in English class is important"

	Category of Responses on the Scale				
	1 Not at all true	**2**	**3**	**4**	**5** Very true
Frequency of Responses in Each Category	30	70	213	314	318

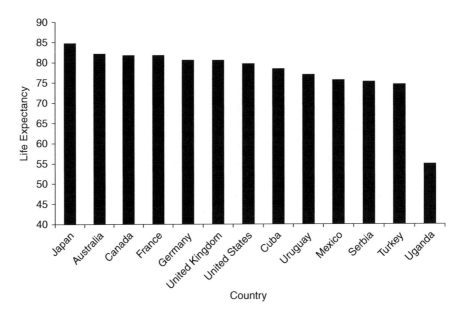

FIGURE 2.3 Life expectancy at birth in several countries.

lower end), they pull the mean toward that end of the distribution. To provide a better sense of the effects of an outlier on the mean of a distribution, I present two graphs showing the average life expectancy, at birth, of people in several different countries. In Figure 2.3, the life expectancy for 13 countries is presented in a column graph and the countries are arranged from the longest life expectancy (Japan) to the shortest (Uganda). As you can see, there is a gradual decline in life expectancy from Japan through Turkey, but then there is a dramatic drop off in life expectancy for Uganda. In this distribution of nations, Uganda is an outlier. The average life expectancy for all of the countries *except* Uganda is 79.34 years, whereas the average life expectancy for all 13 countries in Figure 2.3 *including* Uganda drops to 77.46 years. The addition of a single country, Uganda, drops the average life expectancy for *all* of the 13 countries combined by almost 2 full years. Two years may not sound like a lot, but when you consider that this is about the same amount that separates the top 5 countries in Figure 2.3 from each other, you can see that 2 years can make a lot of difference in the ranking of countries by the life expectancies of their populations.

The effects of outliers on the mean are more dramatic with smaller samples because the mean is a statistic produced by combining all of the members of the distribution together. With larger samples, one outlier does not produce a very dramatic effect. But with a small sample, one outlier can produce a large change in the mean. To illustrate such an effect, I examined the effect of Uganda's life expectancy on the mean for a smaller subset of nations than appeared in Figure 2.3. This new analysis is presented in Figure 2.4. Again, we see that the life expectancy in Uganda (about 52 years) is much lower than the life expectancy in Japan, the U.S., and the United Kingdom (all around 80 years). The average life expectancy across the three nations besides Uganda was 81.66 years, but this mean fell to 74.98 years when Uganda was included. The addition of a single outlier pulled the mean down by nearly 7 years. In this small dataset, the median would be between the United Kingdom and the U.S., right around 80 years. This example illustrates how an outlier pulls the mean in its direction. In this case, the mean was well below the median.

An illustration of an extreme outlier affecting the mean of a distribution recently appeared in a story in the *San Francisco Chronicle* about the average amount of growth in income for the various counties of the San Francisco Bay Area. Because the Bay Area is home to Silicon Valley, the area of high-tech industry, there is a lot of wealth in the area. The story in the newspaper revealed that over the last decade, San Mateo County had the highest average growth in

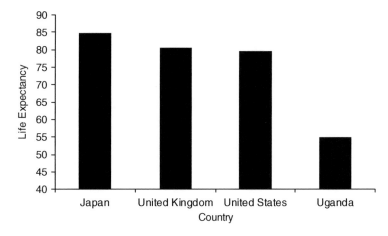

FIGURE 2.4 Life expectancy at birth in four countries.

income. If we focused solely on the mean, we might assume that many wealthy people moved to San Mateo County last quarter, that many of those who already lived there became wealthy, or both. To those of us who live in the San Francisco area, this news was a bit of a surprise, because most of the large tech companies in Silicon Valley are in Santa Clara County, so we assumed that county would have the highest average level of growth in wealth over the previous decade. Further down in the newspaper story, it was revealed that one particularly wealthy resident lives in San Mateo Country: Mark Zuckerberg, co-founder and CEO of Facebook! In this case, one extremely wealthy individual, an outlier, raised the average income level of the entire county. If Mark Zuckerberg's wealth were eliminated from the data, Santa Clara County would have had the highest income growth in the previous decade. The *median* income growth was higher in Santa Clara County than in San Mateo County, because the median is influenced less by a few extreme outliers than is the mean.

Writing it Up

When you encounter descriptions of central tendency in published articles, or when you write up such descriptions yourself, you will find the descriptions to be brief and simple. For the example above about the number of children to whom women gave birth, the proper write-up would be as follows:

In this distribution, the mean (M = 2.60) was slightly higher than the median (P_{50} = 2.00), indicating a slight positive skew.

Wrapping Up and Looking Forward

Measures of central tendency, particularly the mean and the median, are some of the most used and useful statistics for researchers. They each provide important information about an entire distribution of scores in a single number. For example, we know that the average height of a man in the United States is 5 ft 9 in. tall. This single number is used to summarize information about millions of men in this country. But for the same reason that the mean and median are useful, they can often be dangerous if we forget that a statistic such as the mean *ignores* a lot of information about a distribution, including the great amount of variety that exists in many distributions. Without considering the variety as well as the average, it becomes easy to make sweeping generalizations, or stereotypes, based on the mean. The measure of variance is the topic of the next chapter.

Work Problems

Suppose that I have collected data from a random sample of 10 adults and I want to know how much time each of them spends working outside the home in a week. I get the following data:

40   50   40   30   0   35   25   45   5   40

Please answer the following questions using these data.

1. What is the mode of this distribution?
2. What is the median of this distribution?
3. What is the mean of this distribution?
4. Do you believe this distribution is skewed in one direction or another? Why do you think so?
5. If you have calculated the mean and the median correctly, you will notice that the median is larger than the mean. What caused this difference between the mean and the median? Explain your answer.

 For answers to these work problems, and for additional work problems, please refer to the website that accompanies this book.

Note

1 It is also possible to calculate the median of a **grouped frequency distribution.** For an excellent description of the technique for calculating a median from a grouped frequency distribution, see Spatz (2010).

Chapter 3

Measures of Variability

Measures of central tendency, such as the mean and the median described in Chapter 2, provide useful information. But it is important to recognize that these measures are limited and, by themselves, do not provide a great deal of information. There is an old saying that provides a caution about the mean: "If your head is in the freezer and your feet are in the oven, on average you're comfortable." To illustrate, consider this example: Suppose I gave a sample of 100 fifth-grade children a survey to assess their level of depression. Suppose further that this sample had a mean of 10.0 on my depression survey and a median of 10.0 as well. All we know from this information is that the mean and the median are in the same place in my distribution, and this place is 10.0. Now consider what we do not know. We do not know if this is a high score or a low score. We do not know if all of the students in my sample have about the same level of depression or if they differ from each other. We do not know the highest depression score in our distribution or the lowest score. Simply put, we do not yet know anything about the **dispersion** (i.e., the spread) of scores in the distribution. In other words, we do not yet know anything about the variety of the scores in the distribution.

There are three measures of dispersion that researchers typically examine: the **range**, the **variance**, and the **standard deviation**. Of these, the standard deviation is the most widely used because it is both easy to understand and provides a summary statistic of the average amount of variation within a distribution.

Range

The range is simply the difference between the largest score (the **maximum value**) and the smallest score (the **minimum value**) of a distribution. This statistic gives researchers a quick sense of how spread out the scores of a distribution are, but it is not a particularly useful statistic because it can be quite misleading. For example, in our depression survey described earlier, we may have one student that scores a 1 and another that scores a 20, but the other 98 may all score a 10. In this example, the range will be 19 (20 − 1 = 19), but the scores really are not as spread out as the range might suggest. Researchers often take a quick look at the range to see whether all or most of the points on a scale, such as a survey, were covered in the sample.

Another common measure of the range of scores in a distribution is the **interquartile range (IQR).** Unlike the range, which is the difference between the largest and smallest score in the distribution, the IQR is the difference between the score that marks the 75th percentile (the third quartile) and the score that marks the 25th percentile (the first quartile). If the scores in a distribution were arranged in order from smallest to largest and then divided into groups of equal size, the IQR would contain the scores in the two middle quartiles (see Figure 3.1).

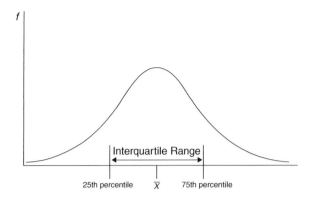

FIGURE 3.1 The interquartile range (IQR).

Variance

The variance provides a statistical average of the amount of dispersion in a distribution of scores. Because of the mathematical manipulation needed to produce a variance statistic (more about this in the next section), variance, by itself, is not often used by researchers to gain a sense of a distribution. In general, variance is used more as a step in the calculation of other statistics (e.g., standard deviation, analysis of variance) than as a stand-alone statistic. But with a simple manipulation, the variance can be transformed into the standard deviation, which is one of the statistician's favorite tools.

Standard Deviation

The best way to understand a standard deviation is to consider what the two words mean. *Deviation*, in this case, refers to the difference between an individual score in a distribution and the average score for the distribution. So if the average score for a distribution is 10, and an individual child has a score of 12, the deviation is 2. The other word in the term standard deviation is *standard*. In this case, standard means typical, or average. So a standard deviation is roughly the typical, or average, deviation between individual scores in a distribution and the mean for the distribution.[1] This is a very useful statistic because it provides a handy measure of how much spread there is in the scores in the distribution. When combined, the mean and the standard deviation provide a pretty good picture of what the distribution of scores is like.

In a sense, the range provides a measure of the total spread in a distribution (i.e., from the lowest to the highest scores), whereas the variance and standard deviation are measures of the average amount of spread within the distribution. Researchers tend to look at the range when they want a quick snapshot of a distribution, such as when they want to know whether all of the response categories on a survey question have been used (i.e., did people use all 5 points on the 5-point Likert scale?) or when they want a sense of the overall balance of scores in the distribution. The standard deviation is a very useful statistic that researchers constantly examine to provide the most easily interpretable and meaningful measure of the average dispersion of scores in a distribution.

Measures of Variability in Depth

Calculating the Variance and Standard Deviation

There are two central issues that I need to address when considering the formulas for calculating the variance and standard deviation of a distribution: (a) whether to use the formula for the sample or the population, and (b) how to make sense of these formulas.

It is important to note that the formulas for calculating the variance and the standard deviation differ depending on whether you are calculating these statistics for sample data or calculating parameters for an entire population. The reason these two formulas are different is quite complex and requires more space than allowed in a short book like this. I provide an overly brief explanation here and then encourage you to find a more thorough explanation in a traditional statistics textbook. Briefly, when we do not know the population mean, we must use the sample mean as an estimate. But the sample mean will probably differ from the population mean. Assuming that the sample mean and the population mean are different, when we calculate the variance using the sample mean, that variance will be different than it would have been had we used the population mean to calculate it. Because only the sample mean would produce the smallest possible variance for the sample data, if we had used the population mean instead of the sample mean, the result would have been a *larger* variance than we got using the sample mean. In other words, the variance we calculated using the sample mean was *smaller* than the variance we would have produced using the population mean. And this smaller variance that we got by using the sample mean results in a smaller standard deviation. In other words, when we calculate a standard deviation using the sample mean, we can assume that the standard deviation would have been *larger* if we had used the population mean, because the population mean most likely differs from the sample mean. Therefore, when we use the sample mean to generate an *estimate* of the population variance or standard deviation, we will actually *under*estimate the size of the true variance in the population. To adjust for this underestimation, we use $n - 1$ in the denominator of our sample formulas. Smaller denominators produce larger overall variance and standard deviation statistics, which will be more accurate estimates of the population parameters.

SAMPLE STATISTICS AS ESTIMATES OF POPULATION PARAMETERS

It is important to remember that most statistics, although generated from sample data, are used to make *estimations* about the population. As discussed in Chapter 1, researchers usually want to use their sample data to make some inferences about the population that the sample represents. Therefore, sample statistics often represent estimates of the population parameters. This point is discussed in more detail later in the book when examining inferential statistics. But it is important to keep this in mind as you read about these measures of variation. The formulas for calculating the variance and standard deviation of sample data are actually designed to make these sample statistics better *estimates* of the population parameters (i.e., the population variance and standard deviation). In later chapters (e.g., Chapters 6, 7, and 8), you will see how researchers use statistics like standard errors, confidence intervals, and probabilities to figure out how well their sample data estimate population parameters.

The formulas for calculating the variance and standard deviation of a population and the estimates of the population variance and standard deviation based on a sample are presented in Table 3.1. As you can see, the formulas for calculating the variance and the standard deviation are virtually identical. Because both require that you calculate the variance first, we begin with the formulas for calculating the variance (see the upper row of Table 3.1). This formula is known as the *deviation score formula*.[2]

When working with a population distribution, the formulas for both the variance and the standard deviation have a denominator of N, which is the size of the population. In the real world of research, particularly social science research, we usually assume that we are working with a sample that represents a larger population. For example, if I study the effectiveness of my new reading program with a class of second graders, as a researcher I assume that these particular second graders represent a larger population of second graders, or students more generally. Because of this type of inference, researchers generally think of their research participants as a

TABLE 3.1 Variance and standard deviation formulas

	Population	Estimate Based on a Sample
Variance	$\sigma^2 = \dfrac{\Sigma(X - \mu)^2}{N}$	$s^2 = \dfrac{\Sigma(X - \bar{X})^2}{n - 1}$
	where σ^2 is population variance, Σ is to sum, X is each score in the distribution, μ is the population mean, N is the number of cases in the population.	where s^2 is sample variance, Σ is to sum, X is each score in the distribution, $\bar{X}$ is the sample mean, n is the number of cases in the sample.
Standard Deviation	$\sigma = \sqrt{\dfrac{\Sigma(X - \mu)^2}{N}}$	$s = \sqrt{\dfrac{\Sigma(X - \bar{X})^2}{n - 1}}$
	where σ is population standard deviation, Σ is to sum, X is each score in the distribution, μ is the population mean, N is the number of cases in the population.	where s is sample standard deviation, Σ is to sum, X is each score in the distribution, $\bar{X}$ is the sample mean, n is the number of cases in the sample.

sample rather than a population, and the formula for calculating the variance of a sample is the formula more often used. Notice that the formula for calculating the variance of a sample is identical to that used for the population, except that the denominator for the sample formula is $n - 1$.

How much of a difference does it make if we use N or $n - 1$ in our denominator? Well, that depends on the size of the sample. If we have a sample of 500 people, there is virtually no difference between the variance formula for the population and for the estimate based on the sample. After all, dividing a numerator by 500 is almost the same as dividing it by 499. But when we have a small sample, such as a sample of 10, then there is a relatively large difference between the results produced by the population and the sample formulas.

To illustrate, suppose that I am calculating a standard deviation. After crunching the numbers, I find a numerator of 100. I divide this numerator by four different values depending on the sample size and whether we are dividing by N or $n - 1$. The results of these calculations are summarized in Table 3.2. With a sample size of 500, subtracting 1 from the denominator alters the size of the standard deviation by less than one one-thousandth. With a sample size of 10, subtracting 1 from the denominator increases the size of the standard deviation by nearly two-tenths. Note that in both the population and sample examples, given the same value in the numerator, larger samples produce dramatically smaller standard deviations. This makes sense because the larger the sample, the more likely it is that each member of the sample will have a value near the mean, thereby producing a smaller standard deviation.

The second issue to address involves making sense of the formulas for calculating the variance. In all honesty, there will be very few times that you will need to use this formula. Outside of my teaching duties, I haven't calculated a standard deviation by hand since my first statistics course. Thankfully, all computer statistics and spreadsheet programs, and many calculators, compute the variance and standard deviation for us. Nevertheless, it is interesting and quite informative to examine how these variance formulas work.

To begin this examination, let me remind you that the variance is simply an average of a distribution. To get an average, we need to add up all of the scores in a distribution and divide this sum by the number of scores in the distribution, which is n (remember the formula for calculating the mean in Chapter 2?). With the variance, however, we need to remember that we are not interested in the average *score* of the distribution. Rather, we are interested in the average *difference*, or *deviation*, between each score in the distribution and the mean of the distribution. To get this

TABLE 3.2   Effects of sample size and *n* – 1 on standard deviation

	N or *n* = 500	*N* or *n* = 10
Population	$\sigma = \sqrt{\dfrac{100}{500}} = .44721$	$\sigma = \sqrt{\dfrac{100}{10}} = 3.16$
Sample	$s = \sqrt{\dfrac{100}{499}} = .44766$	$s = \sqrt{\dfrac{100}{9}} = 3.33$

information, we have to calculate a *deviation score* for each individual score in the distribution (see Figure 3.2). This score is calculated by taking an individual score and subtracting the mean from that score. If we compute a deviation score for each individual score in the distribution, then we can sum the deviation scores and divide by *n* to get the average, or standard, deviation, right? Not quite.

The problem here is that, by definition, the mean of a distribution is the mathematical middle of the distribution. Therefore, some of the scores in the distribution will fall above the mean (producing positive deviation scores), and some will fall below the mean (producing negative deviation scores). When we add these positive and negative deviation scores together, the sum will be zero. Because the mean is the mathematical middle of the distribution, we will get zero when we add up these deviation scores no matter how big or small our sample, or how skewed or normal our distribution. And because we cannot find an average of zero (i.e., zero divided by *n* is zero, no matter what *n* is), we need to do something to get rid of this zero.

The solution statisticians came up with is to make each deviation score positive by squaring it. So, for each score in a distribution, we subtract the mean of the distribution and then square the deviation. If you look at the deviation score formulas in Table 3.1, you will see that all that the formula is doing with $(X - \mu)^2$ is taking each score, subtracting the mean, and squaring the resulting deviation score. What you get when you do this is the all-important **squared deviation**, which is used all the time in statistics. If we then put a summation sign in front, we have $\Sigma(X - \mu)^2$. What this tells us is that after we have produced a squared deviation score for each case in our distribution, we then need to add up all of these squared deviations, giving us the **sum of squared deviations**, or the **sum of squares (*SS*)**. Once this is done, we divide by the number of cases in our distribution, and we get an average, or mean, of the squared deviations. This is our variance.

Let's take a quick look at an example. Suppose I want to calculate the variance and standard deviation of the heights of my siblings. I have three of them, so the population of my siblings has *N* = 3. Their heights, in inches, are 68, 70, and 76. The mean for this distribution is (68 + 70 + 76)/3 = 71.33. Now we can use this mean to calculate three squared deviation scores:

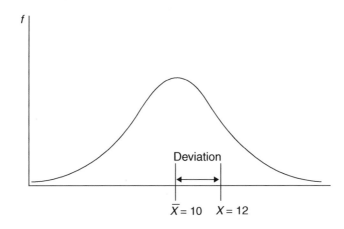

FIGURE 3.2   A deviation.

$$(68 - 71.33)^2 = (-3.33)^2 = 11.09$$
$$(70 - 71.33)^2 = (-1.33)^2 = 1.77$$
$$(76 - 71.33)^2 = (4.67)^2 = 21.81$$

Next, we sum these squared deviations:

$$11.09 + 1.77 + 21.81 = 34.67$$
$$\Sigma(X - \mu)^2 = 34.67$$

This is the sum of our squared deviations. To turn this into a variance, we just divide it by *N*, because this is a population of scores, not a sample:

$$34.67/3 = 11.56$$
$$\sigma^2 = 11.56$$

The final step in this process is to convert the variance into a standard deviation. Remember that in order to calculate the variance, we have to square each deviation score. We do this to avoid getting a sum of zero in our numerator. When we square these scores, we change our statistic from our original scale of measurement (i.e., whatever units of measurement were used to generate our distribution of scores) to a squared score. To reverse this process and give us a statistic that is back to our original unit of measurement, we merely need to take the square root of our variance. When we do this, we switch from the variance to the standard deviation. Therefore, the formula for calculating the standard deviation is exactly the same as the formula for calculating the variance, except that we put a big square root symbol over the whole formula. Notice that because of the squaring and square rooting process, the standard deviation and the variance are always positive numbers.

Returning to our example of my siblings' height, let's convert the variance into a standard deviation:

$$\sigma = \sqrt{11.56}$$

$$\sigma = 3.40$$

So the standard deviation for the population of scores representing the heights of my siblings is 3.40 in.

Why Have Variance?

If the variance is a difficult statistic to understand, and rarely examined by researchers, why not just eliminate this statistic and jump straight to the standard deviation? There are two reasons. First, we need to calculate the variance before we can find the standard deviation anyway, so it is no more work. Second, the fundamental piece of the variance formula, which is the sum of the squared deviations, is used in a number of other statistics, most notably analysis of variance (ANOVA). When you learn about more advanced statistics such as ANOVA (Chapter 9), factorial ANOVA (Chapter 10), and even regression (Chapter 13), you will see that each of these statistics uses the *sum of squares*, which is just another way of saying the sum of the squared deviations. Because the sum of squares is such an important part of so many statistics, the variance statistic has maintained its place in the teaching of basic statistics.

Examples: Examining the Range, Variance, and Standard Deviation

In the examples that follow, we examine the mean, range, variance, and standard deviation of the distribution of scores on a survey item and scores on a short test. These examples come from data that I collected in two different studies. To make sense of these (and all) statistics, you need to know how the survey questions were asked, what kinds of questions were on the test, what the full range of possible responses or correct answers was, and so on. Although this may sound obvious, I mention it here because, if you notice, much of the statistical information reported in the news (e.g., the results of polls) does not provide the exact wording of the questions or the response choices. Similarly, people often get very excited about test scores reported in the news, but they have no idea what the test questions looked like. Without this information, it is difficult to know exactly what the responses mean, and "lying with statistics" becomes easier.

The first example comes from a study I conducted with high school students in ninth and eleventh grades. The study was designed to gain information about students' attitudes toward school and their perceptions of their own goals and abilities. Students completed a survey made up of many items, and one of the survey items was, "If I have enough time, I can do even the most difficult work in this class." This item was designed to measure students' confidence in their abilities to succeed in their classwork. Students were asked to respond to this question by circling a number on a scale from 1 to 5. On this scale, circling the 1 means that the statement is *Not at all true* and the 5 means *Very true*. So students were basically asked to indicate how true they felt the statement was on a scale from 1 to 5, with higher numbers indicating a stronger belief that the statement was true.

I received responses from 491 students on this item. The distribution of responses produced the following sample statistics:

$$Sample\ Size = 491$$

$$Mean = 4.21$$

$$Standard\ Deviation = .98$$

$$Variance = (.98)^2 = .96$$

$$Range = 5 - 1 = 4$$

A graph of the frequency distribution for the responses on this item appears in Figure 3.3. As you can see in this graph, most of the students in the sample circled number 4 or number 5 on the response scale, indicating that they felt the item was quite true (i.e., that they were confident in their ability to do their classwork if they were given enough time). Because most students circled a 4 or a 5, the average score on this item is quite high (4.21 out of a possible 5). This is a negatively skewed distribution.

The graph in Figure 3.3 also provides information about the variety of scores in this distribution. Although our range statistic is 4, indicating that students in the sample circled both the highest and the lowest number on the response scale, we can see that the range does not really provide much useful information. For example, the range does not tell us that most of the students in our sample scored at the high end of the scale. By combining the information from the range statistic with the mean statistic, we can reach the following conclusion: "Although the distribution of scores on this item covers the full range, it appears that most scores are at the higher end of the response scale."

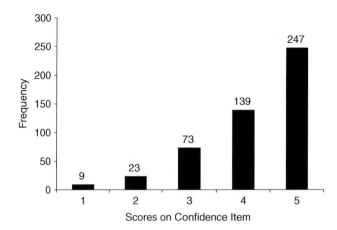

FIGURE 3.3 Frequency distribution of scores on the confidence item.

Now that we've determined that (a) the distribution of scores covers the full range of possible scores (i.e., from 1 to 5), and (b) most of the responses are at the high end of the scale (because the mean is 4.21 out of a possible 5), we may want a more precise measure of the average amount of variance among the scores in the distribution. For this we turn to the variance and standard deviation statistics. In this example, the variance (.96) is almost exactly the same as the standard deviation (.98). This is something of a fluke. Do not be fooled. It is quite rare for the variance and standard deviation to be so similar. In fact, this only happens if the standard deviation is about 1.0, because 1.0 squared is 1.0. So in this rare case, the variance and standard deviation provide almost the same information. Namely, they indicate that the average difference between an individual score in the distribution and the mean for the distribution is about 1 point on the 5-point scale.

Taken together, these statistics tell us the same things that the graph tells us, but more precisely. Namely, we now know that (a) students in the study responding to this item covered the whole range of response choices (i.e., 1–5); (b) most of the students answered at or near the top of the range, because the mean is quite high; and (c) the scores in this distribution generally pack fairly closely together, with most students having circled a number within 1 point of the mean, because the standard deviation was .98. The variance tells us that the average *squared deviation* is .96.

In our second example, I present data from a study I conducted with college students. Part of this study involved taking a short test of vocabulary knowledge that included seven test questions. If students answered none of these test questions correctly, their score on this variable would be 0, and if they answered all of the questions correctly they would receive a score of 7.

One hundred and forty students participated in this study, and the distribution produced the following statistics:

Sample Size = 140

Mean = 3.21

Standard Deviation = 1.60

Variance = $(1.60)^2 = 2.56$

Range = 6 – 0 = 6

Figure 3.4 illustrates the distribution of students' test scores. Notice that the range of scores on this test was 6, and recall that the total possible range of scores on the test was 7. So the range

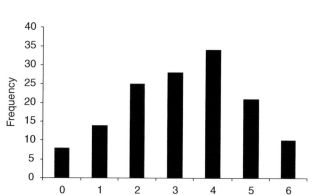

FIGURE 3.4 Frequency distribution of scores on the test.

of 6 tells us that no students in this study got the maximum possible test score of 7. You can see from the statistics provided above that the mean for this distribution was 3.21, which is near the middle of the total possible range of scores on this test. Although it provides an average score, it is impossible from just examining the mean to determine whether most students got 3 or 4 correct answers on the test, or whether roughly equal numbers of students got zero, 1, 2, 3, 4, 5, or 6 correct answers on the test. We could have even had a scenario where slightly less than half of the students in this study got zero correct answers and slightly more than half got 6 correct answers. All three scenarios would produce a mean of about 3.21, because that is roughly the middle of the range.

To get a better picture of this distribution, we need to consider the standard deviation in conjunction with the mean. Before discussing the actual standard deviation for this distribution of scores, let us briefly consider what we would expect the standard deviation to be for each of the three scenarios just described. First, if almost all of the students got either 3 or 4 correct answers on the test, we would expect a fairly small standard deviation, as we saw in the previous example using the confidence survey item. The more similar the responses are to an item, the smaller the standard deviation. However, if half of the students got zero correct answers and the other half got 6 correct answers, we would expect a large standard deviation (about 3.0) because each score would be about three units away from the mean (i.e., if the mean is about 3.0 and each test score is either 0 or 6, each response is about three units away from the mean). Finally, if the test scores are spread out across the range of test scores, we would expect a moderately sized standard deviation (about 1.60).

Now, when we look at the actual mean for this distribution (3.21) and the actual standard deviation (1.60), we can develop a rough picture of the distribution in our minds. Because we know that the test scores ranged from 0 to 6, a mean of 3.21 indicates that the average test score was close to the middle of this range. Furthermore, because we've got a moderately sized standard deviation of 1.60, we know that the scores are pretty well spread out, with a fair number of students receiving each of the 7 test scores in the range, but more students in the test score areas closer to the mean. If more students had scored near the extremes of the range (i.e., 0 or 6), a larger standard deviation would have been produced. Our standard deviation is of a moderate size (i.e., about one fourth the width of the range), so we know that we didn't get an overwhelming number of students scoring 3 on the test and we didn't have a situation where all of the students scored either 0 or 6 on the test. At this point, this is about all we can say about this distribution: The mean is near the middle of the scale, and the responses are pretty well spread out across the range, with more scores near the mean than at the extremes. To say any more, we would need to look at the number of scores in each category, as shown by the graph presented in Figure 3.4.

As we look at the actual distribution of scores presented in the graph in Figure 3.4, we can see that the predictions we generated from our statistics about the spread of the scores in the distribution are pretty accurate. The test scores are spread out across the range, with more scores near the mean than at the extreme ends. Notice that we did not need to consider the variance at all,

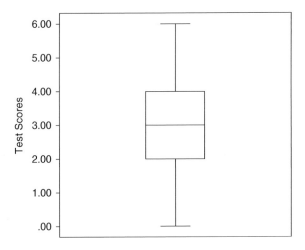

FIGURE 3.5 Boxplot for the test scores variable.

because the variance in this example (2.56) is on a different scale of measurement than our original 5-point response scale, and therefore is very difficult to interpret. Variance is an important statistic for the calculation of many statistics (e.g., ANOVA, regression), but it does little to help us understand the spread of a distribution of scores. The mean, standard deviation, and range, when considered together, can provide a rough picture of a distribution of scores. Often, a rough picture is all a researcher needs or wants. Sometimes, however, researchers need to know more precisely the characteristics of a distribution of scores. In that case, a picture, such as a graph, may be worth a thousand words.

Another useful way to examine a distribution of scores is to create a **boxplot**. In Figure 3.5, a boxplot is presented for the same variable that is represented in Figure 3.4, scores on a test. This boxplot was produced in the SPSS statistical software program. The box in this graph contains some very useful information. First, the line in the middle of the box represents the median of this distribution of scores. The top line of the box represents the 75th percentile of the distribution and the bottom line represents the 25th percentile. Therefore, the top and bottom lines of the box reveal the IQR for this distribution. In other words, 50 percent of the scores on this variable in this distribution are contained within the upper and lower lines of this box (i.e., 50 percent of the scores are between a score of 2 and a score of 4). The vertical lines coming out of the top and bottom of the box and culminating in horizontal lines reveal the largest and smallest scores in the distribution, or the range. These scores are 6 and 0, producing a range of 6 – 0 = 6. As you can see, the boxplot in Figure 3.5 contains a lot of useful information about the spread of scores on this variable in a single picture.

Worked Examples

In this section of the chapter I demonstrate how to calculate the range, variance, and standard deviation of a set of data. Because the variance and standard deviation formulas are slightly different for sample data and population data, I will calculate these twice using the same data.

I am a big baseball fan and like to go to games when I get the chance. For the last five games that I attended, the total number of runs scored by both teams combined were as follows:

4   6   7   10   13

Let's treat this as a sample of five games and calculate the range, variance, and standard deviation. First, the range is the difference between the largest value and the smallest value in the sample: 13 – 4 = 9. So the range for this distribution is 9.

TABLE 3.3 Raw scores and squared deviations for runs-scored-per-game example

Game	Runs Scored	Squared Deviation
Game 1	4	$(4 - 8)^2 = 16$
Game 2	6	$(6 - 8)^2 = 4$
Game 3	7	$(7 - 8)^2 = 1$
Game 4	10	$(10 - 8)^2 = 4$
Game 5	13	$(13 - 8)^2 = 25$
	Mean = 8	SS = 50

Next, we can calculate the variance. The first step is to find the mean. The sum of the values is $4 + 6 + 7 + 10 + 13 = 40$. When we divide this sum by the number of scores in the distribution, we get $40/5 = 8$. So the mean for this distribution is 8 runs per game.

Once we know the mean of the distribution, we can use it to calculate the squared deviations between the mean and each value in the distribution. Remember that you need to do what is in the parentheses *first*, then square that value. So subtract the mean from the score first, then square that difference (a.k.a. deviation). These calculations are presented in Table 3.3.

Once you have calculated the squared deviation between each score in the distribution and the mean for the distribution, we add up all of those squared deviations to find the sum of the squared deviations (*SS*). In this example, *SS* = 50.

Now that we have our *SS*, we use it to find the sample variance. Remember that with sample data, we divide the *SS* by $n - 1$. In this example, $n = 5$, so $n - 1 = 4$:

$$s^2 = \frac{50}{4} = 12.50$$

Finally, we convert this variance into a standard deviation by finding its square root:

$$s = \sqrt{12.50} = 3.54$$

So the standard deviation for this sample is 3.54 runs per game. Now let's suppose that these five games represented all of the games I attended last year. Now, instead of a sample, these games form the *population* of baseball games that I saw in person last year. If we want to find the range, variance, and standard deviation for this population, we can use a lot of the work that we've already completed when calculating the sample statistics. The range is the same: $13 - 4 = 9$. The mean is the same: $M = 8$. The sum of squared deviations is the same: *SS* = 50. To find the variance for this population, we divide the *SS* by *N* (instead of $n - 1$):

$$\sigma^2 = \frac{50}{5} = 10$$

Finally, to find the population's standard deviation, we find the square root of the variance:

$$\sigma = \sqrt{10} = 3.16$$

Notice that the difference between the sample standard deviation ($s = 3.54$) and the population standard deviation ($\sigma = 3.16$) is quite large, roughly 10 percent of the size of the standard deviation. That is because the sample size is so small, so the $n - 1$ we used in the formula for calculating the sample standard deviation made quite a difference.

For a video demonstrating how to calculate the range, variance, and standard deviation of a distribution, please refer to the website that accompanies this book.

Wrapping Up and Looking Forward

Measures of variation, such as the variance, standard deviation, and range, are important descriptive statistics. They provide useful information about the spread of the scores in a distribution, while measures of skew and kurtosis (described in detail in Chapter 4) provide information about the shape of the distribution. Perhaps even more important than their function as descriptors of a single distribution of scores is their role in more advanced statistics such as those coming in later chapters (e.g., ANOVA in Chapters 9, 10, and 11). In the next chapter, we examine the properties of the normal distribution, a distribution with a specific shape and characteristics. Using some of the concepts from Chapter 3, we can see how the normal distribution can be used to make inferences about the population based on sample data.

Work Problems

Suppose that I wanted to know something about the age of customers at my new pizza palace. I take the first six people that walk through the door and ask their age in years. I get the following scores:

6   20   34   42   50   56

1. Calculate and report the range of this distribution.
2. Calculate and report the variance of this distribution.
3. Calculate and report the standard deviation of this distribution.
4. Write a sentence or two in which you explain, using your own words, what a standard deviation is (in general, not this particular standard deviation).
5. Pretend that this distribution of scores represents a population rather than a sample. Calculate and report the standard deviation and explain what it tells you.
6. Explain why the standard deviation you reported for Question 3 differs from the standard deviation you reported for Question 5.
7. Think of an example that illustrates why it is important to know about the standard deviation of a distribution.

 For answers to these work problems, and for more work problems, please refer to the website that accompanies this book.

Notes

1 Although the standard deviation is technically not the "average deviation" for a distribution of scores, in practice this is a useful heuristic for gaining a rough conceptual understanding of what this statistic is. The actual formula for the average deviation would be $\Sigma(|X - \text{mean}|)/N$.

2 It is also possible to calculate the variance and standard deviation using the *raw score formula*, which does not require that you calculate the mean. The raw score formula is included in most standard statistics textbooks.

CHAPTER 4

The Normal Distribution

The **normal distribution** is a concept most people have some familiarity with, even if they have never heard the term. A more familiar name for the normal distribution is the **bell curve**, because a normal distribution forms the shape of a bell. The normal distribution is extremely important in statistics and has some specific characteristics that make it so useful. In this chapter, I briefly describe what a normal distribution is and why it is so important to researchers. Then I discuss some of the features of the normal distribution, and of sampling, in more depth.

Characteristics of the Normal Distribution

In Figure 4.1, I present a simple line graph that depicts a normal distribution. Recall from the discussion of graphs in Chapter 1 that this type of graph shows the frequency, i.e., number of cases, with particular scores on a single variable. So in this graph, the *Y* axis shows the frequency of the cases and the *X* axis shows the scores on the variable of interest. For example, if the variable were scores on an IQ test, the *X* axis would have the scores ranging from smallest to largest. The mean, median, and mode would be 100, and the peak of the line would show that the frequency of cases is highest at 100 (i.e., the mode). As you move away from the mode in either direction, the height of the line goes down, indicating fewer cases (i.e., lower frequencies) at those other scores.

If you take a look at the normal distribution shape presented in Figure 4.1, you may notice that the normal distribution has three fundamental characteristics. First, it is **symmetrical**, meaning that the higher half and the lower half of the distribution are mirror images of each other. Second, the mean, median, and mode are all in the same place, in the center of the distribution (i.e., the peak of the bell curve). Because of this second feature, the normal distribution is highest in the middle, so it is **unimodal**, and it curves downward toward the higher values at the right side of the distribution and toward the lower values on the left side of the distribution. Finally, the normal distribution is **asymptotic**, meaning that the upper and lower tails of the distribution never actually touch the baseline, also known as the *X* axis. This is important because it indicates that the probability of a score in a distribution occurring by chance is never zero. (I present a more detailed discussion of how the normal distribution is used to determine probabilities in Chapter 5.)

Why Is the Normal Distribution So Important?

When researchers collect data from a sample, sometimes all they want to know are the characteristics of the sample. For example, if I wanted to examine the eating habits of 100 first-year college students, I would just select 100 students, ask them what they eat, and summarize my data. These data might give me statistics such as the average number of calories consumed each day by the 100 students in my sample, the most commonly eaten foods, the variety of foods eaten, and

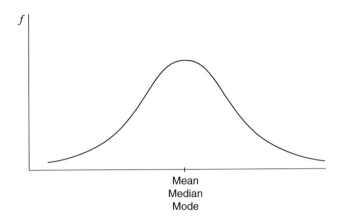

FIGURE 4.1 The normal distribution.

so on. All of these statistics simply *describe* characteristics of my sample, and are therefore called **descriptive statistics**. Descriptive statistics generally are used only to describe a specific sample. When all we care about is describing a specific sample, it does not matter whether the scores from the sample are normally distributed or not.

Many times, however, researchers want to do more than simply describe a sample. Sometimes they want to know what the exact probability is of something occurring in their sample just due to chance. For example, if the average student in my sample consumes 2,000 calories a day, what are the chances, or probability, of having a student in the sample who consumes 5,000 calories or more a day? The three characteristics of the normal distribution are each critical in statistics because they allow us to make good use of **probability** statistics.

In addition, researchers often want to be able to make inferences about the **population** based on the data they collect from their **sample**. To determine whether some phenomenon observed in a sample represents an actual phenomenon in the population from which the sample was drawn, **inferential statistics** are used. For example, suppose I begin with an assumption that in the population of men and women there is no difference in the average number of calories consumed in a day. This assumption of no difference is known as a **null hypothesis** (see Chapter 7 for more information on hypotheses). Now suppose that I select a sample of men and a sample of women, compare their average daily calorie consumption, and find that the men eat an average of 200 calories more per day than do the women. Given my null hypothesis of no difference, what is the probability of finding a difference this large between my samples *by chance?* To calculate these probabilities, I need to rely on the normal distribution, because the characteristics of the normal distribution allow statisticians to generate exact probability statistics. In the next section, I will briefly explain how this works.

The Normal Distribution in Depth

It is important to note that the normal distribution is what is known in statistics as a **theoretical distribution**. That is, one rarely, if ever, gets a distribution of scores from a sample that forms an exact, normal distribution. Rather, what you get when you collect data is a distribution of scores that may or may not approach a normal, bell-shaped curve. Because the theoretical normal distribution is what statisticians use to develop probabilities, a distribution of scores that is not normal may be at odds with these probabilities. Therefore, there are a number of statistics that begin with the assumption that scores are normally distributed. When this assumption is violated (i.e., when the scores in a distribution are not normally distributed), there can be dire consequences.

The most obvious consequence of violating the assumption of a normal distribution is that the probabilities associated with a normal distribution are not valid. For example, if you have a normal distribution of scores on some variable (e.g., IQ test scores of adults in the United States), you can use the probabilities based on the normal distribution to determine exactly what percentage of the scores in the distribution will be 120 or higher on the IQ test (see Chapter 5 for a description of how to do this). But suppose the scores in our distribution do not form a normal distribution. Suppose, for some reason, we have an unusually large number of high scores (e.g., over 120) and an unusually small number of low scores (e.g., below 90) in our distribution. If this were the case, when we use probability estimates based on the normal distribution, we would underestimate the actual number of high scores in our distribution and overestimate the actual number of low scores in our distribution.

The Relationship Between the Sampling Method and the Normal Distribution

As I discussed in Chapter 1, researchers use a variety of different methods for selecting samples. Sometimes samples are selected so that they represent the population in specific ways, such as the percentage of men or the proportion of wealthy individuals (**representative sampling**). Other times, samples are selected randomly with the hope that any differences between the sample and the population are also random, rather than systematic (**random sampling**). Often, however, samples are selected for their convenience rather than for how they represent the larger population (**convenience sampling**). The problem of violating the assumption of normality becomes most problematic when our sample is not an adequate representation of our population.

The relationship between the normal distribution and the sampling methods is as follows. The probabilities generated from the normal distribution depend on (a) the shape of the distribution and (b) the idea that the sample is not somehow systematically different from the population. If I select a sample randomly from a population, I know that this sample may not look the same as another sample of equal size selected randomly from the same population. But any differences between my sample and other random samples of the same size selected from the same population would differ from each other randomly, not systematically. In other words, my sampling method was not **biased** such that I would continually select a sample from one end of my population (e.g., the more wealthy, the better educated, the higher achieving) if I continued using the same method for selecting my sample. Contrast this with a convenience sampling method. If I only select schools that are near my home or work, I will continually select schools with similar characteristics. For example, if I live in the "Bible Belt" (an area of the southern United States that is more religious, on average, than other parts of the country), my sample will probably be biased in that my sample will likely hold more fundamentalist religious beliefs than the larger population of schoolchildren. Now, if this characteristic is not related to the variable I am studying (e.g., achievement), then it may not matter that my sample is biased in this way. But if this bias is related to my variable of interest (e.g., "How strongly do American schoolchildren believe in God?"), then I may have a problem.

Suppose that I live and work in Cambridge, Massachusetts. Cambridge is in a section of the country with an inordinate number of highly educated people because there are a number of high-quality universities in the immediate area (Harvard, MIT, Boston College, Boston University, etc.). If I conduct a study of student achievement using a convenience sample from this area, and try to argue that my sample represents the larger population of students in the United States, probabilities that are based on the normal distribution may not apply. That is because my sample will be more likely than the national average to score at the high end of the distribution. If, based on my sample, I try to predict the average achievement level of students in the United States, or the percentage that score in the bottom quartile, or the score that marks the 75th percentile, all of these predictions will be off, because the probabilities that are generated by the normal distribution assume that the sample is not biased. If this assumption is violated, we cannot trust our results.

Skew and Kurtosis

Two characteristics used to describe a distribution of scores are **skew** and **kurtosis**. When a sample of scores is not normally distributed (i.e., not the bell shape), there are a variety of shapes it can assume. One way a distribution can deviate from the bell shape is if there is a bunching of scores at one end and a few scores pulling a tail of the distribution out toward the other end. If there are a few scores creating an elongated tail at the higher end of the distribution, it is said to be **positively skewed** (see Figure 4.2). If the tail is pulled out toward the lower end of the distribution, the shape is called **negatively skewed** (See Figure 4.3). As you can see, and as discussed in Chapter 2, the mean in a skewed distribution is pulled in the direction of the tail. Skew does not affect the median as much as it affects the mean, however. So a positively skewed distribution will have a higher mean than median, and a negatively skewed distribution will have a lower mean than median. If you recall that the mean and the median are the same in a normal distribution, you can see how the skew affects the mean relative to the median.

As you might have guessed, skewed distributions can distort the accuracy of the probabilities based on the normal distribution. For example, if most of the scores in a distribution occur at the lower end with a few scores at the higher end (positively skewed distribution), the probabilities that are based on the normal distribution will underestimate the actual number of scores at the lower end of this skewed distribution and overestimate the number of scores at the higher end of the distribution. In a negatively skewed distribution, the opposite pattern of errors in prediction will occur.

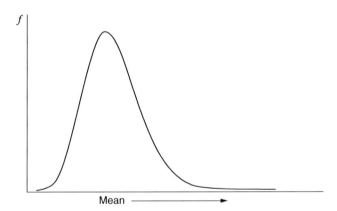

FIGURE 4.2 A positively skewed distribution.

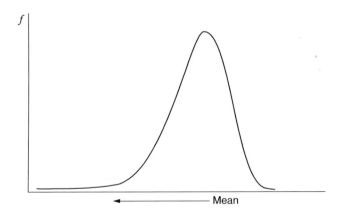

FIGURE 4.3 A negatively skewed distribution.

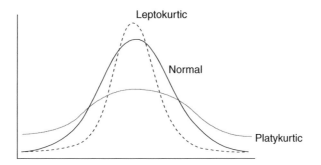

FIGURE 4.4 A comparison of normal, platykurtic, and leptokurtic distributions.

Kurtosis refers to the shape of the distribution in terms of height, or flatness. When a distribution is symmetrical but has a peak that is higher than that found in a normal distribution, it is called **leptokurtic**. When a distribution is flatter than a normal distribution, it is called **platykurtic**. Because the normal distribution contains a certain percentage of scores in the middle area (i.e., about 68 percent of the scores fall between one standard deviation above and one standard deviation below the mean), a distribution that is either platykurtic or leptokurtic will likely have a different percentage of scores near the mean than will a normal distribution. Specifically, a leptokurtic distribution will probably have a greater percentage of scores closer to the mean and fewer in the upper and lower tails of the distribution, whereas a platykurtic distribution will have more scores at the ends and fewer in the middle than will a normal distribution. These different shapes of distributions are presented in Figure 4.4.

Example 1: Applying Normal Distribution Probabilities to a Normal Distribution

In Chapter 5, I go into much more detail explaining how the normal distribution is used to calculate probabilities and percentile scores. In this chapter, I offer a more general example to provide you with an idea of the utility of the normal distribution.

In Figure 4.5, I present a graphic of the normal distribution divided into standard deviation intervals. In a normal distribution, we know that a certain proportion of the population is contained between the mean and one standard deviation above the mean. Because the normal distribution is symmetrical, we also know that the same proportion of the population is contained between the mean and one standard deviation *below* the mean. Because the normal distribution has the mode in the middle, where the mean of the population is, we also know that the further we get from the mean, the smaller the proportion of the population we will find. Therefore, there is a smaller proportion of the population contained between one and two standard deviations above the mean than there is between the mean and one standard

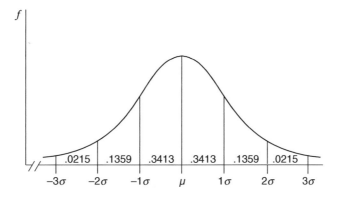

FIGURE 4.5 The normal distribution divided into standard deviation intervals.

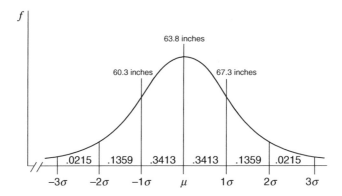

FIGURE 4.6 The normal distribution divided into standard deviation intervals with heights indicated for the mean and one standard deviation above and below the mean.

deviation above the mean. For example, .3413 (or 34.13 percent) of the population will have scores between the mean and one standard deviation above the mean in a normal distribution, but only .1359 (or 13.59 percent) will have scores between one standard deviation and two standard deviations above the mean.

We can use this information to understand where an individual score in a distribution falls in relation to the rest of the scores in the population. For example, if I know that the average height for an adult woman is 63.8 in., with a standard deviation of 3.5 in., I can use the normal distribution to determine some height characteristics of the population. For example, as seen in Figure 4.6, I know that 34.13 percent of women will be between 63.8 and 67.3 in. tall, because 63.8 in. is the mean and 67.3 in. is the mean plus one standard deviation (i.e., 63.8 + 3.5 = 67.3). Similarly, I know that 68.26 percent of women will be between and 60.3 and 67.3 in. tall, because that is the proportion of the population that is contained between one standard deviation below and one standard deviation above the mean. As we will discuss in Chapter 5, the normal distribution allows us to determine, very specifically, the proportion of scores in a population (or normally distributed sample) that falls below or above an individual score, and the probability of randomly selecting an individual with a score that is above or below that score. This is the basis of many statistics that you may have encountered (e.g., what your percentile score was on a standardized test, or what percentage of the population you are taller than), as well as the inferential statistics that we will discuss in the latter chapters of this book.

The normal distribution, and the ability to use the normal distribution to calculate probabilities, is used in the real world all the time. For example, the weight of infants and toddlers at various ages has a normal distribution. Pediatricians use these normal distributions to determine whether young children are growing normally. When toddlers or infants are severely underweight for their age, they may be diagnosed with a condition called failure to thrive. This is a serious medical condition that often requires immediate treatment. But babies and toddlers come in a variety of sizes, so how should doctors decide whether a baby is just small as opposed to dangerously unhealthy? One way to make this determination is to compare the child with other children of the same age. Using the normal distribution, doctors can determine how the weight of one baby compares to the weight of all babies in the population. When a baby weighs less than 95 percent of all babies of the same age, that is one indication that the baby may be failing to thrive.

Another example of the use of the normal distribution comes from the world of intelligence testing and IQ scores. Traditional IQ tests have a mean of 100, and a standard deviation of 15, and the scores form a normal distribution in the population. Individuals who score two standard deviations or more below the mean are often considered as having an intellectual disability. If you look at Figure 4.5, you will notice that only 2.15 percent of the normal distribution scores at least two standard deviations below the mean, so this is the proportion of the population that would be expected to have an intellectual disability. These probabilities associated with the normal distribution have important legal consequences. For example, in some states in the U.S., individuals with IQ scores below 70 are protected from the death penalty because they are not considered intelligent enough to fully understand the crimes they have committed or the nature of the death penalty. To determine who deserves such protection, probabilities associated with the normal distribution are used. Only that small proportion of the distribution with IQ scores of two standard deviations or more below the mean receive such protection from the death penalty in many states. (In 2014, a man in a Florida prison with an IQ score of around 70 was spared from the death penalty when the Supreme Court decided that IQ scores alone were not a sound basis for deciding whether someone was intelligent enough to understand the death penalty.) These are just two of many examples of the use of the normal distribution, and the probabilities that are associated with it, in real life.

Example 2: Applying Normal Distribution Probabilities to a Nonnormal Distribution

To illustrate some of the difficulties that can arise when we try to apply the probabilities that are generated from using the normal distribution to a distribution of scores that is skewed, I present a distribution of sixth-grade students' scores on a measure of self-esteem. In these data, 677 students completed a questionnaire that included four items designed to measure students' overall sense of self-esteem. Examples of these items included "On the whole, I am satisfied with myself" and "I feel I have a number of good qualities." Students responded to each item of the questionnaire using a 5-point rating scale with 1 = *Not at all true* and 5 = *Very true*. Students' responses on these four items were then averaged, creating a single self-esteem score that ranged from a possible low of 1 to a possible high of 5. The frequency distribution for this self-esteem variable is presented in Figure 4.7.

As you can see, the distribution of scores presented in Figure 4.7 does not form a nice, normal, bell-shaped distribution. Rather, most of the students in this sample scored at the high end of the distribution, and a long tail extends out toward the lower end of the scale. This is a negatively skewed distribution of scores. The happy part of this story is that most of the students in this sample appear to feel quite good about themselves. The sad part of the story is that some of the assumptions of the normal distribution are violated by this skewed distribution. Let's take a look at some specifics.

One of the qualities of a normal distribution is that it is symmetrical, with an equal percentage of scores between the mean and one standard deviation below the mean as there are between the mean and one standard deviation above the mean. In other words, in a normal distribution,

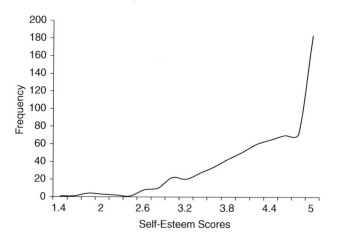

FIGURE 4.7 Frequency distribution for self-esteem scores.

there should be about 34 percent of the scores within one standard deviation above the mean and another 34 percent within one standard deviation below the mean. In our distribution of self-esteem scores presented earlier, the mean is 4.28 and the standard deviation is .72. A full 50 percent of the distribution falls between the mean and one standard deviation above the mean in this group of scores (see Figure 4.7). So, although I might predict that about 16 percent of my distribution will have scores more than one standard deviation above the mean in a normal distribution, in my skewed distribution of self-esteem scores, I can see that there are no students with scores more than one standard deviation above the mean. In Chapter 5, I present a more thorough discussion of how to use the normal distribution to calculate standard deviation units, probabilities, and percentile scores in a normal distribution.

As this example demonstrates, the probabilities that statisticians have generated using the normal distribution may not apply well to skewed or otherwise nonnormal distributions of data. This should not lead you to believe, however, that nonnormal distributions of scores are worthless. In fact, even if you have a nonnormal distribution of scores in your sample, these scores can create normal sampling distributions for use in inferential statistics (a sampling distribution is a theoretical distribution of sample statistics drawn from many samples taken from a single population – see Chapter 6). What is perhaps most important to keep in mind is that a nonnormal distribution of scores may be an indication that your sample differs in important and systematic ways from the population that it is supposed to represent. When making inferences about a population based on a sample, be very careful to define the population precisely and to be aware of any biases you may have introduced by your method of selecting your sample. It is also important to note, however, that not all variables are normally distributed in the population. Therefore, nonnormal sample data may be an accurate representation of nonnormal population data, as well as an indication that the sample does not accurately represent the population. The normal distribution can be used to generate probabilities about the likelihood of selecting an individual or another sample with certain characteristics (e.g., distance from the mean) from a population. If your sample is not normal and your method of selecting the sample may be systematically biased to include those with certain characteristics (e.g., higher than average achievers, lower than average income, etc.), then the probabilities of the normal distribution may not apply well to your sample.

Wrapping Up and Looking Forward

The theoretical normal distribution is a critical element of statistics, primarily because many of the probabilities that are used in inferential statistics are based on the assumption of normal distributions. As you will see in the coming chapters, statisticians use these probabilities to determine the probability of getting certain statistics and to make inferences about the population based on the sample. Even if the data in a sample are not normally distributed, it is possible that the data in the population from which the sample was selected may be normally distributed. In Chapter 5, I describe how the normal distribution, through the use of z scores and standardization, is used to determine the probability of obtaining an individual score from a sample that is a certain distance away from the sample mean. You will also learn about other fun statistics like percentile scores in Chapter 5.

Work Problems

1. In statistics, the word "distribution" comes up a lot.
    a. In your own words, explain what a distribution is.
    b. Then, again in your own words, explain what a "normal distribution" is.
2. What does "asymptotic" mean and why is it important?

3. In statistics, we use the normal distribution a lot.
   a. What is so great about it? In other words, what does it do for us?
   b. Describe something that the normal distribution lets us, as statisticians, do that we cannot do without it.

4. Many believe that most human traits form a normal distribution. Height, weight, intelligence, musical ability, friendliness, attractiveness, etc. are all examples of things that might form a normal distribution.
   a. First, explain whether you agree with this assumption, and why or why not.
   b. Second, think of an example of a trait that does NOT form a normal distribution in the population.

5. If you know that in the population of adults, the average number of hours slept per night is 7, with a standard deviation of 2, what proportion of the population would you expect to sleep between 7 and 9 hours per night?

 For answers to these work problems, and for additional work problems, please refer to the website that accompanies this book.

CHAPTER 5

Standardization and z Scores

If you know the mean and standard deviation of a distribution of scores, you have enough information to develop a picture of the distribution. Sometimes researchers are interested in describing individual scores within a distribution. Using the mean and the standard deviation, researchers are able to generate a **standard score**, also called a **z score**, to help them understand where an individual score falls in relation to other scores in the distribution. Through a process of **standardization**, researchers are also better able to compare individual scores in the distributions of two separate variables. Standardization is simply a process of converting each score in a distribution to a z score. A z score is a number that indicates how far above or below the mean a given score in the distribution is in standard deviation units. So standardization is simply the process of converting individual **raw scores** in the distribution into standard deviation units.

Suppose that you are a college student taking final exams. In your biology class, you take your final exam and get a score of 65 out of a possible 100. In your statistics final, you get a score of 42 out of 200. On which exam did you get a "better" score? The answer to this question may be more complicated than it appears. First, we must determine what we mean by "better." If better means the percentage of correct answers on the exam, clearly you did better on the biology exam. But if your statistics exam was much more difficult than your biology exam, is it fair to judge your performance solely on the basis of the percentage of correct responses? A fairer alternative may be to see how well you did compared to other students in your classes. To make such a comparison, we need to know the mean and standard deviation of each distribution. With these statistics, we can generate z scores (a.k.a. standard scores).

Suppose the mean on the biology exam was 60 with a standard deviation of 10. That means you scored 5 points above the mean, which is half of a standard deviation above the mean (higher than the average for the class). Suppose further that the average on the statistics test was 37 with a standard deviation of 5. Again, you scored 5 points above the mean, but this represents a full standard deviation over the average. Using these statistics, on which test would you say you performed better? To fully understand the answer to this question, let's examine standardization and z scores in more depth.

Standardization and z Scores in Depth

As you can see in the previous example, it is often difficult to compare two scores for two variables when the variables are measured using different scales. The biology test in the example was measured on a scale from 1 to 100, whereas the statistics exam used a scale from 1 to 200. When variables have such different scales of measurement, it is almost meaningless to compare the raw scores (i.e., 65 and 42 on these exams). Instead, we need some way to put these two exams on the same scale, or to *standardize* them. One of the most common methods of standardization used in statistics is to convert raw scores into standard deviation units, or z scores. The formula for doing this is very simple and is presented in Table 5.1.

TABLE 5.1 Formula for calculating a z score

$$z = \frac{\text{raw score} - \text{mean}}{\text{standard deviation}}$$

or

$$z = \frac{X - \mu}{\sigma}$$

or

$$z = \frac{X - \bar{X}}{s}$$

where X is the raw score,
μ is the population mean,
σ is the population standard deviation,
$\bar{X}$ is the sample mean,
s is the sample standard deviation.

As you can see from the formulas in Table 5.1, to standardize a score (i.e., to create a z score), you simply subtract the mean from an individual raw score and divide this by the standard deviation. So if the raw score is above the mean, the z score will be positive, whereas a raw score below the mean will produce a negative z score. When an entire distribution of scores is standardized, the average (i.e., mean) z score for the standardized distribution will always be zero, and the standard deviation of this distribution will always be 1.0.

Notice that there are actually two formulas presented in Table 5.1. The first one includes the population mean (μ, ***mu***) and the population standard deviation (σ, ***sigma***). This is the formula that you use when you are working with a distribution of scores from a population, and you know the population mean and standard deviation. When you are working with a distribution of scores from a sample, the correct formula to use for calculating standard scores (i.e., z scores) is the bottom formula in Table 5.1. This uses the sample mean ($\bar{X}$, ***x-bar***) and the sample standard deviation (s).

Interpreting z Scores

z scores tell researchers instantly how large or small an individual score is relative to other scores in the distribution. For example, if I know that one of my students got a z score of −1.5 on an exam, I would know that student scored 1.5 standard deviations below the mean on that exam. If another student had a z score of .29, I would know the student scored .29 standard deviation units above the mean on the exam.

Let's pause here and think for a moment about what z scores do *not* tell us. If I told you that I had a z score of 1.0 on my last spelling test, what would you think of my performance? What you would know for sure is that (a) I did better than the average person taking the test, (b) my score was one standard deviation above the mean, and (c) if the scores in the distribution were normally distributed (Chapter 4), my score was better than about 84 percent of the scores in the distribution. But what you would *not* know would be (a) how many words I spelled correctly, (b) if I am a good speller, (c) how difficult the test was, (d) if the other people that took the test are good spellers, (e) how many other people took the test, and so on. As you can see, a z score alone does not provide as much information as we might want. To further demonstrate this point, suppose that after I told you I had a z score of 1.0 on the spelling test, I went on to tell you that the average score on the test was 12 out of 50 and that everyone else who took the test was seven years old. Not very impressive in that context, is it?

Now, with the appropriate cautions in mind, let's consider a couple more uses of z scores and standardization. One of the handiest features of z scores is that, when used with a normally

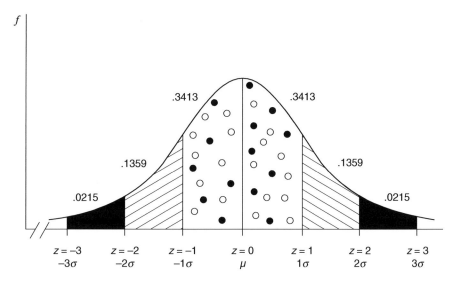

FIGURE 5.1 The standard normal distribution. This is the normal distribution divided into standard deviation units, and it shows the proportion of the normal distribution that falls between each z score.

distributed set of scores, they can be used to determine **percentile scores**. Percentile scores are scores that indicate the percentage of the distribution that falls below a given score. For example, the score that marks the 75th percentile in a distribution is the score at which 75 percent of the distribution falls below, and 25 percent falls above. If you have a normal distribution of scores, you can use z scores to discover which score marks the 90th percentile of a distribution (i.e., that raw score at which 90 percent of the distribution scored below and 10 percent scored above). This is because statisticians have demonstrated that in a normal distribution, a precise percentage of scores will fall between the mean and one standard deviation above the mean. Because normal distributions are perfectly symmetrical, we know that the exact same percentage of scores that falls between the mean and one standard deviation *above* the mean will also fall between the mean and one standard deviation *below* the mean. In fact, statisticians have determined the precise percentage of scores that will fall between the mean and any z score (i.e., number of standard deviation units above or below the mean). A table of these values is provided in Appendix A. When you also consider that in a normal distribution the mean always marks the exact center of the distribution, you know that the mean is the spot in the distribution in which 50 percent of the cases fall below and 50 percent fall above. With this in mind, it is easy to find the score in a distribution that marks the 90th percentile, or any percentile, for that matter. In Figure 5.1, we can see the percentages of scores in a normal distribution that fall between different z score values. This figure contains the *standard normal distribution*.

TIME OUT FOR TECHNICALITY: INTERPRETING APPENDIX A

Using the values in Appendix A is simple once you get the hang of it. The left column shows the z score value to the nearest tenth. If you need to get more precise than that, you can use the values in the top row. For example, if you have a z score of .15, then you find the intersection of the .1 row with the .05 column to create your z value of .15. If you go to that intersection, you will see that you get a value of .5596. This number indicates the proportion of the normal distribution that falls *below* this z value. So using Appendix A, we can conclude that .5596, or 55.96 percent, of the distribution has a z score of .15 *or less*. To find the proportion of the normal distribution that would be above a z score of .15, you simply subtract .5596 from the total of 1.0: 1.0 – .5596 = .4404. This value tells us that the probability of getting a z score of .15 *by chance* is .4404. In statistics, the probability of getting a particular statistic by chance is called a *p* value. As the z values get larger, the proportion of the normal distribution below (i.e., to the left of) the z value increases, and the *p* value becomes smaller. For a z score of 3.0, the area below the z value is .9987, and the *p* value is .0013. The second table in Appendix A shows you the *p* values for several large z scores. As you can see, the *p* values become tiny as the z scores increase. Remember that the larger the z score, the further out the score will be in the tail of the normal distribution, and the smaller the frequencies. Also, keep in mind that because the normal distribution is symmetrical, everything that applies to the positive (i.e., right) side of the distribution also applies to the negative (i.e., left) side. So a z value of –3.0 will also have a corresponding *p* value of .0013.

 For a video demonstration of how to read and use Appendix A, see the video on the companion website for this book.

Let us consider an example. The Scholastic Aptitude Test (SAT) is an exam many high school students in the United States take when they are applying to college. One portion of the SAT covers mathematics and has a range of 200–800 points. Suppose I know that the average SAT math score for males is 517, with a standard deviation of 100, which forms a normal distribution. In this distribution, I already know that the score that marks the 50th percentile is 517. Suppose I want to know the score that marks the 90th percentile. To find this number, I have to follow a series of simple steps.

Step 1: Using the z score table in Appendix A, find the z score that marks the 90th percentile. To do this, we need to remember that the 90th percentile is the score at which 90 percent of the distribution falls below and 10 percent of the distribution falls above. In Appendix A, the values represent the proportion of the normal distribution that falls to the left of (i.e., *below*) the given z values. So in this example we are looking for the value in Appendix A that is closest to .90, because that is the value that marks the 90th percentile. In Appendix A, the closest value we can find to .90 is .8997, and that corresponds to a z value of 1.28 (i.e., where the z = 1.2 row intersects the .08 column). So z = 1.28 in this example.

Step 2: Convert this z score back into the original unit of measurement. Remember that the SAT math test is measured on a scale from 200 to 800. We now know that the mean for males who took the test is 517, and that the 90th percentile score of this distribution is 1.28 standard deviations above the mean (because z = 1.28). So what is the actual SAT math score that marks the 90th percentile? To answer this, we have to convert our z score from standard deviation units into raw score units and add them to the mean. The formula for doing this is

$$X = \mu + (z)(\sigma)$$

In this equation, X is the raw score we are trying to discover, μ is the average score in the distribution, z is the z score we found, and σ is the standard deviation for the distribution. Plugging our numbers into the formula, we find that

$$X = 517 + (1.28)(100)$$

$$X = 517 + 128$$

$$X = 645$$

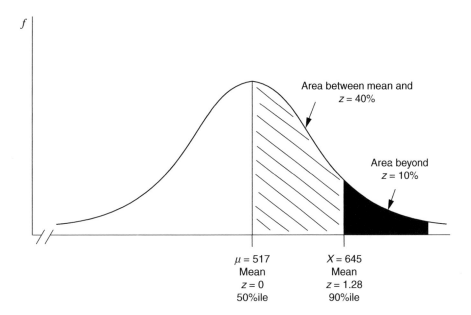

FIGURE 5.2 The score that marks the 90th percentile of this distribution.

Step 3: Now we can wrap words around our result and answer our original question. When doing this, it is often helpful to use the original question when stating our finding, as follows.

Question: *What is the score that marks the 90th percentile of the distribution of male students' SAT math scores?*

Answer: *The score of 645 marks the 90th percentile of the distribution of male students' SAT math scores. This z score, the percentile score, and the corresponding raw score are depicted in Figure 5.2.*

Just as we can use z scores to find the raw score that marks a certain percentile in a distribution, we can also use z scores to help us convert a known raw score into a percentile score. For example, if I know that a student in my distribution has a score of 425 on the SAT math test, I might want to know the percentage of the distribution that scored above and below 425. This is the type of conversion that has happened when students' standardized test scores are published in the local newspaper using percentiles under headlines such as "California Students Score in 45th Percentile on National Test!" Similarly, when a proud parent exclaims "My Johnny is in the top 10 percent in height for his age group!" a conversion from a raw score to a percentile score has taken place, with the help of a z score. Here's how it's done:

Step 1: We must begin by converting the raw score into a z score. In our example, the raw score is 425 ($X = 425$). To convert this into a z score, we simply recall our mean ($\mu = 517$) and our standard deviation ($\sigma = 100$) and then plug these numbers into the z score formula:

$$z = \frac{425 - 517}{100}$$

$$z = \frac{-92}{100}$$

$$z = -.92$$

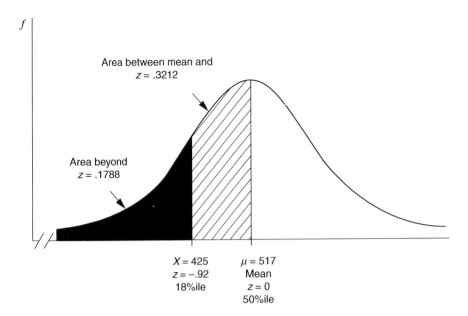

FIGURE 5.3 The percentage of the distribution scoring above and below 425.

Step 2: Now that we have a z score, we need to look in Appendix A to find the percentage of the normal distribution that falls below a z score of –.92. Notice that we are dealing with a negative z score in our example. Most z score tables only report positive z scores, but because normal distributions are symmetrical, the percentage of the distribution that falls below a negative z score is the same as the percentage that falls above the same positive z score value. Similarly, the percentage that falls above a positive z score is identical to the percentage that falls below a negative z score. My z score table in Appendix A tells me that 82.12 percent of the normal distribution will fall below a z value of .92 and 17.88 percent will fall above it (because 1 – .8212 = .1788, or 17.88 percent). The fact that the normal distribution is symmetrical tells us that 17.88 percent of the normal distribution will fall *below* a z score of –.92. So 17.88 percent of the population would be expected to score 425 or lower on the math portion of the SAT and 82.12 percent would score above 425. Figure 5.3 shows the raw score of 425, the corresponding z score, and the proportion of the normal distribution that falls below and above this z score and raw score.

z scores used with a normal distribution can also be used to figure out the proportion of scores that fall between two raw scores. For example, suppose that you got a score of 417 on the SAT math test and your friend got a score of 567. "Wow!" your friend says. "I blew you away! There must be about 50 percent of the population that scored between you and me on this test." Your ego bruised, you decide to see if your friend is right in his assessment. Here's what you need to do.

Step 1: First, convert each raw score into z scores. Recall the mean (μ = 517) and standard deviation (σ = 100) and then plug these numbers into the z score formula: Your z score:

$$z = \frac{417 - 517}{100}$$

$$z = \frac{-100}{100}$$

$$z = -1.00$$

Your friend's z score:

$$z = \frac{567 - 517}{100}$$

$$z = \frac{50}{100}$$

$$z = .50$$

Step 2: Now that we have the z scores, we need to look in Appendix A to find the percentage of the normal distribution that falls between the mean and a z score of −1.00, and the percentage of the distribution that falls between the mean and a z score of .50. Notice that we are dealing with one negative and one positive z score in our example. Our z score table tells me that 84.13 percent of the scores in a normal distribution will fall below a z score of 1, so 34.13 percent (i.e., .8413 − .50, because 50 percent of the normal distribution will fall below the mean) of the normal distribution of scores will fall between the mean and a z score of −1.00. Similarly, 69.15 percent of the normal distribution will fall below a z score of .50, so 19.15 percent will fall between the mean and a z score of .50. To determine the total proportion of scores that fall between these two z scores, we need to add the two proportions together: .3413 + .1915 = .5328. Note that we are *adding* the two proportions together because one of the raw scores (417) was *below* the mean and the other (567) was *above* the mean.

Step 3: Admit defeat in a bitter and defensive way. "Ha ha," you say to your friend. "It is not 50 percent of the population that scored between you and me on the SAT math test. It was 53.28 percent!" (See Figure 5.4 for a depiction of the proportion of the normal distribution that is contained between these two z scores.)

Finally, we can use z scores and percentile scores to determine the proportion of scores in a normal distribution that fall between two raw scores on the same side of the mean. For example,

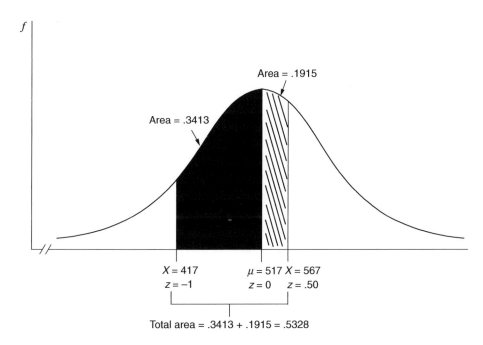

FIGURE 5.4 Proportion of scores in a distribution between two raw scores.

suppose you have another friend who got a raw score of 617 on the SAT math test. Now you want to determine the proportion of the population that scored between 567 and 617 on the test. Here is what you do.

Step 1: First, convert the raw scores into z scores. Recall the mean (μ = 517) and the standard deviation (σ = 100) and then plug these numbers into the z score formula. Friend 1's z score:

$$z = \frac{567 - 517}{100}$$

$$z = \frac{50}{100}$$

$$z = .50$$

Friend 2's z score:

$$z = \frac{617 - 517}{100}$$

$$z = \frac{100}{100}$$

$$z = 1.00$$

Step 2: Now that we have the z scores, we need to look in Appendix A to find the percentage of the normal distribution that falls between the mean and a z score of 1.00, and the percentage of the distribution that falls between the mean and a z score of .50. Notice that now we are dealing with two positive z scores in our example because both of the raw scores were above the population mean. Our z score table tells us that 84.13 percent of the normal distribution will fall below a z score of 1.0, so if we subtract 50 percent from that (i.e., the proportion of the distribution that falls below the mean), we find that 34.13 percent of the normal distribution of scores will fall between the mean and a z score of 1.00. Using a similar process, we find that 19.15 percent of the normal distribution will fall between the mean and a z score of .50. To determine the total proportion of scores that fall between these two z scores, we need to *subtract* the smaller proportion from the larger proportion: .3413 – .1915 = .1498.

Step 3: Rub the results in Friend 1's face. "Ha ha! My *new* best friend got a score that was 14.98 percentile points higher than yours!" (See Figure 5.5 for a graph illustrating the proportion of the normal distribution between two z scores.)

The examples just presented represent handy uses of z scores for understanding both an entire distribution of scores and individual scores within that distribution. It is important to note that using z scores to find percentile scores is only appropriate when the data in the distribution are *normally distributed*. When you do not have a normal distribution, the z scores that you calculate will *not* produce accurate percentile scores. (See Chapter 4 for a discussion of the importance of normal distributions.) It *is* possible to calculate percentile scores without having a normal distribution. To do this, you do not convert z scores to percentile scores. Rather, you rank order your data and find the score at which a certain percentage of the scores fall above and a certain

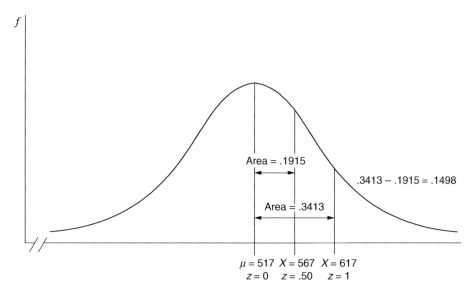

FIGURE 5.5 Proportion of scores in a distribution between two raw scores (both above the mean).

percentage fall below. This is exactly the procedure you used to find the median of a simple frequency distribution in Chapter 3. The median is, after all, simply the score that marks the 50th percentile in a distribution.

Standardized scores are used in a variety of statistics and are perhaps most helpful for comparing scores that are measured using different scales of measurement. As discussed earlier in this chapter, it is difficult to compare two scores that are measured on different scales (e.g., height and weight) without first converting them into a common unit of measurement. Standardizing scores is simply this process of conversion. In the final section of this chapter, I present and briefly describe two distributions of scores described by both raw scores and z scores.

Examples: Comparing Raw Scores and z Scores

To illustrate the overlap between raw scores and standardized z scores, I first present data from a sample of elementary and middle school students from whom I collected data a few years ago. I gave these students a survey to assess their motivational beliefs and attitudes about a standardized achievement test they were to take the following week. One of the items on the survey read, "The ITBS test will measure how smart I am." Students responded to this question using an 8-point scale with 1 = *Strongly disagree* and 8 = *Strongly agree*. The frequency distribution, along with the z scores that correspond to each raw score, is presented in Figure 5.6. This distribution has a mean of 5.38 and a standard deviation of 2.35.

As you can see, this is not a normal, bell-shaped distribution. This distribution has an odd sort of shape where there is the hint of a normal distribution in scores 2 through 7, but then there are "spikes" at each end, particularly at the higher end. The result is an asymmetrical distribution. If you compare the z scores on top of each column with the raw scores at the bottom of each column, you can see how these scores are related to each other. For example, we can see that all of the raw scores of 5 or lower have negative z scores. This is because the mean of a distribution always has a z score of zero, and any raw scores below the mean will have negative z scores. In this distribution, the mean is 5.38, so all raw scores of 5 and below have negative z scores and all raw scores of 6 or above have positive z scores.

Another feature of this distribution that is clearly illustrated by the z scores is that there is a larger range of scores below the mean than above the mean. This is fairly obvious, because the mean is well above the midpoint on this scale. The highest scores in this distribution are just a little more than one standard deviation above the mean (z = 1.12), whereas the lowest scores are

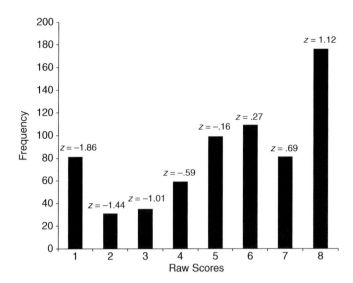

FIGURE 5.6 Frequency distribution, with z scores associated with each raw score, for the item "The test will show how smart I am."

nearly two standard deviations below the mean ($z = -1.86$). Finally, the inclusion of standard deviation scores with each raw score allows us to immediately determine how many standard deviations away from the mean a particular raw score falls. For example, we can see that a student who had a raw score of 3 on this variable scored just about exactly one standard deviation below the mean ($z = -1.01$).

For our second example, I have chosen a variable with a much smaller standard deviation. Using the same 8-point scale described earlier, students were asked to respond to the item "I think it is important to do well on the ITBS test." Students overwhelmingly agreed with this statement, as the mean (7.28) and relatively small standard deviation (1.33) revealed. The frequency distribution for the scores on this item is presented in Figure 5.7.

In this graph, we can see that the distribution is highly skewed, with most students circling the number 8 on the scale. Because so many students answered similarly, the standard deviation is quite small, with only relatively few scores at the lower end of the distribution. The small standard deviation coupled with the high mean create a situation where very low scores on the scale have extremely small z scores. For example, the few students with a raw score of 1 on the scale ($n = 7$) had z scores of -4.72, indicating that these students were more than 4⅔ standard

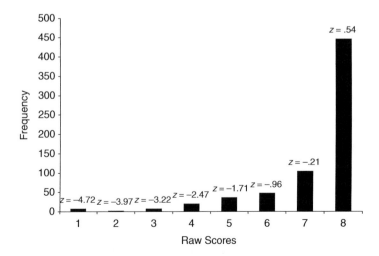

FIGURE 5.7 Frequency distribution for the item "Important to do well."

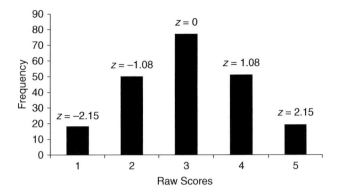

FIGURE 5.8 Frequency distribution for performance-approach goals.

deviations below the mean. Those students with the highest score on the scale were only about half a standard deviation above the mean because, with such a high mean, it was impossible to get a score very far above the mean.

The two examples provided above both illustrate the relation between the z scores and the raw scores for distributions that are skewed. Please note that because these data were not normally distributed, it would be inappropriate to calculate percentile scores from the z scores derived from these data. If you did need to calculate percentile scores from a skewed or otherwise non-normal distribution, you could use the ranking method described earlier in the chapter. In both of the distributions presented in Figures 5.6 and 5.7, the means were above the midpoint on the scale, and subsequently there was a greater range of z scores below than above the mean. This is not the case when the scores are normally distributed. To illustrate this, I use data from a different dataset. I used surveys to measure a sample of high school students' motivational goals in school. One goal that I measured is known as a performance-approach goal. This goal reflects a concern, or a desire, to outperform classmates and peers for the sake of demonstrating superior ability. The items on the survey were measured using a scale from 1 to 5 (1 = *Not at all true* and 5 = *Very true*). The frequency distribution is presented in Figure 5.8.

This distribution of scores had a mean of 3.00 and a standard deviation of .92. As you can see, the data are quite normally distributed. When the data are normally distributed, we would expect most of our cases to have z scores at or near zero because in a normal distribution, most of the cases are near the mean. Also notice that as we move farther away from the mean (i.e., z scores over 2.0 or less than −2.0), there are fewer cases. In a normal distribution, then, the probability of finding a particular z score becomes smaller as the value of the z score moves further away from zero. As Figures 5.6 and 5.7 illustrate, this is not always the case in skewed distributions.

Worked Examples

In this section I will work through three examples to demonstrate how to calculate and wrap words around a standard score (i.e., a z score), how to find the proportion of the normal distribution that would fall beyond a certain raw score, and how to find the proportion of the normal distribution that would fall between two raw scores.

Suppose that in the population of college students in the U.S. the average number of units taken per semester is 15 with a standard deviation of 4. What is the standard score for a person in this population that takes 12 units per semester?

$$z = \frac{12 - 15}{4}, \text{ so } z = -.75$$

Wrapping words around this result, we would say that a student who takes 12 units per semester is .75 standard deviations below the mean for units taken per semester by college students in the U.S.

Now, what proportion of the population would you expect to take 20 units or more in a semester?

$$z = \frac{20-15}{4}, \text{ so } z = 1.25$$

In Appendix A, we see that .8944 of the normal distribution falls below a z score of 1.25, so .1056, or 10.56 percent, would fall above this z score. Therefore, we would expect 10.56 percent of this population to take 20 units or more per semester.

Now, what proportion (and percentage) of the population would we expect to take between 17 and 20 units per semester? We already know that .1056 of the distribution would take 20 units or more. So now we need to calculate the z score for the raw score of 17:

$$z = \frac{17-15}{4}, \text{ so } z = .50$$

In Appendix A, we see that .6915 of the normal distribution falls below a z score of .50, and .3085 falls above. To find the proportion of the distribution that falls *between* the z scores of 1.25 and .50, we subtract one proportion from the other:

$$.3085 - .1056 = .2029$$

Now we can wrap words around our results: .2029, or 20.29 percent, of this population would be expected to take between 17 and 20 units per semester.

 For brief videos demonstrating how to calculate and interpret z scores, probabilities, and percentile scores, please refer to the website that accompanies this book.

Wrapping Up and Looking Forward

z scores provide a handy way of interpreting where a raw score is in relation to the mean. We can use z scores to quickly and easily determine where an individual score in a distribution falls relative to other scores in the distribution, either by interpreting the z score in standard deviation units or by calculating percentile scores. Using the table of probabilities based on the normal distribution presented in Appendix A, we can also use z scores to determine how unusual a given score in a distribution is (i.e., the probability of obtaining an individual score of that size when selecting the individual at random). In the next chapter, I will use information about the mean, standard deviation, normal distributions, z scores, and probability to explain one of the most important concepts in statistics: the standard error.

Work Problems

Suppose you know that in the population of full-time employees in the United States, the average number of vacation days taken off work per year is 10 with a standard deviation of 4. Please answer the following questions using this information, assuming that the number of vacation days taken forms a normal distribution.

1. What percentage of the population takes at least 7 vacation days off per year?
2. What is the number of vacation days that marks the 30th percentile of this distribution?
3. What proportion of the distribution takes between 6 and 10 vacation days off per year?
4. What percentage of the distribution takes between 6 and 15 vacation days off per year?
5. Suppose that you randomly select an individual from the population who takes 20 vacation days off per year. Calculate that person's z score and interpret it. What does it tell you?
6. What is the probability of randomly selecting an individual from the population who takes 8 vacation days or more off?

 For the answers to these work problems, and for additional work problems, please refer to the website that accompanies this book.

CHAPTER 6

Standard Errors

The concept of **standard error** is one that many students of statistics find confusing when they first encounter it. In all honesty, there are many students, and many researchers, who never fully grasp the concept. I am convinced that many people have problems with understanding standard errors because they require a bit of a leap into the abstract and because, with the advent of computer programs, it is possible to lead a long and productive research life without having to think about or analyze a standard error for years at a time. Therefore, many researchers choose to gloss over this abstract concept. This is a mistake. I hold this opinion because, as a teacher of statistics, I have learned that when one is able to truly understand the concept of standard error, many of our most beloved inferential statistics (*t* tests, ANOVA, regression coefficients, correlations) become easy to understand. So let me offer this piece of advice: Keep trying to understand the contents of this chapter, and other information you get about standard errors, even if you find it confusing the first or second time you read it. With a little effort and patience, you can understand standard errors and many of the statistics that rely on them.

As I often tell my students, inferential statistics is all about using information collected from samples to reach conclusions about the populations the samples came from. In the inferential statistics that we will discuss in this book, the formulas are all basically the same: How large is the effect that you observe in your sample data compared to the amount of error you would expect to get just due to chance? (In inferential statistics, *chance* means **random sampling error,** or the error you would expect just due to random sampling.) As you will see when we discuss *t* tests (Chapter 8), *F* values (Chapters 9, 10, and 11), and correlation coefficients (Chapter 12), the formulas for the inferential statistics all have this same general formula, with the observed effect in the sample as the numerator of the formulas and the error due to chance as the denominator. This error that forms the denominator is the standard error. Because this basic formula of observed difference divided by the standard error is repeated, in various forms, in so many inferential statistics, if you can hang in there and understand the basic idea of the standard error, the rest of the statistics you encounter in this book will be much easier to understand.

What Is a Standard Error?

The standard error is *the measure of how much* random *variation we would expect from samples of equal size drawn from the same population.* Look at the preceding sentence, think about it, and rest assured that it is explained in more detail in the next few pages. Until then, here are a few more points to keep in mind. First, the term **error** in statistics has a very specific meaning that is different from our everyday usage of the word. In statistics, error does not mean "mistake." Error refers to random variation that is due to random sampling. This notion of error is discussed in more detail later in this chapter and in subsequent chapters of the book. Second, the standard error is, in effect, the standard deviation of the **sampling distribution** of some statistic (e.g., the mean, the difference between two means, the correlation coefficient, etc.). I realize that this makes no sense until you know what a sampling distribution is, and I explain this in the next section of this chapter. Third, the standard error is the denominator in the formulas used to calculate many inferential statistics. In the following chapters, you will see the standard error as the denominator in many formulas.

Standard Errors in Depth

The Conceptual Description of the Standard Error of the Mean

To begin this more detailed discussion of standard errors, I introduce the abstract component of the concept. This is a section that you may need to read several times to let it sink in. Although there are standard errors for all statistics, we will focus on the standard error of the mean in this chapter. (Standard errors for other statistics—correlation coefficient, differences between sample means—are discussed in more detail in the chapters in which these statistics are described.)

When we think of a distribution of scores, we think of a certain number of scores that are plotted in some sort of frequency graph to form a distribution (see Chapters 2 and 4). In these distributions, each case has a score that is part of the distribution. Just as these simple frequency distributions are plotted, or graphed, we can also plot distributions of sample means. Imagine that we want to find the average shoe size of adult women in a particular country. In this study, the population we are interested in is all adult women in the country. But it would be expensive and tedious to measure the shoe sizes of all adult women in a country. So we select a sample of 100 women, at random, from our population. At this point, it is very important to realize that our sample of 100 women may or may not look like the typical women in the country (in terms of shoe size). When we select a sample at random, it is possible to get a sample that represents an extreme end of the population (e.g., a sample with an unusually large average shoe size). If we were to throw our first sample of women back into the general population and choose another random sample *of the same size* (i.e., 100), it is possible that this second sample may have an average shoe size that is quite different from our first sample.

Once you realize that different random samples of equal size can produce different mean scores on some variable (i.e., different average shoe sizes), the next step in this conceptual puzzle is easy: If we were to take 1,000 different random samples, each of 100 women, and compute the average shoe size of each sample, these 1,000 sample means would form their own distribution. This distribution would be called the **sampling distribution of the mean**.

To illustrate this concept, let's consider an example with a small population ($N = 5$). Suppose my population consists of five college students enrolled in a seminar on statistics. Because it is a small seminar, these five students represent the entire population of this seminar. These students each took the final exam, which was scored on a scale from 1 to 10, with lower scores indicating poorer performance on the exam. The scores for each student are presented in Table 6.1, arranged in ascending order according to how well they did on the exam.

If I were to select a random sample of two students from this population ($n = 2$), I might get Student 2 and Student 5. This sample would have a mean of 7.5 because [$(6 + 9) \div 2 = 7.5$]. If I were to put those two students back into the population and randomly select another sample of two, I might get Student 4 and Student 5. This sample would have a mean of 8 because [$(7 + 9) \div 2 = 8$]. I put those students back into the population and randomly select another

TABLE 6.1 Population of students' scores on their final exam

Students	Score on Final Exam
Student 1	3
Student 2	6
Student 3	6
Student 4	7
Student 5	9

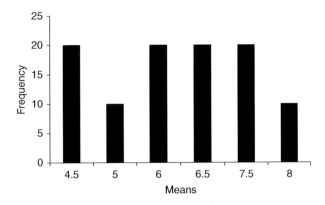

FIGURE 6.1 Sampling distribution of the mean created by selecting multiple random samples (*n* = 2) from a population and calculating the mean of each sample.

sample of two, such as Students 1 and 3. This sample would have a mean of 4.5. As you can see, just by virtue of those included in each random sample I select from my population, I get different sample means. Now, if I were to repeat this process of randomly selecting samples of two students from my population, calculating their mean, and returning the members of the sample to the population (called sampling with replacement), eventually I would get a distribution of sample means that would look something like the distribution presented in Figure 6.1. As you can see, these means form a distribution. This example illustrates how random samples of a given size selected from a population will produce a distribution of sample means, eventually forming a sampling distribution of the mean.

 For a brief video illustrating how to produce a sampling distribution of the means, please refer to the website that accompanies this book.

Just as the other distributions we have discussed have a mean and a standard deviation, this sampling distribution of the mean also has these characteristics. To distinguish a sampling distribution from a simple frequency distribution, the mean and the standard deviation of the sampling distribution of the mean have special names. The mean of the sampling distribution of the mean is called the **expected value of the mean**. It is called the expected value because the mean of the sampling distribution of the mean is the same as the population mean. When we select a random sample from the population, our best guess is that the mean for the sample will be the same as the mean for the population, so our *expected* mean will be the population mean. The standard deviation of the sampling distribution of the mean is called the standard error. So the standard error is simply the standard deviation of the sampling distribution.

The final step in understanding the concept of standard error of the mean is to understand what this statistic tells us. If you recall the discussion about standard deviations in Chapter 3, you will remember that the standard deviation tells us the average difference, or deviation, between an individual score in the distribution and the mean for the distribution. The standard error of the mean provides essentially the same information, except it refers to the average difference between the expected value (e.g., the population mean) and an individual sample mean. So one way to think about the standard error of the mean is that it tells us how confident we should be that a sample mean represents the actual population mean. Phrased another way, the standard error of the mean provides a measure of how much *error* we can expect when we say that a sample mean represents the mean of the larger population. That is why it is called a standard *error*. Knowing how much error we can expect when selecting a sample of a given size from a population is critical in helping us determine whether our sample statistic, such as the sample mean, is *meaningfully* different from the population parameter, such as the population mean. This is the foundation of all the inferential statistics that are discussed in later chapters. A graph depicting a sampling distribution of the mean, with the expected value and the standard error, is presented in Figure 6.2.

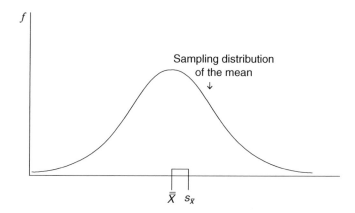

FIGURE 6.2 Sampling distribution of the mean with the expected value and the standard error shown.

How to Calculate the Standard Error of the Mean

Most of the time, researchers do not draw 1,000 samples of equal size from the population and then figure out the mean and standard deviation of this distribution of sample means. In fact, most of the time, researchers collect data from only a single sample, and then use this sample to make inferences about the population from which the sample was drawn. How can we make inferences about a larger population on the basis of a single sample?

To do this, researchers must use what they know about their sample to make educated guesses, or estimates, about the population. I demonstrate this concept using the shoe-size example mentioned earlier. Suppose that I have a random sample of 100 women. Now, if this sample were truly selected at random (i.e., every adult woman in the country had an equal chance of being selected), my most logical assumption would be that this sample represents the larger population accurately. Therefore, I would have to assume that the mean shoe size of my sample (suppose it is 6) is also the mean shoe size of the larger population. Of course, I cannot know if this is true. In fact, as discussed earlier, there is good reason to believe that my sample may not represent my population well. But if the only information I have about adult women's shoe sizes comes from my sample of 100 women, my *best guess* about what the larger population of women looks like must be that they are similar to this sample of 100 women. Now I am faced with a critical question: When I guess that the population of women in the country where I am conducting the study has an average shoe size of 6 (based on my sample average), how much *error* can I *expect* to have in this estimation? In other words, what is the *standard error*?

To answer this question, I must examine two characteristics of my sample. First, how large is my sample? The larger my sample, the less error I should have in my estimate about the population. This makes sense because the larger my sample, the more my sample should look like my population, and the more accurate my estimates of my population will be. If there are 50 million women in the country where the study is being conducted and I use a sample of 25 million to predict their average shoe size, I would expect this prediction to be more accurate than a prediction based on a sample of 100 women. Therefore, the larger my sample, the smaller my standard error.

The second characteristic of my sample that I need to examine is the standard deviation. Remember that the standard deviation is a measure of how much variation there is in the scores in my sample. If the scores in my sample are very diverse (i.e., a lot of variation and therefore a large standard deviation), I can assume that the scores in my population are also quite diverse. So, if some women in my sample have a shoe size of 2 and others have a shoe size of 14, I can also assume that there is a pretty large variety of shoe sizes in my population. On the other hand, if all of the women in my sample have shoe sizes of either 5, 6, or 7, I can assume that most of

TABLE 6.2 Formulas for calculating the standard error of the mean

$$\sigma_{\bar{x}} = \frac{\sigma}{\sqrt{n}}$$

or

$$s_{\bar{x}} = \frac{s}{\sqrt{n}}$$

where σ is the standard deviation for the population,
   s is the sample estimate of the standard deviation,
   n is the size of the sample.

the women in the larger population have an equally small variety of shoe sizes. Although these assumptions about the population may not be true (e.g., I may have selected a biased sample from the population), I must rely on them because this is all the information I have. So, the larger the sample standard deviation, the greater the assumed variation of scores in the population, and consequently the larger the standard error of the mean. (*Note:* In those instances where I know the population standard deviation, I can use that in my calculation of the standard error of the mean. See Table 6.2 for that formula.)

An examination of the formula for calculating the standard error of the mean reveals the central role of the sample standard deviation (or population standard deviation, if known) and the sample size in determining the standard error. As you can see, the formula is simply the standard deviation of the sample or population divided by the square root of n, the sample size. As with all fractions, as the numerator gets larger, so does the resulting standard error. Similarly, as the size of the denominator decreases, the resulting standard error increases. Small samples with large standard deviations produce large standard errors, because these characteristics make it more difficult to have confidence that our sample accurately represents our population. In contrast, a large sample with a small standard deviation will produce a small standard error, because such characteristics make it more likely that our sample accurately represents our population.

The Central Limit Theorem

Simply put, the **central limit theorem** states that as long as you have a reasonably large sample size (e.g., $n = 30$), the sampling distribution of the mean will be normally distributed, even if the distribution of scores in your sample is not. In earlier chapters (i.e., Chapters 2 and 4), I discussed distributions that were not in the shape of a nice, normal, bell curve. What the central limit theorem proves is that even when you have such a nonnormal distribution in your population, the sampling distribution of the mean will most likely approximate a nice, normal, bell-shaped distribution as long as you have at least 30 cases in your sample. Even if you have fewer than 30 cases in your sample, the sampling distribution of the mean will probably be near normal if you have at least 10 cases in your sample. Even in our earlier example where we had only two cases per sample, the sampling distribution of the mean had the beginning of a normal shape.

 To see a brief video demonstration of how means taken from small, random samples will produce an approximately normal distribution, refer to the website that accompanies this book.

Although we do not concern ourselves here with why the central limit theorem works, you need to understand why this theorem is so important. As I discussed in Chapter 4, a number of statistics rely on probabilities that are generated from normal distributions. For example, I may want to know whether the average IQ test scores of a sample of 50 adults in California is different from the larger population of adults. If my sample has an average IQ test score of 110, and the national average is 100, I can see that my sample average differs from the population average by 10 points. Is 10 points a meaningful difference or a trivial one? To answer that question, I must be able to discover the probability of getting a difference of 10 points by random chance alone. (In statistics, the probability of obtaining a statistic by chance is known as the *p* **value**.) In other words, if I were to select another random sample of 50 adults from California and compute their average IQ test score, what are the odds that they will have an average that is 10 points higher than the national average of 100? To determine this probability, I must have a normal distribution of sample means, or a normal sampling distribution of the mean. The central limit theorem indicates that as long as I have a sample size of at least 30, my sampling distribution of the mean is likely to approximate a normal distribution.

The Normal Distribution and *t* Distributions: Comparing *z* Scores and *t* Values

In Chapter 5, we learned how to determine the probability of randomly selecting an individual case with a particular score on some variable from a population with a given mean on that variable. We did this by converting the raw score into a *z* score. Now that we know how to compute a standard error, we can use *z* scores again to determine the probability of randomly selecting a sample with a particular mean on a variable from a population with a given mean on the same variable. We can also use the family of *t* distributions to generate *t* values to figure out the same types of probabilities. To explain this, I will begin by comparing the normal distribution with the family of *t* distributions.

As discussed in Chapter 4, the normal distribution is a theoretical distribution with a bell shape and is based on the idea of population data. We also know that the probabilities associated with *z* scores are associated with the normal distribution (Chapter 5). In addition, we know that a standard deviation derived from sample data is only an *estimate* of the population standard deviation (Chapter 3). Because the formula for calculating the sample standard deviation has $n - 1$ in the denominator, we also know that the smaller the sample, the less precisely the sample standard deviation estimates the population standard deviation. Finally, we know that the standard error formula (Table 6.2) is based partly on the standard deviation.

When we put all of this information together, we end up with a little bit of a dilemma. If we can use the standard error to generate *z* scores and probabilities, and these *z* scores and probabilities are based on the normal distribution, what do we do in those cases where we are using sample data and we have a small sample? Won't our small sample influence our standard error? And won't this standard error influence our *z* scores? Will our *z* scores and probabilities be accurate if we have a small sample? Fortunately, these concerns have already been addressed by brains larger than my own. It turns out that the normal distribution has a close family of relatives: the family of *t* distributions. These distributions are very much like the normal distribution, except the shape of *t* distributions is influenced by sample size. With large samples (e.g., > 120), the shape of the *t* distribution is virtually identical to the normal distribution. As the sample size decreases, however, the shape of the *t* distribution becomes flatter in the middle and higher at the ends. In other words, as the sample size decreases, there will be fewer cases near the mean and more cases away from the mean, out in the tails of the distribution. Like the normal distribution, *t* distributions are still symmetrical.

Just as we use the *z* table (Appendix A) to find probabilities associated with the normal distribution, we use the table of *t* values (Appendix B) to find probabilities associated with the *t* distributions. Down the left column of Appendix B are numbers in ascending order. These are **degrees of freedom** and they are directly related to sample size. To use this table, you simply calculate a *t* value (using basically the same formula that you would use to find a *z* score) and then, using the appropriate degrees of freedom, figure out where your *t* value falls in Appendix B to determine the probability of finding a *t* value of that size. Whenever you don't know the population standard deviation and must use an estimate from a sample, it is wise to use the family of *t* distributions. Here is an example to illustrate these ideas.

 For a video explaining how to read and interpret Appendix B, please refer to the website that accompanies this book.

In Chapter 5, we used this formula to calculate a *z* score from a raw score:

$$z = \frac{\text{raw score} - \text{mean}}{\text{standard deviation}}$$

or

$$z = \frac{X - \mu}{\sigma}$$

where *X* is a raw score,

  μ is the population mean,

  σ is the standard deviation.

The formula for converting a sample mean into a *z* score is almost identical, except the individual raw score is replaced by the sample mean and the standard deviation is replaced by the standard error. In addition, if we do not know the population standard deviation, the standard deviation estimate from the sample must be used and we are computing a *t* value rather than a *z* score. These formulas are found in Table 6.3.

Now, suppose that I know that the average man exercises for 60 minutes a week. Suppose, further, that I have a random sample of 144 men and that this sample exercises for an average of 65 minutes per week with a standard deviation of 10 minutes. What is the probability of getting

---

TABLE 6.3 *z* score and *t* value formulas

When σ is known

$$z = \frac{\text{sample mean} - \text{population mean}}{\text{standard error}}$$

or

$$z = \frac{\bar{X} - \mu}{\sigma_{\bar{x}}}$$

When σ is not known

$$t = \frac{\text{sample mean} - \text{population mean}}{\text{standard error}}$$

or

$$t = \frac{\bar{X} - \mu}{s_{\bar{x}}}$$

where μ is the population mean,

  $\sigma_{\bar{x}}$ is the standard error of the mean using population standard deviation,

  $\bar{X}$ is the sample mean,

  $s_{\bar{x}}$ is the sample estimate of the standard error of the mean.

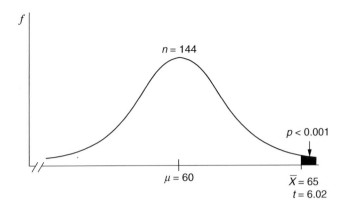

FIGURE 6.3 Probability of finding this difference between the means by chance when *n* = 144.

a random sample of this size with a mean of 65 if the actual population mean is 60 *by chance*? To answer this question, I compute a *t* value:

$$t = \frac{65 - 60}{10 / \sqrt{144}}$$

$$t = \frac{5}{.83}$$

$$t = 6.02$$

If we look in Appendix B, using the row with ∞ degrees of freedom, we can see that the probability (i.e., *p* value) of getting a *t* value of this size or larger *by chance* with a sample of this size is less than .001. Notice that if we had calculated a *z* score rather than a *t* score (i.e., if the *population* standard deviation had been 10), our *z* value would have been the same (i.e., *z* = 6.02) and our probability, as found in Appendix A, would have been about *p* = .0000000009, which is also less than .001 (see Figure 6.3). The normal distribution (associated with *z* scores) and the *t* distributions are virtually identical when the sample size is larger than 120.

Finally, to illustrate the difference between the *t* distributions and the normal distribution, suppose that our sample size had been 25 rather than 144. We would have calculated the *t* value just as we did before, but our standard error would have been different (because our sample size was smaller), thereby producing a smaller *t* value:

$$t = \frac{65 - 60}{10 / \sqrt{25}}$$

$$t = \frac{5}{2}$$

$$t = 2.50$$

Now, looking at our table of *t* values with 24 degrees of freedom, we find that the probability of getting a *t* value of this size or larger is just about *p* = .02 (see Figure 6.4). Notice that if we had had our larger sample size of 144, the probability of getting a *t* value of 2.50 or larger would have been closer to *p* = .01.

So when the sample size is large, the normal distribution and the *t* distribution are virtually identical. But as our sample size decreases, the *t* distribution changes and so do the

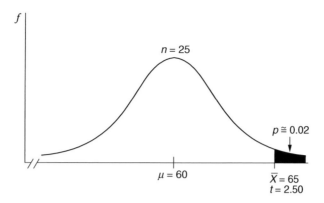

FIGURE 6.4 Probability of finding this difference between the means by chance when *n* = 25.

probabilities associated with it. When the population standard deviation is known (a rare occurrence in most social science research), the normal distribution can be used. But when the population standard deviation is not known, or the sample size is small, the family of *t* distributions should be used. Now we can turn our attention to how standard errors are used in other statistics.

The Use of Standard Errors in Inferential Statistics

Some type of standard error is used in many inferential statistics, including those discussed in this book (*t* tests, ANOVA, correlation, regression, etc.). In **inferential statistics**, we want to know whether something that we observe in our sample represents a similar phenomenon in the larger population from which the sample was drawn. For example, if I compare the average weight of a sample of 100 men to that of a sample of 100 women and find that, on average, men in my sample weigh 60 pounds more than women in my sample, I may want to know whether I should conclude that, on average, men in the larger population weigh more than women in the population. Similarly, if I find a correlation (see Chapter 12) of *r* = .45 between height and weight in my sample of 100 men, I might want to know whether this relationship means that there is probably a relationship between these two variables in the larger population of men. To answer these questions, I need to use standard errors.

In many inferential statistics formulas, I need to see whether the phenomenon I observed in my sample(s) is large or small relative to my standard error. Recall from the definition of standard error presented earlier in this chapter that the standard error is a measure of the average amount of variance, or difference, that we can expect from different samples of the same size selected randomly from a population. So, the question we are asking with many inferential statistics is whether some statistic that we see in our sample is big or small compared to the amount of variance (or error) we would expect if we had randomly selected a *different* sample of the same size. This question can be summarized with the following fraction:

$$\frac{\text{size of sample statistic}}{\text{standard error}}$$

As an illustration, let us return to the example comparing the average weight of men and women. We already know that, in my samples, the difference between the average weight of men and women was 60 pounds. The statistic that I am interested in here is the *difference* between the two means (i.e., the average weight of men and the average weight of women). If I were to select two different samples of the same size from the populations of men and women and find the difference between those two sample means, I would probably find a difference that was either larger or smaller than the difference I found in the comparison of the first two samples. If I kept selecting different samples and compared their means, I would eventually get a **sampling distribution of the differences between the means**, and this sampling distribution would have a standard error. Suppose that the standard error of this sampling distribution was 10. Let's plug that standard error into our fraction formula presented earlier:

$$\frac{\text{sample statistic} = 60}{\text{standard error} = 10}$$

From this formula, I can see that the difference between my two sample means is six times larger than the difference I would expect to find just due to random sampling error. This suggests that the difference between my two sample means is probably not due to chance. (Note that the word *chance* refers to the chance selection of a sample with a set of scores from an extreme end of the distribution.) Using a table of probabilities based on the *t* distribution (see Chapter 8 and Appendix B), I can calculate the exact probability of getting a ratio this large (i.e., 60:10, or 6:1). So, to summarize, the standard error is often used in inferential statistics to see whether our sample statistic is larger or smaller than the average differences in the statistic we would expect to occur by chance due to differences between samples. I now discuss some examples to demonstrate the effect of sample size and the standard deviation on the size of the standard error of the mean.

Example: Sample Size and Standard Deviation Effects on the Standard Error

To illustrate the effect that sample size and standard deviation have on the size of the standard error of the mean, let's take a look at a variable from a set of data I collected a few years ago. The purpose of the study was to examine students' motivational beliefs about standardized achievement tests. I examined whether students thought it was important to do well on the standardized test they were about to take in school, whether they had anxiety about the test, whether they expected to do well on the test, whether they thought of themselves as good test takers, and so on.

One of the goals of the study was to compare the motivational beliefs of elementary school students with those of middle school students. The sample for the study included 137 fifth graders in elementary school and 536 seventh and eighth graders in middle school. Suppose we wanted to know the standard error of the mean on the variable "I expect to do well on the test" for each of the two groups in the study, the elementary school students and the middle school students. To calculate these standard errors, we would need to know the standard deviation for each group on our variable and the sample size for each group. These statistics are presented in Table 6.4.

A quick glance at the standard deviations for each group reveals that they are very similar (*s* = 1.38 for the elementary school sample, *s* = 1.46 for the middle school sample). However, because there is quite a large difference in the size of the two samples, we should expect somewhat different standard errors of the mean for each group. Which group do you think will have the larger standard error of the mean?

TABLE 6.4   Standard deviations and sample sizes

	Elementary School Sample		Middle School Sample	
	Standard Dev.	Sample Size	Standard Dev.	Sample Size
Expect to Do Well on Test	1.38	137	1.46	536

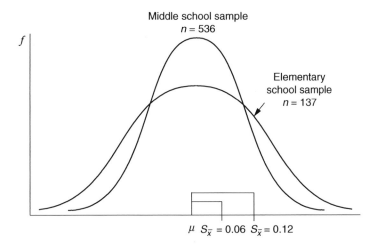

FIGURE 6.5 The two curves and the two standard errors of the mean show the effect of sample size on the shape of the sampling distribution of the mean and the size of the standard errors.

Recall from the formula presented earlier in this chapter that to find the standard error of the mean, we simply need to divide the standard deviation by the square root of the sample size. For the elementary school sample, we need to divide 1.38 by the square root of 137. The square root of 137 = 11.70. When we divide 1.38 by 11.70, we get .12. So the standard error of the mean for the elementary sample is .12. Following the same procedure for the middle school sample, we find that the standard error of the mean for this group will equal 1.46 divided by the square root of 546. The square root of 546 = 23.37. When we divide 1.46 by 23.37, we get .06. As you can see, the standard error of the mean for the middle school sample ($s_{\bar{x}} = 0.6$) is half the size of the standard error of the mean for the elementary school sample ($s_{\bar{x}} = .12$). Because the standard deviations are roughly equal for these two groups, virtually all of the difference in their standard errors is attributable to differences in sample size (see Figure 6.5)

To illustrate the effect of the standard deviation on the size of the standard error, let's take a look at a second variable from this study: students' scores on the verbal portion of the standardized achievement tests. Scores on this portion of the test range from a possible low of 0 to a possible high of 100. In the elementary school sample, the standard deviation on this variable was 23.81. The sample size is still 137. To find the standard error of the mean, we must divide 23.81 by the square root of 137, which we know from our previous example is 11.70. And 23.81 divided by 11.70 equals 2.04. So the standard error of the mean in this example is 2.04. When we compare this number with the standard error of the mean for the elementary school sample on the "Expect to do well on the test" variable ($s_{\bar{x}} = .12$), we see that the larger standard deviation for the test score variable created a much larger standard error, even though the sample size remained the same, 137.

As these examples demonstrate, the size of the standard error of the mean depends on the size of the standard deviation and the size of the sample. As sample size increases, and the standard deviation remains constant, the standard error of the mean decreases. As the size of the standard deviation increases, the size of the standard error of the mean increases as well. Remember that the standard error is generally used in the denominator of the formulas statisticians use to calculate inferential statistics. Therefore, smaller standard errors will produce larger statistics, such as z scores and t values (because smaller denominators produce larger overall numbers than larger denominators do when the numerators are equal). Larger statistics are more likely to be judged by the researcher to indicate a meaningful, or **statistically significant,** effect in the sample. In other words, a large statistic like a t value or a z score is more likely than a small statistic to indicate that a phenomenon observed in a sample represents a meaningful phenomenon in the population as well. (Statistical significance is discussed in greater detail in Chapter 7.) Therefore, all else being equal, larger sample sizes are more likely to produce statistically significant results because larger sample sizes produce smaller standard errors.

Worked Examples

In this section of the chapter I provide two examples of how to calculate and interpret standard errors of the mean, once when the population standard deviation is known, and once when it is not. In each example, the standard errors that I calculate will be used to calculate a *z* score and a *t* value and the probabilities associated with each.

Suppose that in the population of teenagers in Spain, the average number of texts sent by each teenager in a day is 20 with a standard deviation of 8. I select a random sample of 100 Spanish teens and find that they send an average of 19 texts per day. I want to know the probability of selecting a random sample of 100 Spanish teens with a mean number of texts sent that is this different from the population mean, by chance. How do I find this probability?

First, I need to calculate the standard error of the mean. For this, I need the sample size ($n = 100$) and the population standard deviation ($\sigma = 8$). I plug these into the standard error formula that was presented in Table 6.2:

$$\sigma_{\bar{x}} = \frac{8}{\sqrt{100}}$$

$$\sigma_{\bar{x}} = \frac{8}{10}$$

$$\sigma_{\bar{x}} = .8$$

This standard error of the mean tells me that the average difference between the population mean and the sample means, when the samples are randomly selected and the *n*'s = 100, is .8, or eight-tenths of a text. In other words, when I select random samples of 100 Spanish teenagers from the population of Spanish teenagers, I expect there to be a difference between the population mean and the sample mean of .8 of a text sent per day.

Now that I have calculated the standard error of the mean, I can use it to help me find the probability of randomly selecting a sample from this population with a mean of 19 texts sent per day. For this problem, I will need to use the population mean (20), the sample mean (19), and the standard error of the mean (.8). I plug these numbers into the top formula that was presented in Table 6.3:

$$z = \frac{19 - 20}{.8}$$

$$z = \frac{-1}{.8}$$

$$z = -1.25$$

Once I know that my *z* value is –1.25, I can look this value up in Appendix A and find a value of .8944. If I subtract this value from 1.0 (which is the total area under the normal curve), I get 1.0 – .8944 = .1056. This tells me that 10.56 percent of the normal distribution falls *above* a *z* score of 1.25, and 89.44 percent of the normal distribution falls below that *z* value. But my *z* score in this problem is negative. Because the normal distribution is symmetrical, I know that the area of the normal distribution that is beyond my negative *z* score (i.e., further away from the mean) will be identical to the area of the normal distribution that is *beyond* my positive *z* score of the same absolute value. Therefore, I can just flip my values around: If the probability of getting

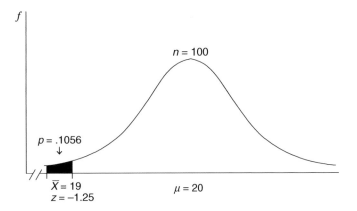

FIGURE 6.6 The probability of obtaining a sample mean of 19 or lower, by chance, when the population mean is 20, the sample size is 100, and the standard deviation of the population is 8.

a z value of *positive* 1.25 or larger is .1056, the probability of getting a z score of *negative* 1.25 *or below* is also .1056 (see Figure 6.6). In other words, 10.56 percent of randomly selected samples (with $n = 100$) from this population would be expected to have a mean of 19 *or less*. Now I am ready to wrap words around my results: The probability of randomly selecting a sample of 100 Spanish teenagers who send 19 texts per day (or fewer), when the population mean is 20, is .1056 (i.e., $p = .1056$). Notice how even a small difference between the sample mean and the population mean can be somewhat unlikely to occur by chance when the sample is fairly large and the standard deviation is relatively small.

Here is another worked example. Suppose that I want to know something about how many grams of sugar children in Australia consume per day. I happen to know that the population mean for this question is 153 grams of sugar consumed per day. I want to know whether a random sample of 25 children selected from Melbourne eat more or less sugar than the average Australian child. My sample has a mean of 160 grams of sugar consumed per day with a standard deviation of 25. What is the probability of getting a difference between the sample mean and the population mean this large *by chance?*

Again, we begin by calculating the standard error of the mean:

$$s_{\bar{x}} = \frac{25}{\sqrt{25}}$$

$$s_{\bar{x}} = \frac{25}{5}$$

$$s_{\bar{x}} = 5$$

This standard error of the mean tells us that the average difference between the population mean of 153 and the sample mean, when samples are randomly selected and $n = 25$, is 5 grams of sugar consumed per day. Next, I use this standard error to calculate a t value. Note that I am calculating a t value rather than a z score because I do not know the population standard deviation in this example.

$$t = \frac{160 - 153}{5}$$

$$t = \frac{7}{5}$$

$$t = 1.40$$

Using Appendix B, we can get an estimate of the probability of obtaining this *t* value by chance. Determining probabilities using Appendix B is a little tougher than it was in the previous example using Appendix A, because Appendix A is more detailed than Appendix B. But we can use Appendix B to get a rough estimate of probability.

In the current problem, we have one sample with a sample size of 25. Our degrees of freedom (*df*) for this problem will be *n* – 1, so 25 – 1 = 24. Now we can look in Appendix B under *df* = 24. We are looking for the two values in that *df* = 24 row that are closest to the *t* value that we calculated, which was *t* = 1.40. In the first column of that row, we find a value of 1.318. In the second column, there is a value of 1.711. Our calculated *t* value, 1.40, is between those two values from Appendix B (1.318 < 1.40 < 1.711). Now, if you look in Appendix B at the very top of those two columns where we found the values of 1.318 and 1.711, you will see the alpha levels for two-tailed tests. (I explain what an alpha level is in Chapter 7.) These are the probabilities of obtaining the *t* values that are presented in this table by chance. We can see that the probability of obtaining a *t* value of 1.318 by chance is .20, and the probability of obtaining a *t* value of 1.711 by chance is .10. Now we know that the probability of obtaining our calculated *t* value, 1.40, by chance, is between .10 and .20. In other words, we would expect somewhere between 10 and 20 percent of randomly selected samples of *n* = 25, from this population, to consume 160 grams of sugar (or more) per day.

 For a short video demonstrating how to calculate and interpret a standard error of the mean, and for video examples demonstrating how to use the standard error of the mean to calculate probabilities, please refer to the website that accompanies this book.

Wrapping Up and Looking Forward

Standard error is often a difficult concept to grasp the first time it is encountered (or the second or the third). Because it is such a fundamental concept in inferential statistics, however, I encourage you to keep trying to make sense of both the meaning and the usefulness of standard errors. As we learned in this chapter, standard errors can be used to determine probabilities of sample statistics (such as the mean) in much the same way that we used standard scores to determine probabilities associated with individual scores in Chapter 4. Because of the usefulness of standard errors in determining probabilities, standard errors play a critical role in determining whether a statistic is statistically significant. Because standard errors are influenced by sample size, statistical significance will also be influenced by sample size. In the next chapter, the issue of statistical significance, and the effects of sample size on statistical significance, are discussed in more depth.

Work Problems

Suppose that in the population of children in the United States, the average number of minutes per day spent exercising is 45 with a standard deviation of 10. I select a random sample of 16 children and find that they spend an average of 50 minutes exercising with a standard deviation of 12. Please use this information to answer the following questions.

1. Calculate two standard errors of the mean, one using the population standard deviation and the other using the sample standard deviation. Describe what each of these standard errors tells you.
2. Using the standard error of the mean that you calculated using the population standard deviation, determine the probability of getting a difference between the sample mean and the population mean that is this large *by chance*. (*Note*: This is a *z* score problem.)
   a. Describe your results. What does this probability tell you?

3. Using the standard error of the mean that you calculated using the sample standard deviation, develop an estimate of the probability of getting a difference between the sample mean and the population mean that is this large *by chance*. (*Note*: This is a *t* value problem.)

    a. Describe your results. What does this probability tell you?

4. Compare the two standard errors that you calculated in Questions 2 and 3. Why are they different?

5. Suppose that instead of a sample size of 16, you had a sample size of 36.

    a. How would this affect the size of the standard error of the mean?
    b. Why does it make sense that a larger sample size has this effect on the size of the standard error of the mean?

6. Using this larger sample size of 36, and the standard deviation from the population, calculate a new probability of obtaining a difference between the sample mean and the population mean that is this large by chance.

    a. Compare this probability with the probability that you obtained in Question 2. How do they differ?

7. Explain why it makes sense that the larger sample size produces the difference in the two probabilities that you obtained in Questions 2 and 5.

8. Explain how you would decide whether to calculate a *z* score or a *t* value to determine the probability of randomly selecting a sample with a given mean by chance from a population?

 For answers to these problems, and for additional work problems, refer to the website that accompanies this book.

CHAPTER 7

Statistical Significance, Effect Size, and Confidence Intervals

When researchers use the data collected from samples to make inferences about the population (or populations) from which the samples were selected, they need to have some way of deciding how *meaningful* the sample data are. Are the differences between two samples (e.g., a group of adults from Alaska and a group of adults from New York) in their average levels of happiness large enough to conclude that the populations of adults from these two states actually differ in how happy they are? Is the relationship between years of education and income among a sample of 50 American adults strong enough to determine that income is related to education in the larger population of American adults? How do researchers reach important conclusions about how well sample statistics generalize to the larger population?

Three of the common tools used by researchers to reach such conclusions include testing for **statistical significance** and calculating **effect sizes** and **confidence intervals.** All of these tools provide indexes of how meaningful the results of statistical analyses are. Despite their frequent appearance in reports of quantitative research (particularly measures of statistical significance), these concepts are poorly understood by many researchers. The purpose of this chapter is to provide you, the reader, with a solid foundation of the concepts of statistical significance, effect size, and confidence intervals. Because statistical significance, effect size, and confidence intervals can be calculated for virtually any statistic, it is not possible in this short chapter to provide instructions on how to determine statistical significance or calculate an effect size or confidence interval across all research situations. Therefore, the focus of this chapter is to describe what these concepts mean and how to interpret them, as well as to provide general information about how statistical significance and effect sizes are determined.

Statistics are often divided into two types: **descriptive statistics** and **inferential statistics.** As I mentioned in Chapter 1, descriptive statistics are those statistics that *describe* the characteristics of a given set of data. For example, if I collect weight data for a group of 30 adults, I can use a variety of statistics to describe the weight characteristics of these 30 adults (e.g., their average, or mean, weight, the range from the lowest to the highest weight, the standard deviation for this group, etc.). Notice that all of these descriptive statistics do nothing more than provide information about this specific group of 30 individuals from whom I collected the data.

Although descriptive statistics are useful and important, researchers are often interested in extending their results beyond the specific group of people from whom they have collected data (i.e., their sample, or samples). From their sample data, researchers often want to determine whether there is some phenomenon of interest occurring in the larger population(s) that these samples represent. For example, I may want to know whether, in the general population, boys and girls differ in their levels of physical aggression. To determine this, I could conduct a study in which I measure the physical aggression levels of every boy and girl in the United States and see whether boys and girls differ. This study would be very costly, however, and very time-consuming. Another approach is to select a sample of boys and a sample of girls, measure their levels of physical aggression, see if they differ, and from these sample data *infer* about differences in the larger populations of boys and girls. If I eventually conclude that my results are statistically significant, in essence I am concluding that the differences I observed in the average levels of aggression of the boys and girls in my two samples represent a likelihood that there is also a difference in the average levels of aggression in the populations of boys and girls from which these samples were selected.

As the name implies, *inferential* statistics are always about making inferences about the larger population(s) on the basis of data collected from a sample or samples. To understand how this works, we first need to understand the distinction between a population and a sample and get comfortable with some concepts from probability. Once we have developed an understanding of statistical significance, we can then compare the concepts of statistical significance and **practical significance.** This distinction leads us to the second major concept covered in this chapter, which is effect size. Briefly, effect size is a measure of how large an observed effect is without regard to the size of the sample. In the earlier example examining levels of aggression, the effect that I am interested in is the difference in boys' and girls' average levels of aggression. Finally, we can calculate a confidence interval to provide a range of values that we are confident, to a certain degree of probability, contain the actual population parameter.

Statistical Significance in Depth

Samples and Populations

The first step in understanding statistical significance is to understand the difference between a **sample** and a **population.** This difference has been discussed earlier in Chapter 1. Briefly, a sample is an individual or group from whom or from which data are collected. A population is the individual or group that the sample is supposed to represent. For the purposes of understanding the concept of statistical significance, it is critical that you remember that when researchers collect data from a sample, they are often interested in using these data to make inferences about the population from which the sample was drawn. Statistical significance refers to the likelihood, or probability, that a statistic derived from a *sample* represents some genuine phenomenon in the *population* from which the sample was selected. In other words, statistical significance provides a measure to help us decide whether what we observe in our sample is also going on in the population that the sample is supposed to represent.

One factor that often complicates this process of making inferences from the sample to the population is that in many, if not most, research studies in the social sciences, the population is never explicitly defined. This is somewhat problematic, because when we argue that a statistical result is statistically significant, we are essentially arguing that the result we found in our sample is representative of some effect in the population from which the sample was selected. If we have not adequately defined our population, it is not entirely clear what to make of such a result (see Chapter 1 for a more detailed discussion of defining populations). For the purposes of this chapter, however, suffice it to say that samples are those individuals or groups from whom or from which data are collected, whereas populations are the entire collection of individuals or cases from which the samples are selected.

Probability

As discussed earlier in Chapters 4 and 6, probability plays a key role in inferential statistics. When it comes to deciding whether a result in a study is statistically significant, we must rely on probability to make the determination. Here is how it works.

When we calculate an inferential statistic, that statistic is part of a sampling distribution. From our discussion of standard errors in Chapter 6, you will recall that whenever we select a sample from a population and calculate a statistic from the sample, we have to keep in mind that if we had selected a different sample *of the same size from the same population*, we would probably get a slightly different statistic from the new sample. For example, if I randomly selected a sample of 1,000 men from the population of men in the United States and measured their shoe size, I might find an average shoe size of 10 for this sample. Now, if I were to randomly select a new sample of 1,000 men from the population of men in the United States and calculate their average shoe size, I might get a different mean, such as 9. If I were to select an infinite number of random samples of 1,000 and calculate the average shoe sizes of each of these samples, I would end up with a sampling distribution of the mean, and this sampling distribution would have a standard deviation, called the standard error of the mean (see Chapter 6 for a review of this concept). Just as there is a sampling distribution and a standard error of the mean, so there are sampling distributions and standard errors for all statistics, including correlation coefficients, *F* ratios from ANOVA, *t* values from *t* tests, regression coefficients, and so on.

Because these sampling distributions have certain stable mathematical characteristics, we can use the standard errors to calculate the exact probability of obtaining a specific sample statistic, from a sample of a given size, using a specific known or hypothesized population parameter. It's time for an example. Suppose that, from previous research by the shoe industry, I know that the average shoe size for the population of men in the United States is size 9. Because this is the known average for the *population*, this average is a *parameter* and not a statistic. Now suppose I randomly select a sample of 1,000 men and find that their average shoe size is 10, with a standard deviation of 2. Notice that the average for my sample (10) is a *statistic* because it comes from my sample, not my population. With these numbers, I can answer two slightly different but related questions. First, if the average shoe size in the population is really 9, what is the probability of selecting a random sample of 1,000 men who have an average shoe size of 10? Second, is the difference between my population mean (9) and my sample mean (10) *statistically significant?* The answer to my first question provides the basis for the answer to my second question. Notice that simply by looking at the two means, I can clearly see that they are different (i.e., 9 is different from 10). So I am trying to answer a deeper question than whether they differ. Rather, I am trying to determine whether the difference between my sample and population means is *statistically significant.* In other words, I am trying to determine whether the difference between my sample and population means is too large to have likely occurred by chance (i.e., because of who I happened to get in my sample).

Notice that if I do not select my sample at random, it would be easy to find a sample of 1,000 men with an average shoe size of 10. I could buy customer lists from shoe stores and select 1,000 men who bought size 10 shoes. Or I could place an advertisement in the paper seeking men who wear size 10 shoes. But if my population mean is really 9, and my sample is really selected at random, then there is some probability, or *chance*, that I could wind up with a sample of 1,000 men with an average shoe size of 10. In statistics, this *chance* is referred to as **random sampling error** or **random chance.**

Back to the example. If my population mean is 9, and my random sample of 1,000 men has a mean of 10 and a standard deviation of 2, I can calculate the standard error by dividing the standard deviation by the square root of the sample size (see Chapter 6 for this formula):

$$s_{\bar{x}} = 2 \div \sqrt{1000}$$

$$s_{\bar{x}} = 2 \div 31.62$$

$$s_{\bar{x}} = .06$$

where $s_{\bar{x}}$ is the standard error of the mean.

Now that I know the standard error is .06, I can calculate a *t* value to find the approximate probability of getting a sample mean of 10 *by random chance* if the population mean is really 9. (*Note:* For sample sizes larger than 120, the *t* distribution is almost identical to the normal distribution. Therefore, for large sample sizes, *t* values and *z* values, and their associated probabilities, are virtually identical. See Chapters 4 and 6 for more information.)

$$t = \frac{10 - 9}{.06}$$

$$t = \frac{1}{.06}$$

$$t = 16.67$$

When using the *t* distribution to find probabilities, we can simply take the absolute value of *t*. Once we have our absolute value for *t* (*t* = 16.67), we can consult the *t* table in Appendix B and see that, when the degrees of freedom equal infinity (i.e., greater than 120), the probability of getting a *t* value of 16.67 or greater is less than .001. In fact, because the critical *t* value associated with a probability of .001 is only 3.291, and our actual *t* value is 16.67, we can conclude that the random chance of getting a sample mean of 10 when the population mean is 9 is *much* less than .001 (see Figure 7.1). In other words, when we randomly select a sample of 1,000 men and calculate their average shoe size, when we know that the average shoe size of men in the population is 9, we would *expect* to get a sample mean of 10 much less than one time in 1,000. With our table of *t* values, that is as accurate as we can get.

 To watch a brief video demonstration of how to calculate a *t* value and determine the probability of obtaining a *t* value of a given size by chance, please refer to the website that accompanies this book.

It is important to reiterate a point that was raised earlier, in Chapters 4, 5, and 6. In the normal distribution and the family of *t* distributions, values near the middle of the distribution occur more often than values away from the middle. (This is what creates the bell shape of these distributions.) These infrequently occurring values are out at the ends of the distributions, and these ends are known as the **tails** of the distributions. For example, in Figure 7.1, notice that the *t* value we calculated was at the extreme upper (or positive) tail of the distribution. Because the values in the tails of the distributions are less likely to occur by chance than the values near the middle, that is where we find the statistically significant values. We will return to this point when we discuss one-tailed and two-tailed hypotheses later in the chapter.

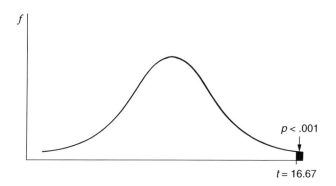

FIGURE 7.1 A statistically significant *t* value.

So we have already calculated that the probability, or random chance, of finding a sample mean of 10 when the population mean is 9 is very small, less than one in a thousand, when the sample size is 1,000 and is randomly selected. This probability is known as a *p* **value**, with *p* standing for *probability*. In our current example, we would say that we found *p* < .001, which is the way *p* values are generally reported in research reports and scholarly journals. Now we can turn our attention to the second question: Is the difference between a population mean of 9 and a sample mean of 10 statistically significant? Well, the quick answer is "Yes." The longer answer requires us to delve into the world of hypothesis testing.

Hypothesis Testing and Type I Errors

The idea here is simple. Before we calculate the statistic and decide whether a result is statistically significant, we should establish a standard, or benchmark. To do this, we develop a hypothesis and establish a criterion that we will use when deciding whether to retain or reject our hypothesis. The primary hypothesis of interest in social science research is the **null hypothesis (H_0).** Because the word "null" means zero, the null hypothesis always suggests that there will be an *absence* of effect. For example, the null hypothesis suggests that a sample mean will not be different from the population mean, or that two population means (e.g., boys and girls) will not differ, or that two variables (e.g., education and income) will not be related to each other in the population. Notice that the null hypothesis always refers to an absence of effect *in the population*. To illustrate, let us return to the shoe-size example. Recall that we already knew our population average shoe size was 9. Given this, we would expect that if we were to randomly select a sample from that population, and calculate the average shoe size for the sample, that average would also be 9. We might know that there is a *chance* our sample would have a different mean than our population, but our best guess is that our sample would have the same mean as our population. Therefore, our null hypothesis would be that our population mean and our sample mean would not differ from each other (i.e., no effect). We could write this hypothesis symbolically as follows:

$$H_0 : \mu = \bar{X}$$

where μ represents the population mean,
$\bar{X}$ represents the sample mean.

Notice that at this point, we have not yet selected our sample of 1,000 men and we have not yet calculated a sample mean. This entire hypothesis building process occurs *a priori* (i.e., *before* we conduct our test of statistical significance). Of course, where there is one hypothesis (the null), it is always possible to have alternative hypotheses. One alternative to the null hypothesis is the opposite hypothesis. Whereas the null hypothesis is that the sample and population means will equal each other, an alternative hypothesis could be that they will not equal each other. This **alternative hypothesis (H_A or H_1)** would be written symbolically as

$$H_A : \mu \neq \bar{X}$$

where μ is the population mean,
$\bar{X}$ is the sample mean.

Notice that our alternative hypothesis does not include any speculation about whether the sample mean will be larger or smaller than the population mean, only that the two will differ. This is known as a **two-tailed** alternative hypothesis. I could have proposed a different alternative hypothesis. For example, I might have proposed that my sample mean would be larger than my population mean because the population mean was calculated several years ago and men (and their feet) are getting larger with each new generation. When my alternative hypothesis is *directional* (i.e., it includes speculation about which value will be larger), I have a **one-tailed** alternative hypothesis. In the example about shoe size, my one-tailed alternative hypothesis would look like this:

$$H_A : \mu < \bar{X}$$

where μ is the population mean,
$\bar{X}$ is the sample mean.

Let's suppose, for this example, that we are using the two-tailed hypothesis and that the population mean and the sample mean are different from each other, with no direction of difference specified. At this point in the process, we have established our null and alternative hypotheses. You may assume that all we need to do is randomly select our 1,000 men, find their average shoe size, and see if it is different from or equal to 9. But, alas, it is not quite that simple. Suppose that we get our sample and find that their average shoe size is 9.00001. Technically, that is different from 9, but is it different enough to be considered meaningful? Keep in mind that whenever we select a sample at random from a population, there is always a chance that it will differ slightly from the population. Although our best guess is that our sample mean will be the same as our population mean, we have to remember that it would be almost impossible for our sample to look *exactly* like our population. So our question becomes this: How different does our sample mean have to be from our population mean before we consider the difference meaningful, or *significant*? If our sample mean is just a little different from our population mean, we can shrug it off and say, "Well, the difference is probably just due to *random sampling error*, or *chance*." But how different do our sample and population means need to be before we conclude that the difference is probably *not* due to chance? That's where our **alpha level** comes into play. The alpha level is the standard, set by the researcher, that is used to determine whether a result is statistically significant. Frequently, researchers use an alpha level of .05, meaning that if the probability of a result occurring by chance is less than this alpha level of .05, the researcher will conclude that the result did not occur by chance, and is therefore statistically significant.

As I explained earlier in this chapter, and in Chapters 4 and 6, sampling distributions and standard errors of these distributions allow us to compute probabilities for obtaining sample statistics of various sizes. When I say "probability," this is in fact shorthand for "the probability of obtaining this sample statistic due to *chance* or *random sampling error*." Given that samples generally do not precisely represent the populations from which they are drawn, we should expect some difference between the sample statistic and the population parameter simply due to the luck of the draw, or random sampling error. If we reach into our population and pull out another random sample, we will probably get slightly different statistics again. So some of the difference between a sample statistic, like the mean, and a population parameter will always be due to who we happened to get in our random sample, which is why it is called random sampling error. Recall from Chapter 6 that, with a statistic like the mean, the sampling distribution of the mean is a normal distribution. So our random sampling method will produce many sample means that are close to the value of the population mean and fewer that are further away from the population mean. The further the sample mean is from the population mean, the less likely it is to occur by chance, or random sampling error.

Before we can conclude that the differences between the sample statistic and the population parameter are probably *not* just due to random sampling error, we have to decide how unlikely the chances are of getting a difference between the statistic and the population parameter just by chance *if the null hypothesis is true*. In other words, before we can *reject the null hypothesis*, we want to be reasonably sure that any difference between the sample statistic and the population parameter is not just due to random sampling error, or chance. In the social sciences, the convention

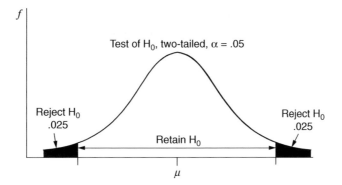

FIGURE 7.2 Regions of rejection for a two-tailed test.

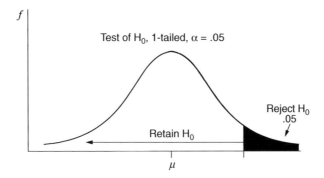

FIGURE 7.3 Region of rejection for a one-tailed test.

is to set that level at .05. (This is the alpha level.) In other words, social scientists generally agree that if the probability of getting a difference between the sample statistic and the population parameter *by chance* is less than 5 percent, we can reject the null hypothesis and conclude that the differences between the statistic and the parameter are probably not due to chance. In Figures 7.2 and 7.3, I present graphs that illustrate the regions of rejection for two-tailed and one-tailed tests of statistical significance, using an alpha level of .05.

The agreed-upon probability of .05 (symbolized as $\alpha = .05$) represents the **Type I error** rate that we, as researchers, are willing to accept *before we conduct our statistical analysis.* (Notice that in Figure 7.2, this alpha of .05 is divided into the two tails of the distribution, and the "Reject H_0" areas represent the upper and lower 2.5 percent extremes of the distribution. In Figure 7.3, in contrast, the entire 5 percent of the distribution that is associated with the alpha level of .05 is at the top end of the distribution.) Remember that the purpose of our analysis is to determine whether we should retain or reject our null hypothesis. When we decide to reject the null hypothesis, what we are saying, in essence, is that we are concluding that the difference between our sample statistic and our population parameter is *not* due to random sampling error. But when we make this decision, we have to remember that it is *always* possible to get even very large differences just due to random sampling error, or chance. In our shoe-size example, when I randomly selected 1,000 men, it is possible that, just due to some fluke, I selected 1,000 men with an average shoe size of 17. Now this is extremely unlikely, but it is always possible. You never know what you're going to get when you select a random sample. In my earlier example, where my sample had an average shoe size of 10, I found that the probability of getting a sample mean of 10 when my population mean was 9, by chance, was less than one in a thousand. Though unlikely, *it is still possible* that this difference between my sample and population means was just due to chance. So because my p value ($p < .001$) is much smaller than my alpha level ($\alpha = .05$), I will reject the null hypothesis and conclude that my sample mean is actually different from my population mean, that this is probably not just a fluke of random sampling, and that my result is statistically significant. When I reach this conclusion, I may be wrong. In fact, I may be rejecting the null hypothesis even though the null hypothesis is true. Such errors (rejecting the null hypothesis when it is true) are called Type I errors. Another type of error in hypothesis testing, **Type II errors**, occur when the null hypothesis is retained even though it is false and should have been rejected.

To summarize, when we do inferential statistics, we want to know whether something that we observe in a sample represents an actual phenomenon in the population. So we set up a null hypothesis that there is no real difference between our sample statistic and our population parameter, and we select an alpha level that serves as our benchmark for helping us decide whether to reject or retain our null hypothesis. If our p value (which we get *after* we calculate our statistic) is smaller than our selected alpha level, we will reject the null hypothesis. When we reject the null hypothesis, we are concluding that the difference between the sample statistic and the population parameter is probably not due to chance, or random sampling error. However, when we reach this conclusion, there is always a chance that we will be wrong, having made a Type I error. One goal of statistics is to avoid making such errors, so to be extra safe we may want to select a more conservative alpha level, such as .01, and say that unless our p value is smaller than .01, we will retain our null hypothesis. In our shoe-size example, our p value was much smaller than either .05 or .01, so we reject the null hypothesis and conclude that, for some reason, our sample of 1,000 men had a statistically significantly larger average shoe size than did our general population. Because we concluded that this difference was probably not due to random sampling error, or chance, we must conclude that our sample represents a different population. Perhaps the population mean of 9 represents the population of men born from an earlier generation and the sample mean of 10 represents a population of (larger) men born more recently.

Limitations of Statistical Significance Testing

As an indication of the importance of a result in quantitative research, statistical significance has enjoyed a rather privileged position for decades. Social scientists have long given the "$p < .05$" rule a sort of magical quality, with any result carrying a probability greater than .05 being quickly discarded into the trash heap of "non-significant" results and statistically significant results being heralded as important. Recently, however, researchers and journal editors have begun to view statistical significance in a slightly less flattering light, recognizing some of its major shortcomings. For example, the sixth edition of the *Publication Manual of the American Psychological Association* (2009) calls for authors to include information about effect size and confidence intervals, not just measures of statistical significance, in all publications that conform to their guidelines. Organizations across the social science disciplines are also emphasizing the importance of effect size and confidence interval reporting. As a result, more and more researchers are becoming aware of the importance of effect size and are increasingly including reports of effect size in their work.

Two limitations of the hypothesis-testing, statistical significance model have received the most attention. First, this model creates a situation where researchers are looking to answer a dichotomous, yes-or-no question that is often not particularly informative. Specifically, because tests of statistical significance are designed to examine whether the null hypothesis should be rejected, researchers find themselves examining whether an effect is significantly different from zero. Is the difference between two sample means significantly different from zero? Is a sample correlation coefficient significantly different from zero? These are important questions to answer, but most research questions are designed to go beyond this simple yes-or-no answer. Researchers also want to know how large the observed effect is, and how confident they can be that the effect observed in the sample data reflects what is happening in the population. The answer to these questions comes from effect sizes and confidence intervals. Although tests of statistical significance can allow researchers to determine whether their statistical effects are due to chance (i.e., random sampling error), the answer to this question is just the beginning of what we want to find out from our data, not the end.

A second limitation of testing for statistical significance is that these tests are heavily influenced by sample size. To determine whether a statistic is statistically significant, we follow the same general sequence regardless of the statistic (*z* scores, *t* values, *F* values, correlation coefficients, etc.). First, we find the difference between a sample statistic and a population parameter (either the actual parameter or, if this is not known, a hypothesized value for the parameter). Next, we divide that difference by the standard error. Finally, we determine the probability of getting a ratio of that size due to chance, or random sampling error. (For a review of this process, refer to the earlier section in this chapter when we calculated the *t* value for the shoe-size example.)

The problem with this process is that when we divide the numerator (i.e., the difference between the sample statistic and the population parameter) by the denominator (i.e., the standard error), the sample size plays a large role. In all of the formulas that we use for standard error, the larger the sample size, the smaller the standard error (see Chapter 6). When we plug the standard error into the formula for determining *t* values, *F* values, and *z* scores, we see that the smaller the standard error, the larger these values become, and the more likely it is that they will be considered statistically significant. Because of this effect of sample size, we sometimes find that even very small differences between the sample statistic and the population parameter can be statistically significant if the sample size is large. In Figure 7.4, the influence of sample size on statistical significance is depicted graphically. The left side of the graph shows a fairly large difference between the sample mean and the population mean, but this difference is not statistically significant with a small sample size (*n* = 4). In contrast, a small difference between sample means with a large sample size (*n* = 1,600) can produce a statistically significant result, as shown on the right side of Figure 7.4.

To illustrate this point, let us consider an example with two different sample sizes. Suppose we know that the average IQ score for the population of adults in the United States is 100. Now suppose that I randomly select two samples of adults. One of my samples contains 25 adults, the other 1,600. Each of these two samples produces an average IQ score of 105 and a standard deviation of 15. Is the difference between 105 and 100 statistically significant? To answer this question, I need to calculate a *t* value for each sample. The standard error for our sample with 25 adults will be

$$s_{\bar{x}} = 15 \div \sqrt{25} \Rightarrow 15 \div 5 \Rightarrow 3$$

The standard error for our second sample, with 1,600 adults, will be

$$s_{\bar{x}} = 15 \div \sqrt{1600} \Rightarrow 15 \div 40 \Rightarrow .375$$

where $s_{\bar{x}}$ is the standard error of the mean.

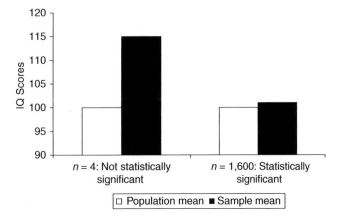

FIGURE 7.4   The effect of sample size on the likelihood of finding a statistically significant difference between means.

Plugging these standard errors into our *t* value formulas, we find that the *t* value for the 25-person sample is $(105 - 100) \div 3$, or 1.67. Looking in our table of *t* distributions (Appendix B), we can see that the *p* value for a *t* value of 1.67 is between .10 and .20. The *t* value for the sample with 1,600 adults is $(105 - 100) \div .375$, or 13.33, with a corresponding *p* value of $p < .0001$. If we are using an alpha level of .05, then a difference of 5 points on the IQ test would not be considered statistically significant if we only had a sample size of 25, but would be highly statistically significant if our sample size were 1,600. Because sample size plays such a big role in determining statistical significance, many statistics textbooks make a distinction between statistical significance and practical significance. With a sample size of 1,600, a difference of even 1 point on the IQ test would produce a statistically significant result ($t = 1 \div .375 \Rightarrow t = 2.67, p < .01$). However, if we had a very small sample size of 4, even a 15-point difference in average IQ scores would not be statistically significant ($t = 15 \div 7.50 \Rightarrow t = 2.00, p > .10$). (See Figure 7.4 for a graphic illustration of this.) But is a difference of 1 point on a test with a range of over 150 points really important in the real world? And is a difference of 15 points not meaningful? In other words, is it a significant difference in the *practical* sense of the word *significant*? One way to answer this question is to examine the effect size.

Effect Size in Depth

Different statistics have different effect sizes associated with them. For example, for correlation and regression it is common to use measures of how much of the variance in one variable is explained by another variable, or variables (i.e., r^2 or R^2). These will be discussed in Chapters 12 and 13. Common measures of effect size for ANOVA analyses are eta squared and partial eta squared, and these will be discussed in more detail in Chapters 9, 10, and 11. For chi-square analyses (Chapter 14), phi and Cramer's V are two commonly used measures of effect size. In this chapter, we will examine **Cohen's *d*,** a common effect size formula used with *t* tests. The formulas for calculating many inferential statistics, including *t* tests, involve a ratio of a numerator (such as the difference between a sample mean and a population mean in a one-sample *t* test) divided by a standard error. To calculate the Cohen's *d*, the standard error must be converted into a standard deviation, thereby eliminating the effect of the sample size that is built into the standard error formula and creating a measure of the standardized difference between the means.

We can examine one form of effect size that is commonly used for *t* tests, the Cohen's d,[1] by returning to our examples using IQ scores. Remember that we have a population with an average IQ score of 100. We also had two samples, each with an average IQ score of 105 and a standard deviation of 15: one with a sample size of 25 and the other with a sample size of 1,600. Also recall that to find the standard error for calculating our *t* scores, we simply divided the standard deviation by the square root of the sample size. So for the sample with 25 members, our standard error was

$$s_{\bar{x}} = 15 \div \sqrt{25} \Rightarrow 15 \div 5 \Rightarrow 3$$

where $s_{\bar{x}}$ is the standard error of the mean.

To calculate an effect size, what we need to do is convert this standard error back into a standard deviation. If we *divide* the standard deviation by the square root of the sample size to find the standard error, we can *multiply* the standard error by the square root of the sample size to find the standard deviation. When we do this, we find that

$$s = 3\sqrt{25} \Rightarrow 3 \times 5 \Rightarrow 15$$

where *s* is the sample standard deviation.

Notice that the standard deviation would be exactly the same if we calculated it for the larger sample size of 1,600, even though the standard error was much smaller for that sample:

$$s = .375\sqrt{1600} \Rightarrow .375 \times 40 \Rightarrow 15$$

Once we have our standard deviation, it is easy to calculate a Cohen's *d* effect size, which has the symbol *d*. In the IQ example, we could determine the effect size as follows:

$$d = \frac{105 - 100}{15}$$

$$d = \frac{5}{15}$$

$$d = .33$$

where *d* is the effect size.

As you can see, the formula for the effect size translates the numerator into standard deviation units. When the numerator represents some sort of difference score (e.g., the difference between two or more group means, the difference between a sample statistic and a population parameter), the effect size will represent that difference in standard deviation units. This is similar to representing the difference in standard error units, as most inferential statistics do (e.g., *t* values, *F* values, correlation coefficients), except that sample size is *eliminated* from the process.

There are no hard and fast rules regarding the interpretation of Cohen's *d* effect sizes. A common rule-of-thumb is that Cohen's *d* effect sizes smaller than .20 are small, those between .20 and .75 are moderate, and those over .75 are large. When determining whether an effect size is meaningful, it is important to consider what you are testing and what your perspective is. If I am comparing the mortality rates of two samples trying two different experimental drugs, even small effect sizes are important, because we are talking about life and death. But if I'm comparing two different samples' preferences for ice cream flavors, even fairly large effect sizes may have little more than trivial importance to most people. Keep in mind, however, that what is trivial to one person may be vitally important to another. Although I do not care about even large differences in people's preferences for certain ice cream flavors, the CEO of an ice cream company may care very much about even small differences in preference. In fact, a small preference for chocolate over vanilla can mean millions of dollars to an ice cream company (and the owners of stock in the company). The point here is that "practical significance" is a subjective concept. Although statistics can provide measures of effect size, interpreting the importance of these effect sizes is an imprecise science.

The recent push by some researchers to focus more heavily on effect sizes than on statistical significance reminds me that I should conclude this section of the chapter by urging you to take both effect size *and* statistical significance into consideration as you read and conduct research. Notice that in the previous examples, the exact same effect size was produced with the 25-person sample as with the 1,600-person sample. These results suggest that sample size does not matter. In fact, sample size is very important. Stated simply, it is easier to come up with fluke, or *chance* results with smaller sample sizes than with larger sample sizes. Our tests of statistical significance, which are sensitive to sample size, tell us the probability that our results are due to random sampling error, or chance. Because larger sample sizes have a better likelihood of representing the populations from which they were selected, the results of studies that use larger sample sizes are more *reliable* than those using smaller sample sizes, if all else is equal (e.g., how the samples were selected, the methods used in the study, etc.). When used together, tests of statistical significance and measures of effect size can provide important information regarding the reliability and importance of statistical results. Of course, our own judgments about the meaning, causes, and consequences of our results are also important factors.

Confidence Intervals in Depth

Confidence intervals are becoming increasingly common in reports of inferential statistics, in part because they provide another measure of effect size.[2] When researchers use sample data to make inferences about populations, they usually do not really know the actual value of the population parameters. All they have is their sample data. By using probability and confidence intervals, they can make educated predictions about the approximate values of the population parameters.

To illustrate how confidence intervals work, let's return to the shoe-size example from earlier in the chapter. But let me slightly rephrase the statement about the average shoe size in the population. Instead of saying, as I did earlier, "In the population of American men, the average shoe size is 9," let me say, "*Suppose* that the average shoe size of American men is 9." This is technically more accurate because, assuming the average shoe size in the population was determined some time ago, we do not really know the average shoe size of the current population of American men. So our hypothesized value of the average shoe size in the population is 9, and our observed shoe size in our sample of 1,000 men is 10, with a standard deviation of 2. Using these data, we can calculate a confidence interval.

Recall that in our earlier example, using the same values for the sample mean, standard deviation, and sample size, we calculated a standard error of .06. Using these data, we can calculate a confidence interval. The confidence interval provides a range of values that we are confident, to a certain degree of probability, contains the population parameter (e.g., the population mean). Most of the time, researchers want to be either 95 percent or 99 percent confident that the confidence interval contains the population parameter. These values correspond with *p* values of .05 and .01, respectively. The formulas for calculating 95 percent and 99 percent confidence intervals are provided in Table 7.1. Notice that the formula for the confidence interval involves building the interval around the sample statistic (both greater than and less than the sample statistic). Because the confidence interval involves values both greater and less than the sample statistic, we always use the alpha level for the *two-tailed* test to find our *t* value, even if we had a one-tailed alternative hypothesis when testing for statistical significance.

If we look in Appendix B for a two-tailed test with $df = \infty$ and $\alpha = .05$, we find $t_{95} = 1.96$. Plugging this value into our confidence interval formula, we get the following:

$$\text{CI}_{95} = 10 \pm (1.96)(.06)$$

$$\text{CI}_{95} = 10 \pm .12$$

$$\text{CI}_{95} = 9.88, 10.12$$

TABLE 7.1 Formulas for calculating confidence intervals for the mean

$$\text{CI}_{95} = \bar{X} \pm (t_{95})(s_{\bar{x}})$$

$$\text{CI}_{99} = \bar{X} \pm (t_{99})(s_{\bar{x}})$$

where CI_{95} is a 95% confidence interval,
CI_{99} is a 99% confidence interval,
$\bar{X}$ is the sample mean,
$s_{\bar{x}}$ is the standard error of the mean,
t_{95} is the *t* value for a two-tailed test with an alpha level of .05 and a given number of degrees of freedom,
t_{99} is the *t* value for a two-tailed test with an alpha level of .01 and a given number of degrees of freedom.

To wrap words around this result, we would say that we are 95 percent confident that the population mean is contained within the interval ranging from 9.88 to 10.12. In other words, given our sample mean of 10, and not knowing our population mean, we are 95 percent confident that the population that this sample represents has a mean between 9.88 and 10.12. Notice that this confidence interval does not contain the value of 9.00, which we hypothesized to be our population mean. It turns out that our sample most likely does not represent a population with a mean shoe size of 9. That is why, when we compared our sample mean of 10 with the population mean of 9, we found the two means to be statistically significantly different from each other.

If we want to create an interval that we are even more confident contains our population mean, notice that we just need to widen the interval a little. To calculate a 99 percent confidence interval using these data, we look in Appendix B for a two-tailed test with $df = \infty$ and $\alpha = .01$, and we find $t_{99} = 2.576$. Plugging these numbers into the confidence interval formula, we get

$$CI_{99} = 10 \pm (2.576)(.06)$$

$$CI_{99} = 10 \pm .15$$

$$CI_{99} = 9.85, 10.15$$

Now we can conclude that we are 99 percent confident that the population mean is contained within the interval between 9.85 and 10.15. This interval also does not contain the value of 9.00. This tells us that the sample mean of 10 is statistically significantly different from the hypothesized population mean of 9.00 at the $p < .01$ level.

 To watch a video demonstration of how to calculate and interpret a confidence interval, please refer to the website that accompanies this book.

You may have noticed that these two confidence intervals that we built around the sample mean of a shoe size of 10 are both very small. In other words, we are quite confident that the mean of the population from which this sample of 1,000 men was drawn is very close to 10. This is useful information to researchers, because it tells us that although we do not know the actual population mean, we can be quite certain that it is close to 10. Had we found a wide confidence interval (e.g., $CI_{95} = 8, 12$), this would tell us that we do not really have a very good idea about what the actual population mean is. So the confidence interval provides us with information about how much faith we can have that our sample statistic is an accurate representation of our population parameter.[3]

One reason that our analyses produced such narrow confidence intervals is because our sample was quite large (i.e., $n = 1,000$). Generally speaking, the larger the sample, the more accurately it should represent the population. To illustrate the effects of sample size on confidence intervals, let's calculate 95 percent and 99 percent confidence intervals for the shoe-size example, but this time let's suppose that our sample size is 25. The standard deviation is still 2 and the sample mean is still 10. First, we need to re-calculate the standard error of the mean, using our smaller sample size of $n = 25$:

$$s_{\bar{x}} = 2 \div \sqrt{25}$$

$$s_{\bar{x}} = 2 \div 5$$

$$s_{\bar{x}} = .40$$

where $s_{\bar{x}}$ = the standard error of the mean.

Next, we need to find two new *t* values from Appendix B using our smaller sample. Because $n = 25$, and the number of degrees of freedom when we have a single sample is $n - 1$, we are going to look in Appendix B for the row with 24 degrees of freedom ($df = 25 - 1 = 24$). We are looking for two *t* values in Appendix B, one for our 95 percent confidence interval and one for a 99 percent confidence interval. In Appendix B, this means looking at the "alpha level for two-tailed test" for alpha levels of .05 and .01. With 24 degrees of freedom and a two-tailed alpha level of .05, we find a *t* value of 2.064. And with an alpha level of .01, $t = 2.797$. Now we can plug these values into our confidence interval formulas.

Our 95 percent confidence interval calculation looks like this:

$$CI_{95} = 10 \pm (2.064)(.40)$$

$$CI_{95} = 10 \pm .83$$

$$CI_{95} = 9.17, 10.83$$

And our 99 percent confidence interval calculation looks like this:

$$CI_{99} = 10 \pm (2.797)(.40)$$

$$CI_{99} = 10 \pm 1.12$$

$$CI_{99} = 8.88, 11.12$$

The results of the confidence intervals for sample sizes of 1,000 and 25 are presented graphically in Figure 7.5. As you can see, the confidence intervals are quite a bit narrower when $n = 1,000$ than when $n = 25$. This makes sense, as we should be less confident that our sample statistics accurately represent the population parameters when samples are small than when they are large, assuming that the samples were selected using the same method.

Example: Statistical Significance, Confidence Interval, and Effect Size for a One-Sample *t* Test of Motivation

To illustrate the concepts of statistical significance, effect size, and confidence intervals, I present the results from a one-sample *t* test that I conducted using data from research I conducted with high school students. In this study, 490 students were given surveys in their social studies classrooms to measure their motivation, beliefs, and attitudes about school and school work. One of the constructs that my colleague and I measured was a motivational orientation called *performance-approach goals*. Performance-approach goals refer to students' perceptions that one purpose of trying to succeed academically is to demonstrate to others how smart they are, sometimes by outperforming other students. We used a measure of performance-approach goals that was developed by Carol Midgley and her colleagues at the University of Michigan (Midgley et al., 1998). This measure includes five items: (1) "I'd like to show my teacher that I'm smarter than the other students in this class"; (2) "I would feel successful in this class if I did better than most of the other students"; (3) "I want to do better than other students in this class"; (4) "Doing better than other students in this class is important to me"; and (5) "I would feel really good if I were the only one who could answer the teacher's questions in this class." Students responded to each of these questions using a 5-point Likert scale (with 1 = *Not at all true* and 5 = *Very true*). Students' responses to these five items were then averaged, creating a performance-approach goal scale with a range from 1 to 5.

I wanted to see whether my sample of high school students in California had a different mean on this performance-approach goal scale than the larger population of high school students in the United States. Suppose that previous research conducted with a large sample of high school

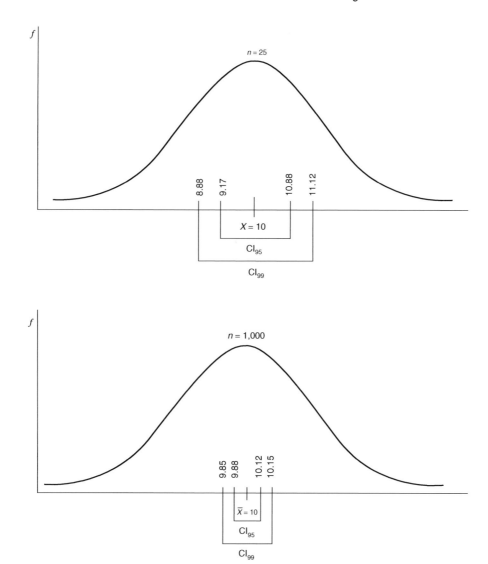

FIGURE 7.5 The effect of sample size on the widths of the confidence intervals.

students that accurately represented the larger population of high school students throughout the United States found that the average score on the performance-approach goal scale was 3.00. Some might argue that students in California, with the sunshine and relatively easy lifestyle, are less competitive than students in the rest of the country. So we might expect students in the California sample to have lower average scores on the performance-approach goal scale when compared with the average scores in the American population of high school students. Others think this is hogwash. California is more expensive and has more competition for jobs than other parts of the country, so perhaps these students are *more* competitive than the typical American student. Because both sides of the argument are presented, our alternative hypothesis is two-tailed. What we are testing is the null hypothesis (H_0: $\mu = \bar{X}$) against the two-tailed alternative (H_A: $\mu \neq \bar{X}$).

So I used the SPSS statistics program to conduct a one-sample t test. In Table 7.2, the actual SPSS output from the t test is presented. In this output, the top part of the table shows the sample size ($n = 490$), the mean for the sample ($\bar{X} = 3.0449$, or 3.04), the standard deviation ($s = .98199$, or .98), and the standard error of the mean ($s_{\bar{x}} = .04436$, or .04). The lower part of Table 7.2 provides the t value ($t = 1.012$), the degrees of freedom ($df = 489$), the p value for this t (Sig. 2-Tailed = .312), and the difference between the sample mean and the hypothesized

TABLE 7.2 SPSS output for a one-sample *t* test

One-Sample Statistics				
	n	Mean	Std. Deviation	Std. Error Mean
Performance Approach Goals	490	3.0449	.98199	.04436

One-Sample Test						
Test Value = 3.00						
				Mean Difference	95% Confidence Interval of the Difference	
	t	df	Sig. 2-Tailed		Lower	Upper
Performance Approach Goals	1.012	489	.312	.0449	−.0423	.1321

population mean ($\bar{X} - \mu = .0449$). Finally, the 95 percent confidence interval for the *difference* between the sample and population means is provided (CI$_{95}$ = −.0423, .1321).

If we are using the conventional alpha level of .05 (i.e., α = .05), then we can see that our *p* value is larger than our alpha level, and we would retain the null hypothesis of no differences between the average scores of the sample of California high school students and the national population of high school students on the performance-approach goal scale. Therefore, we would conclude that our results are not statistically significant and we can make a more far-reaching conclusion: "The *population* of California high school students does not differ from the larger population of American high school students on the performance-approach goal measure" (assuming this sample represents the larger population of California high school students).

Using the information in Table 7.2 and the table of *t* values presented in Appendix B, we can recreate this *t* test, see why it is not statistically significant, and calculate the effect size and confidence interval. First, using the means and the standard error of the sample mean, we can reproduce the equation used to generate the *t* value:

$$t = \frac{3.0449 - 3.00}{.04436}$$

$$t = \frac{.0449}{.04436}$$

$$t = 1.012$$

Next, using the degrees of freedom (*df* = 489), we can look in Appendix B to find the approximate probability of finding a *t* value of this size or larger by chance. Because our degrees of freedom are larger than 120, we must look in the row labeled with the infinity symbol (∞). Because the absolute value of our observed *t* value is 1.01, which is considerably smaller than the value of 1.96 that is associated with an α = .05 (two-tailed test), we must retain our null hypothesis. Our SPSS output confirms this, placing the probability at a more precise number, *p* = .312, considerably larger than the .05 cut-off level for rejecting the null hypothesis. This would *not* be considered statistically significant if we were using the conventional alpha level of .05.

Now let's use this data to calculate two 95 percent confidence intervals: one for the sample mean and one for the difference between the sample and population means. Both will provide similar information about the magnitude of the differences between the sample and population means. First, the sample mean:

$$CI_{95} = 3.0449 \pm (1.96)(.04436)$$

$$CI_{95} = 3.0449 \pm .0869$$

$$CI_{95} = 2.958, 3.132$$

This confidence interval tells us that, based on the sample mean, we are 95 percent confident that the population that this sample represents has a mean between the values of 2.958 and 3.132. This is quite a narrow interval, indicating that we are confident that the actual population mean is quite close to our sample mean. Because that interval *contains* the hypothesized value of the population mean (3.0) for American high school students on this variable, we *must* conclude that the population represented by our sample does not differ significantly from the population of American high school students. If our sample represents California high school students, then we say, "There is no difference between the population of California high school students and the population of American high school students in their average scores on the performance-approach goal measure."

Now let's compute the confidence interval for the difference between the sample and population means:

$$CI_{95} = .0449 \pm (1.96)(.04436)$$

$$CI_{95} = .0449 \pm .0869$$

$$CI_{95} = -.0420, .1318$$

Once again, we can see that our 95 percent confidence interval contains the hypothesized difference between the sample and population means presented in the *null* hypothesis (H_0: $\mu = \bar{X}$, so $\mu - \bar{X} = 0$). Therefore, we must retain our null hypothesis, just as we did with the other confidence interval we calculated for these data.

Finally, we can calculate an effect size for these data. Although our result was not statistically significant, and our effect size is likely to be quite small, it is still instructive to calculate an effect size. So let's do it:

$$d = \frac{\bar{X} - \mu}{S}$$

where d is the effect size,

$\bar{X}$ is the sample mean,

μ is the population mean,

S is the standard deviation for the effect size.

Although we have a standard deviation for the sample in the study, we do not yet have a standard deviation to use in our effect size formula. To find it, we multiply the standard error by the square root of the sample size, as we did in our earlier example:

$$S = \sqrt{490} \times .04436$$

$$S = 22.14 \times .04436$$

$$S = .98$$

Now that we have our standard deviation, we can easily calculate the effect size:

$$d = \frac{3.049 - 3.00}{.98}$$

$$d = \frac{.0449}{.98}$$

$$d = .05$$

Our effect size of .05 is very small, as we might expect from a non-statistically significant result. When we combine the results of our analysis of statistical significance with our effect size and confidence interval results, we have a consistent picture: High school students in California do not really differ from students in the rest of the country in their endorsement of performance-approach goals. If we were to write these results up for a journal article, it would look something like this: "The difference between the average levels of performance-approach goal orientation for the sample of California students ($M = 3.04$) and the population of students in the U.S. ($M = 3.00$) was not statistically significant ($t_{(489)} = 1.02, p = .31, CI_{95} = -.04, .13$). The effect size was also quite small ($d = .05$), indicating a lack of practical significance for the difference between the means."

Wrapping up and Looking Forward

For several decades, statistical significance has been the measuring stick used by social scientists to determine whether the results of their analyses are meaningful. Testing for statistical significance is important, because it allows researchers to determine whether the effect they observe in their sample data was likely just due to random sampling error, or something more substantial. But as we have seen in this chapter and in our discussion of standard errors in Chapter 6, tests of statistical significance are quite dependent on sample size. With large samples, even trivial effects are often statistically significant, whereas with small sample sizes, quite large effects may not reach statistical significance. Because of this, there has recently been an increasing appreciation of, and demand for, measures of practical significance as well. When determining the practical significance of your own results, or of those you encounter in published articles or books, you are well advised to consider all of the measures at your disposal. Is the result statistically significant? How large is the effect size? And, as you look at the effect in your data and place your data in the context of real-world relevance, use your judgment to decide whether you are talking about a meaningful or a trivial result. In the chapters to come, we will encounter several examples of inferential statistics. Use what you have learned in this chapter to determine whether the results presented should be considered practically significant.

Work Problems

Suppose that in the population of adults in the United States, the average number of hours spent per year riding a bicycle is 20. I select a random sample of 36 adults from Ohio to see if their average amount of time riding a bike differs from the population in the U.S. The mean for the Ohio sample is 18 with a standard deviation of 3. Please answer the following questions using this information.

1. Write the null and alternative hypotheses for this problem, once using symbols and again in sentence form.
2. Is the difference between the sample mean and the population mean statistically significant?
3. Calculate a Cohen's *d* statistic and interpret it. Would this be considered a small, moderate, or medium effect size?

4. Calculate two confidence intervals and explain what they indicate.
   a. First, calculate a 95 percent confidence interval for the sample mean.
   b. Then calculate a 99 percent confidence interval for the difference between the sample mean and the population mean, assuming the population mean is actually 20 hours of bike riding per year.
5. What, exactly, does a *p* value tell you?
6. What does it mean to say that a result is statistically significant?
7. If we know that a result is statistically significant, why should we calculate an effect size and a confidence interval? What additional information is gained from these statistics?
   a. Please discuss the difference between practical significance and statistical significance in this answer.
8. How does sample size affect whether a result is statistically significant?

 For answers to these work problems, and for additional work problems, please refer to the website that accompanies this book.

Notes

1 There are other types of effect sizes frequently reported in research. One of the most common of these is the percentage of variance explained by the independent variable. I mention this in later chapters as I discuss the concept of explained variance.

2 Many researchers have begun to report the confidence intervals *of* effect size statistics, like Cohen's *d*. The specifics of how to calculate confidence intervals for effect size statistics are a bit beyond the scope of this book, but there are a few references at the end of this book if you are interested in learning more about this (Cumming & Finch, 2001; Howell, 2010; Steiger & Fouladi, 1997).

3 Of course, this confidence regarding how well our sample statistics represent population parameters rests on several factors besides the confidence interval, including how the sample was selected and how accurately we have measured the variables in our study.

CHAPTER 8

t Tests

What Is a *t* Test?

Because there is a distinction between the common statistical description of *t* tests and the more technical definition, *t* tests can be a little confusing. The common-use definition or description of *t* tests is simply comparing two means to see if they are significantly different from each other. The more technical definition or description of a *t* test is any statistical test that uses the *t*, or Student's *t*, family of distributions. In this chapter, I will briefly describe the family of distributions known as the *t* distribution. Then I will discuss the three most commonly conducted *t* tests: the **one-sample *t* test**, the **independent samples *t* test**, and the **paired** or **dependent samples *t* test**.

---

t Distributions

In Chapters 4 and 5, I discussed the normal distribution and how to use the normal distribution to find *z* scores. The probabilities that are based on the normal distribution are accurate when (a) the population standard deviation is known, and/or (b) we have a large sample (i.e., *n* > 120). If neither of these is true, then we cannot assume that we have a nicely shaped bell curve and we cannot use the probabilities that are based on this normal distribution. Instead, we have to adjust our probability estimates by taking our sample size into account. As I discussed in Chapter 6, we are fortunate to have a set of distributions that have already been created for us that do this, and this is known as the family of *t* distributions. Which specific *t* distribution you use for a given problem depends on the size of your sample. There is a table of probabilities based on the different *t* distributions in Appendix B.

 For a brief video describing how to read and interpret Appendix B, please refer to the website that accompanies this book.

The One-Sample *t* Test

We examined the one-sample *t* test in some detail in Chapters 6 and 7, so I will not spend too much time on it in this chapter. As the name implies, a one-sample *t* test is performed when you want to compare the mean from a single sample to a population mean. For example, suppose I wanted to compare the scores on a standardized mathematics test of the students of a particular teacher to the test scores of all the students in the school. The students in the school represent the population and I select a random sample of 25 students who all have the same particular teacher for mathematics. I calculate the mean of my sample and compare it to the mean of the population to see whether they differ. If the difference between the sample mean and the population mean is statistically significant, I would conclude that the sample represents a different population (i.e., the population of students who have this particular teacher for mathematics) than the larger population of students in the school. However, if the one-sample *t* test produces a result that was not statistically significant, I would conclude that the sample does not represent a different population than the rest of the students in the school; they are all part of the same population in terms of their mathematics test scores. (I provide a worked example of how to calculate a one-sample *t* test later in this chapter.)

The Independent Samples *t* Test

One of the most commonly used *t* tests is the independent samples *t* test. You use this test when you want to compare the means of two *independent* samples on a given variable. For example, if you wanted to compare the average height of 50 randomly selected men to that of 50 randomly selected women, you would conduct an independent samples *t* test. Note that the sample of men is not related to the sample of women, and there is no overlap between these two samples (i.e., one cannot be a member of both groups). Therefore, these groups are *independent*, and an independent samples *t* test is appropriate. To conduct an independent samples *t* test, you need one **categorical** or **nominal independent variable** and one **continuous** or **intervally scaled dependent variable**. A dependent variable is a variable on which the scores may differ, or *depend* on the value of the independent variable. An independent variable is the variable that may cause, or simply be used to predict, the value of the dependent variable. The independent variable in a *t* test is simply a variable with two categories (e.g., men and women, fifth graders and ninth graders, etc.). In this type of *t* test, we want to know whether the average scores on the dependent variable differ according to which group one belongs to (i.e., the level of the independent variable). For example, we may want to know if the average height of people (height is the dependent, continuous variable) *depends* on whether the person is a man or a woman (the gender of the person is the independent, categorical variable).

In the real world of research, you can find many examples of independent *t* tests. Comparisons of genders, groups in experiments (i.e., treatment vs. control), and any number of other two-group comparisons can be found. One example that I found was a study examining the stress levels of Hispanic adolescents (Goldbach et al., 2015). The researchers compared a sample of Hispanic adolescents who drank alcohol in the previous 30 days with a sample that did not. Using independent *t* tests, the researchers found that the sample of Hispanic adolescents who used alcohol had significantly higher average levels of stress in several areas (e.g., violence in their community, economic stress in the family, discrimination) than did Hispanic adolescents who did not use alcohol. In this example, the group variable (i.e., Hispanic adolescents who used alcohol, Hispanic adolescents who did not use alcohol) was the categorical, independent variable, and the level of stress was the dependent, interval variable.

Dependent (Paired) Samples *t* Test

A dependent samples *t* test is also used to compare two means on a single dependent variable. Unlike the independent samples test, however, a dependent samples *t* test is used to compare the means of a single sample or of two **matched** or **paired samples**. For example, if a group of students took a math test in March and that same group of students took the same math test two months later in May, we could compare their average scores on the two test dates using a dependent samples *t* test. Or, suppose that we wanted to compare a sample of boys' Scholastic Aptitude Test (SAT) scores with their fathers' SAT scores. In this example, each boy in our study would be matched with his father. In both of these examples, each score is matched, or paired, with a second score. Because of this pairing, we say that the scores are *dependent* upon each other, and a dependent samples *t* test is warranted.

In the real world of research, dependent *t* tests are often used to examine whether the scores on some variable change significantly from one time to another. For example, a team of researchers at the University of California, San Diego conducted a study to examine whether wearing a backpack reduced blood flow to the shoulders, arms, and hands (Neuschwander et al., 2008). The researchers measured the blood flow of eight adults before wearing a backpack and again while wearing a 26-pound backpack for 10 minutes. They found that after wearing the backpack, blood flow to the arms and hands had decreased, which is known to cause fatigue and problems with fine motor control. The use of dependent *t* tests is common in this kind of before-and-after research design.

Independent Samples *t* Tests in Depth

To understand how *t* tests work, it may be most helpful to first try to understand the conceptual issues and then move on to the more mechanical issues involved in the formulas. Because the independent and dependent forms of the *t* tests are quite different, I discuss them separately. Let's begin with the independent samples *t* test.

Conceptual Issues with the Independent Samples *t* Test

The most complicated conceptual issue in the independent samples *t* test involves the standard error for the test. If you think about what this *t* test does, you can see that it is designed to answer a fairly straightforward question: Do two independent samples differ from each other *significantly* in their average scores on some variable? Using an example to clarify this question, we might want to know whether a random sample of 50 men differs *significantly* from a random sample of 50 women in their average enjoyment of a new television show. Suppose that I arranged to have each sample view my new television show and than rate, on a scale from 1 to 10, how much they enjoyed the show, with higher scores indicating greater enjoyment. In addition, suppose that my sample of men gave the show an average rating of 7.5 and my sample of women gave the show an average rating of 6.5.

In looking at these two means, I can clearly see that my sample of men had a higher mean enjoyment of the television show than did my sample of women. But if you look closely at my earlier question, you'll see that I did not ask simply whether my sample of men differed from my sample of women in their average enjoyment of the show. I asked whether they differed *significantly* in their average enjoyment of the show. The word *significantly* is critical in much of statistics, so I discuss it briefly here as it applies to independent *t* tests (for a more thorough discussion, see Chapter 7).

When I conduct an independent samples *t* test, I generally must collect data from two samples and compare the means of these two samples. But I am interested not only in whether these two samples differ on some variable, but also whether the differences in the two sample means are large enough to suggest that there are also differences in the two *populations* that these samples represent. So, returning to our previous example, I already know that the 50 men in my sample enjoyed the television show more, on average, than did the 50 women in my sample. So what? Who really cares about these 50 men and these 50 women, other than their friends and families? What I really want to know is whether the difference between these two samples of men and women is large enough to indicate that men *in general* (i.e., the population of men that this sample represents) will like the television show more than women *in general* (i.e., the population of women that this sample represents). In other words, is this difference of 1.0 between my two samples large enough to represent a real difference between the populations of men and women on this variable? The way of asking this question in statistical shorthand is to ask, "Is the difference between the means of these two samples statistically significant?" (or **significant** for short).

To answer this question, I must know how much difference I should *expect* to see between two samples of this size drawn from these two populations. On the one hand, my null hypothesis says that I am expecting no difference in my population means, and I am conducting this *t* test to determine whether to retain or reject my null hypothesis. But from a statistical sampling perspective, we know that when we select random samples from populations, there is likely to be some difference between the sample means and the population means. (See the discussion of standard errors in Chapter 6.) If I were to randomly select a different sample of 50 men and a different sample of 50 women, I might get the opposite effect, where the women outscore the men. Or I might get an even larger difference, where men outscore the women by 3 points rather than 1. So the critical question here is this: If I were to repeatedly select random samples of this size ($n = 50$) from each of these populations, what would be the *average expected difference between the means*? In other words, *what is the* **standard error of the difference between the means?**

As I have said before, understanding the concept of standard error provides the key to understanding how inferential statistics work, so take your time and reread the preceding four paragraphs to make sure you get the gist. Regarding the specific case of independent samples *t* tests, we can conclude that the question we want to answer is whether the difference between our two sample means is large or small compared to the difference we would expect to see just by selecting two different random samples. Phrased another way, we want to know whether our *observed* difference between our two sample means is large relative to the standard error of the difference between the means. The general formula for this question is as follows:

$$t = \frac{\text{observed difference between sample means}}{\text{standard error of the difference between the means}}$$

or

$$t = \frac{\bar{X}_1 - \bar{X}_2}{s_{\bar{x}1 - \bar{x}2}}$$

where $\bar{X}_1$ is the mean for sample 1,
   $\bar{X}_2$ is the mean for sample 2,
   $s_{\bar{x}1 - \bar{x}2}$ is the standard error of the difference between the means.

The Standard Error of the Difference between Independent Sample Means

The standard error of the difference between independent sample means is a little bit more complex than the standard error of the mean discussed in Chapter 6. That's because instead of dealing with a single sample, now we have to find a single standard error involving two samples. Generally speaking, this involves simply combining standard errors of the two samples. In fact, when the two samples are roughly the same size, the standard error for the difference between the means is similar to simply combining the two sample standard errors of the mean, as the formula presented in Table 8.1 indicates.

When the two samples are not roughly equal in size, there is a potential problem with using the formulas in Table 8.1 to calculate the standard error. Because these formulas essentially blend the standard errors of each sample together, they also essentially give each sample equal weight

TABLE 8.1   Formula for calculating the standard error of the difference between independent sample means when the sample sizes are roughly equal

$$s_{\bar{x}1 - \bar{x}2} = \sqrt{s_{\bar{x}1}^2 + s_{\bar{x}2}^2}$$

$s_{\bar{x}1}$ is the standard error of the mean for the first sample.
$s_{\bar{x}2}$ is the standard error of the mean for the second sample.

and treat the two samples as one new, larger sample. But if the two samples are not of equal size, and especially if they do not have equal standard deviations, then we must adjust the formula for the standard error to take these differences into account. The only difference between this formula and the formula for the standard error when the sample sizes are equal is that the unequal sample size formula adjusts for the different sample sizes. This adjustment is necessary to give the proper weight to each sample's contribution to the overall standard error. Independent *t* tests assume that the size of the variance in each sample is about equal. If this assumption is violated, and one sample is considerably larger than the other, you could end up with a situation where a small sample with a large variance is creating a larger standard error than it should in the independent *t* test. To keep this from happening, when sample sizes are not equal, the formula for calculating the standard error of the independent *t* test needs to be adjusted to give each sample the proper weight. (If the variances of the two samples are grossly unequal, the sample sizes are very different, and/or the data are not normally distributed, a nonparametric alternative to the *t* test – the Mann–Whitney U test – should be considered.)

In practice, let us hope that you will never need to actually calculate any of these standard errors by hand. Because statistical computer programs compute these for us these days, it may be more important to understand the concepts involved than the components of the formulas themselves. In this spirit, try to understand what the standard error of the difference between independent sample means is and why it may differ if the sample sizes are unequal. Simply put, the standard error of the difference between two independent sample means is the average expected difference between any two samples of a given size randomly selected from two populations on a given variable. In our example comparing men's and women's enjoyment of the new television show, the standard error would be the average (i.e., *standard*) amount of difference (i.e., error) we would expect to find between any two samples of 50 men and 50 women selected randomly from the larger populations of men and women.

TIME OUT FOR TECHNICALITY: STANDARD ERROR FOR INDEPENDENT *t* TEST WITH UNEQUAL SAMPLE SIZES

In the formula for the standard error that was provided for the independent samples *t* test, you may have noticed that we simply combined the standard errors of the means for each sample together. This is known as the pooled variance method. This method works well when the two sample sizes are equal (or roughly equal). But if the sample sizes are not equal (and they often are not in social science research), just pooling the variances of the two samples is not accurate. There needs to be an adjustment to the standard error formula used in the independent *t* test to account for different sample sizes. This formula for calculating the standard error of the differences between the independent sample means includes an adjustment, or weighting, for unequal sample sizes:

$$s_{\bar{x}_1 - \bar{x}_2} = \sqrt{\frac{SS_1 + SS_2}{n_1 + n_2 - 2}\left(\frac{1}{n_1} + \frac{1}{n_2}\right)}$$

In this formula, SS_1 and SS_2 represent the sum of squares for each sample. The sum of squares is shorthand for the sum of the squared deviations from the mean. We discussed how to calculate the sum of squared deviations from the mean back in Chapter 3 when we learned about variance and standard deviation. The sum of squares is discussed again in Chapter 9 when we learn about ANOVA. For now, notice that the right side of this formula includes adjustments for sample sizes by building in the $1/n_1$ and $1/n_2$.

Large differences between the sample sizes are most problematic when the assumption of homogeneity of variance is violated. The results of an independent *t* test can be quite misleading when the variances between the two groups are unequal and the sample sizes are quite different. When the sample sizes are similar, unequal variances are not a serious problem. But when the variances are unequal and the sample sizes are unequal, it is wise to adjust the effective degrees of freedom using the Welch–Satterthwaite equation. (In an SPSS analysis, this adjustment to the degrees of freedom is made automatically when the program detects unequal variances between the groups.)

Determining the Significance of the *t* Value for an Independent Samples *t* Test

Once we calculate the standard error and plug it into our formula for calculating the *t* value, we are left with an *observed t* value. How do we know if this *t* value is statistically significant? In other words, how do we decide if this *t* value is large enough to indicate that the difference between my sample means probably represents a real difference between my population means? To answer this question, we must find the probability of getting a *t* value of that size by chance. In other words, what are the odds that the difference between my two sample means is just due to the luck of the draw when I selected these two samples at random, rather than some real difference between the two populations? Fortunately, statisticians have already calculated these odds for us, and a table with such odds is included in Appendix B. Even more fortunately, statistical software programs used on computers calculate these probabilities for us, so there will hopefully never be a need for you to use Appendix B. I provide it here because I think the experience of calculating a *t* value by hand and determining whether it is statistically significant can help you understand how *t* tests work.

In Chapter 5, we saw how statisticians generated probabilities based on the normal distribution. With *t* distributions, the exact same principles are involved, except that now we have to take into account the size of the samples we are using. This is because the shape of the *t* distribution changes as the sample size changes, and when the shape of the distribution changes, so do the probabilities associated with it. The way that we take the sample size into account in statistics is to calculate degrees of freedom (*df*). The explanation of exactly what a degree of freedom is may be a bit more complicated than is worth discussing here (although you can read about it in most statistics textbooks if you are interested). At this point, suffice it to say that in an independent samples *t* test, you find the degrees of freedom by adding the two sample sizes together and subtracting 2. So the formula is $df = n_1 + n_2 - 2$. Once you have your degrees of freedom and your *t* value, you can look in the table of *t* values in Appendix B to see if the difference between your two sample means is significant.

To illustrate this, let's return to our example comparing men's and women's enjoyment of the new television program. Let's just suppose that the standard error of the difference between the means is .40. When I plug this number into the *t* value formula, I get the following:

$$t = \frac{7.5 - 6.5}{.40}$$

$$t = \frac{1.0}{.40} = 2.50$$

$$df = 50 + 50 - 2 = 98$$

Now that we have a *t* value and our degrees of freedom, we can look in Appendix B to find the probability of getting a *t* value of this size (*t* = 2.50) or larger by chance when we have 98 degrees of freedom. Because 98 degrees of freedom is between 60 and 120, I will look in the *df* = 60 row to be on the safe side. Choosing the smaller degrees of freedom gives me a more

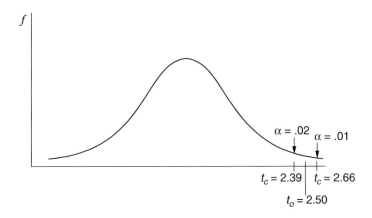

FIGURE 8.1 A statistically significant observed *t* value that falls between critical *t* values for alpha levels of .01 and .02.

conservative test (meaning that if my result is statistically significant at the *df* = 60 level, it will certainly be significant at the *df* = 98 level). Looking across the *df* = 60 row, and using the values for a two-tailed test, I can see that my observed *t* value (t_o = 2.50) is between the critical *t* values of 2.390 and 2.660. I can see that the alpha levels associated with these two critical *t* values in Appendix B are .02 and .01. Therefore, my table tells me that the probability of getting a *t* value this large by chance (i.e., due strictly to random sampling) is between 1 percent and 2 percent. In other words, when we randomly select two samples of 50 each from two different populations, we would expect to have a *t* value of this size less than 2 percent of the time *when there is no real difference between the population means* (for a more thorough discussion of this issue, see Chapter 7). Because this is such a small probability, I conclude that the difference between my sample of 50 men and my sample of 50 women that I observed in the average ratings of enjoyment of the television show probably represents a real difference between the larger populations of men and women, rather than some fluke difference that emerged simply because of who I happened to get in my samples (i.e., *random sampling error*; see Figure 8.1 for an illustration of where the observed *t* value falls in comparison to critical *t* values for alpha levels of .01 and .02).

It is important to remember that although this difference between the means was *statistically* significant (if we were using an alpha level of .05), that does not necessarily mean that it is *practically* significant (refer to the discussion about effect size in Chapter 7). Just as the standard error of the mean is influenced by the size of the sample, the standard error of the *difference* between the means is also affected by the sample size. The larger the samples, the smaller the standard error and the more likely it is that you will find a statistically significant result. To determine whether this difference between men and women is *practically* significant, we should consider the actual *raw score* difference. Men in our sample scored an average of 1 point higher on a 10-point scale than did women. Is that a big difference? Well, that is a judgment call. I would consider that a fairly inconsequential difference because we are talking about preferences for a television show. I don't consider a 1-point difference on a 10-point scale regarding television preferences to be important. But potential advertisers might consider this a meaningful difference. Those wanting to advertise female-oriented products may not select this show, which seems to appeal more to male viewers.

Another way to determine whether this difference in the means is practically significant is to calculate an effect size. The formula for the effect size for an independent samples *t* test is presented in Table 8.2. To calculate the effect size, you must first calculate the denominator. Using our example where the sample size for one group is 50 and the standard error of the difference between the means is .40, we get the following:

$$\hat{S} = \sqrt{50}(.40)$$
$$\hat{S} = 7.07(.40)$$
$$\hat{S} = 2.83$$

TABLE 8.2 Formula for the effect size for an independent samples *t* test

$$d = \frac{\bar{X}_1 - \bar{X}_2}{\hat{s}}$$

$$\hat{S} = \sqrt{n_1}(s_{\bar{x}1-\bar{x}2})$$

where $\bar{X}_1$ is the mean for the first sample,

$\bar{X}_2$ is the mean for the second sample,

n_1 is the sample size *for one sample,*

$\hat{s}$ is the standard deviation estimate for the effect size,

$(s_{\bar{x}1-\bar{x}2})$ is the standard error of the difference between the means.

We can then plug this into the formula for the effect size, along with the two sample means:

$$d = \frac{7.5 - 6.5}{2.83} \Rightarrow d = .35$$

So our effect size for this problem is .35, which would be considered a small- to medium-size effect.

Paired or Dependent Samples *t* Tests in Depth

Most of what I wrote before about the independent samples *t* test applies to the paired or dependent samples *t* test as well. We are still interested in determining whether the difference in the means that we observe in some sample(s) on some variable represents a true difference in the population(s) from which the sample(s) were selected. For example, suppose I wanted to know whether employees at my widget-making factory are more productive after they return from a two-week vacation. I randomly select 30 of my employees and calculate the average number of widgets made by each employee during the week before they go on vacation. I find that, on average, my employees made 250 widgets each during the week. During the week after they return from vacation, I keep track of how many widgets is made by *the same sample* of 30 employees and find that, on average, they made 300 widgets each during the week after returning from their vacations.

Just as with the independent samples *t* test, here I am concerned not only with whether this sample of 30 employees made more or fewer widgets after their vacation. I can look at the pre-vacation and post-vacation averages and see that these 30 employees, on average, made an average of 50 more widgets a week after their vacation. That is quite a lot. But I also want to know whether what I observed in this sample represents a likely difference in the productivity of the larger population of widget makers after a vacation. In other words, is this a statistically significant difference? The only real distinction between this dependent samples *t* test and the independent samples *t* test is that rather than comparing two samples on a single dependent variable, now I am comparing the average scores of a single sample (i.e., the same group of 30 employees) on two variables (i.e., pre-vacation widget-making average and post-vacation widget-making average). To make this comparison, I will again need to conduct a *t* test in which I find the difference between the two means and divide by the standard error of the difference between two *dependent sample* means. This equation looks like this:

$$t = \frac{\text{observed difference between post-vacation means}}{\text{standard error of the difference between the means}}$$

or

$$t = \frac{\overline{X} - \overline{Y}}{s_{\overline{D}}}$$

where $\overline{X}$ is the pre-vacation mean,

$\overline{Y}$ is the post-vacation mean,

$s_{\overline{D}}$ is the standard error of the difference between the means.

The formula for calculating the standard error of the difference between the means for dependent samples is slightly different than the one for independent samples, but the principles involved (i.e., what the standard error represents) are the same. Keep in mind that if I were to continually randomly select a samples of 30 widget makers and compare their pre-vacation and post-vacation productivity, I could generate a distribution of difference scores. For some samples, there would be no difference between pre-vacation and post-vacation productivity. For others, there would be increases in productivity and for still other samples there would be decreases in productivity. This distribution of difference scores (i.e., differences between pre-vacation and post-vacation averages) would have a mean and a standard deviation. The standard deviation of this distribution would be the standard error of the differences between dependent samples. The formula for this standard error is presented below in Table 8.3.

As you can see in Table 8.3, the easiest way to find the standard error is to follow a two-step process. First, we can find the standard deviation of the difference scores for my sample. Then we can divide this by the square root of the sample size to find the standard error. This formula is very similar to the formula for finding the standard error of the mean.

Another difference between dependent and independent samples *t* tests can be found in the calculation of the degrees of freedom. Whereas we had to add the two samples together and subtract 2 in the independent samples formula, for dependent samples we find the number of pairs of scores and subtract 1. In our example of widget makers, we have 30 pairs of scores because we have two scores for each person in the sample (one pre-vacation score and one post-vacation score). In the case of a paired *t* test where we have two paired samples (e.g., fathers and their sons), we use the same formula for calculating the standard error and the degrees of freedom. We must simply remember to match each score in one sample with a corresponding score in the second sample (e.g., comparing each father's score with only his son's score).

Once we've found our *t* value and degrees of freedom, the process for determining the probability of finding a *t* value of a given size with a given number of degrees of freedom is exactly the same as it was for the independent samples *t* test.

TABLE 8.3 **Formula for the standard error of the difference between dependent sample means**

Step 1: $s_{\overline{D}} = \dfrac{s_D}{\sqrt{N}}$

Step 2: $s_D = \sqrt{\dfrac{\Sigma D^2 - \dfrac{(\Sigma D)^2}{N}}{N-1}}$

where $s_{\overline{D}}$ is the standard error of the difference between dependent sample means,

s_D is the standard deviation of the difference between dependent sample means,

D is the difference between each pair of X and Y scores (i.e., $X - Y$),

N is the number of pairs of scores.

Example 1: Comparing Boys' and Girls' Grade Point Averages

To illustrate how *t* tests work in practice, I provide one example of an independent samples *t* test and one of a dependent samples *t* test using data from a longitudinal study conducted by Carol Midgley and her colleagues. In this study, a sample of students was given surveys each year for several years beginning when the students were in the fifth grade. In the examples that follow, I present two comparisons of students' grade point averages (GPAs). The GPA is an average of students' grades in the four core academic areas: math, science, English, and social studies. Grades were measured using a 14-point scale with 13 = "A+" and 0 = "F".

In the first analysis, an independent samples *t* test was conducted to compare the average grades of sixth-grade boys and girls. This analysis was conducted using SPSS computer software. Thankfully, this program computes the means, standard error, *t* value, and probability of obtaining the *t* value by chance. Because the computer does all of this work, there is nothing to compute by hand, and I can focus all of my energy on interpreting the results. I present the actual results from the *t* test conducted with SPSS in Table 8.4.

SPSS presents the sample sizes for boys (*n* = 361) and girls (*n* = 349) first, followed by the mean, standard deviation ("SD"), and standard error of the mean ("SE of mean") for each group. Next, SPSS reports the actual difference between the two sample means ("Mean Difference = −1.5604"). This mean difference is negative because boys are the X_1 group and girls are the X_2 group. Because girls have the higher mean, when we subtract the girls' mean from the boys' mean (i.e., $\bar{X}_1 - \bar{X}_2$) we get a negative number. Below the mean difference we see "Levene's Test for Equality of Variances."[1] We can see that the *F* value for this test equals .639 and *p* = .424. This test tells us that there is not a significant difference between the variances of the two groups on the dependent variable (GPA) because our *p* value is larger than .05. Below the test for equality of variances, SPSS prints two lines with the actual *t* value (−7.45), the degrees of freedom ("*df*" = 708), the *p* value ("Sig. 2-Tailed" = .000), and the standard error of the difference between the means ("SE of Diff." = .210 and .209). These two lines of statistics are presented separately depending on whether we have equal or unequal variances. (See the "Time Out for Technicality" box for more information about the effects of unequal variances and sample sizes in independent *t* tests.) Because we had equal variances (as determined by Levene's test), we should interpret the top line, which is identified by the "Equal" name in the left column. Notice that these two lines of statistics are almost identical. That is because the variances are not significantly different between the two groups, and because the sample sizes were almost equal. If the variances and sample sizes were more different, the statistics presented in these two lines would differ more dramatically.

TABLE 8.4   SPSS results of independent samples *t* test

Variable	Number of Cases	Mean	SD	SE of Mean
Sixth-Grade GPA				
Male	361	6.5783	2.837	.149
Female	349	8.1387	2.744	.147

Mean Difference = −1.5604
Levene's Test for Equality of Variances: *F* = .639, *p* = .424

	t Test for Equality of Means			
Variances	*t* Value	*df*	2-Tailed Sig.	SE of Diff.
Equal	−7.45	708	.000	.210
Unequal	−7.45	708.00	.000	.209

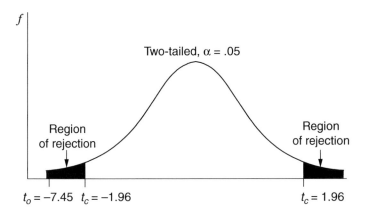

FIGURE 8.2 Results of a statistically significant *t* value for an independent *t* test comparing the average GPAs of boys and girls. Regions of rejection, critical *t* values, and observed *t* value for a two-tailed, independent samples *t* test are shown.

If we take the difference between the means and divide by the standard error of the difference between the independent sample means, we get the following equation for *t*:

$$t = -1.5604 \div .210$$

$$t = -7.45$$

The probability of getting a *t* value of −7.45 with 708 degrees of freedom is very small, as our *p* value ("Sig. Two-Tailed") of .000 reveals. Because *t* distributions are symmetrical (as are normal distributions), there is the exact same probability of obtaining a given negative *t* value by chance as there is of obtaining the same positive *t* value. For our purposes, then, we can treat negative *t* values as absolute numbers. (If you were testing a one-tailed alternative hypothesis, you would need to take into account whether the *t* value is negative or positive. See Chapter 7 for a discussion of one-tailed and two-tailed tests.)

The results of the *t* test presented in Table 8.4 indicate that our sample of girls had higher average GPAs than did our sample of boys, and that this difference was statistically significant. In other words, if we kept randomly selecting samples of these sizes from the larger populations of sixth-grade boys and girls and comparing their average GPAs, the odds of finding a difference between the means that is this large *if there is no real difference between the means of the two populations* is .000. This does not mean there is absolutely no chance. It just means that SPSS does not print probabilities smaller than .001 (e.g., .00001). Because this is such a small probability, we conclude that the difference between the two sample means probably represents a genuine difference between the larger populations of boys and girls that these samples represent. Notice in Figure 8.2 that this observed *t* value falls in the region of rejection, further indication that we should reject the null hypothesis of no difference between the means of boys and girls. Girls have *significantly* higher GPAs than boys (see Figure 8.2). Reminder: Statistical significance is influenced by sample size. Our sample size was quite large, so a difference of about 1.56 points on a 14-point scale was statistically significant. But is it practically significant? You can compute an effect size to help you decide.

Example 2: Comparing Fifth- and Sixth-Grade GPAs

Our second example involves a comparison of students' GPAs in fifth grade (when children are usually 10 or 11 years old) with the same sample's GPAs a year later, at the end of sixth grade. For each student in the sample (*n* = 689), there are two scores: one GPA for fifth grade and one GPA for sixth grade. This provides a total of 689 pairs of scores, and leaves us with 688 degrees of freedom (*df* = number of pairs − 1). A quick glance at the means reveals that, in this sample, students had slightly higher average GPAs in fifth grade (8.0800) than they did a year later in sixth grade (7.3487). But is this a *statistically significant* difference? To find out, we must conduct a dependent samples t test, which I did using SPSS (see Table 8.5).

This analysis produced a t value of 8.19, which my SPSS program told me had a probability of occurring less than one time in a thousand due to chance ("Sig. 2-Tailed" = .000). Therefore, I conclude that the difference between fifth- and sixth-grade GPAs in my sample probably represents a real difference between the GPAs of the larger population of fifth and sixth graders that my sample represents. My observed t value falls squarely in the region of rejection (see Figure 8.3), indicating that I should reject the null hypothesis of no difference between the means of fifth and sixth graders.

Although this difference is statistically significant, notice that it is a difference of only about .73 points on a 14-point scale. Also notice that the SPSS program also provides a measure of the correlation between the two variables ("Corr" = .635) and indicates that this correlation coefficient is statistically significant. This tells you that students' fifth-grade GPAs are strongly related to their sixth-grade GPAs, as you might expect. Finally, notice that at the bottom left of Table 8.5, the difference between the means ("Paired Differences Mean"), the standard deviation of the difference between the means ("SD"), and the standard error of the difference between the means ("SE of Mean") are presented. The differences between the means divided by the standard error of the difference between the means produces the t value.

Writing it Up

Writing up t test results for publication is generally similar for independent, dependent, and single-sample t tests. Usually, what gets reported are the means for the groups being compared, the t value, and the degrees of freedom (df). The write-up for the results of the paired t test described in Table 8.5 and Figure 8.3 would be as follows:

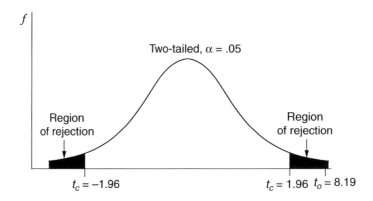

FIGURE 8.3 Region of rejection, critical t value, and observed t value for a two-tailed, dependent samples t test comparing fifth-grade and sixth-grade GPAs of one sample of students.

TABLE 8.5 SPSS results for dependent samples t test comparing fifth- and sixth-grade GPA

Variable	Number of Pairs	Corr	2-Tail Sig.	Mean	SD	SE of Mean
Fifth-Grade GPA				8.0800	2.509	.096
	689	.635	.000			
Sixth-Grade GPA				7.3487	2.911	.111

Paired Differences					
Mean	SD	SE of Mean	t Value	df	2-Tailed Sig.
.7312	2.343	.089	8.19	688	.000

"A paired *t* test was calculated to compare the grade point averages (GPAs) of students when they were in fifth grade and a year later when they were in sixth grade. The analysis produced a significant *t* value ($t_{(688)} = 8.19, p < .001$). An examination of the means revealed that students had higher GPAs in fifth grade ($M = 8.08$) than they did in sixth grade ($M = 7.35$)."

The write-up for the independent *t* test summarized in Table 8.4 would be very similar:

"I performed an independent *t* test to compare the grade point averages (GPAs) of sixth-grade boys and girls. The analysis produced a significant *t* value ($t_{(708)} = -7.45, p < .001$). An examination of the means revealed that boys had lower GPAs ($M = 6.58$) than did girls ($M = 8.14$)."

Worked Examples

In this section I present three worked examples of *t* tests: a one-sample *t* test, an independent samples *t* test, and a paired or dependent samples *t* test.

One-Sample *t* Test

For the one-sample *t* test, suppose I want to know whether students at my university differ from other students in the country in the amount of time they spend on school work outside of class. I happen to know that in the U.S., university students spend an average of 15 hours per week working on school work outside of class. I select a random sample of 36 students from my university and find that they spend an average of 14 hours per week on school work, with a standard deviation of 3 hours. Is the difference between the sample mean and the population mean significant, either practically or statistically?

The first step in the process of answering this question is to realize that I am actually trying to determine whether the *population* that my sample represents differs from the population of students at universities in the U.S. in terms of hours spent on school work outside of class. So my null hypothesis is that the population mean of students at my university will equal the population mean of students at universities in the U.S. Because this is a two-tailed test (i.e., my research question is whether the means *differ*), my alternative hypothesis is that the population mean of students at my university will differ (either be larger or smaller) than the population mean of university students in the U.S.

Next, I calculate a standard error of the mean using the sample size (36) and the sample standard deviation (3):

$$s_{\bar{x}} = \frac{3}{\sqrt{36}}$$

$$s_{\bar{x}} = \frac{3}{6}$$

$$s_{\bar{x}} = .5$$

Now that I have my standard error of the mean, I can calculate my observed *t* value:

$$t = \frac{14 - 15}{.5} = -2.0$$

To determine whether my results are statistically significant, I compare the *t* value that I calculated to a critical *t value* that I will look up in Appendix B. Remember, with a two-tailed test, we can use the absolute value of the observed *t* value, so I will compare the critical *t* value that I find in Appendix B with an observed *t* value of 2.0. With a sample size of 36 and one sample,

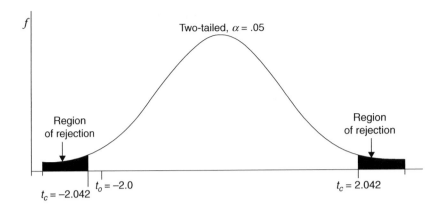

FIGURE 8.4 Regions of rejection, critical *t* values, and observed *t* value for a two-tailed, one-sample *t* test comparing a sample and population of college students on the number of hours spent studying.

my degrees of freedom will be 36 − 1 = 35. Appendix B lists *t* values for 30 *df* or 40 *df*, so I will use those two and find the average. With an alpha level of .05, I find a critical *t* value of 2.042 for *df* = 30 and 2.021 for a *df* = 40. The average of those two values is about 2.031 for a *df* of 35, and this critical *t* value is larger than my observed *t* value of 2.0. Therefore, using a two-tailed alpha level of .05, the difference between my sample mean and the population mean is *not* statistically significant. There is no difference between the average number of hours spent on school work outside of class between the students in my university and the university students in the U.S. population. (See Figure 8.4 for an illustration of the two-tailed regions of rejection, critical *t* values, and my observed *t* value.)

I also want to report an effect size for this *t* test, so I will calculate a Cohen's *d* value:

$$d = \frac{14 - 15}{3} = -.33$$

The Cohen's *d* is expressed in standard deviation units (Cohen, 1988). This effect size of .33 is considered a weak-to-moderate effect size, meaning that the difference between the means has little practical significance. Combined with the lack of statistical significance, we would conclude that the population of students at my university does not really differ from the larger population of university students in the U.S. on this variable.

Independent Samples *t* Test

Suppose I work for a marketing firm and I want to know whether men and women differ in their enjoyment of a new movie that my client has produced. I select random samples of 25 men and 25 women, show them the movie, and ask them to rate, on a 10-point scale, how much they enjoyed the movie. The average movie-enjoyment rating for my sample of men was 7 with a standard deviation of 3, and the average for women was 6 with a standard deviation of 4. Is this a meaningful difference between the means?

The first step in solving this problem is to calculate the standard error of the difference between the means. This involves finding the standard errors of the means for each sample:

$$\text{For men}: s_{\bar{x}} = \frac{3}{\sqrt{25}} = .60$$

$$\text{For women}: s_{\bar{x}} = \frac{4}{\sqrt{25}} = .80$$

Now that I have calculated the standard errors of the mean for each sample, I need to square each one and add them together:

$$.60^2 = .36$$

$$.80^2 = .64$$

$$.36 + .64 = 1$$

The final step in the process of calculating the standard error of the difference between the means is to calculate the square root of this sum:

$$s_{\bar{x}1-\bar{x}2} = \sqrt{1} = 1$$

Once I've calculated the standard error of the difference between the sample means, I can plug that into my formula for calculating the observed t value:

$$t = \frac{7-6}{1} = 1.0$$

Notice that in this t value formula I placed the mean for men first, creating a positive t value. Had I placed the mean for women first and produced a negative t value, it would not have mattered as the research question created a two-tailed test (i.e., testing whether there is a *difference* between the means without any statement about the direction of that difference).

To determine whether my observed t value is statistically significant, I will compare it to a critical t value that I find in Appendix B. The degrees of freedom for an independent samples t test is $n + n - 2$, so in this situation we have $df = 25 + 25 - 2 = 48$. In Appendix B, the closest I can get to a df of 48 is a df of 40, so I will look in that row for my critical t value. Using an alpha level of .05 and a two-tailed test, the critical t value is 2.021. Because my $t_c > t_o$, I conclude that the difference between the sample means of men and women is *not* statistically significant. Therefore, I conclude that there is no difference between the population means of men and women in their enjoyment of this movie. I will market the movie to both genders. (See Figure 8.5 for an illustration of the regions of rejection, the critical t values, and the observed t value for this analysis.)

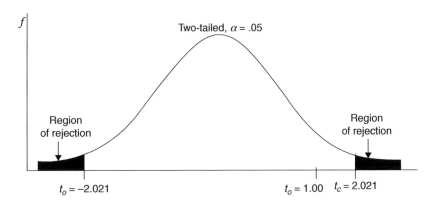

FIGURE 8.5 Regions of rejection, critical t values, and observed t value for a two-tailed, independent samples t test comparing men and women on average enjoyment of a movie.

To provide more information about the differences between these sample means, I will calculate an effect size (*d*) and a confidence interval. First, I need to calculate the standard deviation of the estimate of the effect size:

$$\hat{s} = \sqrt{25}(1) = 5$$

Then I plug that into my effect size formula to find *d*:

$$d = \frac{7-6}{5} = .20$$

This is quite a small effect size, supporting our previous finding of no statistically significant difference between the means of men and women. Finally, let's calculate a 95 percent confidence interval for the difference between the means:

$$\text{CI}_{95} = (7 - 6) \pm (1)(2.021)$$

$$\text{CI}_{95} = 1 \pm 2.021$$

$$\text{CI}_{95} = -1.021, 3.021$$

This confidence interval tells us that we can be 95 percent confident that the actual difference between the population means of men and women in their enjoyment of this movie is between women rating their enjoyment of the movie about 1 point higher than men up to men rating their enjoyment of the movie about 3 points higher than women. This is a fairly large range (about 4 points on a 10-point scale) that includes the value of 0 (i.e., no difference between the population means), again indicating that there are no reliable differences between the population means on this variable.

Dependent/Paired *t* Test

Suppose that I have developed a drug that is supposed to improve mental focus and memory. To test whether it works, I select a random sample of 64 adults and ask them to play a game where they are presented with a set of 50 pictures, one at a time, on a computer screen. After a 5-minute break, they are presented with another set of 50 pictures, some of which appeared in the first set that was presented. During this second presentation of pictures, my participants have to indicate whether the picture shown on the screen was also presented in the first presentation of pictures, or is new to the second presentation. Scores for this game range from 0 to 50.

In my experiment, participants have to play this game twice. After playing the game once, I give everyone in my sample the new drug I have created to improve mental focus and memory, and wait an hour for the drug to take effect. Then, when the hour is over, I have my participants play the game again. The first time they play the game, my sample gets an average of 30 correct answers. The second time, the sample average is 32 correct answers.

As you can see in Table 8.3, the formula for calculating the standard error of the differences between the means for a dependent *t* test requires that you either know the scores for each individual in the sample or are given the standard *deviation* of the differences between the means. For the sake of brevity, let's just suppose that the standard *deviation* of the differences between the means is 4. Notice that the number of *pairs* of scores in this problem is 64, because each participant created one *pair* of scores (i.e., had two scores on the game). Now we can calculate the standard *error* of the difference between the mean:

$$s_{\overline{D}} = \frac{s_D}{\sqrt{N}}$$

$$s_{\overline{D}} = \frac{4}{\sqrt{64}} = .5$$

Now I can plug my sample means and the standard error into the t value formula to find my observed t value. Note that scores from the first test are my X variable and scores from the second test are my Y variable:

$$t = \frac{\overline{X} - \overline{Y}}{s_{\overline{D}}}$$

$$t = \frac{30 - 32}{.5} = -4.0$$

The next step is to determine whether this is a statistically significant result. In this situation, it is reasonable to argue that this is a one-tailed test. I created the drug assuming it would enhance focus and memory. If this assumption is true, I would expect the test scores to be higher after taking the drug (i.e., the Y variable) than before taking the drug (the X variable). So in this situation, my null and alternative hypotheses would be as follows:

Null hypothesis (H_0): $\mu_X = \mu_Y$
Alternative hypothesis (H_A): $\mu_X < \mu_Y$

Because the formula for calculating the t value for the dependent t test involves subtracting the mean of Y from the mean of X, my alternative hypothesis would produce a negative t value. For a one-tailed test, I am only going to be looking at the negative side of the distribution and will only consider my results to be statistically significant if my observed t value is *less than* my critical t value. The critical t value, from Appendix B, with 60 *df*, an alpha level of .05, and a one-tailed test is –1.671. This critical value is *larger* than my observed t value of –4.0. In other words, my observed t value is *beyond* (i.e., further out in the tail than) my critical t value. Therefore, my results *are* statistically significant, and I conclude that, in the population of adults, test scores are higher, on average, after taking my new drug than before taking it. (See Figure 8.6

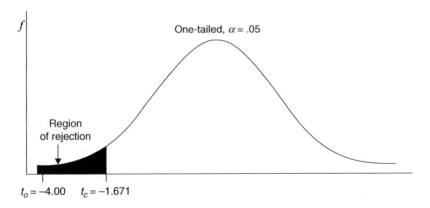

FIGURE 8.6 Region of rejection, critical t value, and observed t value for a one-tailed, dependent samples t test comparing test scores of adults before and after taking my new memory drug.

for an illustration of the one-tailed region of rejection, the critical *t* value, and the observed *t* value for this analysis.)

 For brief videos demonstrating how to calculate one-sample, independent, and dependent *t* tests, see the website that accompanies this book.

Wrapping Up and Looking Forward

The two types of *t* tests described in this chapter share two things in common. First, they both test the equality of means. Second, they both rely on the *t* distribution to produce the probabilities used to test statistical significance. Beyond that, these two types of *t* tests are really quite different. The independent samples *t* test is used to examine the equality of means from two independent groups. Such a test has much in common with one-way ANOVA (Chapter 9) and factorial ANOVA (Chapter 10). In contrast, the dependent samples *t* test is used to examine whether the means of *related* groups, or of two variables examined within the same group, are equal. This test is more directly related to repeated-measures ANOVA as discussed in Chapter 11.

Work Problems

1. I want to know whether Californians, who tend to be pretty health conscious, eat fewer hot dogs than the general population of Americans. Suppose that in the population of adults, the average number of hot dogs eaten per year is 15. I select a random sample of 25 adults from California and find that they eat an average of 17 hot dogs with a standard deviation of 3.

   a. State the null and alternative hypotheses.
   b. Choose an alpha level.
   c. Decide whether you are doing a one-tailed or two-tailed test (explain why).
   d. State your degrees of freedom.
   e. Find and report your critical value for *t*.
   f. Compute your observed *t* value.
   g. Decide whether to reject or fail to reject H_0.
   h. Describe your results. Is this a statistically significant difference?

2. Suppose you want to know whether men and women who take a college statistics class differ in their enjoyment of statistics. Enjoyment of statistics is measured by asking people to rate "How much do you enjoy statistics?" on a 10-point scale (1 = *"I hate it"* and 10 = *"I love it"*). I select a random sample of 20 women who took statistics and 20 men who took statistics. I find that the women had a mean of 4 and a standard deviation of 1.5 whereas the men had a mean of 4.5 and a standard deviation of 2.

   a. State the null and alternative hypotheses.
   b. Choose an alpha level.
   c. Decide whether you are doing a one-tailed or two-tailed test (explain why).
   d. Decide whether to reject or fail to reject H_0.
   e. Describe your results. What do they tell you?
   i. Is this a statistically significant difference?
   f. Calculate a 99 percent confidence interval for the difference between the means and explain what this confidence interval tells you.
   g. Calculate an effect size (*d*) and describe what it means.

3. I think people are getting taller. I select a random sample of 15 fathers and their adult sons to take part in a study. I find that the fathers have an average height of 71 in. and their sons have an average height of 73 in. The standard *deviation* of the difference between the means is 1.3.

   a. Write the null and alternative hypotheses.
   b. Select an alpha level.
   c. Is this a statistically significant difference? (Do the calculations and explain what your results mean.)

 For answers to these work problems, and for additional work problems, see the website that accompanies this book.

Note

1 As noted in the "Time Out for Technicality" box, unequal variances between the two samples on the dependent variable in the independent *t* test can create unreliable probability estimates. When unequal variances are detected, the degrees of freedom must be adjusted. SPSS uses Levene's test to determine whether the sample variances are equal and adjusts the degrees of freedom automatically, as the example presented in Table 8.4 indicates.

CHAPTER 9

One-Way Analysis of Variance

The purpose of a one-way analysis of variance (**one-way ANOVA**) is to compare the means of two or more groups (the independent variable) on one dependent variable to see if the group means are significantly different from each other. In fact, if you want to compare the means of two independent groups on a single variable, you can use either an independent samples t test or a one-way ANOVA. The results will be identical, except that instead of producing a t value, the ANOVA will produce an F ratio, which is simply the t value squared (more about this in the next section of this chapter). Because the t test and the one-way ANOVA produce identical results when there are only two groups being compared, most researchers use the one-way ANOVA only when they are comparing three or more groups. To conduct a one-way ANOVA, you need to have a categorical (or nominal) variable that has at least two independent groups (e.g., a race variable with the categories African-American, Latino, and Euro-American) as the independent variable and a continuous variable (e.g., achievement test scores) as the dependent variable. It is assumed in ANOVA that the variance in the dependent variable is equal in each of the groups being compared.

In many fields of research, including the social sciences, one-way ANOVA is an extremely popular statistical technique. Experiments that involve comparisons among more than two groups often employ one-way ANOVA. For example, a researcher may conduct an experiment to examine whether a new treatment for diabetes is more effective than an existing treatment, or than a placebo. These three groups would be compared using one-way ANOVA. Researchers conducting correlational research (i.e., not manipulating the independent variable) also often use one-way ANOVA. For example, a researcher who wants to compare the academic performance of students from different countries might use one-way ANOVA. Because so much research involves comparing the means of multiple groups, there are thousands of studies across many disciplines that have used one-way ANOVA. In this chapter, we consider the most basic form of ANOVA, one-way ANOVA, involving one independent variable and one dependent variable. In Chapters 10 and 11, we consider more complex forms of ANOVA that involve multiple independent variables.

ANOVA vs. Independent *t* Tests

Because the independent t test and the one-way ANOVA are so similar, people often wonder, Why don't we just use t tests instead of one-way ANOVAs? Perhaps the best way to answer this question is by using an example. Suppose that I want to go into the potato chip business. I've got three different recipes, but because I'm new to the business and don't have a lot of money, I can produce only one flavor. I want to see which flavor people like best and produce that one. I randomly select 90 adults and randomly divide them into three groups. One group tries my BBQ-flavored chips, the second group tries my ranch-flavored chips, and the third group tastes my cheese-flavored chips. All participants in each group fill out a rating form after tasting the chips to indicate how much they liked the taste of the chips. The rating scale goes from a score of 1 (*"Hated it"*) to 7 (*"Loved it"*). I then compare the average ratings of the three groups to see which group liked the taste of their chips the most. In this example, the chip flavor (BBQ, Ranch, Cheese) is my categorical, independent variable and the rating of the taste of the chips is my continuous, dependent variable.

To see which flavor received the highest average rating, I could run three separate independent *t* tests comparing (a) BBQ with Ranch, (b) BBQ with Cheese, and (c) Ranch with Cheese. The problem with running three separate *t* tests is that each time we run a *t* test, we must make a decision about whether the difference between the two means is meaningful, or statistically significant. This decision is based on probability, and every time we make such a decision, there is a slight chance we might be wrong (see Chapter 7 on statistical significance). The more times we make decisions about the significance of *t* tests, the greater the chances are that we will be wrong. In other words, the more *t* tests we run, the greater the chances become of us deciding that a *t* test is significant (i.e., that the means being compared are really different) when it really is not. In still other words, running multiple *t* tests increases the likelihood of making a Type I error (i.e., rejecting the null hypothesis when in fact it is true). A one-way ANOVA fixes this problem by adjusting for the number of groups being compared. To see how it does this, let's take a look at one-way ANOVA in more detail.

One-Way ANOVA in Depth

The purpose of a one-way ANOVA is to divide up the variance in some dependent variable into two components: the variance attributable to **between-group** differences, and the variance attributable to **within-group** differences, also known as *error*. When we select a sample from a population and calculate the mean for that sample on some variable, that sample mean is our best predictor of the population mean. In other words, if we do not know the mean of the population, our best guess about what the population mean is would have to come from the mean of a sample drawn randomly from that population. Any scores in the sample that differ from the sample mean are believed to include what statisticians call error. For example, suppose I have a sample of 20 randomly selected fifth graders. I give them a test of basic skills in math and find out that, in my sample, the average number of questions answered correctly on my test is 12. If I were to select one student in my sample and find that she had a score of 10 on the test, the difference between her score and the sample mean would be considered error, as indicated in Figure 9.1.

The variation that we find among the scores in a sample is not just considered error. In fact, it is thought to represent a specific kind of error: **random error**. When we select a sample at random from a population, we expect that the members of that sample will not all have identical

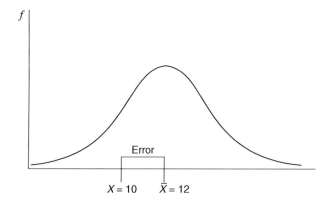

FIGURE 9.1 An example of within-group error.

TABLE 9.1 Formula for the *F* value

$$F = \frac{mean\ square\ between}{mean\ square\ error}$$

or

$$F = \frac{MS_b}{MS_e}$$

where *F* is the *F* value,

MS_b is the mean square between groups,

MS_e is the mean square error, or within group error.

---

scores on our variable of interest (e.g., test scores). That is, we expect that there will be some variability in the scores of the members of the sample. That's just what happens when you select members of a sample randomly from a population. Therefore, the variation in scores that we see among the members of our sample is just considered random error.

The question that we can address using ANOVA is this: Is the average amount of difference, or variation, between the scores of members of *different* samples large or small compared to the average amount of variation *within* each sample, otherwise known as random error (a.k.a. error)? To answer this question, we have to determine three things. First, we have to calculate the average amount of variation within each of our samples. This is called the **mean square error (MS_e)**, also referred to as the **mean square within (MS_w)** in some textbooks and websites. Second, we have to find the average amount of variation *between* the groups. This is called the **mean square between (MS_b)**. Once we've found these two statistics, we must find their ratio by dividing the mean square between by the mean square error. This ratio provides our ***F*** **value**, and when we have our *F* value we can look at our family of *F* distributions to see if the differences between the groups are statistically significant (see Table 9.1).

Note that, although it may sound like analysis of variance is a whole new concept, in fact it is virtually identical to the independent *t* test discussed in Chapter 8. Recall that the formula for calculating an independent *t* test also involves finding a ratio. The top portion of the fraction is the difference between two sample means, which is analogous to the mean square between (MS_b) just presented. The only differences between the two are (a) rather than finding a simple difference between two means as in a *t* test, in ANOVA we are finding the *average* difference between means, because we are often comparing more than two means; and (b) we are using the squared value of the difference between the means. (Notice that because we are squaring the values we use to calculate an *F* value, the *F* value will always be positive.) The bottom portion of the fraction for the *t* test is the standard *error* of the difference between two sample means. This is exactly the same as the *average*, or standard, error within groups. In the formula used to calculate the *F* value in ANOVA, we must square this average within-group error. So, just as in the *t* test, in ANOVA we are trying to find the average difference *between* group means relative to the average amount of variation *within* each group.

To find the MS_e and MS_b, we must begin by finding the **sum of squares error (SS_e)** and the **sum of squares between (SS_b)**. This sum of squares idea is not new. It is the same sum of squares as introduced in Chapter 3 in the discussion about variance and standard deviation. Sum of squares is actually short for *sum of squared deviations*. In the case of ANOVA, we have two types of deviations. The first is the deviation between each score in a sample and the mean for that sample (i.e., error). The second type of deviation is between each sample mean and the mean for all of the groups combined, called the **grand mean** (i.e., between groups). These two types of deviations are presented in Figure 9.2. Notice that the deviation between the individual score (X_{3i}) is considered random error and is part of the SS_e, and the deviation between the group mean and the grand mean is part of the between-groups SS_b.

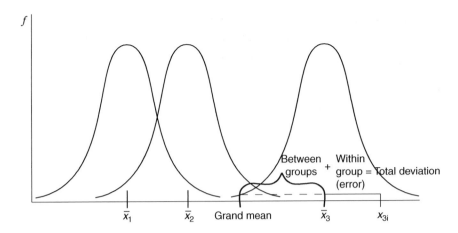

FIGURE 9.2 Illustrations of between-group and within-group deviations.

 For a video explanation of how variance is partitioned in a one-way ANOVA, please refer to the website that accompanies this book.

To find the sum of squares error (SS_e):

1. Calculate the mean for each group: $\bar{X} = \dfrac{\Sigma X}{n}$
2. Subtract the group mean from each individual score in each group: $X - \bar{X}$
3. Square each of these deviation scores: $\left(X - \bar{X}\right)^2$
4. Add them all up for each group: $\Sigma\left(X - \bar{X}\right)^2$
5. Then add up all of the sums of squares for all of the groups:

$$\Sigma\left(X_1 - \bar{X}_1\right)^2 + \Sigma\left(X_2 - \bar{X}_2\right)^2 + \ldots + \Sigma\left(X_k - \bar{X}_k\right)^2$$

Note: The subscripts indicate the individual groups, through to the last group, which is indicated by the subscript k.

The method used to calculate the sum of squares between groups (SS_b) is just slightly more complicated than the SS_e formula. To find the SS_b:

1. Subtract the grand mean from the group mean: $(\bar{X} - \bar{X}_T)$; T indicates total, or the mean for all of the cases across all of the groups
2. Square each of these deviation scores: $(\bar{X} - \bar{X}_T)^2$
3. Multiply each squared deviation by the number of cases in the group: $[\,n(\bar{X} - \bar{X}_T)^2\,]$
4. Add these squared deviations from each group together: $\Sigma\left[n\left(\bar{X} - \bar{X}_T\right)^2\right]$

The only real differences between the formulas for calculating the SS_e and the SS_b are:

1. In the SS_e we subtract the group mean from the individual scores in each group, whereas in the SS_b we subtract the grand mean from each group mean.
2. In the SS_b we multiply each squared deviation by the number of cases in each group. We must do this to get an approximate deviation between the group mean and the grand mean *for each case in every group.*

If we were to add the SS_e to the SS_b, the resulting sum would be called the **sum of squares total (SS_T)**. A brief word about the SS_T is in order. Suppose that we have three randomly selected samples of students. One is a sample of fifth graders, the second is a sample of eighth graders, and the third is a sample of eleventh graders. If we were to give each student in each sample a spelling test, we could add up the scores for all of the students in the three samples combined and divide by the total number of scores to produce one average score. Because we have combined the scores from all three samples, this overall average score would be called the grand mean, or total mean, which would have the symbol $\bar{X}_T$. Using this grand mean, we could calculate a squared deviation score for each student in all three of our samples combined using the familiar formula $\left(X - \bar{X}\right)^2$. The interesting thing about these squared deviations is that, for each student, the difference between each student's score and the grand mean is the sum of that student's deviation from the mean of his or her own group and the deviation of that group mean from the grand mean. So, suppose Jimmy is in the fifth-grade sample. Jimmy gets a score of 25 on the spelling test. The average score for the fifth-grade sample is 30, and the average score for all of the samples combined (i.e., the grand mean) is 35. The difference between Jimmy's score (25) and the grand mean (35) is just the difference between Jimmy's score and the mean for his group (25 – 30 = –5) plus the difference between his group's mean and the grand mean (30 – 35 = –5). Jimmy's deviation from the grand mean is –10 (see Figure 9.3). If we square that deviation score, we end up with a squared deviation of 100 for Jimmy.

Now, if we calculated a deviation score for each student in all three samples and added up all of these deviation scores using the old $\sum\left(X - \bar{X}_T\right)^2$ formula, the result would be the sum of squares total, or the SS_T. (Notice that this formula is the same one that we used way back in Chapter 3! It is the numerator for the variance formula!) The interesting thing about this SS_T is that it is really just the sum of the SS_b and the SS_e. $SS_T = SS_b + SS_e$. This makes sense, because, as we saw with Jimmy, the difference between any individual score and the grand mean is just the sum of the difference between the individual score and the mean of the group that the individual is from plus the difference between that group mean and the grand mean. This is the crux of ANOVA.

Deciding if the Group Means Are Significantly Different

Once we have calculated the SS_b and the SS_e, we have to convert them to average squared deviation scores, or MS_b and MS_e. This is necessary because there are far more deviation scores in the SS_e than there are in the SS_b, so the sums of squares can be a bit misleading. What we want to know in an ANOVA is whether the *average* difference between the group means is large or small relative to the *average* difference between the individual scores and their respective group means,

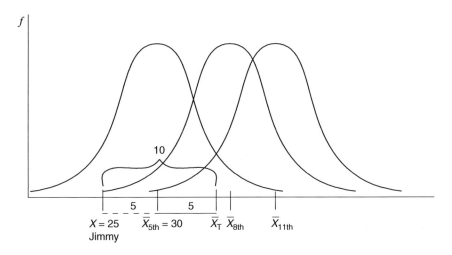

FIGURE 9.3 Within- and between-group deviations for a particular individual.

or the average amount of error within each group. To convert these sums of squares into mean squares, we must divide the sums of squares by their appropriate degrees of freedom.

For the SS_b, remember that we are only making comparisons between each of the groups. The number of degrees of freedom for the SS_b is always the number of groups minus 1. If we use K to represent the number of groups, and df to represent the degrees of freedom, then the formula for the between-group degrees of freedom is $df = K - 1$. So, to convert an SS_b to an MS_b, we divide the SS_b by $K - 1$. The number of degrees of freedom for the SS_e is found by taking the number of scores in each group and subtracting 1 from each group. So, if we have three groups, our df for the SS_e will be $(n_1 - 1) + (n_2 - 1) + (n_3 - 1)$. Notice that this is the same formula for the degrees of freedom as was used for the independent samples t test in Chapter 8. The only difference is that we have one more group here. A simpler way to write this df formula is $N - K$, where N is the total number of cases for *all* groups combined and K is the number of groups. Once we have this df, we can convert the SS_e into an MS_e by simply dividing the SS_e by $N - K$. Table 9.2 contains a summary of the formulas for converting the sums of squares into mean squares.

Once we have found our MS_b and our MS_e, all we have to do is divide the MS_b by the MS_e to find our F value. Once we've found our F value, we need to look in our table of F values (Appendix C) to see whether it is statistically significant. This table of F values is similar to the table of t values we used in Chapter 8, with one important difference. Unlike t values, the significance of F values depends on both the number of cases in the samples (i.e., the df for the MS_e) *and* the number of groups being compared (i.e., the df for the MS_b). This second df is critical, because it is what is used to control for the fact that we are comparing more than two groups. Without it, we might as well conduct multiple t tests, and this is problematic for the reasons discussed at the beginning of the chapter. In Appendix C, we can find critical values for F associated with different alpha levels. If our observed value of F (F_o) is larger than our critical value of F (F_c), we must conclude that there are statistically significant differences between the group means. In Figure 9.4, you can see that the observed F value is in the shaded area beyond the critical value of F that indicates the region of rejection, therefore indicating that we should reject the null hypothesis of no difference between the population means.

Post-Hoc Tests

Our work is not done once we have found a statistically significant difference between the group means. Remember that when we calculated the MS_b, we ended up with an *average* difference between the group means. If we are comparing three group means, we might find a relatively large average difference between these group means even if two of the three group means are identical. Therefore, a statistically significant F value tells us only that somewhere there is a meaningful difference between my group means. But it does not tell us *which* groups differ from each other significantly. To do this, we must conduct **post-hoc tests**. If the overall F value of the ANOVA was not statistically significant, there is no need to conduct the post-hoc tests.

There are a variety of post-hoc tests available. Some are more conservative, making it more difficult to find statistically significant differences between groups, whereas others are more liberal. All post-hoc tests use the same basic principle. They allow you to compare each group mean to each other group mean and determine if they are significantly different, while controlling for

TABLE 9.2 Converting sums of squares into mean squares

$$MS_b = \frac{SS_b}{K - 1} \qquad\qquad MS_e = \frac{SS_e}{N - K}$$

MS_b is the mean squares between groups.
SS_b is the sum of squares between groups.
K is the number of groups.

MS_e is the mean square error.
SS_e is the sum of squares error.
K is the number of groups.
N is the number of cases combined across all groups.

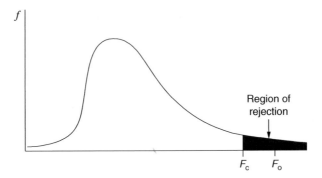

FIGURE 9.4 A statistically significant *F* value.

the number of group comparisons being made. Conceptually, post-hoc tests in ANOVA are like a series of independent *t* tests where each group mean is compared to each other group mean. Unlike *t* tests, however, post-hoc tests keep the Type I error rate constant by taking into consideration how many groups are being compared. As we saw in Chapters 7 and 8, to determine if the difference between two group means is statistically significant, we subtract one group mean from the other and divide by a standard error. The difference between the various types of post-hoc tests is what each test uses for the standard error. Some formulas are designed to take different sample sizes for different groups into account (e.g., Tukey–Kramer) and others are designed to handle situations where the variances are not equal across all of the groups in the independent variable (e.g., Dunnett's test, the Games–Howell test).

In this book, for the purposes of demonstration, we will consider the **Tukey HSD** (HSD stands for Honestly Significantly Different) post-hoc test. I chose the Tukey HSD test because it is one of the simpler formulas and it allows me to demonstrate how to calculate a post-hoc test by hand more simply than another, more complicated formula would. But the Tukey HSD is not better than other post-hoc tests and is only appropriate to use when the sample sizes and variances of all the groups in the ANOVA are equal. This is a fairly liberal test, meaning that it is more likely to produce statistically significant differences than some other tests (e.g., the Scheffé test). When tests are more liberal, they are more likely to produce statistically significant results, even when they should not (i.e., Type I errors). In general, more conservative tests allow researchers to be more confident that when they proclaim a result is statistically significant, they are not making a Type I error.

The Tukey test compares each group mean to each other group mean by using the familiar formula described for *t* tests in Chapter 8. Specifically, it is the mean of one group minus the mean of a second group divided by the standard error:

$$\text{Tukey HSD} = \frac{\bar{X}_1 - \bar{X}_2}{s_{\bar{x}}}$$

where $s_{\bar{x}} = \sqrt{\dfrac{MS_e}{n_g}}$

and n_g = the number of cases *in each group.*

When we solve this equation, we get an *observed* Tukey HSD value. To see if this observed value is significant, and therefore indicative of a statistically significant difference between the two groups being compared, we must compare our observed Tukey HSD value with a critical value. We find this critical value in Appendix D, which we read in pretty much the same way that we read the *F*-value table. That is, the number of groups being compared is listed on the top row of the table and the *df* error is along the left column. In this table, only the critical values for an alpha level of .05 are presented.

Once we have calculated a Tukey HSD for each of the group comparisons we need to make, we can say which groups are significantly different from each other on our dependent variable. Notice that, because the standard error used in the Tukey HSD test assumes that each group has an equal number of cases, this is not the best post-hoc test to use if you have groups with unequal sample sizes.

Effect Size

In addition to the calculation of effect size (*d*) presented in Chapters 7 and 8, another common measure of effect size is the percentage of variance in the dependent variable that is explained by the independent variable(s). In ANOVA analyses, **eta squared** is the statistic that reveals the percentage of variance in the dependent variable that is explained by an independent variable, and is the most common measure of effect size. Remember that in a one-way ANOVA, the independent variable is always categorical. Therefore, the eta squared statistic tells us how much of the variance in the dependent variable can be explained by differences between groups in the independent variable. If I am comparing the average temperature in January (dependent variable) in Maine, California, and Sydney, Australia, I would expect a fairly large eta squared value because the average temperatures vary widely by location (independent variable). In other words, a large amount of the variation in January temperatures is explained by the location. (For a more detailed discussion of explained variance, see Chapters 12 and 13.) To illustrate how this works, I present the results of an analysis using the SPSS computer software program to analyze a set of fictional data that I made up.

Suppose that I want to test a drug that I developed to increase students' interest in their school work. I randomly select 75 third-grade students and randomly assign them to one of three groups: a "High Dose" group, a "Low Dose" group, and a "Placebo" group. After dividing the students into their respective groups, I give them the appropriate dosage of my new drug (or a placebo) and then give them all the exact same school work assignment. I measure their interest in the school work by asking them to rate how interesting they thought the work was on a scale from 1 (*Not interesting*) to 5 (*Very interesting*). Then I use SPSS to conduct an ANOVA on my data, and I get the output from the program presented in Table 9.3.[1]

The results produced by SPSS include descriptive statistics such as the means, standard deviations, and sample sizes for each of the three groups, as well as the overall mean ("Total") for the entire sample of 75 students. In the descriptive statistics, we can see that the "Low Dose" group has a somewhat higher average mean on the dependent variable (i.e., interest in the school work) than do the other two groups. Turning now to the ANOVA results below the descriptive statistics in Table 9.3, there are identical statistics for the "Corrected Model" row and the "Group" row. The

TABLE 9.3   SPSS output for ANOVA examining interest by drug treatment group

Descriptive Statistics

Independent Variable	Mean	Std. Deviation	N
High Dose	2.7600	1.2675	25
Low Dose	3.6000	1.2583	25
Placebo	2.6000	.9129	25
Total	2.9867	1.2247	75

ANOVA Results

Source	Type III Sum of Squares	df	Mean Square	F	Sig.	Eta Squared
Corrected Model	14.427	2	7.213	5.379	.007	.130
Intercept	669.013	1	669.013	498.850	.000	.874
Group	14.427	2	7.213	5.379	.007	.130
Error	96.560	72	1.341			

"Model" row includes all effects in the model, such as all independent variables and interaction effects (see Chapter 10 for a discussion of these multiple effects). In the present example, there is only one independent variable, so the "Model" statistics are the same as the "Group" statistics.

Let's focus on the "Group" row. This row includes all of the between-group information, because "Group" is our independent group variable. Here we see the sum of squares between (SS_b),[2] which is 14.427. The number of degrees of freedom ("df") here is 2, because with three groups, $K - 1 = 2$. The sum of squares divided by the degrees of freedom produces the mean square (MS_b), which is 7.213. The statistics for the sum of squares error (SS_e), degrees of freedom for the error component, and the mean square error (MS_e) are all in the row below the "Group" row. The F value ("F") for this ANOVA is 5.379, which was produced by dividing the mean square from the "Group" row by the mean square from the "Error" row. This F value is statistically significant ("Sig." = .007). The "Sig." is the same thing as the p value (described in Chapter 7). Finally, in the "Eta Squared" column, we can see that we have a value of .130 in the "Group" row. Eta squared is a measure of the association between the independent variable ("Group") and the dependent variable (the interest variable). It indicates that 13 percent of the variance in the scores on the interest variable can be explained by the group variable. In other words, I can account for 13 percent of the variance in the interest scores simply by knowing whether students were in the "High Dose," "Low Dose," or "Placebo" group. Eta squared is similar to the coefficient of determination (r^2) discussed in Chapters 12 and 13.

Now that we know that there is a statistically significant difference between the three groups in their level of interest, and that group membership accounts for 13 percent of the variance in interest scores, it is time to look at our Tukey post-hoc analysis to determine which groups significantly differ from each other. The SPSS results of this analysis are presented in Table 9.4. The far left column of this table contains the reference group (I), and the column to the right of this shows the comparison groups (J). So, in the first comparison, the mean for the "High Dose" group is compared to the mean for the "Low Dose" group. We can see that the "Mean Difference" between these two groups is –.8400, indicating that the "High Dose" group had a mean that was .84 points lower than the mean of the "Low Dose" group on the interest variable. In the last column, we can see that this difference is statistically significant ("Sig." = .033). So we can conclude that students in the "Low Dose" group, on average, were more interested in their work than were students in the "High Dose" group. In the next comparison, between "High Dose" and "Placebo," we find a mean difference of .16, which was not significant ("Sig." = .877). Looking at the next set of comparisons, we see that the "Low Dose" group is significantly different from both the "High Dose" group (we already knew this) and the "Placebo" group. At this point, all of our comparisons have been made and we can conclude that, on average, students in the "Low Dose" group were significantly more interested in their work than were students in the "High Dose" and "Placebo" groups, but there was no significant difference between the interest of students in the "High Dose" and "Placebo" groups.

 For a video demonstration of how to interpret the SPSS output for a one-way ANOVA, please refer to the website that accompanies this book.

TABLE 9.4 SPSS results of Tukey HSD post-hoc tests comparing three drug-treatment groups

(*I*) Treatment 1, Treatment 2, Control	(*J*) Treatment 1, Treatment 2, Control	Mean Difference (*I – J*)	Std. Error	Sig.
High Dose	Low Dose	–.8400	.328	.033
	Placebo	.1600	.328	.877
Low Dose	High Dose	.8400	.328	.033
	Placebo	1.0000	.328	.009
Placebo	High Dose	–.1600	.328	.877
	Low Dose	–1.0000	.328	.009

TABLE 9.5 Data for 5-, 8-, and 12-year-olds' hours slept per day

5-Year-Olds	8-Year-Olds	12-Year-Olds
12	12	10
11	10	9
11	10	8
10	9	8
9	9	7
$Mean_1 = 10.6$	$Mean_2 = 10.0$	$Mean_3 = 8.4$

Example: Comparing the Sleep of 5-, 8-, and 12-Year-Olds

Suppose that I've got three groups: 5-year-olds, 8-year-olds, and 12-year-olds. I want to see whether children at these different age levels differ in the amount of sleep they get per day, on average. I get the data presented in Table 9.5. From the individual scores presented for each group, all of the additional data can be calculated. Let's walk through these steps.

Step 1: Find the mean for each group.

To find the mean for each group, add the scores together within the group and divide by the number of cases in the group. These group means have been calculated and are presented in Table 9.5.

Step 2: Calculate the grand mean.

This can be done either by adding up all of the 15 scores across the groups and dividing by 15 or, because each group has the same number of cases in this example, by adding up the three group means and dividing by 3: 10.6 + 10.0 + 8.4 = 29 / 3 = 9.67.

Step 3: Calculate the sum of squares error (SS_e).

First, we must find the squared deviation between each individual score and the group mean. These calculations are presented in Table 9.6. When we sum the three sums of squares, we get SS_e = 16.40.

Step 4: Calculate the sum of squares between groups (SS_b).

Recall that to find the SS_b we need to subtract the grand mean from the group mean, square it, and multiply by the number of cases in the group. Then we add each of these numbers together. So for our three groups we get:

$$\text{Group 1: } 5(10.6 - 9.67)^2 = 5(.86) = 4.30$$

$$\text{Group 2: } 5(10.0 - 9.67)^2 = 5(.11) = .55$$

$$\text{Group 3: } 5(8.4 - 9.67)^2 = 5(1.61) = 8.05$$

$$\textit{Sum: } 4.30 + .55 + 8.05 = 12.90$$

TABLE 9.6 Squared deviations for the ANOVA example

5-Year-Olds	8-Year-Olds	12-Year-Olds
$(12 - 10.6)^2 = 1.96$	$(12 - 10.0)^2 = 4.0$	$(10 - 8.4)^2 = 2.56$
$(11 - 10.6)^2 = .16$	$(10 - 10.0)^2 = 0$	$(9 - 8.4)^2 = .36$
$(11 - 10.6)^2 = .16$	$(10 - 10.0)^2 = 0$	$(8 - 8.4)^2 = .16$
$(10 - 10.6)^2 = .36$	$(9 - 10.0)^2 = 1.0$	$(8 - 8.4)^2 = .16$
$(9 - 10.6)^2 = 2.56$	$(9 - 10.0)^2 = 1.0$	$(7 - 8.4)^2 = 1.96$
$SS_1 = 5.20$	$SS_2 = 6.00$	$SS_3 = 5.20$

Step 5: Calculate the mean square error (MS_e).

To find the MS_e we divide the SS_e by the degrees of freedom for the error (df_e). The df_e is $N - K$. In this example we have 15 cases across three groups, so the degrees of freedom are $15 - 3 = 12$. When we divide the SS_e by 12 we get

$$MS_e = 16.40/12 = 1.37$$

Step 6: Calculate the mean square between groups (MS_b).

To find the MS_b we divide the SS_b by the degrees of freedom between groups (df_b). The df_b is $K - 1$. In this example we have three groups, so the degrees of freedom are $3 - 1 = 2$. When we divide the SS_b by 2 we get

$$MS_b = 12.90/2 = 6.45$$

Step 7: Calculate the F ratio.

The F ratio can be found by dividing the MS_b by the MS_e:

$$F = \frac{6.45}{1.37} = 4.71$$

Step 8: Find the critical value for F from Appendix C.

Looking in Appendix C, with 2 degrees of freedom in the numerator and 12 degrees of freedom in the denominator, we find a critical value of F of 3.88 (with $\alpha = .05$).

 For a brief video explaining how to read and interpret Appendix C, please refer to the website that accompanies this book.

Step 9: Decide whether the F value is statistically significant.

By comparing our observed F value of 4.71 with the critical F value of 3.88, we can see that $F_o > F_c$. Therefore, we conclude that our results are statistically significant (see Figure 9.5).

Assuming we selected an alpha level of .05, we now know that we have a statistically significant F value. This tells us that there is a statistically significant difference between the means of our three groups in the average amount of sleep they get per day. But I do not yet know which of my three groups differ. To figure this out, I need to conduct post-hoc tests. So, I conduct Tukey

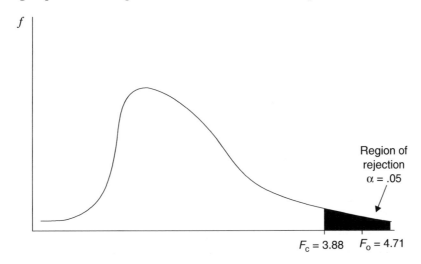

FIGURE 9.5 Critical and observed F values for the ANOVA example.

tests to compare my three groups. Recall that the formula for the Tukey test is the mean of one group minus the mean of another group divided by the standard error. When all of our groups have equal numbers of cases, then the standard error for the Tukey test is the same for each comparison of groups. In our example, we have equal numbers of cases in each group, so we only need to calculate the standard error once:

$$s_{\bar{x}} = \sqrt{\frac{MS_e}{n_g}}$$

$$s_{\bar{x}} = \sqrt{\frac{1.37}{5}}$$

$$s_{\bar{x}} = \sqrt{.27} \Rightarrow .52$$

With our standard error for the Tukey tests in place, we can compare the means for each of the three groups:

$$\text{Tukey}_{1-2} = \frac{10.6 - 10.0}{.52} \Rightarrow \frac{.6}{.52} \Rightarrow 1.15$$

$$\text{Tukey}_{1-3} = \frac{10.6 - 8.4}{.52} \Rightarrow \frac{2.2}{.52} \Rightarrow 4.23$$

$$\text{Tukey}_{2-3} = \frac{10.0 - 8.4}{.52} \Rightarrow \frac{1.6}{.52} \Rightarrow 3.08$$

The final step in our analysis is to determine whether each of these Tukey HSD values is statistically significant. To do this, we must look at the table of critical values for the **studentized range statistic** in Appendix D. The values in this table are organized in a similar way to those presented in the table of *F* values in Appendix C. However, instead of using the degrees of freedom between groups to find the appropriate column, we use the number of groups. In this example, we have three groups, so we find the column labeled "3." To find the appropriate row, we use the degrees of freedom for the error. In this example our df_e was 12. So, with an alpha level of .05, our Tukey value must be larger than 3.77 before we consider it statistically significant. I know this because the critical Tukey value in Appendix D for 3 groups and 12 degrees of freedom is 3.77.

 For a brief video illustration of how to read Appendix D, please refer to the website that accompanies this book.

My Tukey value comparing Groups 1 and 2 was only 1.15. Because this is smaller than the value of 3.77, I conclude that Groups 1 and 2 do not differ significantly in how much they sleep per day, on average. The Tukey values for the comparison of Group 1 with Group 3 produced a Tukey value of 4.23, which is larger than 3.77, so I can conclude that Group 1 is different from Group 3. My third Tukey test produced a value of 3.08, indicating that Group 2 is not significantly different from Group 3. By looking at the means presented for each group in Table 9.5, I can see that, on average, 5-year-olds sleep more than 12-year-olds, but 5-year-olds do not differ significantly from 8-year-olds and 8-year-olds do not differ significantly from 12-year-olds in how much sleep they get per day, on average. In Figure 9.6, each of these observed (i.e., calculated) Tukey values are presented, along with the critical Tukey value (3.77). As you can see, only the Tukey value for the comparison of 5-year-olds and 12-year-olds falls in the region of rejection, indicating that it is the only statistically significant difference between the three groups being compared.

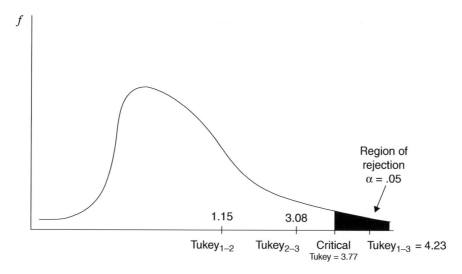

FIGURE 9.6 Results of the Tukey test.

For the sake of comparison, I analyzed the same data using the SPSS computer program. The results of this analysis are presented in Table 9.7. You will notice some minor differences in the values produced by SPSS and those that I calculated above. For example, we calculated $SS_b = 12.90$, but SPSS reported an $SS_b = 12.933$ (under the "Type III Sum of Squares" for the age variable). This difference is due simply to rounding error. This rounding error also produced a small difference between the MS_b values and the observed F values. Nonetheless, both my analysis and the SPSS analysis found a statistically significant F value. The SPSS output, in the box

TABLE 9.7 SPSS output for one-way ANOVA comparing different age groups' average hours of sleep per day

Descriptive Statistics
Dependent Variable: Sleep

Age	Mean	Std. Deviation	N
5.00	10.6000	1.14018	5
8.00	10.0000	1.22474	5
12.00	8.4000	1.14018	5
Total	9.6667	1.44749	15

Levene's Test of Equality of Error Variances
Dependent Variable: Sleep

F	df_1	df_2	Sig.
.023	2	12	.977

Tests of Between-Subjects Effects
Dependent Variable: Sleep

Source	Type III Sum of Squares	df	Mean Square	F	Sig.	Partial Eta Squared
Corrected Model	12.933[1]	2	6.467	4.732	.031	.441
Intercept	1401.667	1	1401.667	1025.610	.000	.988
Age	12.933	2	6.467	4.732	.031	.441
Error	16.400	12	1.367			
Total	1431.000	15				
Corrected Total	29.333	14				

labeled "Levene's Test of Equality of Error Variances," revealed that the assumption of equality of variances across our three groups was not violated, because this F value was not statistically significant. In the next box of SPSS output ("Tests of Between-Subjects Effects"), in the last column, we can see that the partial eta squared for our independent variable of age was .441. This tells us that 44.1 percent of the variance in hours slept per night is explained by which age group children were in. This is quite a large amount of variance explained.

Writing it Up

To summarize these results in a form that you might see in a published journal I would write the following: "A one-way ANOVA was conducted to compare the average amount of sleep per day among samples of 5-year-olds, 8-year-olds, and 12-year olds. This analysis produced a statistically significant result ($F_{(5,12)}$ = 4.73, p = .031). The independent variable of age explained 44.1 percent of the variance in the dependent variable of hours slept per day (eta squared = .441). Post-hoc Tukey tests revealed that the only significant difference between groups was found between 5-year-olds (M = 10.6) and 12-year-olds (M = 8.4), with the younger children sleeping significantly more than the older children."

Worked Example

Suppose I work for a drug company and we have developed a new weight-loss drug. The new drug, Lose-A-Lot, is given to a random sample of 7 adult men. The old weight-loss drug, Meltaway, is given to a different random sample of 7 adult men. A third random sample of 7 adult men take a placebo (i.e., a water-filled capsule that they believe is a weight-loss drug). After one month of taking the pills, the men are weighed to see how much weight each man has lost (or gained) during the month. The data are summarized in Table 9.8.

As you can see, the table includes some blank boxes that will allow me to demonstrate how to do each of the necessary calculations in a one-way ANOVA. The first step in any ANOVA calculation is to find the mean for each group. In this example, the means for the Lose-A-Lot and Meltaway groups are provided in the table, but the mean for the Placebo group needs to be calculated. The raw scores for the Placebo group are provided in the table. To find the mean, or average, of these values we first need to add them together to find their sum:

$$5 + 4 + 7 + 9 + 11 + 15 + 12 = 63$$

TABLE 9.8   Comparison of three weight-loss groups for a one-way ANOVA example

	Lose-A-Lot		Meltaway		Placebo	
	X	$(X - \overline{X})^2$	X	$(X - \overline{X})^2$	X	$(X - \overline{X})^2$
Man 1	2	7.34	6	0.08	5	16
Man 2	5	0.08	4	☐	4	25
Man 3	4	0.50	8	2.92	7	4
Man 4	6	1.66	7	0.50	9	0
Man 5	8	10.82	9	7.34	11	4
Man 6	5	☐	6	0.08	15	36
Man 7	3	2.92	4	5.24	12	9
Group means	$\overline{x}$ = 4.71		$\overline{x}$ = 6.29		☐	
SS (each group)	☐	23.40			☐	94
Grand mean						

Then we divide this sum by the number of scores in the group (7) to find the mean:

$$\bar{X} = \frac{63}{7} = 9$$

Once we know the means for each group, we can complete the rest of the missing information in the table. First, let's calculate the grand mean. This is the average of all the scores, across all of the groups. When we have an even number of cases in each group, as we do in this example, we can simply average the three group means together to find the grand mean:

$$GM = \frac{4.71 + 6.29 + 9}{3} = 6.67$$

Next we can find the values for the missing deviation scores in the table. First, there is a missing deviation score $(X - \bar{X})^2$ in the Lose-A-Lot group. To find this score I take the raw score (X) and subtract the group mean from it: $(5 - 4.71)^2 = (.29)^2 = .08$. Next, we do the same process to find the missing deviation score for the Meltaway group: $(4 - 6.29)^2 = (-2.29)^2 = 5.24$.

Now that we have all of the deviation scores for each group, we can calculate the sum of the squared deviations for each group. For the Lose-A-Lot group, the sum of the squared deviations is 23.4. For the Placebo group, the sum of the squared deviation is 94. Both of these sums of squared deviations are provided in the table. For the Meltaway group, we need to add together the squared deviations to find the sum for that group:

$$.08 + 5.24 + 2.92 + .50 + 7.34 + .08 + 5.24 = 21.40$$

We have now found all of the missing values from Table 9.8, and the completed table can be found in Table 9.9. With all of the pieces of the table in place, we can move on to calculating the necessary statistics for our F value. First, with the sums of squared deviations for each group known, we can calculate the sum of squares within (SS_w), also known as the sum of squares error (SS_e). To find this value we simply add together the sums of squared deviations from each of the three groups in our analysis:

$$SS_e = 23.40 + 21.40 + 94$$

$$SS_e = 138.80$$

TABLE 9.9 Completed table for weight-loss comparison example with missing values added

	Lose-A-Lot		Meltaway		Placebo	
	X	**(X − X̄)²**	**X**	**(X − X̄)²**	**X**	**(X − X̄)²**
Man 1	2	7.34	6	0.08	5	16
Man 2	5	0.08	4	5.24	4	25
Man 3	4	0.50	8	2.92	7	4
Man 4	6	1.66	7	0.50	9	0
Man 5	8	10.82	9	7.34	11	4
Man 6	5	.08	6	0.08	15	36
Man 7	3	2.92	4	5.24	12	9
Group mean	x̄ = 4.71		x̄ = 6.29		9	
SS (each group)		23.40		21.40		94
Grand mean	6.67					

Next, we use the group means and the grand mean to calculate the sum of squares between (SS_b) groups. Remember from earlier in the chapter that we need to multiply each deviation between the group mean and the grand mean by the number of cases in the group:

Lose-A-Lot: $7(4.71 - 6.67)^2 = 7(-1.96)^2 = 7(3.84) = 26.89$

Meltaway: $7(6.29 - 6.67)^2 = 7(-.38)^2 = 7(.14) = .98$

Placebo: $7(9 - 6.67)^2 = 7(2.33)^2 = 7(5.43) = 38.01$

To find the SS_b we add these values together:

$$SS_b = 26.89 + .98 + 38.01 = 65.88$$

The next step is to convert our SS_e and SS_b into the values that make up the F value: the MS_e and the MS_b. We accomplish this by dividing the two SS values by their respective degrees of freedom, or df. For the SS_e, the degrees of freedom are the total number of cases, across all of the groups, minus the number of groups. In this example there are 21 cases across 3 groups, so $df_e = 21 - 3 = 18$. The degrees of freedom for the SS_b is the number of groups minus 1: $df_b = 3 - 1 = 2$.

To find the MS_e we divide the SS_e by the df_e: $MS_e = \dfrac{138.8}{18} = 7.71$

To find the MS_b we divide the SS_b by the df_b: $MS_b = \dfrac{65.88}{2} = 32.94$

Now we are ready to calculate the observed F value by dividing the MS_b by the MS_e:

$$F = \frac{32.94}{7.71} = 4.27$$

So now we know that our observed F value for this problem is 4.27. But is that statistically significant? To make that determination we need to find the *critical F* value and compare it to our observed F value. Remember that the two degrees of freedom values that we found are 2 and 18. Using Appendix C, the number of degrees of freedom for the numerator of the F value is 2, and the number of degrees of freedom for the denominator is 18. Using an alpha level of .05, we find a critical F value of 3.55. When we compare this to our observed F value of 4.27, we can see that 4.27 > 3.55, so our observed F value > our critical F value. Therefore, we conclude that our results are statistically significant. The three populations represented by the samples in the Lose-A-Lot, Meltaway, and Placebo groups differ in their average weight lost, but we do not yet know which groups differ from which other groups. For that, we need to perform Tukey post-hoc tests.

The first step in performing a Tukey test is to calculate the standard error that we will use as the denominator in our Tukey comparisons. To do this, we need to know the MS_e, which you may recall from our F value is 7.71, and the number of cases in each group, which is 7. Then we plug those numbers into our standard error formula for the Tukey test:

$$s_{\bar{x}} = \sqrt{\frac{MS_e}{n_g}}$$

$$s_{\bar{x}} = \sqrt{\frac{7.71}{7}}$$

$$s_{\bar{x}} = \sqrt{1.10} = 1.05$$

Now that we have our standard error, we can use the Tukey HSD formula to compare the means of each group to each other group:

$$\text{Tukey HSD} = \frac{\overline{X}_1 - \overline{X}_2}{s_{\overline{x}}}$$

Lose - A - Lot–Meltaway: $\text{Tukey HSD} = \dfrac{4.71 - 6.29}{1.05} = -1.50$

Lose - A - Lot–Placebo: $\text{Tukey HSD} = \dfrac{4.71 - 9.0}{1.05} = -4.09$

Placebo–Meltaway: $\text{Tukey HSD} = \dfrac{9.0 - 6.29}{1.05} = 2.58$

We now have three, calculated, observed Tukey HSD values. We can compare each one of them to the critical Tukey value that we will look up in Appendix D, using 3 for the number of levels of the independent variable (because we are comparing three different groups) and 18 for our *df* error. This gives us a critical Tukey value of 3.61 if we are using an alpha level of .05. Comparing our observed Tukey values to the critical Tukey value, we can conclude that only the difference between the Lose-A-Lot group and the Placebo group is statistically significant. Therefore, we would conclude that, in the populations of these three groups, the average amount of weight loss does not differ for the Lose-A-Lot and the Meltaway groups, or for the Meltaway and the Placebo groups, but the Placebo group lost significantly more weight than did those in the Lose-A-Lot group, on average.

 For a video demonstration of how to calculate and interpret a one-way ANOVA and post-hoc tests, please refer to the website that accompanies this book.

Wrapping Up and Looking Forward

One-way ANOVA, when combined with post-hoc tests, is a powerful technique for discovering whether group means differ on some dependent variable. The *F* value from a one-way ANOVA tells us whether, overall, there are significant differences between our group means. But we cannot stop with the *F* value. To get the maximum information from a one-way ANOVA, we must conduct the *post-hoc* tests to determine *which* groups differ. ANOVA incorporates several of the concepts that I have discussed in previous chapters. The sum of squares used in ANOVA is based on the squared deviations first introduced in Chapter 3 in the discussion of variance. The comparisons of group means is similar to the information about independent samples *t* tests presented in Chapter 8. And the eta squared statistic, which is a measure of association between the independent and dependent variables, is related to the concepts of shared variance and variance explained discussed in Chapters 12 and 13, as well as the notion of effect size discussed in Chapter 7.

In this chapter, a brief introduction to the most basic ANOVA model and post-hoc tests was provided. It is important to remember that many models are not this simple. In the real world of social science research, it is often difficult to find groups with equal numbers of cases. When groups have different numbers of cases, the ANOVA model becomes a bit more complicated. I encourage you to read more about one-way ANOVA models, and I offer some references to help you learn more. In the next two chapters, I examine two more advanced types of ANOVA techniques: factorial ANOVA and repeated-measures ANOVA.

In this chapter and those that preceded it, I examined several of the most basic, and most commonly used, statistics in the social sciences. These statistics form the building blocks for most of the more advanced techniques used by researchers. For example, *t* tests and one-way

ANOVA represent the basic techniques for examining the relations between nominal or categorical independent variables and continuous dependent variables. More advanced methods of examining such relations, such as factorial ANOVA and repeated-measures ANOVA, are merely elaborations of the more basic methods I have already discussed. Techniques for examining the associations among two or more continuous variables are all based on the statistical technique discussed in Chapter 12, correlations. More advanced techniques, such as factor analysis and regression, are based on correlations.

Work Problems

1. What type of research question would you use ANOVA to answer?
2. Why would we use ANOVA rather than multiple t tests?
3. Describe what an F ratio is. What does it tell you?
4. How should we interpret a significant F ratio? That is, what does a statistically significant F ratio tell us? What does it not tell us?
5. Suppose I want to know whether drivers in Ohio, Texas, and California differ in the average number of miles they commute to work each day. So I select random samples of 5 drivers from each state and ask them how far they drive to work. I get the data that is summarized in Table 9.10. Please answer the following questions based on these data.

   a. Calculate the missing values in the blank cells in the table.
   b. Perform all of the necessary calculations to determine whether the F value is statistically significant with an alpha level of .05. DO NOT perform the Tukey tests here.
   c. Interpret your results. What can you say now about the differences between the population means?
   d. Conduct the Tukey post-hoc tests to determine which means differ significantly using an alpha level of .05, then interpret your results. Now what can you say about the differences between the population means?

TABLE 9.10 Data for numbers of hours Ohio, Texas, and California drivers spend commuting per day

	Ohio		Texas		California	
	X	$(X - \bar{X})^2$	X	$(X - \bar{X})^2$	X	$(X - \bar{X})^2$
Driver 1	11	.36	11	23.04	13	49
Driver 2	5	29.16	13	7.84	16	16
Driver 3	12	☐	15	.64	19	1
Driver 4	16	31.36	19	☐	24	16
Driver 5	8	5.76	21	27.04	28	64
Group means	10.40		☐		20.00	
SS (each group)	☐	69.20		☐		146
Grand mean						

6. I recently conducted an experiment with college students to examine whether telling them about the expectations for how well they would perform on a test influenced how well they actually performed. Students were randomly assigned to one of three groups: Neutral, in which students were simply told they would be given a test and to try to do well; Encouraged, in which students were told they were expected to do well because they were good students attending a good school; and Disrespected, in which they were told the test was created for students at a more prestigious school so the test creator did not expect them to do very well. Then the students in my study completed a set of test questions. I conducted a one-way ANOVA to compare the means of the participants in the three groups, and the SPSS results of this analysis are presented in Table 9.11. In this analysis, test performance is the total

number of test questions that were correctly answered by the participants. The independent variable is labeled "Group" in the SPSS output. Take a look at the results presented in Table 9.11 and answer the following questions.

a. Report the means for each group.
b. Report whether the assumption of equal variances is violated and explain how you know.
c. Report the F value for the one-way ANOVA examining differences between the groups.
    i. Is this a statistically significant F value? How do you know?
d. Report the effect size for the independent group variable and explain what it means.
e. Write a sentence or two to summarize what this ANOVA reveals about the differences in test performance between the groups.

TABLE 9.11   SPSS output for one-way ANOVA comparing test performances of three groups (Neutral, Encouraged, and Disrespected)

Descriptive Statistics
Dependent Variable: Test performance

Group	Mean	Std. Deviation	N
1 = Neutral	10.9423	2.60778	52
2 = Encouraged	10.5577	2.93333	52
3 = Disrespected	9.8519	2.92940	54
Total	10.4430	2.84749	158

Levene's Test of Equality of Error Variances
Dependent Variable: Test performance

F	df_1	df_2	Sig.
.887	2	155	.414

Tests of Between-Subjects Effects
Dependent Variable: Test performance

Source	Type III Sum of Squares	df	Mean Square	F	Sig.	Partial Eta Squared
Corrected Model	32.519[1]	2	16.259	2.032	.135	.026
Intercept	17250.573	1	17250.573	2155.507	.000	.933
Group	32.519	2	16.259	2.032	.135	.026
Error	1240.469	155	8.003			
Total	18504.000	158				
Corrected Total	1272.987	157				

Note: 1 R Squared = .026 (Adjusted R Squared = .013)

 You can find the answers to these work problems, as well as additional work problems, on the website that accompanies this book.

Notes

1   There are actually two different ways to conduct a one-way ANOVA in SPSS. In this chapter I presented the results from the "General Linear Model → Univariate" option. This method allowed me to present the eta squared statistic. The other approach in SPSS is to choose the "Compare Means → One-way ANOVA" option. This method does not produce an eta squared statistic, but it does produce a Levene's test of homogeneity of variance to examine whether this assumption of ANOVA has been violated.

2   SPSS generally reports this as the Type III sum of squares. This sum of squares is known as the "residual" sum of squares because it is calculated after taking the effects of other independent variables, covariates, and interaction effects into account.

CHAPTER **10**

Factorial Analysis of Variance

In the previous chapter, we examined one-way ANOVA. In this chapter and the one that follows it, we explore the wonders of two more advanced methods of analyzing variance: factorial ANOVA and repeated-measures ANOVA. These techniques are based on the same general principles as one-way ANOVA. Namely, they all involve the partitioning of the variance of a dependent variable into its component parts (e.g., the part attributable to between-group differences, the part attributable to within-group variance, or error). In addition, these techniques allow us to examine more complex, and often more interesting, questions than allowed by simple one-way ANOVA. As mentioned at the end of the last chapter, these more advanced statistical techniques involve much more complex formulas than those we have seen previously. Therefore, in this chapter and those that follow, only a basic introduction to the techniques is offered. You should keep in mind that there is much more to these statistics than described in these pages, and you should consider reading more about them in the suggested readings at the end of the book.

When to Use Factorial ANOVA

Factorial ANOVA is the technique to use when you have one continuous (i.e., interval or ratio scaled) dependent variable and two or more categorical (i.e., nominally scaled) independent variables. For example, suppose I want to know whether boys and girls differ in the amount of television they watch per week, on average. Suppose I also want to know whether children in different regions of the United States (i.e., East, West, North, and South) differ in their average amount of television watched per week. In this example, average amount of television watched per week is my dependent variable, and gender and region of the country are my two independent variables. This is known as a 2 × 4 factorial analysis, because one of my independent variables has two levels (gender) and one has four levels (region). If I were writing about this analysis in an academic paper, I would write, "I conducted a 2 (gender) × 4 (region) factorial ANOVA."

Now when I run my factorial ANOVA, I get three interesting results. First, I get two **main effects**: one for my comparison of boys and girls and one for my comparison of children from different regions of the country. These results are similar to the results I would get if I simply ran two one-way ANOVAs, with one important difference, which I describe in the next section. In addition to these main effects, my factorial ANOVA also produces an **interaction effect,** or simply an **interaction**. An interaction is present when the differences between the groups of one independent variable on the dependent variable vary according to the level of a second independent variable. Interaction effects are also known as **moderator** effects. I discuss interactions in greater detail in the next section as well. For now, suffice it to say that interaction effects are often very interesting and important pieces of information for social scientists.

As I discussed in Chapter 1, research designs that involve randomly assigning participants to different groups and then comparing them on some dependent variable (i.e., **randomized controlled trials or randomized controlled study, or RCT or RCS)** are very common in a variety of disciplines, including the social sciences. In such studies, researchers often include two (or more) independent variables and examine the interactions between them. For example, Miyake et al. (2010) wanted to know whether the gender difference in college physics courses (males tend to perform better than females in college physics courses) could be reduced or eliminated by having students affirm their values at the beginning of the course. This technique, known as values affirmation, has found that some students perform better after reminding themselves what they value, or think is important, in their lives. Because women tend to perform poorly in physics classes relative to men, and because there is a negative stereotype about the ability of women in this field, the researchers hypothesized that this values affirmation would benefit women more than men. Participants were randomly divided into two groups (values affirmation vs. no values affirmation), and this was one independent variable. Gender was a second independent variable. They found that there was a significant gender by values affirmation interaction: women in the no-values-affirmation group did much worse on their exams in physics than did men in the no-values-affirmation group, on average. In contrast, the gender gap was almost completely eliminated in the values affirmation group as women in this group performed much better than did women in the no-values-affirmation condition. Factorial ANOVA is a very useful statistic for examining main effects and interaction effects in these kinds of randomized controlled studies.

Some Cautions

Just as with one-way ANOVA, when conducting a factorial ANOVA one of the assumptions is that the amount of variance within each group is roughly equal (known as **homogeneity of variance**). As discussed in the previous chapter, the ideal situation in ANOVA is to have roughly equal sample sizes in each group and a roughly equal amount of variation (e.g., the standard deviation) in each group. If the variances are not roughly equal, there can be difficulties with the probabilities associated with tests of statistical significance. These problems can be exacerbated when the groups have different sample sizes, a situation that often occurs in factorial ANOVA because the sample is being divided up into so many categories. So it is important to test whether the groups being compared have similar standard deviations.

Returning to our previous example on children's amount of television watched, suppose we have 40 boys and 40 girls in the entire sample. In addition, suppose that we have 20 children from each of the four regions in our sample. To test the main effects, these numbers are acceptable. That is, it is reasonable to compare 40 boys to 40 girls if we want to know whether boys and girls differ in their average amount of television viewing. Similarly, it is reasonable to compare 20 children from each of the four different regions of the country. But suppose that in the West, our sample of 20 children includes only 5 girls and 15 boys, whereas in the North our sample includes 15 girls and only 5 boys. When we divide up our sample by *two* independent variables, it is easy to wind up with **cell sizes** that are too small to conduct meaningful ANOVAs. A *cell* is a subset of cases representing one unique point of intersection between the independent variables. In the aforementioned example, there would be eight cells: girls from the West, boys from the West, girls from the South, boys from the South, and so on. When you consider that factorial ANOVAs can have more than two independent variables, the sample can be subdivided a number of times. Without a large initial sample, it is easy to wind up with cells that contain too few cases. As a general rule, cells that have fewer than 10 cases are too small to include in ANOVAs; cell sizes of at least 20 are preferred.

Factorial ANOVA in Depth

When dividing up the variance of a dependent variable, such as hours of television watched per week, into its component parts, there are a number of components that we can examine. In this section, we examine three of these components: main effects, interaction effects, and **simple**

effects. In addition, I also present an introduction to the idea of **partial** and **controlled effects**, an issue that is revisited in Chapter 13 on multiple regression.

Main Effects and Controlled or Partial Effects

As mentioned earlier, a factorial ANOVA will produce main effects for each independent variable in the analysis. These main effects will each have their own *F* value, and are very similar to the results that would be produced if you just conducted a one-way ANOVA for each independent variable on the dependent variable. However, there is one glorious benefit of looking at the main effects in a factorial ANOVA rather than separate one-way ANOVAs: When looking at the main effects from a factorial ANOVA, it is possible to test whether there are significant differences between the groups of one independent variable on the dependent variable while controlling for, or partialing out, the effects of the other independent variable(s) on the dependent variable. Let me clarify this confusing sentence by returning to my example of television viewing.

Suppose that when I examine whether boys and girls differ in the average amount of television they watch per week, I find that there is a significant difference: boys watch significantly more television than girls. In addition, suppose that children in the North watch, on average, more television than children in the South. Now, suppose that, in my sample of children from the northern region of the country, there are twice as many boys as girls, whereas in my sample from the South there are twice as many girls as boys. Now I've got a potential problem. How do I know whether my finding that children in the North watch more television than children in the South is not just some artifact caused by the greater proportion of boys in my northern sample? By "artifact" I mean that the North–South difference is merely a *by-product* of the difference between boys and girls; region of the country is not an important factor in and of itself. Think about it: If I already know that boys watch more television, on average, than girls, then I would *expect* my northern sample to watch more television than my southern sample because there is a greater proportion of boys in my northern sample than in the southern sample. So my question is this: How can I determine whether there is a difference in the average amount of television watched by children in the North and South *beyond* the difference caused by the unequal proportions of boys and girls in the samples from these two regions. Phrased another way, is there an effect of region on television viewing beyond or in addition to the effect of gender?

To answer this intriguing question, I must examine the main effect of region on television viewing after *controlling for,* or *partialing out,* the effect of gender. I can do this in a factorial ANOVA. To understand how this is accomplished, keep in mind that what we are trying to do with an ANOVA is to *explain* the variance in our dependent variable (amount of television children watch per week) by dividing that variance up into its component parts. If boys and girls differ in how much they watch television, then part of the variance is explained, or accounted for, by gender. In other words, we can understand a bit of the differences among children in their weekly television viewing if we know their gender. Now, once we remove that portion of the total variance that is explained by gender, we can test whether any *additional* part of the variance can be explained by knowing what region of the country the children are from. If children from the North and South *still* differ in the amount of television they watch, after *partialing out* or *controlling for* the chunk of variance explained by gender, then we know that there is a main effect of region *independent of* the effect of gender. In statistical jargon, we would say, "There is a main effect of region on amount of television watched *after controlling for the effect of gender.*" This is powerful information. In factorial ANOVA, it is possible to examine each main effect and each interaction effect when controlling for *all* other effects in the analysis. See Figure 10.1 for an illustration of two different independent variables explaining portions of variance in a dependent variable. (The notion of shared variance is explained in more detail in Chapter 13.)

Total Variance in Televison Viewing

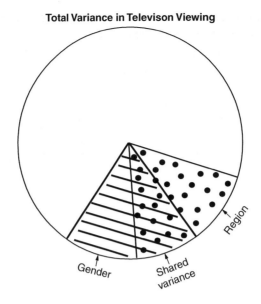

FIGURE 10.1 Partitioning the total variance in television viewing.

Interactions

A second benefit of factorial ANOVA is that it allows researchers to test whether there are any statistical interactions present. Interactions can be a complex concept to grasp. Making the whole issue even more confusing is the fact that the level of possible interactions increases as the number of independent variables increases. For example, when there are two independent variables in the analysis, there are two possible main effects and one possible two-way interaction effect (i.e., the interaction between the two independent variables). If there are three independent variables in the analysis, there are three possible main effects, three possible two-way interaction effects, and one possible three-way interaction effect. The whole analysis can get very complicated very quickly. To keep things simple, let's take a look at two-way interactions first.

In my television-viewing example, suppose that I randomly select 25 boys and 25 girls from each of the four regions of the country, measure the number of hours each child spent watching television, and calculate the averages for each group. (*Note:* Unlike the example provided earlier, there are equal numbers of boys and girls from each region in this sample.) These averages are presented in Table 10.1.

As we see when examining the means in Table 10.1, boys in the North, East, and West watch more television, on average, than girls. The overall averages by gender presented in the last column indicate that there appears to be a main effect for gender, with boys watching an average of 21 hours of television per week and girls watching an average of only 16.5 hours per week. When we look at the overall averages presented for each region (bottom row), we can see that children in the North watch more television, on average, than do children in the other three regions. Therefore, we can tell that there appear to be main effects for gender and region on amount of television watched. Notice that I said "*appear* to be main effects." To determine whether these main effects are statistically significant, we have to determine the probability of

TABLE 10.1   Mean hours of television viewed per week by gender and region

	North	East	West	South	Overall Averages by Gender
Girls	20 hrs.	13 hrs.	13 hrs.	20 hrs.	16.5 hrs.
Boys	25 hrs.	22 hrs.	22 hrs.	15 hrs.	21 hrs.
Overall Averages by Region	22.5 hrs.	17.5 hrs.	17.5 hrs.	17.5 hrs.	

obtaining differences of this size between randomly selected groups of this size (see Chapter 7 for a discussion of significance tests and their meaning).

Once we have examined the main effects, we can turn our attention to the possible interaction effects. To do this, we need to examine the means in each of the eight cells presented in Table 10.1 (i.e., northern boys, northern girls, eastern boys, eastern girls, etc.). When we examine these means, we can see that in the North, East, and West, boys watch an average of 5 to 7 more hours of television per week than do girls. But in the South, *girls* watch an average of 5 more hours of television than *boys*. Therefore, it appears that the differences in the amount of television watched by girls and boys are not uniform across the four regions of the country. In other words, the relationship between gender and amount of television watched *depends on*, or *is moderated by*, the region of the country. Because the definition of a two-way interaction is that the relationship between an independent variable and a dependent variable is moderated by a second independent variable, we appear to have a two-way interaction here.

When we find a statistically significant interaction (again, we must examine the p value of the F ratio for the interaction term to determine if it is statistically significant), we must determine the *nature* of the interaction and then *describe* the interaction. One excellent method for getting a handle on the nature of the interaction is to depict it graphically. To do this, all we need to do is to graph the means. Line graphs and column graphs work best. For the sake of comparing the two different styles of graphs, I have produced a line graph and a column graph that represent the data presented in Table 10.1. These graphs are presented in Figure 10.2.

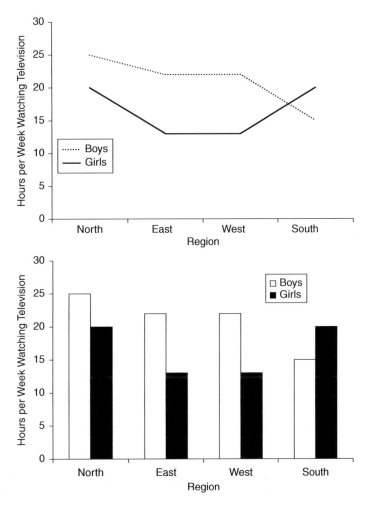

FIGURE 10.2 Interaction plot and column graph for television watching by gender and region.

When we look at these graphs, the nature of the interaction becomes readily apparent. Specifically, what we can see is that there is a consistent pattern for the relationship between gender and amount of television viewed in three of the regions (North, East, and West), but in the fourth region (South) the pattern changes. Specifically, whereas boys watched more television, on average, than girls in the North, East, and West, in the South girls watched more television than boys.

As you look at the graphs presented in Figure 10.2, notice that you can see both the main effects and the interaction effects. Recall that the main effect for gender indicates that, when we combine the scores from all four regions, boys appear to have higher average scores than girls on our dependent variable (i.e., amount of television watched per week). In Figure 10.2 this effect is clear, as we can see that the line for boys is higher than the line for girls in all three of the four regions, and the average for boys appears to be a bit higher than the average for girls when you collapse across the regions (i.e., combine the scores within each gender across the regions). We can also see evidence of a main effect for region. We see the region effect by noting that when we combine the averages for boys and girls, the average amount of television viewing is higher in the North than in the South, East or West regions. This main effect is complicated a little, however, by the presence of the interaction. Notice that whereas the mean is lower in the South than in the North for boys (supporting our main effect for region), the mean for girls in the South is equal to the mean for girls in the North. This raises a difficult question: When we say there is a main effect for region, with children in the North watching more television, on average, than children in the other three regions, are we being accurate? Similarly, when we say that there is a main effect for gender such that boys watch more television than girls, is that a misleading statement given that it is not true in the southern region?

Interpreting Main Effects in the Presence of an Interaction Effect

Researchers do not always agree on the best way to interpret main effects when there is a significant interaction effect. Some argue that it makes little sense to interpret main effects at all when there is an interaction effect present, because the interaction effect essentially modifies (or nullifies) the meaning of the main effect. In the preceding example, the main effect for region that shows that children in the North watch more television than children elsewhere is really only true within the boys' sample. In fact, girls in the South watch as much television as girls in the North, and girls in the North do not watch more television than boys in any region except the South. Therefore, some would argue that we should just describe the nature of the interaction, and not interpret the main effects. The logic of this argument is as follows: If I say that children in the North watch more television than children in other regions, the statement is misleading because it is not true for girls. To be accurate, I should just say that *boys* in the North watch more television than *boys* in other regions.

Others, myself included, think it makes sense to interpret all of the effects and to consider them in relation to each other. Returning to our earlier example, we can see that there is a main effect for gender, with boys watching more television, on average, than girls. We can also see that this effect is not present in the South, where girls watch more television than boys. In addition, we can say that overall, when we *combine* the samples of boys and girls together, there is a main effect for region such that northern children watch more television than children in other regions, on average. When we add the consideration of the interaction effect, we can further argue that this overall effect is due *primarily* to differences within the sample of boys, and less to variation within the sample of girls. It is possible to get an interaction effect without a main effect. (See Figure 10.3. In this example, boys and girls have equal means, as do children in each of the four geographic regions.) Therefore, it makes sense to report and interpret significant main effects, even in the presence of an interaction effect. The key is to provide enough information so that readers of your results can make sense of them. To do this, it may be necessary to discuss your interaction and main effects in relation to each other.

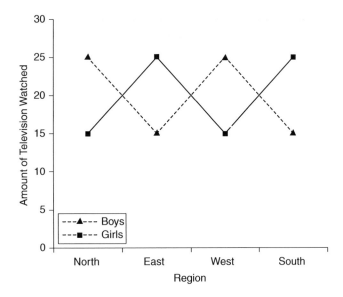

FIGURE 10.3 Interaction with equal means.

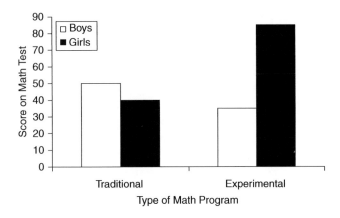

FIGURE 10.4 Interaction of gender by math program.

Here is another example to more clearly illustrate the problems of interpreting main effects in the presence of significant interactions. Suppose that I were to examine the math skills of boys and girls in two different types of mathematics programs. Students in the "Traditional" program study math in the usual way, reading a textbook and working out math problems in class. Students in the "Experimental" program work in groups to solve problems collaboratively and work with more real-world, applied problems. After one year, I give a math test to 25 randomly selected boys and 25 randomly selected girls from each math program. I calculate the averages for these four groups, which are presented in Figure 10.4.

The means presented in the figure clearly show that although boys and girls in the Traditional math program had similar average scores on the math test, girls did much better than boys in the Experimental math program. This is an interaction. In addition, because girls in the Experimental program did so well on their math test, the overall mean for the Experimental group is significantly higher than the overall mean for the Traditional group, thereby creating a main effect for math program. But does it make sense to say that students in the Experimental math program did better on the test than students in the Traditional program? Clearly, this is not the case for the boys, and some would argue that it would be misleading to point out the main effect for math program because the effect is only present for the girls, not the boys. There is not a good, clean answer to this question of how to interpret main effects in the presence of a significant interaction. My advice is to present as much of the data as you can and then clearly describe what is going on. In the example presented in Figure 10.4, I would say the following: "Students in the Experimental group scored higher on the math test, on average, than did students in the Traditional condition, but this main effect of math condition was caused by a significant gender by math condition interaction. Whereas girls in the Experimental math condition did better than girls in the Traditional math group, there was no difference for boys in each condition. So the new mathematics program appeared to work well for girls but had little effect for boys."

Testing Simple Effects

Once we have found our main and interaction effects in factorial ANOVA, we can conduct one final set of analyses to examine the simple effects. The methods used to calculate the simple effects and determine whether they are statistically significant are analogous to the post-hoc tests described in Chapter 9. What simple effects analysis allows us to do is to test whether there are significant differences in the average scores of any particular cells. One of the benefits of simple effects analysis is that it allows us to better understand some of the complexities in our data, particularly how to make sense of significant interaction effects.

Returning to our sample data presented in Figure 10.4, we can see that we have four cells: girls in the Traditional math program, boys in the Traditional program, girls in the Experimental program, and boys in the Experimental program. With a simple effects analysis, we can test whether boys in the Traditional math program ($\bar{X} = 50$) had significantly higher average math test scores than did boys in the Experimental program ($\bar{X} = 35$). We could also test whether boys and girls in the Traditional program differed significantly. Perhaps most importantly for helping us understand the interaction effect, we can test whether girls in the Experimental program had higher average math test scores than students in each of the three other groups. For a detailed description of the methods for calculating simple effects, I recommend reading Hinkle et al. (1998).

Analysis of Covariance

Earlier in this chapter, I suggested that one of the benefits of conducting factorial ANOVAs is that it allows us to determine whether groups differ on some dependent variable while controlling for, or partialing out, the effects of other independent variables. A closely related concept that applies to all types of ANOVA, including one-way, factorial, and repeated-measures, is the use of **covariates** in these analyses. In **analysis of covariance (ANCOVA)**, the idea is to test whether there are differences between groups on a dependent variable after controlling for the effects of a different variable, or set of variables. The difference between an ANCOVA and the types of controlled variance I described earlier is that with an ANCOVA, the variable(s) that we are controlling for, or partialing out the effects of, is not necessarily an independent variable. Let me explain.

In my earlier example, I was able to test whether boys and girls differed in the amount of television they watched while controlling for the effects of which region of the country they lived in (the second independent variable), as well as the interaction between the two independent variables. But in an ANCOVA analysis, we can control for the effects of variables *besides* independent variables. For example, I could use socioeconomic status (SES) as a covariate and test whether children in different regions of the country differ in the amount of television they watch *after* controlling for the effects of their SES. Suppose that my sample of children from the North is less wealthy than my samples from the three other regions. Suppose further that children from poorer families tend to watch more television than children from wealthier families. Because of this, my earlier results that found greater television watching among children in the northern region may simply be due to the fact that these children are less wealthy than children in the other regions. With ANCOVA, I can test whether the difference in the viewing habits of children from different regions is due strictly to differences in SES, or whether there are regional differences *independent* of the effects of SES. This is particularly handy because even though factorial ANOVA only allows us to use categorical (i.e., nominally scaled) independent variables, with ANCOVA we can also control for the effects of continuous (i.e., intervally scaled) variables.

Illustration of Factorial ANOVA, ANCOVA, and Effect Size with Real Data

As I did in Chapter 9, I will illustrate effect size in factorial ANOVA, along with some of the particulars about sums of squares, mean squares, and *F* values, using output from an analysis of my own data using the SPSS computer software program. I collected data from 928 high school students, some of whom were in ninth grade and some of whom were in eleventh grade. I asked these students how much they valued the work they were doing in their English classes, on a scale from 1 to 5, with lower scores indicating lower levels of value. (By "valued" I mean that they thought the work in their English class was interesting, important, and useful to them.) First, I conducted a factorial ANOVA to see whether there were differences between ninth and eleventh graders in valuing of English work (i.e., a main effect for grade level), differences between boys and girls in how much they valued English work (i.e., main effect for gender), and an interaction between grade level and gender. I also asked the SPSS program to provide measures of effect size for each main effect and the interaction effect. The results of this analysis are presented in Table 10.2.

In the first part of Table 10.2, I present the means, standard deviations, and sample sizes for each group in the study. For example, ninth-grade girls in this study had a mean of 3.7427 on the

TABLE 10.2 Summary of results for gender by grade level factorial ANOVA

Descriptive Statistics

Dependent Variable: Value of English Coursework

Gender	Grade	Mean	Std. Deviation	n
Girl	9	3.7427	.85522	296
	11	3.7337	.93071	209
	Total	3.7389	.88634	505
Boy	9	3.7531	.89887	214
	11	3.4833	.92903	209
	Total	3.6198	.92275	423
Total	9	3.7471	.87294	510
	11	3.6085	.93718	418
	Total	3.6846	.90458	928

Tests of Between-Subjects Effects

Dependent Variable: Value of English Coursework

Source	Type III Sum of Squares	df	Mean Square	F	p value	Partial Eta Squared
Corrected Model	10.979[1]	3	3.660	4.523	.004	.014
Intercept	12284.651	1	12284.651	15184.189	.000	.943
1) Gender	**3.268**	**1**	**3.268**	**4.039**	**.045**	**.004**
2) Grade level	**4.414**	**1**	**4.414**	**5.456**	**.020**	**.006**
3) Gender * Grade level	**3.861**	**1**	**3.861**	**4.772**	**.029**	**.005**
Error	747.555	924	.809			
Total	13357.500	928				
Corrected Total	758.534	927				

Note: 1 R Squared = .014 (Adjusted R Squared = .011)

Value of English Coursework measure (on a scale from 1 to 5), and there were 296 ninth-grade girls in this sample. A look at the means in this table indicates that they are quite similar for three of the groups in this study. Girls and boys in ninth grade and girls in eleventh grade all had means around 3.75 on the Value of English Coursework variable. But eleventh-grade boys had a lower mean, around 3.48. Although I can see that there are some differences among the means of my four samples, to see whether these differences are significant I need to look at the ANOVA results presented in the lower portion of Table 10.2.

Turning our attention to the ANOVA results, there are a number of important features to notice. In the far left column titled "Source," there are the various *sources* of variation in our dependent variable, Value of English Coursework. These are the different ways that the variance of the dependent variable is divided up by the independent variables. The first source is called the "Corrected Model." This is the combination of all of the main and interaction effects. If covariates were used, these effects would be included in the "Corrected Model" statistics. Reading from left to right, we can see that the full model has a sum of squares (10.979), which when divided by three degrees of freedom ("*df*") produces a "Mean Square" of 3.660. When we divide this by the mean square error a few rows down ($MS_e = .809$), we get an *F* value of 4.523. This has a *p* value of .004. Because this value is less than .05 (see Chapter 7), the overall model is statistically significant. But is it *practically* significant? In the final column labeled "Eta Squared," we can see that the overall model accounts for only 1.4 percent of the variance in Value of English Coursework scores. In other words, gender, grade level, and the interaction of these two *combined* only explain 1.4 percent of the variance. Although this is *statistically* significant, this may not be a big enough effect size to be considered *practically* significant. Remember that statistical significance is influenced by sample size, and 928 cases is a pretty large sample. An effect size of .014, in contrast, is not affected by sample size and may therefore be a better indicator of practical significance.

In addition to the *F* value, *p* value, and effect size for the entire model, SPSS prints out statistics for each of the main effects as well as the interaction effect. In the table, I have highlighted these results using bold font and numbered them 1, 2, and 3. Here we can see that there is a statistically significant main effect for gender (1), revealing that the overall means for boys and girls on Value of English Coursework differ ($F = 4.039$, $p = .045$). But the effect size of .004 is very small. By looking at the overall means for girls and boys in the top portion of Table 10.2, we can see that boys ($\bar{X}_{boys} = 3.6198$) have slightly lower average Value of English School work than girls ($\bar{X}_{girls} = 3.7389$). The main effect for grade level (2) is also statistically significant ($F = 5.456$, $p = .020$). Again, the effect size is quite small (eta squared = .006). On average, ninth-grade students valued English coursework more than eleventh-grade students. The gender by grade level interaction (3) was also statistically significant ($F = 4.772$, $p = .023$) and has a tiny effect size (eta squared = .005). Overall, then, the statistics presented in Table 10.2 reveal that there are statistically significant main effects for gender and grade level on Value of English Coursework, as well as an interaction of gender by grade level. Although the overall model is statistically significant, these effect sizes are quite small and indicate that gender, grade level, and their interaction do not explain very much of the variance in Value of English Coursework.

There are two other features of the SPSS output presented in Table 10.2 worth noting. First, the sum of squares that SPSS uses by default in a factorial ANOVA is called the "Type III" sum of squares. This means that when SPSS calculates the sum of squares for a particular effect, it does so by accounting for the other effects in the model. So when the sum of squares for the gender effect is calculated, for example, the effect of grade level and the gender by grade level interaction effects have been partialed out already. This allows us to determine the *unique* effect of each main effect and interaction effect. Second, notice that the *F* value for each effect is obtained by dividing the mean square for that effect by the mean square error. This is the same way that *F* values were calculated in one-way ANOVA discussed in Chapter 9.

 To watch a video describing how to read and interpret the SPSS output from a factorial ANOVA analysis, please refer to the website that accompanies this book.

TABLE 10.3   SPSS results for gender by grade level factorial ANCOVA

Tests of Between-Subjects Effects

Dependent Variable: Value of English Coursework

Source	Type III Sum of Squares	df	Mean Square	F	Sig.	Partial Eta Squared
Corrected Model	16.420¹	4	4.105	5.105	.000	.022
Intercept	1922.153	1	1922.153	2390.665	.000	.721
1) Grade in English	**5.441**	**1**	**5.441**	**6.767**	**.009**	**.007**
2) Gender	**2.288**	**1**	**2.288**	**2.846**	**.092**	**.003**
3) Grade Level	**4.660**	**1**	**4.660**	**5.796**	**.016**	**.006**
4) Gender * Grade Level	**3.935**	**1**	**3.935**	**4.894**	**.027**	**.005**
Error	742.114	923	.804			
Total	13357.500	928				
Corrected Total	758.534	927				

Note: 1 R Squared = .022 (Adjusted R Squared = .017)

These results presented in Table 10.2 made me wonder whether the gender differences I found were due to differences in performance. After all, girls tend to do better in English classes than boys, and how well one performs can certainly influence how much he or she values the task. Maybe girls value English more than boys because they perform better in English. So I performed a new analysis using the SPSS statistical software program, this time controlling for (i.e., partialing out) the effects of performance in English, as measured by the grades students received in their English courses. The results of this analysis, as presented by the SPSS program, are given in Table 10.3. I have highlighted some important effects of this ANCOVA in bold and numbered them. First, notice that the covariate in this example, grade in English (1), is statistically significant ($p < .01$), and has the largest effect size (eta squared = .007) of any of the variables in the model. This tells us that the grades students received in their English class are significantly related to how much they valued the work in English. Second, the main effect for gender (2) is no longer statistically significant once the covariate is in the model. In other words, the difference between boys and girls in how much they valued English coursework was explained by how well they performed in their English classes. Finally, notice that the addition of the covariate did not eliminate the significant main effect of grade level (3) nor the significant interaction between gender and grade level (4).

Example: Performance, Choice, and Public vs. Private Evaluation

In a study published in 1987, Jerry Burger, a psychology professor at Santa Clara University, examined the effects of choice and public vs. private evaluation on college students' performance on an anagram-solving task. This experiment involved one dependent variable and two independent, categorical variables. The dependent variable was the number of anagrams solved by participants in a two-minute period. One of the independent variables was whether participants were able to choose the type of test they would perform. There were 55 participants in the study. About half of these were randomly assigned into the "choice" group. This group was told that they could choose one test to perform from a group of three different tests. The "no choice" group was told that they would be randomly assigned one of the tests. In fact, the "choice" and "no choice" groups worked on the same tests, but the choice group was given the perception that they had chosen the type of test they would work on. So this first independent variable has two categories: choice and no choice. The second independent variable also had two categories: public vs. private. Participants were told either that their test score and ranking would be read aloud along with their name (the public condition), or that the test scores and ranks would be read aloud without identifying the name of the test taker (the private

TABLE 10.4   Mean number of anagrams solved for four treatment groups

	Public		Private	
	Choice	No Choice	Choice	No Choice
Number of Anagrams Solved	19.50	14.86	14.92	15.36

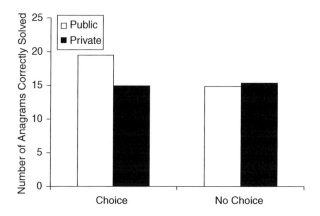

FIGURE 10.5   Interaction of choice by public vs. private evaluation.

condition). Participants were randomly assigned to the public or private groups as well. The resulting ANOVA model for this experiment is a 2 (choice vs. no choice) × 2 (public vs. private feedback) factorial ANOVA.

The average numbers of anagrams solved by the members of each group are presented in Table 10.4. These means are also graphed in Figure 10.5. Burger found a main effect for the choice independent variable, such that participants who thought they were given a choice of which type of test to take solved more anagrams, on average, than those who were not given a choice. In addition, Burger found that participants in the public evaluation condition solved more anagrams, on average, than participants in the private feedback condition. This is a second significant main effect. Finally, he found an interaction between the two independent variables. If you look closely at the means in Table 10.4 and in Figure 10.5, you can see that three of the four groups have very similar means. Only the public/choice group appears to have solved a significantly greater number of anagrams than did students in the other three groups. I could conduct a test of simple effects to determine whether students in the public/choice group scored significantly higher than students in the public/no-choice group.

In this example, the presence of a significant interaction raises questions about how to interpret our statistically significant main effects. Notice that Burger found a main effect for choice, with students in the two choice groups *combined* solving more anagrams, on average, than students in the two no-choice groups *combined*. The problem here is that we can see that students in the private/choice group did not score higher than students in the private/no-choice group, and had very similar scores to students in the public/no-choice group. Therefore, this main effect for choice vs. no choice is caused entirely by the relatively high scores of the public/choice group. So when Burger states that participants solved more anagrams on average when they were given a choice than did participants who had no choice, he must carefully point out that this is only true for students in the public condition. Similarly, the main effect for public over private is also caused solely by the high scores of the public/choice group. By noting that there is a significant interaction of the two independent variables, Burger is in effect telling his readers that they must interpret the main effects very carefully. If we were to simply conclude that students perform better when given a choice, or when their performance is made public, we would miss the intricacy of the story.

Burger's study also provides a good example of the importance of *interpreting* statistical results, and the important role that theory plays in the interpretation. In his study, Burger found that when participants believed they had a choice in the task they completed, their performance improved, but only when participants thought their choice and their performance would be made known to others (i.e., the public condition). But why would this be? Burger's hypothesis was that when people are given the opportunity to choose what they work on, they may also feel an increased sense of responsibility to perform well on the task. After all, if they had the power to choose the task, they had better do well on it. But this added responsibility to perform well on a chosen task is only present if others know that the individual got to choose the task, and that the performance on the task would also be made public. Burger's idea that this heightened concern among participants for how they would be perceived by others who knew that participants got to choose their own tasks would lead to increased effort and performance on the task was supported by his results. In the world of research, the interpretation of what the statistics mean (i.e., why the results turned out as they did) is just as important as the statistics themselves. As I often say to my students, people often agree on the statistical results (e.g., whether a *t* value or an *F* value is statistically significant). The really interesting discussions (and disagreements) are about *why* the statistical results occurred as they did.

Writing it Up

When writing up the results of a factorial ANOVA for publication, it is important to mention all of the main and interaction effects, along with the relevant *F* values and degrees of freedom (*df*) for each. For example, if we were to write up the results of the Burger (1987) study described above, we might write the following: "We performed a 2 (choice vs. no choice) × 2 (public vs. private) factorial ANOVA to examine the main effects and interaction effects of choice and context on the number of anagrams correctly solved. This analysis revealed a significant main effect for the choice condition ($F_{(1,51)}$ = 12.72, p < .001) and for the public–private condition ($F_{(1,51)}$ = 14.10, p < .001). Students in the public condition (*M* = 17.17) solved more anagrams, on average, than did students in the private condition (*M* = 15.15), and students in the choice condition (*M* = 17.20) solved more anagrams than participants in the no-choice condition (*M* = 15.11), on average. These main effects were moderated by the presence of a significant interaction effect ($F_{(1,51)}$ = 17.62, p < .001). The means for each group are presented in Table 10.4 and Figure 10.5. They reveal that participants in the public/choice condition solved more anagrams, on average, than did participants in the other three conditions, and the other three conditions did not differ substantially in the number of anagrams solved."

Wrapping Up and Looking Forward

In this chapter we were able to extend what we learned about ANOVA in Chapter 9 in three important ways. First, we added the concept of *multiple independent variables*. By having more than one independent variable in the model, we are able to more finely divide up, and explain, the variance in the dependent variable. Second, we examined the concept of *controlling* or *partialing out* the effects of other variables in the model, including covariates, to get a better picture of the *unique* relation between an independent and a dependent variable. Finally in this chapter, we considered the importance of statistical interactions. All three of these concepts provide a hint of the amazing power of many different statistical techniques to explore the relations among variables. In the social sciences, as in most fields, variables are related to each other in very complex ways. We live in a complex world. Although *t* tests and one-way ANOVA are useful statistical techniques, they are often unable to examine the most interesting questions in the social sciences. It is the messy world of interactions, shared variance, and multiple predictors that make the statistical life a life worth living. So although the concepts in these last few chapters may seem a bit more difficult than those discussed earlier in the book, they pay rich dividends when finally understood. In the next chapter, we enter the complex yet particularly interesting world of repeated-measures ANOVA.

Work Problems

Because the details of how to calculate the statistics for a factorial ANOVA are not presented in this chapter, I cannot ask you to calculate your own statistics using raw data, as I have in previous chapters. Instead, I present the output tables from a factorial ANOVA that I have conducted using the SPSS statistical software and will ask you to interpret the results of this analysis.

The data presented in Tables 10.5 and 10.6 come from a study I conducted several years ago with a sample of high school students. In this study, I asked students to report their gender and also to tell me in which country they were born and in which country their mothers were born. From this second question I created a variable called "generation." Students who were born in the United States to mothers who were also born in the U.S. are "3+" generation because their families have been in the U.S. for at least three generations (i.e., the student, the student's mother, and the mother's mother all lived in the U.S.). Students who were born in the U.S. to mothers who were born outside of the U.S. are 2nd generation, and students born outside of the U.S. are

TABLE 10.5 Descriptive statistics for GPA by gender and generation

Dependent Variable: Cumulative GPA

Generation	Gender	Mean	Std. Deviation	n
3+ Gen.	Girl	2.80	1.21	143
	Boy	2.63	1.52	106
	Total	2.73	1.35	249
2nd Gen.	Girl	3.06	1.00	206
	Boy	2.76	.92	189
	Total	2.92	.98	395
1st Gen.	Girl	3.18	.75	116
	Boy	2.99	.80	77
	Total	3.10	.77	193
Total	Girl	3.01	1.03	465
	Boy	2.77	1.11	372
	Total	2.90	1.07	837

TABLE 10.6 Summary statistics for the factorial ANOVA with gender, generation, and the gender by generation interaction effects on GPA

Source	Type III Sum of Squares	df	Mean Square	F	Sig.	Partial Eta Squared
Corrected Model	27865418.736[1]	5	5573083.747	4.929	.000	.029
Intercept	6318381546.677	1	6318381546.677	5588.057	.000	.871
Generation	14751468.548	2	7375734.274	6.523	.002	.015
Gender	8953089.504	1	8953089.504	7.918	.005	.009
Generation * Gender	781668.532	2	390834.266	.346	.708	.001
Error	939606563.822	831	1130693.819			
Total	8047918449.299	837				
Corrected Total	967471982.557	836				

Note: 1 R Squared = .029 (Adjusted R Squared = .023)

1st generation. I also collected students' cumulative grade point averages (GPAs) from school records. Using this information, the information presented in Tables 10.5 and 10.6, and information presented earlier in this chapter, try to answer the following questions.

1. Just looking at the means presented in Table 10.5, predict whether there will be statistically significant main effects for gender and generation and a significant interaction between the two.
2. Based on the summary statistics in Table 10.6, is the difference between the GPAs of boys and girls statistically significant?
3. Based on the summary statistics in Table 10.6, what is the effect size for the main effect of generation? What does this effect size tell you?
4. Is there a statistically significant interaction between gender and generation on GPA?
5. Using the degrees of freedom for generation and for error and the values in Appendix C, what is the critical value for F if the alpha level is .05?

 For a brief video explaining how to read and interpret Appendix C, please refer to the website that accompanies this book.

6. Combining the information for the three main tests of effects (i.e., main effects for gender and generation, interaction effect for gender × generation), write a sentence that summarizes these tests of statistical significance.
7. How much of the variance in GPA is explained by gender, generation, and their interaction combined?

 For answers to these work problems, and for additional work problems on factorial ANOVA, please refer to the website that accompanies this book.

Repeated-Measures Analysis of Variance

One type of *t* test discussed in Chapter 8 was the paired *t* test. One type of study in which a paired *t* test would be used is when we have two scores for a single group on a single measure. For example, if we had a group of third-grade students and we gave them a test of their math abilities at the beginning of the school year and again at the end of the school year, we would have one group (third graders) with two scores on one measure (the math test). In this situation, we could also use a **repeated-measures analysis of variance (ANOVA)** to test whether students' scores on the math test were different at the beginning and end of the academic year.

Repeated-measures ANOVA has a number of advantages over paired *t* (i.e., dependent *t*) tests, however. First, with repeated-measures ANOVA, we can examine differences on a dependent variable that has been measured at more than two time points, whereas with a dependent *t* test we can only compare scores on a dependent variable from two time points. Second, as discussed in Chapter 10 on factorial ANOVA, with repeated-measures ANOVA we can control for the effects of one or more covariates, thereby conducting a repeated-measures analysis of covariance (ANCOVA). Third, in repeated-measures ANOVA, we can also include one or more independent categorical, or **group variables**. This type of mixed model is a particularly useful technique and is discussed in some detail later in the chapter.

When to Use Each Type of Repeated-Measures Technique

The most basic form of a repeated-measures ANOVA occurs when there is a single group (e.g., third graders) with two scores (e.g., beginning of the year, end of the year) on a single dependent variable (e.g., a mathematics test). This is a very common model that is often used in simple laboratory experiments. For example, suppose I want to know whether drinking alcohol affects the reaction times of adults when driving. I could take a group of 50 adults and test their stop reaction times by flashing a red light at each one of them when they are driving and measuring how long it takes for each one to apply the brakes. After calculating the average amount of time it takes this group to apply the brakes when sober, I could then ask each member of my group to consume two alcoholic drinks and then again test their reaction time when driving, using the same methods. In this example, I've got one group (50 adults) with two scores on one dependent variable (reaction time when driving). After the second measure of reaction time, I could ask each of my participants to consume two more alcoholic drinks and again test their reaction time. Now I've got three measures of reaction time that I can use in my repeated-measures ANOVA. Notice that my dependent variable is always the same measure (reaction time), and my group is always the same (sample of 50 adults). The results of my repeated-measures ANOVA will tell me whether, on average, there are differences in the reaction times across my three trials. If there are, I might logically conclude that drinking alcohol affects reaction time, although there may be other explanations for my results (e.g., my participants may be getting tired or bored with the experiment, they may

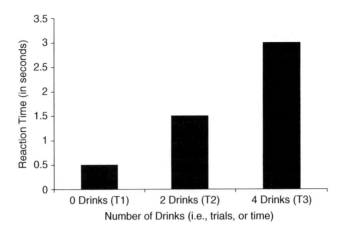

FIGURE 11.1 Driving reaction times over three trials with increasing numbers of drinks.

be getting used to the test situation, etc.). The average reaction times for my sample at three time points (i.e., after no drinks, 2 drinks, and 4 drinks) are presented in Figure 11.1.

In a slightly more advanced form of the reaction time test, I could include a covariate. In the previous example, suppose that I found the reaction time was fastest when my participants were sober, a bit slower after two drinks, and a lot slower after four drinks. Suppose that I publish these results and the national beer, wine, and liquor companies become worried that, because of my study, people will stop drinking their products for fear of getting in automobile accidents. These producers of alcoholic drinks begin to criticize my study. They suggest that because equal amounts of alcohol generally have greater effects on those who weigh less than on heavier people, my results may have been skewed by the effects of alcohol on the lighter people in my study. "Although the effects of two alcoholic drinks may impair the reaction times of lighter people, even four alcoholic drinks will not impair the reaction times of heavier people" said the United Alcohol Makers of America (a fictitious group).

Stung by the criticism of the UAMA, I decide to replicate my study, but this time I use weight as a covariate. Again, I measure participants' reaction times when driving completely sober, after two alcoholic drinks, and after four alcoholic drinks. In addition, this time I weigh each of my participants. Now when I analyze my data, I include my weight covariate. I find that, after controlling, or partialing out, the effects of weight, the difference in the average reaction times of participants before they have any drinks and after they have two drinks is reduced slightly compared with the results I got before I included the weight covariate, but after four drinks my participants reacted more slowly, on average, than they did after zero or two drinks (Figure 11.2). These results suggest that drinking may increase the reaction times of lighter people more than

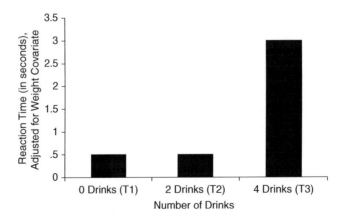

FIGURE 11.2 Driving reaction times over three trials, controlling for the weight of the individuals in the sample.

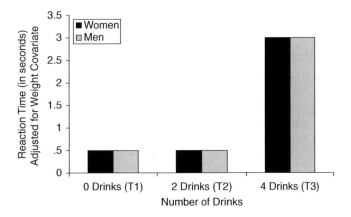

FIGURE 11.3 Driving reaction times over three trials by gender, controlling for weight.

heavier people after only two drinks, but it seems to impair the reaction times of people, regardless of weight, after four drinks. (Please keep in mind that these results are fictional. It is never a good idea to drive after having two drinks, whatever your weight or gender.)

Still bothered by my results, the UAMA suggests that my results are skewed because I did not look at the effects of drinking on reaction time separately for men and women. "Women are more dramatically affected by alcohol than men, regardless of weight," claims the UAMA. They argue that although consuming four alcoholic drinks may slow the reaction times of women, it will not have an effect on heavy men. Though I am dubious of the argument that heavy men should have their rights to drink and drive protected, in the name of science I decide to conduct one final study. In this study, again with 50 adults (25 women and 25 men) of various weights, I again test their reaction times while driving after zero, two, and four alcoholic drinks. Now I've got one dependent variable (reaction time) measured at three time points, one covariate (weight), and one independent group variable (gender of participant). Notice that although number of drinks is technically an independent variable, it is *not* a categorical, or group, variable. In other words, I do not have three independent groups (the zero-drinks group, the two-drinks group, and the four-drinks group). Rather, I have three *dependent,* or repeated, measures of the same dependent variable, reaction time.

When I examine the results of my study, I find that, after controlling for the effects of my covariate (weight), there is still a small difference in reaction time measured after zero and two drinks, and still a much slower reaction time, on average, after four drinks. In addition, I find no interaction between gender and number of drinks on reaction time. This tells me that *both* men and women have slower reaction times after four drinks, regardless of their weight (see Figure 11.3).

To summarize, my three different repeated-measures ANOVAs produced the following results. The first one found that adults' reaction times while driving were slower, on average, after two drinks, and slower still after four drinks. My second test included the covariate of weight, and I found that when we control for the effects of weight, the difference in reaction time between zero and two drinks is reduced, but reaction time becomes much slower after four drinks. Finally, in my third analysis, I examined whether changes in reaction time after two and four drinks, when controlling for weight, were different for men and women. I found that they were not. These three analyses provide a snapshot of how repeated-measures ANOVA works and what information it can provide. Now let's take a closer look.

Repeated-Measures ANOVA in Depth

Repeated-measures ANOVA is governed by the same general principles as all ANOVA techniques. As with one-way ANOVA and factorial ANOVA, in repeated-measures ANOVA we are concerned with dividing up the variance in the dependent variable. Recall that in a one-way ANOVA, we separated the total variance in the dependent variable into two parts: that attributable to differences between the groups, and that attributable to differences among individuals in the same group (a.k.a. the **error variance**). In a repeated-measures ANOVA with no independent group variable, we are still interested in the error variance. However, we also want to find out how much of the total variance can be attributed to **time**, or **trial**, that is, how much of the total variance in the dependent variable is attributable to differences *within individuals* across the times they were measured on the dependent variable.

Consider an example. Suppose that I am interested in examining whether a group of students increase their knowledge and skills from one academic year to the next. To do this, I give my sample a standardized vocabulary test (with a possible range of 1 to 100), once when they are finishing third grade and again when they are finishing fourth grade. When I do this, suppose I get the data presented in Table 11.1.

For each of the 10 cases in Table 11.1, we have two test scores, giving us a total of 20 scores in the table. We could find an average for these 20 scores combined, a standard deviation, and a variance. The variance that we calculated for these 20 scores would represent the total variance in the dependent measure. In repeated-measures ANOVA, we want to try to partition this total variance into different pieces. In the most basic form of repeated-measures ANOVA, there are two ways that we can slice up this variance. First, there is the portion of variance that is attributable to differences among the individual cases in their scores on the dependent variable (i.e., test scores). These differences among individuals within a sample are considered **random variance**, and are called error variance in ANOVA.

In repeated-measures ANOVA, this error variance can be further divided into two parts. First, there is the usual random variation in the scores of different cases within the same sample. But there is also variability in the scores of *individuals* within samples on two or more variables. For example, in the first case in Table 11.1, the student has a score of 40 in the vocabulary test at Time 1 and a score of 60 at Time 2. As Figure 11.4 clearly shows, some subjects had large increases in their test scores from Time 1 to Time 2 (e.g., Subjects 1, 8, 9, and 10), whereas others had more modest increases, one had no change (Subject 2), and one actually had a lower score at Time 2 (Subject 5). In other words, the size of the increase in test score from third to fourth grade depends on which subject we are looking at. This variability within *individual* cases across different times of measurement is another source of variance that is accounted for in repeated-measures ANOVA.

What we are really interested in when we conduct a basic repeated-measures ANOVA is whether there is a substantial portion of the total variance that is attributable to changes in scores on the dependent variable within all of the individuals in the sample, on average. An important source of variation in the scores involves the **within-subject variance**, or differences, between Time 1 and Time 2 scores. As we can see by looking at the scores in Table 11.1, it appears that

TABLE 11.1 Vocabulary test scores at two time points

Case Number	Test Score, Time 1 (Third Grade)	Test Score, Time 2 (Fourth Grade)
1	40	60
2	55	55
3	60	70
4	40	45
5	75	70
6	80	85
7	65	75
8	40	60
9	20	35
10	45	60
Trial (or Time) Average	$\overline{X} = 52$	$\overline{X} = 61.5$

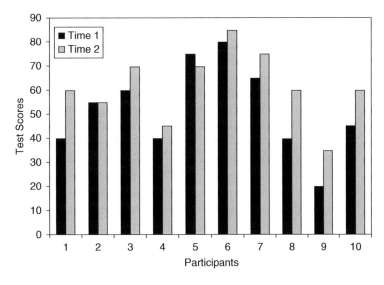

FIGURE 11.4 Time 1 and Time 2 test scores.

students, on average, had different scores on the vocabulary test at Time 1 than they did at Time 2. These intra-individual, or within-subject, differences between Time 1 and Time 2 scores can be seen more easily in the graph presented in Figure 11.4. These intra-individual changes reflect differences, or variance, *within each individual,* and are therefore called within-subjects effects. What we are interested in is whether, on average, individuals' scores were different at Time 1 (in third grade) than they were at Time 2 (in fourth grade). Notice that we are asking whether there were differences in the scores between Time 1 and Time 2 *on average.* If the scores of some of the cases went up from Time 1 to Time 2, but the scores of other cases went down by the same amount, then these changes would cancel each other out, and there would be no *average* difference between the Time 1 and Time 2 scores. But if the scores either went up or down on average between Time 1 and Time 2, then we could say that some of the total variation can be attributable to within-subject differences across time. A look at the scores in Table 11.1 and Figure 11.4 reveals that scores *appear* to increase from Time 1 to Time 2. To examine whether there are differences in the average scores across time, all we need to do is calculate the average score for each time and find the difference between these average scores and the overall average. In Table 11.1, we can see that the average score for Time 1 is 52, and the average score for Time 2 is 61.5. So we can see that there is some variance in the average scores at the two times (i.e., third and fourth grade), suggesting that there may be a within-subjects effect.

Using these three sources of variance, we can then calculate an F ratio and determine whether there are statistically significant differences in the average scores at Time 1 and at Time 2. To do this, we divide the **mean square for the differences between the trials**, or time, averages (MS_T) by the **mean square for the subject by trial interaction** ($MS_{s \times T}$). This subject by trial interaction refers to differences among individuals in how much their scores changed on the dependent variable over time, or trial (e.g., Time 1 to Time 2). The degrees of freedom for the F ratio is the number of trials minus 1 ($T - 1$) and ($T - 1$)($S - 1$), where S represents the number of subjects in the sample. What we get when we calculate this F ratio is an answer to the following question: How large is the difference between the average scores at Time 1 and Time 2 relative to (i.e., divided by) the average amount of variation among subjects in their change from Time 1 to Time 2? Because differences in the rate of change across time are just considered random fluctuations among individuals, this F ratio, like all F ratios, is a measure of *systematic* variance in scores divided by *random* variance in scores. (*Note:* For a more detailed discussion of these sources of variance, including how to calculate the sum of squares for each source, see Glass and Hopkins, 1996.)

TABLE 11.2 Summary of repeated-measures ANOVA results comparing test scores at two time points

	Sum of Squares	df	Mean Squares	F Value	Partial Eta Squared
Within-Subject Effects (Time)	451.25	1	451.25	13.05[1]	.59
Error	311.25	9	34.58		

Note: 1 indicates $p < .01$

Using the data presented in Table 11.1, I calculated a repeated-measures ANOVA using the SPSS statistics software program. I have summarized the results of the analyses in Table 11.2. In this simple form of repeated-measures ANOVA, the variance in our dependent variable—test scores—is divided into two parts: the part that is attributable to differences in test scores, on average, at the two time points, and error. Recall that, on average, there was an increase of 9.5 points on the vocabulary test from Time 1 to Time 2. This difference has an F value of 13.05, and this F value is statistically significant at $p < .01$ level. The eta square reported in this table is a measure of effect size, and it reveals that 59 percent of the variance in test scores is explained by time. In other words, changes within subjects in their test scores from Time 1 to Time 2 (i.e., third grade to fourth grade) had a large effect size. Given that we are measuring growth in vocabulary between the end of third grade and the end of fourth grade, and that this is typically a period of rapid vocabulary growth in children, we would expect to find a large change in vocabulary test scores within individuals during this year of school.

In this most basic form of repeated-measures ANOVA, notice that what we are primarily concerned with is whether there is a systematic pattern of differences *within individuals*, or *subjects*, in the scores on the dependent variable measured at two time points. Also notice that if we had three points of data (e.g., test scores from third, fourth, and fifth grades), our question would remain the same: Is there a pattern of differences in the scores *within subjects* over time? Keep in mind that when I say "a pattern" or "a systematic pattern," I mean *on average*. So, to rephrase the question, a simple repeated-measures ANOVA can help us detect whether, *on average*, scores differ *within subjects* across multiple points of data collection on the dependent variable. This type of simple repeated-measures ANOVA is sometimes referred to as a **within-subjects design**.

Repeated-Measures Analysis of Covariance (ANCOVA)

A slightly more complicated form of repeated-measures ANOVA can be produced by adding one or more covariates to the model. As discussed earlier in this chapter, as well as in Chapter 10 on factorial ANOVA, covariates can be used to partial out some portion of the variance in the dependent variable. I illustrate how this works by returning to the example data presented in Table 11.1.

One could argue that the results of my repeated-measures ANOVA were skewed by the scores of the more intelligent students in my sample. Although the students in my sample scored higher on the vocabulary test at the end of fourth grade (Time 2) than they did at the end of third grade (Time 1), we must keep in mind that the change in scores over time represents an *average* change. Some students in my sample improved quite a bit over time, whereas others did not improve at all, and one (Subject 5) actually declined. So it is possible that this overall average improvement over time was caused by large increases among the brightest students. To explore this hypothesis, I conduct a new repeated-measures ANOVA, but this time I include a covariate: IQ test scores. The results of this ANCOVA analysis are summarized in Table 11.3.

When I conduct my repeated-measures ANCOVA, I now have three ways of partitioning the total variance in my vocabulary test scores. First, there is the portion of variance that is accounted for by my covariate, IQ test scores. If students' IQ test scores are related to (i.e., correlated with) their vocabulary test scores, then the IQ test scores will explain, or account for, some percentage of the variance in students' vocabulary test scores (see Chapter 13 for a more thorough

TABLE 11.3 Summary of repeated-measures ANCOVA results comparing test scores at two time points, controlling for IQ

	Sum of Squares	df	Mean Squares	F Value	Partial Eta Squared
Covariate Effects (IQ) [1]	1343.31	1	1343.231	3.25	.29
Within-Subject Effects (Time)	27.10	1	27.10	.72	.08
Time × IQ Interaction	11.42	1	11.42	.60	.04
Error	299.83	8	37.48		

Note: 1 indicates that the covariate is a between-subjects effect

explanation of this concept of shared variance). As you can see in Table 11.3, the partial eta squared for my IQ covariate is .29. This indicates that students' IQ explains a substantial portion of the variance in their vocabulary test scores. Second, after partialing out the portion of variance attributable to IQ test scores, I can see whether any of the remaining variance in vocabulary test scores is accounted for by *changes* in vocabulary test scores from third to fourth grade. In other words, once we control for the effects of IQ test scores, do the scores of my sample change significantly from Time 1 (third grade) to Time 2 (fourth grade), on average? Looking at Table 11.3, we can see that the within-subjects effect of time now has a partial eta squared of only .08. If you recall that without the covariate, the partial eta squared for time was .59, it is clear that the addition of the IQ covariate greatly reduced the amount of variance in vocabulary test scores that was explained by time. Next, in Table 11.3, are the results for the time by IQ interaction. This tests whether changes in vocabulary test scores over time vary depending on the IQ levels of the students. The non-significant *F* value and small partial eta squared indicate that this interaction did not explain much of the variance in vocabulary test scores. Finally, after accounting for the variance in vocabulary test scores that is attributable to the covariate (i.e., IQ test scores) and the within-subjects effects (i.e., time and the time × IQ interaction), there will still be some variance in vocabulary test scores that is not explained. This is **error variance**, which is essentially the same as the **random variance** that we normally find between different members of the same sample. Figure 11.5 displays how the variance in the dependent variable, vocabulary test scores, is partitioned among the within-subject independent variable, the covariate, the interaction between IQ and Time, and the error variance.

To reiterate, when a covariate (or several covariates) are added to the repeated-measures ANOVA model, they are simply included to "soak up" a portion of the variance in the dependent variable. Then, we can see whether there are any within-subject differences in the scores on the dependent variable, when *controlling for*, or *partialing out*, that portion of the variance accounted for by the covariate(s). In the example we have been using, the addition of the IQ score covariate allows us to answer this question: Do students' vocabulary test scores change, on average, from

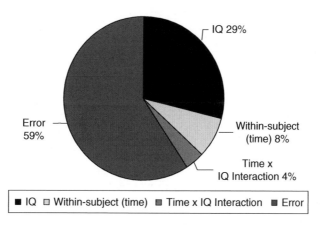

FIGURE 11.5 Partitioning of variance of vocabulary test scores.

third to fourth grade *independently* of their IQ scores? Phrased another way, we can ask whether, when controlling for IQ, students' vocabulary test scores change from third to fourth grade. According to our results, the answer is "No, not much."

Adding an Independent Group Variable

Now that we have complicated matters a bit by adding a covariate to the model, let's finish the job by adding an independent categorical, or *group* variable. Suppose, for example, that my 10 cases listed in Table 11.1 included an equal number of boys and girls. This two-level independent variable may allow us to divvy up the variance in our dependent variable even more, but only if there are differences in the scores of boys and girls.

There are two ways that this independent group variable may explain variance in vocabulary test scores. First, boys and girls may simply differ in their average scores on the vocabulary test. Suppose that when we divide the scores in Table 11.1 by gender, we get the results presented in Table 11.4. If the data were aligned in this way, we would find that at Time 1, the average score on the vocabulary test was 35 for boys and 67 for girls. Similarly, at Time 2, the average score for boys was 52 while for girls it was 71. At both Time 1 and Time 2, boys appear to have lower average scores on the vocabulary test than girls. Therefore, there appears to be a *main effect* for gender. Because this main effect represents a difference between groups of cases in the study, this type of effect is called a **between-groups** or **between-subjects** main effect. In other words, some of the variance in vocabulary test scores can be explained by knowing the group (i.e., gender) to which the student belongs.

The second way that my independent group variable can explain some of the variance in my dependent variable is through an interaction effect. If I were to graph the means for boys and girls at both time points, I would get an interesting picture. As we can see in Figure 11.6, the main effect for gender is clear. In addition, it is also clear that there is a within-subjects effect, because both boys and girls have higher scores at Time 2 than they did at Time 1.

But what also becomes clear in Figure 11.6 is that the *amount* of change from Time 1 to Time 2 appears to be greater for boys than for girls. Whereas the average score for girls increased 4 points from third to fourth grade, it grew 17 points for boys. These different amounts of change represent another source of explained variance in vocabulary test scores: the interaction of the within-subjects effect with the *between-subjects* effect. In other words, there appears to be a gender (i.e., between-subjects) by time (i.e., within-subjects) interaction on vocabulary test scores. Note that questions about how to interpret the main effect in the presence of a statistically

TABLE 11.4 Vocabulary test scores at two time points, divided by gender

Case Number	Test Score, Time 1 (Third Grade)	Test Score, Time 2 (Fourth Grade)
Boys		
9	20	35
4	30	45
8	40	60
1	40	60
10	45	60
	Mean = 35	Mean = 52
Girls		
2	55	55
3	60	70
7	65	75
5	75	70
6	80	85
	Mean = 67	Mean = 71

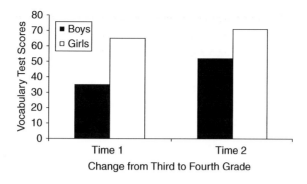

FIGURE 11.6 Gender by time interaction on vocabulary test scores.

significant interaction arise here, just as they did in our discussions of interactions in factorial ANOVAs (Chapter 10). In our current example, the main, within-subjects effect for time (i.e., that test scores went up from Time 1 to Time 2) may be due primarily to the large increase in scores for boys. So it may be misleading to say simply that students' scores increase with time (i.e., the main effect) without also noting that the time by gender interaction reveals a large increase for boys but only a modest increase for girls in test scores over time.

When I ran the repeated-measures ANCOVA with the between-groups variable of gender, I got the results summarized in Table 11.5. If you look down near the bottom of this table, you will see that the main effect for gender, which is a between-subjects effect, is statistically significant and explains a lot of the variance in vocabulary test scores. (You may also notice that the between-subjects effects and the within-subjects effects have their own error variances.) Because this between-subjects effect for gender is quite strong, it reduces the strength of the effects of other variables in the model, such as IQ (the covariate) and time. But the addition of gender also produced a statistically significant time by gender interaction effect. As we suspected when we examined the means in Table 11.4, the change in vocabulary scores from Time 1 to Time 2 differed for boys and girls, and this difference was statistically significant ($F_{(1,7)} = 6.72, p < .05$).

To summarize, our final model has a number of effects, each of which can explain some of the variance in the vocabulary test scores of the cases in my sample. First, some of the variance in vocabulary test scores can be explained by students' IQ test scores. Second, after controlling for IQ, the within-subjects effect of time was not very powerful and did not explain much of the variance in vocabulary test scores. Third, there was a between-subjects effect for gender, so I can explain some of the variance in vocabulary test scores by knowing the gender of the student. Girls had higher scores, on average, than did boys. Fourth, my time by gender interaction explains some additional variance in vocabulary test scores. Although both boys' and girls' scores

TABLE 11.5 Summary of repeated-measures ANCOVA results comparing test scores at two time points, by gender, controlling for IQ

	Sum of Squares	df	Mean Squares	F Value	Partial Eta Squared
Within-Subjects Effects					
Covariate Effects (IQ)[1]	159.40	1	159.40	.75	.10
Time (Third to Fourth Grade)	1.01	1	1.01	.05	.01
Time × IQ Interaction	6.98	1	6.98	.32	.04
Time × Gender Interaction	146.81	1	146.81	6.72*	.49
Error	153.02	7	21.86		
Between-Subjects Effects					
Gender	1817.34	1	1817.34	8.53*	.55
Error	299.83	8	37.48		

Notes: 1 indicates that the covariate is a between-subjects effect; *indicates $p < .05$

improved over time, this improvement was more dramatic among boys, on average. Finally, there is some variance in vocabulary test scores that I cannot explain with my covariate, time, gender, or interaction effects. This is error variance.

Please keep in mind that my different effects (time, gender, interaction, covariate) will only explain variation in my dependent variable if the relations between my dependent variable and these effects are statistically significant (see Chapter 7). With only 10 cases in my sample, many of these effects were not statistically significant.

Example: Changing Attitudes about Standardized Tests

Every year, students across the country take standardized tests of achievement. Several years ago, I conducted a study to explore students' beliefs and attitudes about taking a standardized test, the Iowa Test of Basic Skills (ITBS). The participants in the study included fifth graders from an elementary school and seventh and eighth graders from two middle schools. There were 570 students in the sample. Students were given a survey the week before they took the ITBS and were then given another survey during the week after they took the test. This pre-test–post-test design allowed me to examine how students were thinking about the test before taking it, and then to reassess their thinking soon after taking the test.

The two surveys contained questions about a variety of beliefs and attitudes, including test anxiety, self-concept, attributions for success and failure, and other variables related to motivation. One set of questions assessed students' perceptions about the validity of the test. On the pre-test survey, the measure of validity beliefs included items such as "I think the ITBS test will be a good measure of what I can do in school" and "The ITBS test will measure how smart I am." On the post-test survey, the measure of validity beliefs included such items as "My score on the ITBS test will tell me how smart I am" and "The ITBS test was a good test of how much I have learned in school." Students answered each of these questions using an 8-point scale ranging from 1 (*Strongly disagree*) to 8 (*Strongly agree*). Students' answers to each question were averaged to create a single pre-test validity score (Pre-Test Validity) and a single post-test validity score (Post-Test Validity), each with a range of 1 to 8.

One question that we can ask using these data is whether students' beliefs about the validity of the test, in terms of the test measuring what they know or can do academically, changed, on average, from before they took the test to after. Students may develop a set of beliefs about the test before they take it, perhaps due to what their teachers and school administrators tell them in preparation for the test. But once they take the test, and see what sorts of questions the test contains, they may change their beliefs about what the test really measures. This is a *within-subjects* type of question: Are there changes *within individuals* in attitudes about the validity of the test from Time 1 to Time 2?

One factor that may cause students to change their attitudes about the validity of the ITBS test is how well they performed on the test. When taking the test, those who thought the test was difficult, and knew that they were not doing well on it, may have developed a somewhat defensive perception that the tests were unfair or invalid. On the other hand, those who felt the test was easy and knew they were doing well when taking the test may have developed self-augmenting perceptions of the test, such as the test revealing their intelligence and being a valid measure. To control for these performance-based differences in perceptions of test validity, I add two covariates to the model, both measures of actual test performance. One covariate is the students' scores, in percentile terms, on the math portion of the ITBS test. The other covariate is the students' percentile scores on the verbal portion of the test. The addition of these two variables turns my repeated-measures ANOVA into a repeated-measures ANCOVA. This repeated-measures ANCOVA can be used to answer the following question: When controlling for actual achievement on the test, are there changes *within individuals* in students' attitudes about the validity of the test from Time 1 to Time 2?

Finally, it is possible that boys' and girls' perceptions of the validity of the test may differ. Perhaps one gender is more trusting of standardized measures than the other. In addition, perhaps one gender tends to have more idealized perceptions of the tests' validity before taking the test, but these perceptions change after actually taking the test. The other gender, with no such idealized preconceptions, may not change their attitudes after taking the test. By adding the independent group variable of gender, I can now address all of the following questions for my model:

1. When controlling for the effects of gender and achievement, are there changes *within subjects* in students' attitudes about the validity of the test from Time 1 to Time 2?
2. When controlling for within-subject effects and achievement, are there differences between boys' and girls' average beliefs about the validity of the test (i.e., *between-subjects* effects)?
3. Is there a within-subject by between-subject interaction, such that the size of the change in perceptions about the validity of the tests from Time 1 to Time 2 is different for boys and girls, when controlling for the effects of achievement?

As you can see, there are a number of very interesting questions that I can examine in a single repeated-measures ANCOVA. To examine these questions, I conducted my analysis using SPSS software. The actual SPSS output from the analysis is presented in Table 11.6. I explain each piece of information in the order it appears in Table 11.6.

The first set of information in Table 11.6 shows the means, standard deviations, and sample sizes for the pre-test dependent variable (Pre-Test Validity) and the post-test dependent variable (Post-Test Validity). A quick glance at the separate means for boys and girls on the Pre-Test Validity and Post-Test Validity variables reveals that whereas the girls' averages are virtually identical from Time 1 to Time 2, the boys' mean declines somewhat (from 6.2852 to 6.0076). We can also see that at both Time 1 and Time 2, boys appear to score higher than girls, on average, on the validity perception measures (see Figure 11.7). Whether these differences are statistically significant is still to be determined. Regardless of whether these differences are statistically significant, they may not be *practically* significant: Boys and girls do not appear to differ much in their average perceptions of the validity of the ITBS test.

Below the means and standard deviations in the SPSS output, we find the "Tests for Between-Subjects Effects." Here we see five separate sums of squares (*SS*), degrees of freedom (*df*), and Mean Squares. We also get *F* values, "Sig." *p* values, and our effect size measure, "Eta Squared." The statistics we are most interested in here are the *F* value, the "Sig." *p* value, and the "Eta Squared" effect size for the analysis involving gender. These statistics tell us whether, on average, boys and girls differ in their average perceptions of validity of the ITBS, when controlling for their performance on the test. It is important to remember that this between-subjects test is for the Pre-Test Validity scores and the Post-Test Validity scores *combined*. Because the "Sig." is a *p* value, and this *p* value is much less than .05, we conclude that, on average, *across times*, boys and girls differ in their perceptions of the validity of the tests. If we take a look at the means presented earlier, we can conclude that boys have more faith in the validity of the test scores than do girls, even after controlling for performance on the test. Notice that the eta squared statistic for the gender effect is quite small (eta^2 = .02), indicating that gender accounts for only 2 percent of the variance in the combined Pre-Test and Post-Test Validity scores. This suggests that our *statistically* significant result may not be *practically* significant. The data presented in this part of the table also reveal that there is a significant relationship between one of our covariates (Reading test scores) and our dependent variable (the combined Pre-Test and Post-Test Validity scores).

Continuing down the SPSS output in Table 11.6, we get to the section labeled "Test involving Within-Subjects Effects." Here we are most interested in the results for Validity and the Validity * Gender interaction. Validity is the name that I have given to the combination of the

TABLE 11.6 SPSS output for repeated-measures ANCOVA examining changes in beliefs in the validity of standardized test scores, by gender, controlling for math and reading test scores

Descriptive Statistics

	Gender	Mean	Std. Deviation	N
Pre-Test Validity	Girl	5.7679	1.5762	307
	Boy	6.2852	1.4761	264
	Total	6.0071	1.5510	571
Post-Test Validity	Girl	5.7096	1.5190	307
	Boy	6.0076	1.5324	264
	Total	5.8473	1.5311	571

Tests for Between-Subjects Effects

Source	Type III Sum of Squares	df	Mean Square	F	Sig.	Eta Squared
Intercept	10642.913	1	10642.913	2930.419	.000	.838
Reading Test Score	35.006	1	35.006	9.639	.002	.017
Math Test Score	5.266	1	5.266	1.450	.229	.003
Gender	**41.941**	**1**	**41.941**	**11.548**	**.001**	**.020**
Error	2059.273	567	3.632			

Tests Involving Within-Subjects Effects

Source	Type III Sum of Squares	df	Mean Square	F	Sig.	Eta Squared
Validity	**8.884**	**1**	**8.884**	**10.617**	**.001**	**.018**
Validity * Read Test	.164	1	.164	.196	.659	.000
Validity * Math Test	3.533	1	3.533	4.222	.040	.007
Validity * Gender	**3.670**	**1**	**3.670**	**4.386**	**.037**	**.008**
Error (Validity)	474.437	567	.837			

pre- and post-test scores on the validity measure. When these two scores are combined to create a *within-subjects* factor (which I called Validity), we can conduct a test to see whether there were statistically significant within-subject changes, on average, on the validity measures from Time 1 to Time 2. Because this within-subjects test is concerned with *changes* or *differences* within subjects across the two times, the dependent variable in this analysis is *not* the combined scores on the Pre-Test Validity and Post-Test Validity variables, as it was in the between-subjects test. Rather, the

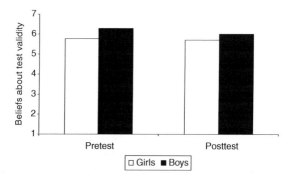

FIGURE 11.7 Change in beliefs about validity of standardized test scores by gender.

dependent variable is the *difference* or *change* in the scores, *within subjects,* from Time 1 to Time 2. Because our *F* value for Validity has a corresponding *p* value of *p* = .001 (as listed in the "Sig." column), we can see that, on average, students' beliefs in the validity of the test did change from Time 1 to Time 2. By looking at the means reported earlier, we can see that, on average, students had more faith in the validity of the test *before* they took the test than they did *after* taking the test. The eta squared statistic for this effect (eta² = .018) indicates that there was a small effect size for this effect. We can also see, from the Validity * Math Test (*F* = 4.222) and the associated *p* value ("Sig." = .040), that there was a significant relationship between the math test covariate and our dependent variable in this analysis. In other words, there was a significant relationship between how well students performed on the math portion of the ITBS test and how much their beliefs in the validity of the test changed over time. There was no significant relationship between performance on the reading portion of the ITBS test and changes in beliefs about the validity of the test.

In addition to the main within-subjects effect, we can see that there is a significant Validity by Gender interaction ("Sig.", or *p* = .037). This tells us that the within-subject changes from Time 1 to Time 2 in beliefs about the validity of the ITBS test were not of equal size among boys and girls. If you recall from the means presented at the top of Table 11.6, this comes as no surprise (see Figure 11.7). We can see that whereas girls' mean scores on the validity variable changed little from Time 1 to Time 2, for boys there was a noticeable decrease in beliefs about the validity of the test from Time 1 to Time 2. It is important to keep in mind that even the statistically significant results in this analysis are all quite modest, as revealed by the small effect sizes (see Chapter 7 for a discussion of effect size).

Now that we have found a significant interaction, we perhaps need to modify our conclusions about the main effects we have found. First, the differences between boys' and girls' average perceptions that the test is valid appear to be due primarily to the relatively large gap in Time 1 scores. Boys' and girls' perceptions of the validity of the test were more similar after they actually took the test, although boys were still slightly more likely to believe the tests were valid. Second, the statistically significant within-subject changes in beliefs about test validity over time appear to be caused entirely by changes in the boys' perceptions from Time 1 to Time 2. Girls barely changed their beliefs about validity over time.

Taken as a group, the results of our repeated-measures ANCOVA reveal a great deal about how boys and girls think about the validity of the ITBS. First, we know that although performance on the English portion of the test is related to beliefs about the validity of the test, it is performance on the math portion of the test that is related to *changes* in beliefs about validity. Second, we know that boys tended to view the tests as more valid than girls, particularly before they took the test, regardless of how well the students performed on the test (i.e., controlling for the effects of test scores). Third, we know that students tended to decline in their beliefs about the validity of the test after taking the test, but this decline appears to only have occurred among boys. Finally, we know that all of these effects are quite small because the small effect sizes tell us so. This is a lot of information, and it demonstrates the power of repeated measures.

 To see a video describing how to interpret SPSS output for a repeated-measures ANOVA, please refer to the website that accompanies this book.

INTERPRETING GRAPHS: A CAUTIONARY TALE

When trying to make sense of a graph, it is important that the reader beware. The same data can look very different depending on the scale used in the graph. If you take a look at Figure 11.7, you'll notice that the bars representing the means for boys and girls look pretty similar, both at the pre-test and the post-test stage. That is because in that graph I used an "honest" *Y* axis. That is to say I used the full range of scores, 1–7, on the *Y* axis that appeared in the original scale of measurement used when I collected the data. By using a less honest, smaller range on my *Y* axis, take a look at what happens to the graph:

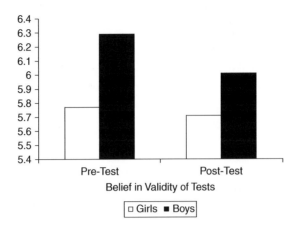

See how much larger the differences between the means appear? I'm presenting the exact same data as I did in Figure 11.7, but it looks different and more impressive here, just because I changed the scale on the *Y* axis. So when reading graphs, pay attention to the *Y* axis.

Writing it Up

To write up the results of the repeated-measures ANCOVA summarized in Table 11.6, I would begin by describing the main effects for both the between-subjects effect and the within-subjects effect. Then I would discuss the interaction effect.

"To examine whether changes in students' beliefs about the validity of standardized achievement tests differed by gender, I performed repeated-measures ANCOVA with gender as a between-subjects factor and with math and reading test scores as covariates. The results revealed a main between-subjects effect for gender ($F_{(1,567)} = 11.55, p < .001$) with boys, on average, having greater faith in the validity of the tests than did girls. There was also a main within-subjects effect for time ($F_{(1,567)} = 10.62, p < .001$). The means indicated that, when combining the two genders and controlling for the covariates, students had greater faith in the validity of the test scores before they took the test than they did after taking it. Finally, there was a significant gender × time interaction ($F_{(1,567)} = 4.39, p < .05$). An examination of the means revealed that whereas the average level of beliefs about the validity of the standardized tests did not appear to change significantly for girls from pre-test to post-test ($M = 5.77$ to $M = 5.71$), there was a larger decline for boys (from $M = 6.29$ to $M = 6.01$ from pre-test to post-test)." (Note that I would need to conduct a test of **simple effects** to determine whether the decline in means for boys and the decline in means for girls were statistically significant.)

Wrapping Up and Looking Forward

In some ways, repeated-measures ANOVA is a simple extension of ideas we have already discussed. The similarities with paired *t* tests (Chapter 8) are clear, as is the idea of parsing the variance of a dependent variable into various components. But the tremendous power of repeated-measures ANOVA can only be appreciated when we take a moment to consider all of the pieces of information that we can gain from a single analysis. The combination of within-subjects and between-subjects variance, along with the interaction between these components, allows social scientists to examine a range of very complex, and very interesting, questions. Repeated-measures ANOVA is a particularly useful technique for examining change over time, either in longitudinal studies or in experimental studies using a pre-treatment/post-treatment design. It is also particularly useful for examining whether patterns of change over time vary for different groups.

In the next two chapters of the book, we shift gears a bit to focus on statistics that examine *associations* among variables. In the chapters on *t* tests and various kinds of ANOVA, we have focused primarily on comparing the means (i.e., averages) of different groups. In the next two chapters, "Correlation" and "Regression," we will explore techniques for examining the strength and direction of the correlations between variables. Some of the statistics that we have already discussed involve correlations (e.g., covariates in ANOVA), but we will discuss the details of correlation more fully in the next chapter. As you finish this chapter and move onto the next, it is important to remember that we are only able to scratch the surface of the powerful techniques presented in the last several chapters of this book. To gain a full appreciation of what factorial ANOVA, repeated-measures ANOVA, regression, and factor analysis can do, you will need to read more about these techniques.

Work Problems

As in Chapter 10, the work problems for this chapter will focus more on interpreting data rather than calculating statistics. The data for these problems were collected from two cohorts of high school students over four semesters. At the beginning of the study, one cohort of students were in their first semester of ninth grade, and the other cohort were in their first semester of eleventh grade. Students in both cohorts completed surveys four times over a two-year period (in the fall and spring of each year), giving us data from the beginning of ninth grade to the end of tenth grade for the first cohort and from the beginning of eleventh grade to the end of twelfth grade for the second cohort.

One of the things I asked students about was their perceptions of how much their teachers cared about students really learning and understanding the material they were being taught. We called this a Mastery Emphasis. Research has shown that many indicators of student motivation decline during the course of a school year (e.g., interest in school tends to be higher in the fall semester than it is in the spring semester). Research has also found that as students get older their interest in school tends to decline. I wanted to see if these within-year and across-grade declines could be found in students' perceptions of how much their teachers cared about their learning and understanding of material. So I calculated a repeated-measures ANOVA with four points of data collection as the within-subjects factor and two cohorts as the between-subjects factor. The results of my SPSS analyses are presented in Table 11.7. Please answer the following questions using the information presented in this table.

1. How many of the participants in this study were in ninth grade and how many were in eleventh grade in the first year of the study?
2. The main effect for grade level is *not* statistically significant. What does that mean, exactly?
3. What is the effect size for the within-subjects effect for Mastery Emphasis?
4. Is the interaction between Mastery Emphasis and grade level statistically significant? What does this interaction tell you?
5. Create two graphs of the means: first a column graph and then a line graph. Be sure to include all four time points for each of the grade levels.

TABLE 11.7 SPSS output for repeated-measures ANOVA for work problems

	Grade	Mean	Std. Deviation	N
Mastery Emphasis, Fall, Year 1	9	3.67	.65	301
	11	3.52	.80	253
	Total	3.60	.73	554
Mastery Emphasis, Spring, Year 1	9	3.41	.80	301
	11	3.49	.79	253
	Total	3.45	.80	554
Mastery Emphasis, Fall, Year 2	10	3.58	.73	301
	12	3.55	.75	253
	Total	3.57	.74	554
Mastery Emphasis, Spring, Year 2	10	3.38	.81	301
	12	3.29	.86	253
	Total	3.34	.83	554

Tests for Between-Subjects Effects

Source	Type III Sum of Squares	df	Mean Square	F	Sig.	Partial Eta Squared
Intercept	26751.461	1	26751.461	19257.280	.000	.972
Grade Level	1.164	1	1.164	.838	.360	.002
Error	766.817	552	1.389			

Tests Involving Within-Subjects Effects

Source	Type III Sum of Squares	df	Mean Square	F	Sig.	Partial Eta Squared
Mastery Emphasis	23.454	3	7.818	23.254	.000	.040
Mastery Emphasis * Grade Level	3.828	3	1.276	3.796	.010	.007
Error (Mastery Emphasis)	556.738	1656	.336			

6. Using the information from the graphs that you created and the statistics about the main effects and the interaction effects, write a summary statement about what you now know about how students' perceptions of their teachers' emphasis on Mastery (i.e., learning and understanding) changed over a two-year period during high school, and how those changes are similar or different for early and later grade levels in high school.

 For answers to these work problems, and for additional work problems, please refer to the website that accompanies this book.

CHAPTER 12

Correlation

In several of the previous chapters, we examined statistics and parameters that describe a single variable at a time, such as the mean, standard deviation, z scores, and standard errors. Although such single-variable statistics are important, researchers are often interested in examining the relations among two or more variables. One of the most basic measures of the association among variables, and a foundational statistic for several more complex statistics, is the **correlation coefficient**. Although there are a number of different types of correlation coefficients, the most commonly used in social science research is the **Pearson product-moment correlation coefficient**. Most of this chapter is devoted to understanding this statistic, with a brief description of three other types of correlations: the **point-biserial coefficient**, the **Spearman rho coefficient**, and the **phi coefficient**.

When to Use Correlation and What it Tells Us

Researchers compute correlation coefficients when they want to know how two variables are related to each other. For a Pearson product-moment correlation, both of the variables must be measured on an interval or ratio scale and are known as **continuous variables**. For example, suppose I want to know whether there is a relationship between the amount of time students spend studying for an exam and their scores on the exam. I suspect that the more hours students spend studying, the higher their scores will be on the exam. But I also suspect that there is not a perfect correspondence between time spent studying and test scores. Some students will probably get low scores on the exam even if they study for a long time, simply because they may have a hard time understanding the material. Indeed, there will probably be a number of students who spend an inordinately long period of time studying for the test precisely *because* they are having trouble understanding the material. On the other hand, there will probably be some students who do very well on the test without spending very much time studying. Despite these "exceptions" to my rule, I still hypothesize that, in general, as the amount of time spent studying increases, so do students' scores on the exam.

There are two fundamental characteristics of correlation coefficients researchers care about. The first of these is the **direction** of the correlation coefficient. Correlation coefficients can be either positive or negative. A **positive correlation** indicates that the values on the two variables being analyzed move in the same direction, and they are associated with each other in a predictable manner. That is, as scores on one variable go up, scores on the other variable go up as well, in general. Similarly, as scores on one variable go down, scores on the other variable go down. Returning to my earlier example, if there is a positive correlation between the amount of time students spend studying and their test scores, I can tell that, in general, the more time students spend studying, the higher their scores are on the test. This is *equivalent* to saying that the *less* time they spend studying, the *lower* their scores are on the test. Both of these represent a *positive* correlation between time spent studying and test scores. (*Note*: I keep saying "in general" because

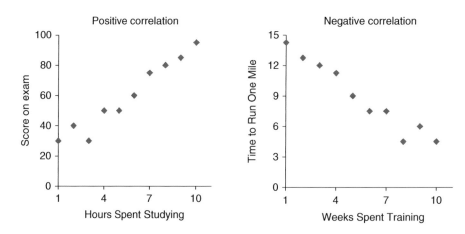

FIGURE 12.1 Examples of positive and negative correlations.

it is important to note that the presence of a correlation between two variables does *not* mean that this relationship holds true for each member of the sample or population. Rather, it means that, in general, there is a relationship of a given direction and strength between two variables in the sample or population.)

A **negative correlation** indicates that the values on the two variables being analyzed move in *opposite* directions. That is, as scores on one variable go up, scores on the other variable go down, and vice versa. For example, the more time runners spend training, the less time it takes them to run a mile. As training time increases, mile time decreases, in general. Similarly, with a negative correlation I would also conclude that the *less* time runners spend training, the *longer* it takes them to run a mile. These positive and negative correlations are represented by the **scattergrams** (also known as **scatterplots** or **scatter graphs**) in Figure 12.1. Scattergrams are simply graphs that indicate the scores of each case in a sample simultaneously on two variables. For example, in the positive correlation scattergram in Figure 12.1, the first case in the sample studied for 1 hour and got a score of 30 on the exam. The second case studied for 2 hours and scored 40 on the exam. Notice that each dot on the scattergram indicates an individual's score on two variables simultaneously.

The second fundamental characteristic of correlation coefficients is the **strength** or **magnitude** of the relationship. The magnitude of the relationship between two variables is indicated by the numerical value of r, regardless of whether the value is positive or negative. Correlation coefficients range in strength from −1.00 to +1.00. A correlation coefficient of .00 indicates that there is no relationship between the two variables being examined. That is, scores on one of the variables are not related in any meaningful way to scores on the second variable. The closer the correlation coefficient is to either −1.00 or +1.00, the stronger the relationship is between the two variables. A **perfect negative correlation** of −1.00 indicates that for every member of the sample or population, a higher score on one variable is related to a lower score on the other variable. A **perfect positive correlation** of +1.00 reveals that for every member of the sample or population, a higher score on one variable is related to a higher score on the other variable.

Perfect correlations are never found in actual social science research. Generally, correlation coefficients stay between −.70 and +.70. Some textbook authors suggest that correlation coefficients between −.20 and +.20 indicate a weak association between two variables; those between

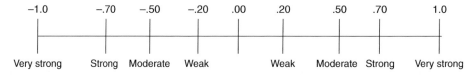

FIGURE 12.2 General guide to the strength of correlation coefficients.

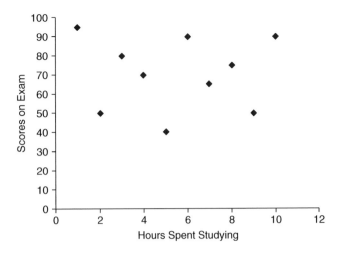

FIGURE 12.3   Scatterplot showing no correlation between hours spent studying and exam scores.

.20 and .50 (either positive or negative) represent a moderate association, and those larger than .50 (either positive or negative) represent a strong association. (See Figure 12.2 for a general guide to interpreting the strength of correlation coefficients.) These general rules of thumb for judging the relevance of correlation coefficients must be taken with a grain of salt. For example, even a "small" correlation between alcohol consumption and liver disease (e.g., +.15) is important, whereas a strong correlation between how much children like vanilla and chocolate ice cream (e.g., +.70) may not be so important.

The scattergrams presented in Figure 12.1 represent very strong positive and negative correlations ($r = .97$ and $r = -.97$ for the positive and negative correlations, respectively; *r* is the symbol for the sample Pearson correlation coefficient). In Figure 12.3, a scattergram representing virtually no correlation between the number of hours spent studying and scores on the exam is presented. Notice that there is no discernible pattern between the scores on the two variables. In other words, the data presented in Figure 12.3 reveal that it would be virtually impossible to predict an individual's test score simply by knowing how many hours the person studied for the exam.

Pearson Correlation Coefficients in Depth

The first step in understanding what the Pearson correlation coefficient is, and what it tells us, is to notice that we are concerned with a sample's scores on *two* variables at the same time. Returning to our previous example of study time and test scores, suppose that we randomly select a sample of five students and measure the time they spent studying for the exam and their exam scores. The data are presented in Table 12.1 (with a scattergram in Figure 12.4).

For these data to be used in a correlation analysis, it is critical that the scores on the two variables are *paired*. That is, for each student in my sample, the score on the *X* variable (hours spent studying) is paired with his or her own score on the *Y* variable (exam score). If I want to determine the relation between hours spent studying and exam scores, I cannot pair Student 1's hours spent studying with Student 4's test score. I must match each student's score on the *X* variable with his or her own score on the *Y* variable. Once I have done this, I can determine whether hours spent studying is related to exam scores.

What the Correlation Coefficient Does, and Does Not, Tell Us

Correlation coefficients such as the Pearson coefficient are very powerful statistics. They allow us to determine whether the values on one variable are *associated with* the values on a second variable. This can be very useful information, but people, including social scientists, are often

TABLE 12.1 Data for the correlation coefficient

	Hours Spent Studying (X Variable)	Exam Score (Y Variable)
Student 1	5	80
Student 2	6	85
Student 3	7	70
Student 4	8	90
Student 5	9	85

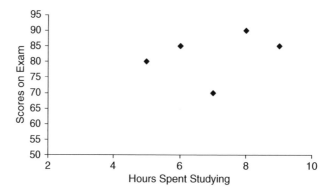

FIGURE 12.4 Scatterplot of data from Table 12.1.

tempted to ascribe more meaning to correlation coefficients than they deserve. Namely, people often confuse the concepts of *correlation* and **causation**. Correlation (co-relation) simply means that variation in the scores on one variable *corresponds* with variation in the scores on a second variable. Causation means that variation in the scores on one variable *causes* or *creates* variation in the scores on a second variable.

When we make the leap from correlation to causation, we may be wrong. As an example, I offer this story, which I heard in my introductory psychology class. As the story goes, one winter shortly after World War II, there was an explosion in the number of storks nesting in some northern European country (I cannot remember which). Approximately nine months later, there was a large jump in the number of babies that were born. Now, the link between storks and babies being what it is, many concluded that this correlation between the number of storks and the number of babies represented a causal relationship. Fortunately, science tells us that babies do not come from storks after all, at least not human babies. However, there is something that storks and babies have in common: both can be "summoned" by cold temperatures and warm fireplaces. It seems that storks like to nest in warm chimneys during cold winters. As it happens, cold winter nights also foster baby-making behavior. The apparent cause-and-effect relationship between storks and babies was in fact caused by a third variable: a cold winter.[1]

For a more serious example, we can look at the relationship between SAT scores and first-year college grade point averages. The correlation between these two variables is about .40. Although these two variables are moderately correlated, it would be difficult to argue that higher SAT scores *cause* higher achievement in the first year of college. Rather, there is probably some other variable, or set of variables, responsible for this relationship. For example, we know that taking a greater number of advanced math courses in high school is associated with higher SAT scores *and* with higher grades in first-year math courses in college.

Although correlations alone cannot tell us whether there is a causal association between two variables, they do allow us to use information from one variable to make **predictions** about scores on a second variable. Returning to our example of the correlation between SAT scores and grades in the first year of college, the positive correlation between these two variables allows us to predict higher first-year college grades for students who have higher SAT scores, and lower first-year college grades for those who have lower SAT scores. Indeed, the primary purpose of the SAT is to help colleges and universities predict how well college applicants will perform once they are in college. The stronger the correlation between the two variables, the more accurate these predictions will be. Because the correlation between SAT scores and first-year college grades is only moderate, we know that the prediction of higher first-year grades among those with higher SAT scores is not especially accurate, and that many students who do not perform well on the SAT will get good grades in college, and vice versa. (We will discuss the predictive power of correlation coefficients in more depth when we discuss regression in Chapter 13.)

The point of these examples is simple: Evidence of a relationship between two variables (i.e., a correlation) does not necessarily mean that there is a causal relationship between the two variables. However, it should also be noted that a correlation between two variables is a *necessary ingredient* of any argument that the two variables are causally related. In other words, I cannot claim that one variable causes another (e.g., that smoking causes cancer) if there is no correlation between smoking and cancer. If I do find a correlation between smoking and cancer, I must rule out other factors before I can conclude that it is smoking that causes cancer.

In addition to the correlation-causation issue, there are a few other important features of correlations worth noting. First, simple Pearson correlations are designed to examine *linear* relations among variables. In other words, they describe *straight* associations among variables. For example, if you find a positive correlation between two variables, you can predict how much the scores in one variable will increase with each corresponding increase in the second variable. But not all relations between variables are linear. For example, there is a **curvilinear** relationship between anxiety and performance on a number of academic and nonacademic behaviors. When taking a math test, for example, a little bit of anxiety may actually help performance. However, once a student becomes too nervous, this anxiety can interfere with performance. We call this a curvilinear relationship because what began as a positive relationship between performance and anxiety at lower levels of anxiety becomes a negative relationship at higher levels of anxiety. This curvilinear relationship is presented graphically in Figure 12.5. Because correlation coefficients show the relation between two variables *in general*, when the relationship between two variables is curvilinear, the correlation coefficient can be quite small, suggesting a weaker relationship than may actually exist.

Another common problem that arises when examining correlation coefficients is the problem of **truncated range**. This problem is encountered when the scores on one or both of the variables in the analysis do not have much variety in the distribution of scores, possibly due to a ceiling or

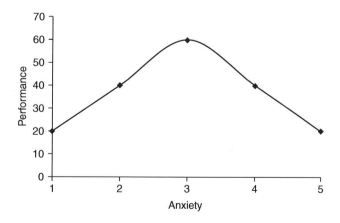

FIGURE 12.5 A curvilinear relationship between anxiety and performance.

TABLE 12.2 Data for the demonstration of truncated range and ceiling effects for association between hours spent studying and exam score

	Hours Spent Studying (X Variable)	Exam Score (Y Variable)
Student 1	5	95
Student 2	7	97
Student 3	1	98
Student 4	3	100
Student 5	12	96
Student 6	10	99
Student 7	6	98
Student 8	8	98
Student 9	4	97
Student 10	2	95

floor effect. For example, suppose that I gave a sample of students a very easy test with a possible high score of 100. Then suppose I wanted to see if there was a correlation between scores on my test and how much time students spent studying for the test. Suppose I got the data presented in Table 12.2.

In this example, all of my students did well on the test, whether they spent many hours studying for it or not. Because the test was too easy, a ceiling effect may have occurred, thereby truncating the range of scores on the exam. (See Figure 12.6 for an illustration of the ceiling effect and the weak correlation produced by the truncated range of test scores.) Although there may be a relationship between how much time students spent studying and their knowledge of the material, my test was not sensitive enough to reveal this relationship. The weak correlation that will be produced by the data in Table 12.2 may not reflect the true relationship between how much students study and how much they learn.

Calculating the Pearson correlation coefficient by hand is a complicated process. There are different formulas for the calculation, some involving z scores and others involving raw scores. Because these formulas are a bit complicated, and because it is easy to calculate correlation coefficients with computer programs and calculators, I have put the details about how to perform these calculations in a separate box in this chapter. Please take a look at the box below if you are interested in the specifics of how to calculate a correlation coefficient.

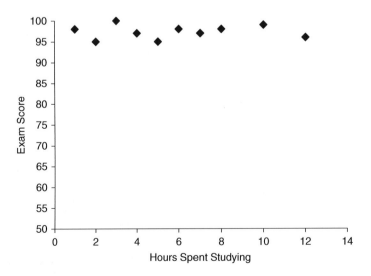

FIGURE 12.6 A small or zero correlation produced by the truncated range of one of the variables, in this case the *Y* variable, test scores.

**UNDERSTANDING THE FORMULA FOR CALCULATING THE
CORRELATION COEFFICIENT**

There are several different formulas that can be used to calculate Pearson product-moment correlation coefficients. These formulas produce the same results and differ only in their ease of use. In fact, none of them is particularly easy to use, and you will probably never need to calculate a correlation coefficient by hand. But it is important to take a look at the formula for calculating the Pearson correlation coefficient (r) so you can gain insights into how this statistic works and what it tells you.

TABLE 12.3 Definitional formula for the Pearson correlation coefficient

$$r = \frac{\Sigma(z_x z_y)}{N}$$

where r is the Pearson product-moment correlation coefficient,
    z_x is a z score for variable X,
    z_y is a paired z score for variable Y,
    N is the number of pairs of X and Y scores.

If you look at the numerator in the formula, you will notice that it is the sum of the z scores (i.e., standardized scores) multiplied together. Each case in the sample will have a score on each of the two variables in the correlation. After standardizing these two variables, each case will have a z score on each of the two variables. So for each case in the sample, multiply the two z scores together, and add up these **cross products**. Recall from Chapter 5 that z scores will be positive for those scores in the sample that are greater than the mean, and negative for those scores that are lower than the mean. If scores above the mean on the first variable (X) are generally associated with scores above the mean on the second variable (Y), the sum of the cross products will be a positive value, and this will produce a positive correlation coefficient. But if scores that are above the mean on the X variable are generally associated with scores that are below the mean on the Y variable, the sum of the cross products will be negative, producing a negative correlation coefficient.

The denominator of the formula in Table 12.3 is N, which refers to the total number of cases in the sample. Whenever we divide by the number of cases, we are getting an average. So in this formula, what we get is the average cross product of standardized scores on the two variables in the correlation. So the correlation coefficient that is produced by this formula tells us the strength and direction of the two standardized variables *in general*. For some cases in our sample, this general pattern will not hold true. For example, some individuals may have scores that are below the mean on the first variable but above the mean on the second variable, even when the overall correlation coefficient for the whole sample is positive.

Now that we have examined the formula for calculating a correlation coefficient, let's take a look at an example of how to apply this formula to some data. I am going to use the data that were presented in Table 12.1 about students, their study time, and their test scores. Take a look at Table 12.4, which has all of the information that we need to calculate a Pearson correlation coefficient.

In Column 1 and Column 2, you will find the scores on the X and Y variables for each student in the sample. These are the raw scores. The first step in calculating the correlation coefficient is to calculate z scores for each case in the sample or population on each of the two variables. In Column 3, you can see each student's z score[2] for the X variable, and in Column 4 I have presented the z scores for each student on the Y variable. Once you have the z scores for each case on each of the two variables, the next step is to multiply the two

TABLE 12.4   Data for calculating the correlation coefficient (r)

	Column 1 Hours Spent Studying (X)	Column 2 Exam Score (Y)	Column 3 z Score for X	Column 4 z Score for Y	Column 5 $z_x z_y$
Student 1	5	80	−1.41	−.29	.42
Student 2	6	85	−.71	.44	−.31
Student 3	7	70	.00	−1.77	.00
Student 4	8	90	.71	1.18	.83
Student 5	9	85	1.41	.44	.63
Mean	7	82			*Sum* = 1.56
Standard Deviation *(Population Formula)*	1.41	6.78			*r* = .31

z scores together for each case. These multiplied z scores are presented in Column 5. Next, you add these z score products together, creating the sum of 1.56 that is presented in the lower right portion of Table 12.4. The final step in the calculation is to divide that sum by the number of cases: 1.56/5 = .31. So our Pearson correlation coefficient in this example is .31, which is a positive, moderately sized correlation. We can take this a step further and calculate the coefficient of determination: $.31^2 = .10$. So we can say that 10 percent of the variance in exam scores is explained by the variance in hours spent studying.

The Coefficient of Determination

Although correlation coefficients give an idea of the strength of the relationship between two variables, they often seem a bit nebulous. If you get a correlation coefficient of .40, is that a strong relationship? Fortunately, correlation coefficients can be used to obtain a seemingly more concrete statistic: the **coefficient of determination**. Even better, it is easy to calculate.

When we want to know if two variables are related to each other, we are really asking a somewhat more complex question: Are the variations in the scores on one variable somehow associated with the variations in the scores on a second variable? Put another way, a correlation coefficient tells us whether we can know anything about the scores on one variable if we already know the scores on a second variable. In common statistical vernacular, what we want to be able to do with a measure of association, like the correlation coefficient, is to be able to *explain* some of the variance in the scores on one variable based on our knowledge of the scores on a second variable. The coefficient of determination tells us how much of the variance in the scores of one variable can be understood, or explained, by the scores on a second variable.

One way to conceptualize **explained variance** is to understand that when two variables are correlated with each other, they *share* a certain percentage of their variance. Consider an example. If we have a sample of 10 people, and we measure their height and their weight, we've got 10 scores on each of two variables. Assuming that my 10 people differ in how tall they are, there will be some total amount of variance in their scores on the height variable. There will also be some total amount of variance in their scores on the weight variable, assuming that they do not all weigh the same amount. These total variances are depicted in Figure 12.7 as two full squares, each representing 100 percent of the variance in their respective variables. Notice how they do not overlap.

When two variables are related, or correlated, with each other, there is a certain amount of **shared variance** between them. In Figure 12.7, the two squares are not touching each other, suggesting that all of the variance in each variable is independent of the other variable. There is no overlap. But when two variables are correlated, there is some *shared* variance. The stronger the correlation, the greater the amount of shared variance, and the more variance you can explain in one variable by knowing the scores on the second variable. The precise percentage of shared, or explained, variance can be determined by squaring the correlation coefficient. This squared correlation coefficient is known as the **coefficient of determination**. Some examples of different

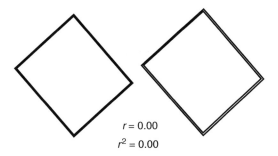

FIGURE 12.7 Uncorrelated variables.

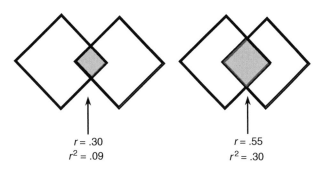

FIGURE 12.8 Examples of different coefficients of determination.

coefficients of determination are presented in Figure 12.8. As the strength of the association between the two variables increases (i.e., larger correlation coefficient), the greater the amount of shared variance, and the higher the coefficient of determination. Notice that on the left side of Figure 12.8, the overlap between the boxes is fairly small, reflecting a correlation coefficient of .30. When this is squared, it produces the coefficient of determination, indicating that 9 percent of the variance in the two variables is shared. On the right side of Figure 12.8, the boxes overlap more, reflecting a larger correlation and more shared variance between the two variables. It is still important to remember that even though the coefficient of determination is used to tell us how much of the variance in one variable can be explained by the variance in a second variable, coefficients of determination do not necessarily indicate a *causal* relationship between the two variables.

Statistically Significant Correlations

When researchers calculate correlation coefficients, they often want to know whether a correlation found in sample data represents the existence of a relationship between two variables in the population from which the sample was selected. In other words, they want to test whether the correlation coefficient is statistically significant (see Chapter 7 for a discussion of statistical significance). To test whether a correlation coefficient is statistically significant, the researcher begins with the null hypothesis that there is absolutely no relationship between the two variables in the population, or that the correlation coefficient in the population equals zero. The alternative hypothesis is that there is, in fact, a statistical relationship between the two variables in the population and that the population correlation coefficient is *not* equal to zero. These two competing hypotheses can be expressed with symbols:

$$H_0 : \rho = 0$$

$$H_0 : \rho \neq 0$$

where ρ is rho, the population correlation coefficient.

TABLE 12.5 Correlation between college students' reports of feeling comfortable at their university and believing that college is not worth the time or money that it costs

	Comfortable/belong	College not worth it
Feel comfortable/belong at this university	$r = 1.00$ $p < .001$	
College is not worth the time or money	$r = -.28$ $p < .01$	$r = 1.00$ $p < .001$

Fortunately, there are many computer programs, and even some calculators, that will compute the correlation coefficient for you and tell you whether it is statistically significant. (If you would like to see how to perform the calculations to test for the statistical significance of r, I have provided instructions and an example below.) In this section of the chapter, I present information from the tests of statistical significance for a correlation coefficient and explain how to interpret the results of this test. Additional examples are presented later in this chapter.

A few years ago, I conducted a study to examine college students' perceptions of college. I asked the students to indicate, on a scale from 1 to 5, how strongly they agreed with each of these statements (1 = *Strongly disagree* and 5 = *Strongly agree*): "I feel comfortable, like I belong, at this university" and "College is not worth the time or the money that it costs."

I used the statistical software program SPSS to calculate the correlation coefficient between these two variables and to indicate whether the correlation coefficient was statistically significant. The results of this analysis are presented in Table 12.5.

There are three boxes in this table that have correlation coefficients and p values presented inside of them. The two boxes along the diagonal of the table are simply variables that are correlated with themselves. These correlations are always perfect and positive (i.e., $r = 1.00$), and are not particularly meaningful. But the correlation between the two variables is presented in the third box, and shows that the scores on these two variables are fairly weakly, negatively correlated ($r = -.28$). This means that, in this sample of 130 college students, those who feel more comfortable at the university are less likely to feel that college is not worth the time or money that it costs. The p value that is reported below the correlation coefficient, $p < .01$, indicates that the probability of obtaining a correlation coefficient this large, from a randomly selected sample of 130, is less than 1 in 100, or less than a 1 percent chance. In Chapter 7, we learned that in most social science research, a p value less than .05 leads us to the conclusion that the result did *not* occur by chance, and is therefore statistically significant. So our correlation coefficient in this example would be considered statistically significant, and we would conclude that in the *population* of college students that this sample represents, there is a negative relationship between feeling that one is comfortable and belongs at the university and the belief that college is not worth the time or money that it costs.

It is important to remember that just because a correlation is statistically significant, that does not mean it is either particularly important or that the association between the two variables is a causal one. The coefficient of determination for this correlation ($-.28^2 = .08$) indicates that only 8 percent of the variance in beliefs about college not being worth it is explained by feelings of comfort and belonging at the university. This is not a lot of variance explained, which suggests that our efforts to predict whether students believe college is worth the cost simply from their feelings of comfort and belonging would not be very accurate. In addition, we cannot tell from this correlation whether feelings of comfort and belonging *affect* whether students feel that college is worth the time and money. The correlation between these two variables may be explained by some third variable that was not included in the analysis, such as how well students are performing in their classes, how well the college football team is performing on the field, or any number of other variables.

If you are interested in the details about how to calculate a t value to determine whether a correlation coefficient is statistically significant, please take a look at the box below.

CALCULATIONS TO TEST FOR STATISTICAL SIGNIFICANCE OF *r*

The *t* distribution is used to test whether a correlation coefficient is statistically significant. Therefore, we must conduct a *t* test. As with all *t* tests, the *t* test that we use for correlation coefficients involves a ratio, or fraction. The numerator of the fraction is the difference between two values. The denominator is the standard error. When we want to see whether a sample correlation coefficient is statistically significant, the numerator of the *t* test formula will be the sample correlation coefficient, *r*, minus the hypothesized value of the population correlation coefficient (ρ), which in our null hypothesis is zero. The denominator will be the standard error of the sample correlation coefficient:

$$t = \frac{r - \rho}{s_r}$$

where *r* is the sample correlation coefficient,

ρ is the population correlation coefficient,

s_r is the standard error of the sample correlation coefficient.

There are two ways to calculate the *t* value for the correlation coefficient. First, we can calculate a standard error for the correlation coefficient, and use that as the denominator of our *t* formula:

$$s_r = \sqrt{\frac{(1 - r^2)}{(N - 2)}}$$

where r^2 is the correlation coefficient squared and

N is the number of cases in the sample.

With the help of a little algebra, we can also use the formula below to calculate a *t* value without going through the process of calculating a separate standard error:

$$t = (r)\sqrt{\frac{N - 2}{1 - r^2}}$$

where **degrees of freedom** is the number of cases in the sample minus two (*df* = *N* − 2).

To illustrate this formula in action, let's consider an example. Some research suggests that there is a relationship between the number of hours of sunlight people are exposed to during the day and their mood. People living at extreme northern latitudes, for example, are exposed to very little sunlight in the depths of winter and may go days or weeks without more than a few hours of sunlight per day. There is some evidence that such sunlight deprivation is related to feelings of depression and sadness. In fact, there is even a name for the condition: seasonal affective disorder, or SAD. To examine this relationship for myself, I randomly select 100 people from various regions of the world, measure the time from sunrise to sunset on a given day where each person lives, and get a measure of each person's mood on a scale from 1 to 10 (1 = *Very sad*; 10 = *Very happy*). Because the members of my sample live at various latitudes, the number of daylight hours will vary. If I conduct my study in January, those participants living in the north will have relatively short days, whereas those living in the south will have long days.

Suppose that I compute a Pearson correlation coefficient with these data and find that the correlation between number of sunlight hours in the day and scores on the mood scale is $r = .25$. Is this a statistically significant correlation? To answer that question, we must find a t value associated with this correlation coefficient and determine the probability of obtaining a t value of this size by chance (see Chapter 7). In this example,

$$t = (.25)\sqrt{\frac{100 - 2}{1 - .25^2}}$$

$$t = (.25)\sqrt{\frac{98}{1 - .25^2}}$$

$$t = (.25)\sqrt{\frac{98}{1 - .0625}}$$

$$t = (.25)\sqrt{\frac{98}{.9375}}$$

$$t = (.25)\sqrt{104.53}$$

$$t = (.25)10.22$$

$$t = 2.56, \; df = 98$$

To see whether this t value is statistically significant, we must look at the table of t values in Appendix B. There we can see that, because our degrees of freedom = 98, we must look at t values in both the $df = 60$ row and the $df = 120$ row. Looking at the $df = 60$ row, we can see that a t value of 2.56 has a probability of between .01 and .02 (for a two-tailed test). We get the same results when looking in the $df = 120$ row. Therefore, we conclude that our p value is between .01 and .02. If our alpha level is the traditional .05, we would conclude that our correlation coefficient is statistically significant. In other words, we would conclude that, on the basis of our sample statistic, in the larger population of adults, the longer the daylight hours, the better their mood, in general. We could convey all of that information to the informed reader of statistics by writing, "We found a significant relationship between number of daylight hours and mood ($r = .25$, $t_{(98)} = 2.56$, $p < .05$)."

This example also provides a good opportunity to once again remind you of the dangers of assuming that a correlation represents a causal relationship between two variables. Although it may well be that longer days cause the average adult to feel better, these data do not prove it. An alternative causal explanation for our results is that shorter days are also associated with *colder* days, whereas longer days are generally associated with *warmer* days. It may be the case that *warmth* causes better moods and the lack of warmth causes depression and sadness. If people had warm, short days, they might be just as happy as if they had warm, long days. So remember: Just because two variables are correlated, it does not mean that one causes the other.

 To watch a video demonstrating how to calculate the t value and determine whether a correlation coefficient is statistically significant, please refer to the website that accompanies this book.

A Brief Word on Other Types of Correlation Coefficients

Although Pearson correlation coefficients are probably the most commonly used and reported in the social sciences, they are limited by the requirement that both variables be measured on interval or ratio scales. Fortunately, there are methods available for calculating the strength of the relationship between two variables even if one or both variables are not measured using interval or ratio scales. In this section, I briefly describe three of these "other" correlation coefficients. It is important to note that all of these statistics are very similar to the Pearson correlation coefficient and each produces a correlation coefficient that is similar to the Pearson *r*. They are simply specialized versions of the Pearson correlation coefficient that can be used when one or both of the variables are not measured using interval or ratio scales.

Point-Biserial Correlation

When one of our variables is a continuous variable (i.e., measured on an interval or ratio scale) and the other is a two-level categorical (a.k.a. nominal) variable (also known as a **dichotomous variable**), we need to calculate a point-biserial correlation coefficient. This coefficient is a specialized version of the Pearson correlation coefficient discussed earlier in this chapter. For example, suppose I want to know whether there is a relationship between whether a person owns a car (yes or no) and their score on a written test of traffic rule knowledge, such as the tests one must pass to get a driver's license. In this example, we are examining the relation between one categorical variable with two categories ("owns a car" or "does not own a car") and one continuous variable (one's score on the driver's test). Therefore, the point-biserial correlation is the appropriate statistic in this instance.

Phi

Sometimes researchers want to know whether two dichotomous variables are correlated. In this case, we would calculate a phi coefficient (Φ), which is another specialized version of the Pearson *r*. For example, suppose I want to know whether gender (male or female) is associated with whether one smokes cigarettes or not (smoker or nonsmoker). In this case, with two dichotomous variables, I would calculate a phi coefficient. (*Note*: Those readers familiar with chi-square analysis will notice that two dichotomous variables can also be analyzed using chi squared.)

Spearman Rho

Sometimes data are recorded as ranks. Because ranks are a form of ordinal data, and the other correlation coefficients discussed so far involve either continuous (interval, ratio) or dichotomous variables, we need a different type of statistic to calculate the correlation between two variables that use ranked data. In this case, the **Spearman rho**, a specialized form of the Pearson *r*, is appropriate. For example, many schools use students' grade point averages (a continuous scale) to rank students (an ordinal scale). In addition, students' scores on standardized achievement tests can be ranked. To see whether a student's rank in their school is related to their rank on the standardized test, a Spearman rho coefficient can be calculated.

Example: The Correlation Between Grades and Test Scores

Student achievement can be measured in a variety of ways. Two of these methods are the grade point average (GPA), usually measured on a scale from 0 to 4 (with 4 = "A"), and standardized test scores. Grades are given to students by their teachers, and standardized test scores indicate how well students have performed on tests produced by test makers who are not affiliated with the students' schools, which are usually scored by computers.

TABLE 12.6   SPSS printout of correlation analysis

	GPA	Naglieri Test Scores
GPA	1.0000 (n = 314)	
Naglieri test scores	.4291 (n = 314) p = .000	1.0000 (n = 314)

My colleague, Carol Giancarlo, and I collected data from a sample of 314 eleventh-grade students at a high school in California. Among the data we collected were their cumulative GPAs (i.e., their GPAs accumulated from the time they began high school up to the time the data were collected). In addition, we gave students the Naglieri Nonverbal Ability Test (NNAT; Naglieri, 1996), a nonverbal test of general mental reasoning and critical thinking skills. To see if there was a statistically significant correlation between these two measures of ability, I used the SPSS statistical software program to calculate a correlation coefficient and a *p* value. The SPSS printout from this analysis is presented in Table 12.6.

The results presented in Table 12.6 provide several pieces of information. First, there are three correlation coefficients presented. The correlations on the diagonal show the correlation between a single variable and itself. Therefore, the first correlation coefficient presented reveals that GPA is correlated with itself perfectly ($r = 1.0000$). Because we always get a correlation of 1.00 when we correlate a variable with itself, these correlations presented on the diagonal are meaningless. That is why there is not a *p* value reported for them. The numbers in the parentheses, just below the correlation coefficients, report the sample size. There were 314 eleventh-grade students in this sample. The correlation coefficient that is *off* the diagonal is the one we're interested in. Here, we can see that students' GPAs were moderately correlated with their scores on the Naglieri test ($r = .4291$). This correlation is statistically significant, with a *p* value of less than .0001 ($p < .0001$).

To gain a clearer understanding of the relationship between GPA and Naglieri test scores, we can calculate a coefficient of determination. We do this by squaring the correlation coefficient. When we square this correlation coefficient ($.4291 \times .4291 = .1841$), we see that GPA explains a little over 18 percent of the variance in the Naglieri test scores. Although this is a substantial percentage, it still leaves more than 80 percent of the ability test scores unexplained. Because of this large percentage of unexplained variance, we must conclude that teacher-assigned grades reflect something substantially different from general mental reasoning abilities and critical thinking skills, as measured by the Naglieri test.

Worked Example: Statistical Significance and Confidence Interval

Suppose that I want to examine whether there is a correlation between how much time high school students spend working on homework and their scores on a standardized achievement test. I select a random sample of 64 high school students and find the correlation between the hours they spend working on homework, per week, and their scores on a standardized achievement test. I find that the correlation between these two variables is $r = .40$. From this statistic I know that, *in this sample*, there is a positive, moderate association between hours spent on homework and scores on the achievement test. But does this correlation in the sample indicate a positive correlation between these two variables in the larger population of high school students? To answer that question we need to calculate a *t* value (see above). Because we are also going to calculate a confidence interval, and because we have already seen a worked example using the simplified *t* test formula earlier in the chapter, this time let's calculate the standard error of the correlation coefficient:

$$s_r = \sqrt{(1 - .4^2) / (64 - 2)}$$
$$s_r = \sqrt{(.84) / (62)}$$
$$s_r = .12$$

When we plug this standard error into the standard *t* test formula for correlation coefficients, we find that our observed *t* value is

$$t = \frac{.40}{.12} = 3.33$$

Using our degrees of freedom of $N - 2$, we find a critical *t* value of 2.000. Notice that we used an alpha level of .05, a two-tailed test, and 60 degrees of freedom in Appendix B because that was the closest value we could find to our actual degrees of freedom. Because our observed *t* value of 3.33 is larger than our critical *t* value of 2.000, we conclude that our sample correlation coefficient is statistically significant. In other words, it is significantly different from zero, which was the value of the correlation coefficient proposed in the null hypothesis. Now we can conclude that in the population of high school students, there is a positive, moderately strong correlation between amount of hours spent doing homework per week and scores on this achievement test. Note that we *cannot* conclude that spending more time on homework *causes* higher scores on the achievement test. There could well be other explanations for this positive correlation.

Now let's calculate a 99 percent confidence interval for the sample correlation coefficient. We already know the standard error and the sample *r*, so we just need to look up the *t* value for 60 *df* and a two-tailed alpha level of .01. In Appendix B we see that this gives us a *t* value of 2.617. (*Note*: Many students make the mistake of plugging the *observed t* value that they calculated for the *t* test into the confidence interval formula. Be sure you use the correct *t* value from Appendix B in your confidence interval formula.)

$$CI_{99} = .4 \pm (.12)(2.617) \rightarrow .4 \pm (.31) \rightarrow .09, .71$$

Now we can wrap words around our results: We are 99 percent confident that the population correlation coefficient is contained within the interval ranging from .09 to .71.

 To watch a video demonstrating how to calculate and interpret a confidence interval for *r*, please refer to the website that accompanies this book.

Writing it Up

When researchers write about bivariate correlations in scientific reports and journal articles, they often present a table that includes the correlation coefficients between the variables, some indication of whether the correlation coefficients are statistically significant, and descriptive statistics (i.e., means and standard deviations) for those variables. In addition, they provide a brief description of the correlations in the text.

In a study that I conducted some time ago, I wanted to compare two different survey measures of achievement goals. Achievement goals represent what students may be trying to accomplish in school, and are divided into mastery goals (the desire to develop knowledge and skills) and performance goals (the desire to do better than others). So I gave a sample of college students two surveys with items assessing mastery and performance goals. One survey was called the Achievement Goals Questionnaire (AGQ; Elliot & McGregor, 2001) and the other was the

TABLE 12.7 SPSS printout of correlation analysis

	Mastery AGQ[1]	Performance AGQ[1]	Mastery PALS[2]	Performance PALS[2]	Mean (s.d.)[3]
Mastery AGQ	1.00				5.56 (.96)
Performance AGQ	.24**	1.00			4.16 (1.46)
Mastery PALS	.75**	.18*	1.00		5.61 (.84)
Performance PALS	.03	.77**	−.02	1.00	4.17 (1.31)

Notes:
1 AGQ: Achievement Goals Questionnaire
2 PALS: Patterns of Adaptive Learning Survey
3 s.d. = standard deviation
* indicates *p* < .05
** indicates *p* < .01

Patterns of Adaptive Learning Survey (PALS; Midgley et al., 1998). I was curious whether these two different surveys were measuring the same thing, so I needed to see how strongly students' scores on the goal measures from one survey were correlated with their scores on the same goal measures from the other survey. The results of the correlation analyses, along with the means and standard deviations for each variable, are presented in Table 12.7.

If I were writing these results up for publication I would write something like the following:

"As the correlation coefficients presented in Table 12.7 reveal, the correlations between the comparable goal variables in the AGQ and the PALS were quite strong. The correlation between the two measures of mastery goals was *r* = .75. The correlation between the performance goal scales of the AGQ and the PALS were similarly strong (*r* = .77). Although these correlations are quite strong, the coefficients of determination (r^2 = .56 and .59 for the mastery and performance goals, respectively) indicate that there is still quite a bit of variance in the goal measures from the PALS that is not explained by the corresponding goal measures of the AGQ. This suggests that there are important differences in students' interpretations of the goal items on these two survey measures."

Wrapping Up and Looking Forward

Correlation coefficients, in particular Pearson correlation coefficients, provide a way to determine both the direction and the strength of the relationship between two variables measured on a continuous scale. This index can provide evidence that two variables are related to each other, or that they are not, but does not, in and of itself, demonstrate a *causal* association between two variables. In this chapter, I also introduced the concepts of explained or shared variance and the coefficient of determination. Determining how much variance in one variable is shared with, or explained by, another variable is at the core of all of the statistics that are discussed in the remaining chapters of this book. In particular, correlation coefficients are the precursors to the more sophisticated statistics involved in multiple regression (Chapter 13). In the next chapter, we examine *t* tests, which allow us to look at the association between a two-category independent variable and a continuous dependent variable.

Work Problems

Suppose you want to know whether there is a correlation between how much time healthy young adults spend exercising and how much sleep they get. You select a random sample of 25 healthy young adults and ask them how many hours they spend exercising per week and how many hours they spend sleeping per week. You find there is a correlation in this sample of .45. Please answer the following questions based on this information.

1. What is the direction of this correlation coefficient? How do you know?
2. What is the strength of this correlation coefficient? How do you know?
3. Interpret this correlation coefficient. What does it tell you?
4. Calculate the coefficient of determination and interpret it. What does it tell you?
5. Using Appendix B and an alpha level of .05, find the critical t value.
6. Calculate the observed t value and decide whether this correlation coefficient is statistically significant using an alpha level of .05. Interpret your results. What do they tell you?
7. Calculate a 95 percent confidence interval for this correlation coefficient and interpret it. What does it tell you?

 For answers to these work problems, and for additional work problems, please refer to the website that accompanies this book.

Notes

1 There is a website that has several excellent examples of **spurious correlations**—correlations between variables that are coincidental or caused by some third variable. Some examples from the website include the number of people who drowned by falling into a pool and how many films Nicolas Cage appeared in across several years ($r = .66$), and a strong correlation ($r = .99$) between the divorce rate in Maine and per capita consumption of margarine over time. For more examples, take a look at the website: http://tylervigen.com/spurious-correlations.

2 When calculating z scores for use in the correlation coefficient, the standard deviation that is used is the standard deviation for the population, not the standard deviation for the sample.

CHAPTER 13

Regression

In Chapter 12, the concept of correlation was introduced. Correlation involves a measure of the degree to which two variables are related to each other. A closely related concept, coefficient of determination, was also introduced in that chapter. This statistic provides a measure of the strength of the association between two variables in terms of percentage of variance explained. Both of these concepts are present in regression. In this chapter, the concepts of **simple linear regression** and **multiple regression** are introduced.

Regression is a very common statistical method in the social sciences. One of the reasons it is such a popular technique is because it is so versatile. Regression, particularly multiple regression, allows researchers to examine the nature and strength of the relations between variables, the relative predictive power of several independent variables on a dependent variable, and the unique contribution of one or more independent variables when controlling for one or more covariates. It is also possible to test for interactions in multiple regression. With all of the possible applications of multiple regression, it is clear that it is impossible to describe all of the functions of regression in this brief chapter. Therefore, the focus of this chapter is to provide an introduction to the concept and uses of regression, and to refer the reader to resources providing additional information.

Simple vs. Multiple Regression

The difference between simple and multiple regression is similar to the difference between one-way and factorial ANOVA. Like one-way ANOVA, simple regression analysis involves a single **independent**, or **predictor variable** and a single **dependent**, or **outcome variable**. This is the same number of variables as used in a simple correlation analysis. The difference between a Pearson correlation coefficient and a simple regression analysis is that while the correlation does not distinguish between independent and dependent variables, in a regression analysis there is always a designated predictor variable and a designated dependent variable (although, just as with correlations, regression analyses do not allow researchers to claim that there is a *causal* association between variables). That is because the purpose of regression analysis is to make *predictions* about the value of the dependent variable given certain values of the predictor variable. This is a simple extension of a correlation analysis. If I am interested in the relationship between height and weight, for example, I could use a simple regression analysis to answer this question: If I know a man's height, what would I *predict* his weight to be? Notice that the variable I am interested in predicting is designated as my dependent variable, and the variable or variables that I am using to predict my dependent variable become my predictor, or independent, variable or variables. Of course, the accuracy of my prediction will only be as good as my correlation will allow, with stronger correlations leading to more accurate predictions. Therefore, simple linear regression is not really a more powerful tool than simple correlation analysis. But it does give me another way of conceptualizing the relation between two variables, a point I elaborate on shortly.

The real power of regression analysis can be found in multiple regression. Like factorial ANOVA, multiple regression involves models that have two or more predictor variables and a single dependent variable. For example, suppose that, again, I am interested in predicting how much a person weighs (i.e., weight is the **dependent variable**). Now suppose that in addition to height, I know how many minutes of exercise that person gets per day, and how many calories a day he consumes. Now I've got three predictor variables (height, exercise, and calories consumed) to help me make an educated guess about the person's weight. Multiple regression analysis allows me to see, among other things, (a) how much these three **predictor variables**, as a group, are related to weight, (b) the strength of the relationship between each predictor variable and the dependent variable *while controlling for the other predictor variables in the model*, (c) the *relative* strength of each predictor variable, and (d) whether there are interaction effects between the predictor variables. As you can see, multiple regression is a particularly versatile and powerful statistical technique.

Variables Used in Regression

As with correlation analysis, in regression the dependent and **independent variables** (a.k.a. the predictor variables) need to be measured on an interval or ratio scale. **Dichotomous** (i.e., categorical variables with two categories) predictor variables can also be used.[1] There is a special form of regression analysis, logit regression, that allows us to examine dichotomous dependent variables, but this type of regression is beyond the scope of this book. In this chapter, we limit our consideration of regression to those types that involve a continuous dependent variable and either continuous or dichotomous predictor variables.

Regression in Depth

Regression, particularly simple linear regression, is a statistical technique that is very closely related to correlations (discussed in Chapter 12). In fact, when examining the relationship between two continuous (i.e., measured on an interval or ratio scale) variables, either a correlation coefficient or a regression equation can be used. Indeed, the Pearson correlation coefficient is nothing more than a simple linear regression coefficient that has been standardized. The benefits of conducting a regression analysis rather than a correlation analysis are (a) regression analysis yields more information, particularly when conducted with one of the common statistical software packages, and (b) the regression equation allows us to think about the association between the two variables of interest in a more intuitive way. Whereas the correlation coefficient provides us with a single number (e.g., $r = .40$), which we can then try to interpret, the regression analysis yields a formula for calculating the **predicted value** of one variable when we know the actual value of the second variable. Here's how it works. There are a few assumptions of regression that must be met or the results of the regression may not be valid. First, as mentioned, the dependent variable should be measured on an interval/ratio scale and the predictor variables should either be interval/ratio or dichotomous variables. Second, it is assumed that there is a linear association between the predictor variable and the dependent variable. (Recall from Chapter 12 that non-linear associations, such as curvilinear relationships, can create difficulties in identifying the true association among the variables.) Third, all of the variables in the regression analysis should have normal distributions. A fourth assumption (of multiple regression in particular) is that the predictor variables are not too strongly correlated with each other. It is also assumed that the errors in prediction are independent of each other. Finally, there is the assumption of **heteroscedasticity**. This means that errors in the prediction of Y are about the same, in both size and direction, at all levels of X.

The key to understanding regression is to understand the formula for the regression equation. So I begin by presenting the most simple form of the regression equation, describing how it works, and then moving on to more complicated forms of the equation. In Table 13.1, the

TABLE 13.1 The regression equation

$$\hat{Y} = bX + a$$

where $\hat{Y}$ is the predicted value of the *Y* variable,
     b is the unstandardized regression coefficient, or the slope,
     X is a given value of the independent variable,
     a is the intercept (i.e., the point where the regression line intercepts the *Y* axis).

regression equation used to find the predicted value of **Y** is presented along with definitions of the components.

In simple linear regression, we begin with the assumption that the two variables are **linearly** related. In other words, if the two variables are actually related to each other, we assume that every time there is an increase of a given size in value on the *X* variable (called the **predictor** or **independent** variable), there is a corresponding increase (if there is a positive correlation) or decrease (if there is a negative correlation) *of a given size* in the *Y* variable (called the **dependent**, **outcome**, or **criterion** variable). In other words, if the value of *X* increases from a value of 1 to a value of 2, and *Y* increases by 2 points, then when *X* increases from 2 to 3, we would predict that the value of *Y* would increase another 2 points.

To illustrate this point, let's consider the following set of data. Suppose I want to know whether there is a relationship between the level of education people have and their monthly income. Education level is measured in years, beginning with kindergarten and extending through graduate school. Income is measured in thousands of dollars. Suppose that I randomly select a sample of 10 adults and measure their level of education and their monthly income, getting the data provided in Table 13.2.

When we look at these data, we can see that, in general, monthly income increases as the level of education increases. This is a general, rather than an absolute, trend because in some cases a person with more years of education makes less money per month than someone with fewer years of education (e.g., Case 10 and Case 9, Case 6 and Case 5). So although not every person with more years of education makes more money, *on average* more years of education are associated with higher monthly incomes. The correlation coefficient that describes the relation of these two variables is $r = .83$, which is a very strong, positive correlation (see Chapter 12 for a more detailed discussion of correlation coefficients).

If we were to plot these data on a simple graph, we would produce a **scatterplot**, such as the one provided in Figure 13.1. In this scatterplot, there are 10 data points, one for each case in the study.

TABLE 13.2 Income and education level data

	Education Level (X) (in Years)	Monthly Income (Y) (in Thousands of Dollars)
Case 1	6	1
Case 2	8	1.5
Case 3	11	1
Case 4	12	2
Case 5	12	4
Case 6	13	2.5
Case 7	14	5
Case 8	16	6
Case 9	16	10
Case 10	21	8
Mean	12.90	4.10
Standard Deviation	4.25	3.12
Correlation Coefficient	.83	

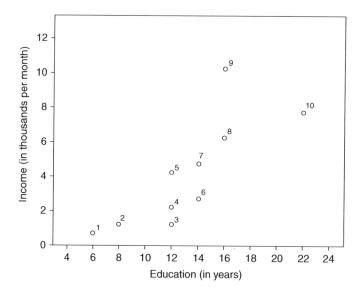

FIGURE 13.1 Scatterplot for education and income.

Note that each data point marks the spot where education level (the X variable) and monthly income (the Y variable) meet for each case. For example, the point that has a value of 10 on the Y axis (income) and 16 on the X axis (education level) is the data point for the 10th case in our sample. These 10 data points in our scatterplot reveal a fairly distinct trend. Notice that the points rise somewhat uniformly from the lower-left corner of the graph to the upper-right corner. This shape is a clear indicator of the positive relationship (i.e., correlation) between education level and income. If there had been a perfect correlation between these two variables (i.e., $r = 1.0$), the data points would be aligned in a perfectly straight line, rising from the lower left to the upper right on the graph. If the relationship between these two variables were weaker (e.g., $r = .30$), the data points would be more widely scattered, making the lower-left to upper-right trend much less clear.

With the data provided in Table 13.2, we can calculate all of the pieces of the regression equation. The regression equation allows us to do two things. First, it lets us find predicted values for the Y variable for any given value of the X variable. In other words, we can predict a person's monthly income if we know how many years of education he or she has. Second, the regression equation allows us to produce the **regression line**. The regression line is the basis for linear regression and can help us understand how regression works.

There are a number of different types of regression formulas, but the most commonly used is called **ordinary least squares regression**, or **OLS**. OLS is based on an idea that we have seen before: the *sum of squares* (see Chapters 3 and 9). If you wanted to, you could draw a number of straight lines that go through the cluster of data points presented in the scatterplot in Figure 13.1. For example, you could draw a horizontal line that extends out from the number 5 on the Y axis. Similarly, you could draw a straight line that extends down from the number 10 on the Y axis to the number 22 on the X axis. No matter how you decide to draw your straight line, notice that at least some of the data points in the scatterplot will not fall exactly *on* the line. Some or all will fall above the line, some may fall directly on the line, and some or all will fall below the line. Any data point that does not fall directly on the line will have a certain amount of distance between the point and the line. Now, if you were to calculate the distance between the data point and the line you have drawn, and then square that distance, you would have a *squared deviation* for that individual data point. If you calculated the squared deviation for each data point that did not fall on the line, and added all of these squared deviations together, you would end up with the *sum of squared deviations*, or *sum of squares*.

Now here is the key: The sum of the squared deviations, or sum of squares, will differ depending on where you draw your line. In any scatterplot, there is only *one* line that produces the *smallest* sum of squares. This line is known as the line of *least squares*, and this is the regression line. So, the reason this type of regression is called ordinary *least squares* regression is because in this form of regression, the regression line represents the straight line that produces the *smallest* sum of squared deviations from the line. This regression line represents the *predicted* values of Y at any given value of X. Of course, when we predict a value of Y for a given value of X, our prediction may be off. This error in prediction is represented by the distance between the regression line and the actual data point(s) in the scatterplot. To illustrate how this works, we first need to calculate the properties of the regression line (i.e., its slope and intercept). Then we draw this regression line into the scatterplot, and you can see how well it "fits" the data (i.e., how close the data points fall to the regression line).

If you take a look at the formula for the regression equation in Table 13.1, you will notice that there are four components: (a) $\hat{Y}$ is the predicted value of the Y variable, (b) b is the unstandardized **regression coefficient**, and also the **slope** of the regression line, (c) X is the value of the X variable, and (d) a is the value of the **intercept** (i.e., where the regression line crosses the Y axis). Because $\hat{Y}$ is the value produced by the **regression equation**, let's save that one for last. And because X is just a given value on the X variable, there is not really anything to work out with that one. So let's take a closer look at a and b.

We cannot calculate the intercept before we know the slope of the regression line, so let's begin there. The formula for calculating the regression coefficient is

$$b = r \times \frac{s_y}{s_x}$$

where b is the regression coefficient,

$\quad$ r is the correlation between the X and Y variables,

$\quad$ s_y is the standard deviation of the Y variable,

$\quad$ s_x is the standard deviation of the X variable.

Looking at the data in Table 13.2, we can see that $r = .83$, $s_y = 3.12$, and $s_x = 4.25$. When we plug these numbers into the formula, we get the following:

$$b = .83 \times \frac{3.12}{4.25}$$

$$b = (.83) \times (.73)$$

$$b = .61$$

Notice that the regression coefficient is simply the correlation coefficient times the ratio of the standard deviations for the two variables involved. When we multiply the correlation coefficient by this ratio of standard deviations, we are roughly transforming the correlation coefficient into the scales of measurement used for the two variables. Notice that there is a smaller range, or less variety, of scores on our Y variable than there is on our X variable in this example. This is reflected in the ratio of standard deviations used to calculate b.

Now that we've got our b, we can calculate our intercept, a. The formula for a is as follows:

$$a = \bar{Y} - b\bar{X}$$

where $\bar{Y}$ is the average value of Y,

$\quad$ $\bar{X}$ is the average value of X,

$\quad$ b is the regression coefficient.

When we plug in the values from Table 13.2, we find that

$$a = 4.1 - (.61)(12.9)$$

$$a = 4.1 - 7.87$$

$$a = -3.77$$

This value of *a* indicates that the intercept for the regression line is –3.77. In other words, the regression line crosses the *Y* axis at a value of –3.77. In still other words, this intercept tells us that when *X* = 0, we would predict the value of *Y* to be –3.77. Of course, in the real world, it is not possible to have a monthly income of negative 3.77 thousand dollars. Such unrealistic values remind us that we are dealing with *predicted* values of Y. Given our data, if a person has absolutely no formal education, we would *predict* that person to make a negative amount of money.

Now we can start to fill out our regression equation. The original formula

$$\hat{Y} = a + bX$$

now reads

$$\hat{Y} = -3.77 + .61X$$

It is important to remember that when we use the regression equation to find predicted values of *Y* for different values of *X*, we are not calculating the *actual* value of Y. We are only making *predictions* about the value of Y. Whenever we make predictions, we will sometimes be incorrect. Therefore, there is bound to be some **error** (*e*) in our predictions about the values of Y at given values of X. The stronger the relationship (i.e., correlation) between my *X* and *Y* variables, the less error there will be in my predictions. The error is the difference between the actual, or observed, value of *Y* and the predicted value of Y. Because the predicted value of *Y* is simply *a* + *bX*, we can express the formula for the error in two ways:

$$e = Y - \hat{Y}$$

$$e = Y - a + bX$$

So, rather than a single regression equation, there are actually two. One of them, the one presented in Table 13.1, is for the *predicted* value of Y ($\hat{Y}$). The other one is for the actual, or *observed* value of Y. This equation takes into account the errors in our predictions, and is written as $Y = bX + a + e$.

Now that we've got our regression equation, we can put it to use. First, let's wrap words around it, so that we can make sure we understand what it is telling us. Our regression coefficient tells us that "For every unit of increase in *X*, there is a corresponding predicted increase of .61 units in Y." Applying this to our variables, we can say that "For every additional year of education, we would *predict* an increase of .61 times $1,000, or $610, in monthly income." We know that the predicted value of *Y* will *increase* when *X* increases, and vice versa, because the regression coefficient is *positive*. Had it been negative, we would predict a decrease in *Y* when *X* increases.

Next, let's use our regression equation to find predicted values of *Y* at given values of *X*. For example, what would we predict the monthly income to be for a person with 9 years of formal education? To answer this question, we plug in the value of 9 for the *X* variable and solve the equation:

$$\hat{Y} = -3.77 + .61(9)$$

$$\hat{Y} = -3.77 + 5.59$$

$$\hat{Y} = 1.82$$

So we would predict that a person with 9 years of education would make $1,820 per month, plus or minus our error in prediction (e).

Finally, we can use our regression equation to compute our regression line. We already know, from the value of the intercept, that our regression line will cross the Y axis at a value of -3.77. To draw a straight line, all we need to do is calculate one additional point. To make sure we include all of the points in our scatterplot, let's just calculate a predicted value of Y for a person with 25 years of education:

$$\hat{Y} = -3.77 + .61(25)$$

$$\hat{Y} = -3.77 + 15.25$$

$$\hat{Y} = 11.48$$

If we were to draw a regression line through our scatterplot, using the two points we found from our intercept and the predicted Y value, we would get something like the line presented in Figure 13.2.

With the regression line added to the scatterplot, some of the concepts mentioned earlier in this chapter may be easier to understand. First, notice that our regression line does not accurately predict the actual Y values for any of our cases except for Case 7. That data point is precisely on the regression line. For each of the other nine cases, there is some amount of error present in the prediction. In some cases, the amount of error is very small (e.g., Case 8), whereas in others the amount of error is quite large (e.g., Case 9). These errors in prediction are known as **residuals**. (See Figure 13.3 for an illustration of the residual for Case 10.) In some cases, our predicted value was less than our **observed value** (e.g., Cases 1, 2, 5, 8, and 9). For these cases, we have **underpredicted** their income based on their level of education. Such underpredictions produce *positive* residuals (because the residual = observed scores – predicted score). For other cases (Cases 3, 4, 6, and 10) we **overpredicted** the Y value, creating *negative* residuals. Second, notice the distance

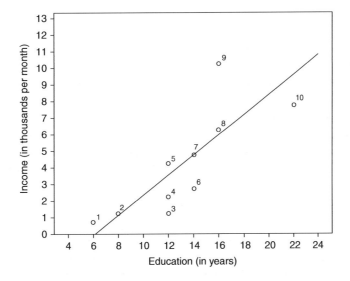

FIGURE 13.2 Scatterplot for education and income with regression line.

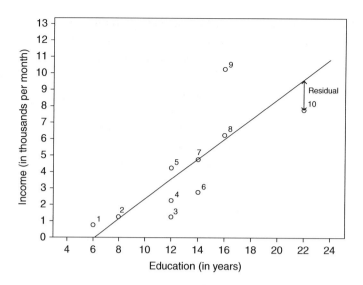

FIGURE 13.3 Illustration of the residual for Case 10.

between each case and the line. When we square each of these distances and then add them all together, we get the sum of squares. Third, notice that the regression line marks the line where the sum of the squared distances is smallest. To test this, try drawing some other lines and note the way this increases the overall amount of error in prediction. Finally, notice where the regression line crosses the *Y* axis (the intercept) and how much higher up the *Y* axis the regression line goes for each increase of one unit value in *X* (the slope). The slope and the intercept will correspond with the values that we found for *b* and *a*, respectively.

Multiple Regression

Now that we've discussed the elements of simple linear regression, let's move on to a consideration of **multiple regression**. Despite the impressive qualities of simple linear regression, the plain truth is that when we only have two variables, simple linear regression does not provide much more information than would a simple correlation coefficient. Because of this, you rarely see a simple linear regression with two variables reported in a published study. But multiple regression is a whole different story. Multiple regression is a very powerful statistic that can be used to provide a staggering array of useful information. At this point, it may be worth reminding you that in a short book like this, we only scratch the surface of what multiple regression can do and how it works. The interested reader should refer to the regression related readings in the bibliography to find more information on this powerful technique.

Multiple regression is such a powerful statistical technique because it allows researchers to examine the associations among several predictor variables and a dependent variable. In the social sciences, researchers are often unable to conduct controlled experiments that isolate a single cause-and-effect relationship between two variables. For example, if I want to know why some students drop out of high school, I cannot conduct an experiment as it would be unethical to cause some students to drop out of school. In addition, in the real world there is not a single cause of dropping out of school; there are multiple influences on this behavior. Low academic achievement, a desire to make money, pressure to help out with childcare and other responsibilities at home, frequent absences, low motivation for school work, and being socially isolated are just some of the factors that may influence a student's decision to drop out of school. In a multiple regression analysis, all of these variables can be entered into the model, and the amount of variance explained in the dependent variable by *each* of the independent variables can be examined, while controlling for the effects of the other variables. This is powerful stuff.

Two examples of real-world uses of multiple regression can demonstrate the power of the technique. First, much of the current data-driven analytics that are being used by companies to sell you products are taking advantage of multiple regression. For example, have you ever noticed which advertisements pop up on your screen when you are on a social media website? Well, it costs a lot of money to advertise on these websites, so advertisers want to make sure they show you ads that are likely to appeal to you. How do they know which ads will catch your attention? Your purchasing behavior is predicted by several factors including your gender, your age, where you live, whether you are single or in a relationship, what your friends like to do, what you like that your friends do, how much money you spend online, and what products you search for online. All of these variables can be plugged into a multiple regression to help companies determine the *strongest* predictor of your shopping behavior and show you advertisements that are targeted toward that predictor. If age is the strongest predictor of shopping behavior, you will see advertisements targeting your age group (e.g., age-related drugs for senior citizens, sugary energy drinks for adolescents and young adults). Some of the earliest adopters of multiple regression analysis techniques were insurance companies. To decide how much to charge each driver for auto insurance, companies look at predictors of safe driving behavior, like age (older drivers tend to be safer), where you live (people who live in more densely populated areas tend to get in more accidents), how well you do in school (higher achievers tend to drive more carefully), and so on.

In one particularly interesting example of an application of multiple regression, described in the book *Freakonomics* (Levitt & Dubner, 2009), researchers examined crime rates in the United States. After many years of rising crime rates that reached a peak in the early 1990s, crime rates began to fall dramatically from the mid-1990s through 2010. What caused this dramatic drop in crime? Several possible explanations have been offered, including more and better policing, tougher sentencing laws for criminals, a strong economy in the 1990s, increased use of capital punishment, tougher gun laws, and an aging population, among other explanations. Using multiple regression, researchers were able to determine how much of the variance in the drop in crime rates could be explained by *each* of these variables, controlling for all of the other variables. They found that some predictor variables (e.g., a strong economy, increased use of capital punishment, tougher gun laws, an aging population) had no effect on the crime rate. It is worth noting that some of these predictor variables—an improving economy in the 1990s, an aging population—were significantly *correlated* with the decrease in crime, but when the effects of other predictor variables were controlled in the multiple regression, these predictor variables were no longer significantly associated with the dependent variable. In contrast, several predictor variables remained significantly associated with the drop in crime, even after controlling for the effects of other variables. More and better policing explained about 10 percent of the drop in crime, tougher sentencing laws explained about 33 percent of the drop in crime, and the bursting of the crime bubble caused by the crack cocaine epidemic explained about 15 percent of the drop in crime. Multiple regression revealed that all of these variables combined explained about 58 percent of the overall drop in crime, leaving about 42 percent of the drop unexplained. (I won't spoil the ending of that chapter of *Freakonomics* by telling you what the authors think may explain the rest of the variance in the crime rate reduction—you'll have to read it yourself.) Multiple regression allowed the researchers to identify the explanatory power of each variable, as well as the combined explanatory power of all the variables in the model combined. Always remember that even though this combination of predictor variables *explained* a large portion of the variance in the drop in crime, this does not prove that these significant predictor variables *caused* the drop in crime. They may have, but regression alone cannot prove that the associations among variables are causal.

An Example Using SPSS

To illustrate some of the benefits of multiple regression, let's add a second *predictor* variable to our previous example predicting monthly income. So far, using the data from Table 13.2, we have examined the relationship between education level and income. In this example, education level has been used as our *predictor* or *independent* variable and income has been used as our *dependent* or *outcome* variable. We found that, on average, in our sample, one's monthly salary is predicted to increase by $610 for every additional year of schooling the individual has received. But there was some error in our predictions, indicating that there are other variables that predict how much money one makes. One such predictor may be the length of time one has been out of school. Because people tend to make more money the longer they have been in the workforce, it stands to reason that those adults in our sample who finished school a long time ago may be making more than those who finished school more recently. Although Case 4 and Case 5 each had 12 years of schooling, Case 5 makes more money than Case 4. Perhaps this is due to Case 5 being in the workforce longer than Case 4.

When we add this second predictor variable to the model, we get the following regression equation:

$$\hat{Y} = a + b_1 X_1 + b_2 X_2$$

where $\hat{Y}$ is the predicted value of the dependent variable,

X_1 is the value of the first predictor variable,

X_2 is the value of the second predictor variable.

b_1 is the regression coefficient for the first independent variable,

b_2 is the regression coefficient for the second independent variable.

This regression equation with two predictor variables will allow me to examine a number of different questions. First, I can see whether my two predictor variables combined are significantly related to, or predictive of, my dependent variable, and how much of the variance my predictor variables explain in my dependent variable. Second, I can test whether each of my predictor variables is significantly related to my dependent variable *when controlling for the other predictor variable*. When I say "controlling for the other predictor variable," I mean that I can examine whether a predictor variable is related to the dependent variable after I partial out, or take away, the portion of the variance in my dependent variable that has already been accounted for by my other independent variable. Third, I can see which of my two predictor variables is the stronger predictor of my dependent variable. Fourth, I can test whether one predictor variable is related to my dependent variable after controlling for the other predictor variable, thus conducting a sort of ANCOVA (see Chapter 10 for a discussion of ANCOVA). There are many other things I can do with multiple regression, but I will limit my discussion to these four.

Suppose that for the 10 cases in my sample, I also measure the number of years that they have been in the workforce, and I get the data presented in Table 13.3. These data reveal that both years of education and years in the workforce are positively correlated with monthly income. But how much of the variance in income can these two predictor variables explain *together*? Will years of education still predict income when we control for the effects of years in the workforce? In other words, after I partial out the portion of the variance in income that is accounted for by years in the workforce, will years of education still be able to help us predict income? Which of these two independent variables will be the stronger predictor of income? And will each make a unique contribution in explaining variance in income?

To answer these questions, I use the SPSS statistical software package to analyze my data. (*Note*: With only 10 cases in my sample, it is not wise to run a multiple regression. I am doing so for illustration purposes only. When conducting multiple regression analyses, you should have at least 30 cases plus 10 cases for each predictor variable in the model.) I begin by computing the Pearson correlation coefficients for all three of the variables in the model. The results are presented in Table 13.4.

These data reveal that both level of education and years in the workforce are correlated with monthly income ($r = .826$ and $r = .695$ for education and workforce with income, respectively). In Table 13.4, we can also see that there is a small-to-moderate correlation between our two predictors, years of education and years in the workforce ($r = .310$). Because this correlation is fairly weak, we can infer that both of these independent variables may predict education level.

TABLE 13.3   Income, years of employment, and education level data

	Education Level (X_1) (in Years)	Years in Workforce (X_2)	Monthly Income (Y) (in Thousands of Dollars)
Case 1	6	10	1
Case 2	8	14	1.5
Case 3	11	8	1
Case 4	12	7	2
Case 5	12	20	4
Case 6	13	15	2.5
Case 7	14	17	5
Case 8	16	22	6
Case 9	16	30	10
Case 10	21	10	8
Mean	12.90	15.00	4.10
Standard Deviation	4.25	7.20	3.12
Correlation With Income	$r = .83$	$r = .70$	

Remember that in a multiple regression, we've got multiple predictor variables trying to explain variance in the dependent variable. For a predictor variable to explain variance in a dependent variable, it must be *related* to the dependent variable (see Chapter 12 and the discussion on the coefficient of determination). In our current example, both of our predictor variables are strongly correlated with our dependent variable, so this condition is met. In addition, for each of our predictor variables to explain a *unique*, or *independent* portion of the variance in the dependent variable, our two predictor variables cannot be too strongly related to *each other*. If our two predictor variables are strongly correlated with each other, they will overlap each other and will not be able to explain unique portions of variance in the dependent variable.

For an illustration of how uncorrelated predictor variables explain unique portions of variance in a dependent variable, see Figure 13.4. In this illustration, 100 percent of the variance in the dependent variable is contained within the hexagon. The two shaded ovals represent two independent variables. Notice that each of the ovals overlaps with the hexagon, but the ovals do not overlap with each other. The portion of each independent variable (i.e., oval) that is overlapping with the dependent variable (i.e., hexagon) is the portion of variance in the dependent variable that is *explained* by the independent variables. In other words, each independent variable is explaining a *unique* portion of the variance in the dependent variable.

Contrast that with Figure 13.5, in which two correlated predictor variables each explain smaller unique portions of variance in the dependent variable. In this illustration, the two ovals representing the predictor variables overlap with each other, signifying that the two predictor variables are correlated with each other. Notice that although each of the ovals overlaps with the hexagon (i.e., each predictor variable is correlated with the dependent variable), there is quite a bit of overlap between the two ovals within the hexagon. The space where the two ovals overlap inside of the hexagon indicates the **shared variance** between the two predictor variables in their explanation of shared variance in the dependent variable. The part of each oval that is inside the hexagon but not overlapping with the other oval is the **unique variance** in the dependent variable that is being explained by the independent variable. You may notice that the portion

TABLE 13.4   Correlations among variables in the regression model

	Years of Education	Years in Workforce	Monthly Income
Years of Education	1.000		
Years in Workforce	.310	1.000	
Monthly Income	.826	.695	1.000

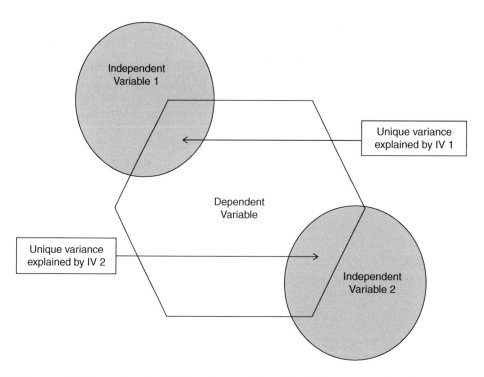

FIGURE 13.4 Portions of unique variance in the dependent variable explained by two uncorrelated independent variables.

of unique variance that is explained by the second independent variable is quite large, but the unique variance explained by the first independent variable is very small.

For example, suppose that scores on a reading test are strongly correlated with scores on a writing test ($r = .70$). Now suppose that I want to use reading and writing test scores to predict students' grades in English class. Because reading and writing test scores are so highly correlated with each other, I will probably not explain any more of the variance in English class grades

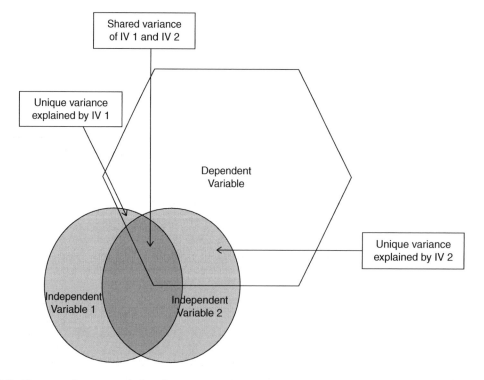

FIGURE 13.5 Portions of unique and shared variance in the dependent variable explained by two correlated independent variables.

using both predictor variables than if I use just one or the other. In other words, once I use reading test scores to predict English class grades, adding writing test scores to my regression model will probably not explain any more of the variance in my dependent variable, because reading and writing test scores are so closely related to each other. This is the concept that is represented graphically in Figure 13.5. Having strong correlations among predictor variables is called **multicollinearity** and it can cause problems in multiple regression analysis because it can make it difficult to identify the unique relation between each predictor variable and the dependent variable.

Returning to our example of using education level and years in the workforce to predict monthly income, when I conduct the regression analysis using SPSS, I get the results presented in Table 13.5. I have included several arrows to highlight particularly important statistics in the output and numbered each arrow to correspond with the discussion of these statistics. There are a variety of results produced with a multiple regression model. These results have been organized into three sections in Table 13.5. I have labeled the first section "Variance Explained." Here, we can see that we get an "*R*" value of .946 (Note 1 in Table 13.5). This is the **multiple correlation coefficient (*R*),** and it provides a measure of the correlation between the two predictors *combined* and the dependent variable. It is also the correlation between the observed value of *Y* and the predicted value of *Y* ($\hat{Y}$). So together, years of education and years in the workforce have a very strong correlation with monthly income. Next, we get an "*R* Squared" value (symbolized as R^2) (Note 2). This is essentially the coefficient of determination (see Chapter 12) for my combined predictor variables and the dependent variables, and it provides us with a percentage of variance explained. So years of education and years in the workforce, combined, explain 89.6 percent of the variance in monthly income. When you consider that this leaves only about 10 percent of the variance in monthly income unexplained, you can see that this is a very large amount of variance explained. The R^2 statistic is the measure of effect size used in multiple regression. Because it is a measure of variance explained (like r^2 in correlation and eta squared in ANOVA), it provides a handy way of assessing the practical significance of the relation of the predictors to the

TABLE 13.5 Annotated SPSS output for regression analysis examining years of education and years in the workforce predicting monthly income

	Variance Explained		
R	***R* Squared**	**Adjusted *R* Squared**	**Std. Error of the Estimate**
Note 1 →.946	Note 2 →.896	.866	1.1405

	ANOVA Results			
	Sum of Square	***df***	**Mean Square**	**F Value**	**p Value**
Regression	78.295	2	39.147	30.095	.000
Residual	9.105	7	1.301		
Total	87.400	9		Note 3	

	Regression Coefficients				
	Unstandardized Coefficients			**Standardized Coefficients**	
	B	**Std. Error**	**Beta**	***t* Value**	**p Value**
Intercept	−5.504 ←Note 4	1.298 Note 7		−4.241	.044 Note 9
Years Education	.495 ←Note 5	.094	→.676	5.270	.001 ←
Years Work	.210 ←Note 6	.056	→.485	3.783	.007 ←
		Note 8			Note 10

dependent variable. In this example, the effect size is large, suggesting practical significance as well as statistical significance. The "Adjusted R Squared" accounts for some of the error associated with multiple predictor variables by taking the number of predictor variables and the sample size into account, thereby adjusting the R^2 value down a little bit. Finally, there is a standard error for the R and R^2 values (see Chapter 6 for a discussion of standard errors).

Moving down the table to the "ANOVA Results" section, we get some statistics that help us determine whether our overall regression model is statistically significant. This section simply tells us whether our two predictor variables, combined, are able to explain a statistically significant portion of the variance in our dependent variable. The F value of 30.095, with a corresponding p value of .000, reveals that our regression model is statistically significant (Note 3 in Table 13.5). In other words, the relationship between years of education and years in the workforce combined (our predictor variables) and monthly income (our dependent variable) is statistically significant (i.e., greater than zero). Notice that these ANOVA statistics are quite similar to those presented in Chapter 10 on gender and GPA predicting valuing of English coursework among high school students. The sum of squares model in Table 10.2 corresponds to the sum of squares regression in Table 13.5. In both cases, we have sums of squares associated with the *combined predictors*, or the overall model.

Similarly, the sum of squares error in Table 10.2 is analogous to the sum of squares residual in Table 13.5. That is because residuals are simply another form of error. Just as the overall F value in Table 10.2 is produced by dividing the mean squares for the model by the mean square error, the overall F value produced in Table 13.5 is produced by dividing the mean square regression by the mean square residual. In both cases, we get an F value and a corresponding significance test, which indicates whether, overall, our predictors are significantly related to our dependent variable.

Finally, in the third section of Table 13.5, we get to the most interesting part of the table. Here we see our intercept (Note 4) and the regression coefficients for each predictor variable. These are the pieces of the regression equation. We can use these statistics to create the regression equation:

$$\hat{Y} = -5.504 + .495X_1 + .210X_2$$

where $\hat{Y}$ is the predicted value of Y,

X_1 is the value of the years of education variable,

X_2 is the value of the years in the workforce variable.

The unstandardized regression coefficients (Notes 5 and 6) can be found in the column labeled "B." Because years of education and years in the workforce are variables with different standard deviations, it is difficult to compare the size of the unstandardized regression coefficients. The variables are simply measured on different scales, making comparisons difficult. However, in the column labeled "Beta", the **standardized regression coefficients** are presented (Notes 7 and 8). These regression coefficients have been standardized, thereby converting the unstandardized coefficients into coefficients with the same scale of measurement (z scores; see Chapter 5 for a discussion of standardization). Here we can see that the two predictors are fairly close in their strength of relation to the dependent variable, but years of education is a bit stronger than years of work. In the next two columns, labeled "t Value" and "p Value," we get measures that allow us to determine whether each predictor variable is statistically significantly related to the dependent variable. Recall that earlier, in the ANOVA section of the table, we saw that the two predictor variables *combined* were significantly related to the dependent variable. Now we can use t tests to see if the slope for *each* predictor variable is significantly different from zero. The p values associated with each predictor variable are much smaller than .05, indicating that each of my independent variables is a significant predictor of my dependent variable. So both years of education (Note 9) and years in the workforce (Note 10) are statistically significant predictors of monthly income.

It is important to note that in this last section of Table 13.5, each regression coefficient shows the strength of the relationship between the predictor variable and the outcome variable *while controlling for the other predictor variable*. Recall that in the simple regression model with one predictor variable, I found that there was a relationship between years of education and monthly income. One of my questions in the multiple regression model was whether this education–income link would remain statistically significant when controlling for, or partialing out, the effects of years in the workforce. As the results presented in Table 13.5 indicate, even when controlling for the effects of years in the workforce, years of education is still a statistically significant predictor of monthly income. Similarly, when controlling for years of education, years in the workforce predicts monthly income as well.

 For a brief video demonstrating how to read SPSS output for a multiple regression analysis, see the website that accompanies this book.

As you can see, multiple regression provides a wealth of information about the relations between predictor variables and dependent variables. Amazingly, in our previous example, we just scratched the surface of all that can be done with multiple regression analysis. Therefore, I strongly encourage you to read more about multiple regression using the references on regression that are provided in the bibliography. I also want to caution you about how to interpret regression analyses, whether they be simple or multiple regressions. Despite the uses of such terms as *predictor* and *dependent* variables, it is important to remember that regression analysis is based on good old correlations. Just as correlations should not be mistaken for proof of causal relationships between variables, regression analyses cannot prove that one variable, or set of variables, causes variation in another variable. Regression analyses can reveal how sets of variables are *related* to each other, but cannot prove causal relations among variables.

Example: Predicting the Use of Self-Handicapping Strategies

Sometimes students engage in behaviors that actually undermine their chances of succeeding academically. For example, they may procrastinate rather than study for an upcoming test, or they may spend time with their friends when they should be doing their homework. These behaviors are called "self-handicapping" because they actually inhibit students' chances of succeeding. One reason that students may engage in such behaviors is to provide an explanation for their poor academic performance, should it occur. If students fear that they may perform poorly on an academic task, they may not want others to think that the reason for this poor performance is that they lack ability, or intelligence. So some students strategically engage in self-handicapping to provide an alternative explanation for their poor performance. That is why these behaviors are called self-handicapping *strategies*.

Because self-handicapping strategies can undermine academic achievement and may be a sign of academic withdrawal on the part of students, it is important to understand the factors that are associated with the use of these strategies. Self-handicapping represents a concern with not appearing academically unable, even if that means perhaps sacrificing performance. Therefore, engaging in self-handicapping behaviors may be related to students' goals of avoiding appearing academically unable to others. In addition, because self-handicapping may be provoked by performance situations in which students expect to fail, it perhaps occurs more commonly among lower achieving students, who have a history of poor academic performance. Moreover, it is reasonable to suspect that when students lack confidence in their academic abilities, they will be more likely to use self-handicapping strategies. Finally, there may be gender differences in how concerned high school students are with appearing academically unable to others. Therefore, I conducted a multiple regression analysis to examine whether avoidance goals, self-efficacy, gender, and GPA, as a group and individually, predicted the use of self-handicapping strategies.

My colleague, Carol Giancarlo, and I collected data from 464 high school students. We used surveys to measure their self-reported use of self-handicapping strategies. In addition, the survey contained questions about their desire to avoid appearing academically unable (called "avoidance goals") and their confidence in their ability to perform academically (called "self-efficacy"). We also collected information about the students' gender (i.e., whether they were boys or girls) and their overall GPA in high school. Self-handicapping, avoidance goals, and self-efficacy were all measured using a 1–5 scale. Low scores indicated that students did not believe the items were true for them (i.e., they did not use self-handicapping strategies, were not confident in their abilities, were not concerned with trying to avoid appearing academically unable), whereas high scores indicated the opposite. Gender was a "dummy"-coded categorical variable (boys = 1, girls = 0), and GPA was measured using a scale from 0 to 4.0 (0 = F, 4.0 = A).

Once again, I used SPSS to analyze my data. The results of this multiple regression analysis are presented in Table 13.6. In the first section of the table, "Variance Explained," there is an R value of .347, and an R^2 value of .12. These statistics tell us that the four predictor variables combined have a moderate correlation with self-handicapping (multiple $R = .347$) and explain the variance in handicapping. This R^2 value is reduced to .113 when adjusted for the error associated with multiple predictor variables. In the second section of the table, "ANOVA Results," I see that I have an F value of 15.686 and a corresponding p value of .000. These results tell me that, as a group, my four predictor variables explain a statistically significant portion of the variance in self-handicapping. In other words, my overall regression model is statistically significant.

In the last section of the table, I find my unstandardized regression coefficients (column labeled "B") for each predictor variable in the model, as well as my intercept. These tell me that GPA and self-efficacy are negatively related to self-handicapping, whereas gender and avoidance goals are positively related to self-handicapping. Scanning toward the right side of the table, I find the standardized regression coefficients (column labeled "Beta"). These coefficients, which are all converted to the same standardized scale, reveal that GPA and self-efficacy appear to be more strongly related to self-handicapping than are avoidance goals and, in particular,

TABLE 13.6 Multiple regression results for predicting self-handicapping

	Variance Explained			
	R	R Squared	Adjusted R Squared	Std. Error of the Estimate
	.347	.120	.113	.9005

	ANOVA Results				
	Sum of Squares	df	Mean Square	F Value	p Value
Regression	50.877	4	12.719	15.686	.000
Residual	372.182	459	.811		
Total	423.059	463			

	Regression Coefficients				
	Unstandardized Coefficients		Standardized Coefficients		
	B	Std. Error	Beta	t Value	p Value
Intercept	3.630	.264		13.775	.000
Avoidance Goals	.132	.045	.130	2.943	.003
Grades (GPA)	−.254	.054	−.209	−4.690	.000
Gender	.105	.085	.055	1.234	.218
Self-Efficacy	−.232	.052	−.198	−4.425	.000

gender. Notice that standardized and unstandardized regression coefficients can be either positive or negative. To make sense of them, it is important to remember how your variables are measured. In the current example, higher values of self-efficacy are actually a *bad* outcome, because self-handicapping is harmful behavior. With this in mind, the negative regression coefficient between GPA and self-handicapping tells us that higher academic achievement is associated with *less* self-handicapping, which is good. Conversely, a positive regression coefficient indicates that higher values on the predictor variable are associated with higher levels of self-handicapping. In this example, higher levels of avoidance goals predict higher levels of self-handicapping.

Continuing to scan toward the right side of the table, I find my *t* values and *p* values for each coefficient. These tell me which of my independent variables are statistically significant predictors of self-handicapping. The *p* values tell me that all of the independent variables, except for gender, are significant predictors of handicapping.

So what can we make of these results? First, my predictors explain a significant percentage of the variance in self-handicapping, although not a particularly large percentage (about 11 percent). Second, as we might expect, students with higher GPAs report engaging in less self-handicapping behavior than students with lower GPAs. Third, students with more confidence in their academic abilities engage in less self-handicapping than do students with less confidence in their abilities. Fourth, students who are concerned with not appearing academically unable in school are more likely to use self-handicapping strategies than are students without this concern. Finally, boys and girls do not differ significantly in their reported use of self-handicapping strategies. Although boys scored slightly higher than girls on the handicapping items (we know this because the regression coefficient was positive, and the gender variable was coded boys = 1, girls = 0), this difference was not statistically significant.

It is important to remember that the results for each independent variable are reported while controlling for the effects of the other independent variables. So the statistically significant relationship between self-efficacy and self-handicapping exists even when we control for the effects of GPA and avoidance goals. This is important, because one may be tempted to argue that the relationship between confidence and self-handicapping is merely a by-product of academic achievement. Those who perform better in school *should* be more confident in their abilities, and therefore *should* engage in less self-handicapping. What the results of this multiple regression reveal is that there is a statistically significant relationship between self-efficacy and self-handicapping *even after controlling for the effects of academic performance.* Confidence is associated with less self-handicapping *regardless* of one's level of academic achievement. Similarly, when students are concerned with not appearing incompetent in school (avoidance goals), *regardless* of their actual level of achievement (GPA), they are more likely to engage in self-handicapping behavior. The ability to examine both the combined and independent relations among predictor variables and a dependent variable is the true value of multiple regression analysis.

Writing it Up

To write up the results of the multiple regression summarized in Table 13.6 for a professional journal or conference, I would only need a few sentences: "A multiple regression analysis was conducted to examine the predictors of self-handicapping. Four predictors were simultaneously entered into the model: avoidance goals, GPA, gender, and self-efficacy. Together, these predictors accounted for 11 percent of the variance in self-handicapping. All of these variables except for gender (β = .06, p < .218) were significant predictors of self-handicapping. GPA (β = −.21, p < .001) and self-efficacy (β = −.20, p < .001) were the strongest predictors and were negatively associated with self-handicapping, whereas avoidance goals were positively associated with self-handicapping (β = .13, p = .003)."

Worked Examples

In this section I present two worked examples, one for a simple linear regression with a single predictor variable and one for multiple regression. For the first example, suppose that my independent variable, *X*, is the number of sugary drinks consumed per month by children between the ages of 10 and 15. Suppose that my dependent variable, *Y*, is weight. I collect data from 10 children, 5 boys and 5 girls, at each age between 10 and 15, giving me a total sample of 60 children (30 boys, 30 girls). I calculate the mean and standard deviation for the number of sugary drinks consumed in a month and weight for the total sample, and I get the data presented in Table 13.7.

With the information in Table 13.7, I can calculate the regression coefficient:

$$b = .59 \times \frac{21.29}{6.22}$$

$$b = .59 \times 3.42$$

$$b = 2.02$$

This regression coefficient tells me that for every increase of one sugary beverage consumed per month, there is a corresponding increase of 2.02 pounds, on average. Now that we have the regression coefficient, we can calculate the intercept:

$$a = 112.12 - (10.88)(2.02)$$

$$a = 112.12 - 21.98$$

$$a = 90.14$$

This intercept tells me that when the number of sugary drinks consumed per month is zero, we would predict the child's weight to be 90.14 pounds.

Now that we know our regression coefficient and our intercept, we can use these to predict *Y* values for various *X* values, using the formula presented in Table 13.1. For example, how much would we expect a child who consumes 10 sugary drinks per month to weigh?

$$\hat{Y} = 2.02(10) + 90.14$$

$$\hat{Y} = 20.20 + 90.14$$

$$\hat{Y} = 110.34$$

We would predict that a child who consumes 10 sugary drinks per month would weigh 110.34.

TABLE 13.7 Means and standard deviations for the number of sugary drinks consumed per month by children, and the correlation between sugary drinks consumed and weight

	Mean	Standard Deviation
Sugary Drinks per Month (*X*)	10.88	6.22
Weight (*Y*)	112.12	21.29
Correlation between *X* and *Y*	*r* = .59	

As we discussed earlier in this chapter, our prediction of 110.34 pounds for a child who has 10 sugary drinks per month is just an educated guess based on a correlation between these two variables. We also know that there are some kids who have 10 sugary drinks per month but weigh 75 pounds, and others who weight 150. Because the predictions based on regression coefficients often have a fair amount of error (i.e., residuals), and because we are smart people who have lived a little, we also know that there are several things that are associated with weight besides how many sugary drinks children consume. In our current example, we might expect the older kids (i.e., 14- and 15-year-olds) to weigh more than the younger kids (i.e., 10- and 11-year-olds), so age is probably a predictor of weight. Come to think of it, age might also be related to how many sugary drinks kids consume. As children get older, they often have more independence from their parents, and also get a little spending money from their parents. When left alone with money in their pockets, early adolescents often spend that money on sugary drinks.

 For a brief video demonstration of how to calculate and interpret a regression coefficient, intercept, and predicted value for *Y*, refer to the website that accompanies this book.

So let's compute another regression, this time using two predictor variables (age and sugary drinks consumed per month) to predict weight. Because the calculations for a multiple regression are a little more complicated due to the shared variance between the predictor variables, I am going to let SPSS do the calculations for us. I'm going to run the regression twice, first with only the number of sugary drinks predicting weight, and then with both predictors (i.e., sugary drinks and age) in the regression model. This will show you how adding a second predictor variable affects the strength of the regression coefficient between the first independent (i.e., predictor) variable and the dependent variable in a regression. But first, let's take a look at Table 13.8 to see the bivariate correlations between the three variables that are going into our regression model.

As you can see from the correlations presented in Table 13.8, as age increased, so did weight, on average ($r = .55$). So our second predictor variable, age, is related to our dependent variable, weight. In addition, we can see that our two predictor variables (age and drinks consumed) are also positively correlated ($r = .44$). Because of this correlation between the two predictor variables, there is a good chance that when they are both put into a regression model, their *independent* association with the dependent variable (weight) will be smaller than the bivariate correlations between each predictor variable and the dependent variable.

Let's take a look. In Table 13.9 I present the results of two regression analyses using SPSS.[2] In the first regression I used sugary drinks consumed per month to predict weight. This is exactly the same analysis that we conducted earlier, and SPSS confirmed our prior results. The unstandardized regression coefficient (*b*) = 2.09 (B in the table), and the intercept (*a*) = 90.14. Notice that the "Beta" in this SPSS output, which is the *standardized* regression coefficient, is .59, and this is the exact same value as our bivariate correlation (*r*) between drinks consumed and weight. When we only have a single predictor variable in a regression, the correlation coefficient is the same as the standardized regression coefficient, also known as the beta. You can also see that the *R* Squared value, which is the percentage of variance in the dependent variable that is explained by the independent variable, is the same as the coefficient of determination: $(.59)^2 = .35$. So 35 percent of the variance in weight can be explained by the sugary drinks consumed variable.

Now if you look at the SPSS output for the second regression in Table 13.9, which is a multiple regression with two predictors of weight, there are a few interesting differences to note.

TABLE 13.8   Correlations between weight, sugary drinks consumed, and age

	Weight	Sugary Drinks	Age
Weight	–		
Sugary Drinks	.59	–	
Age	.55	.44	–

TABLE 13.9 SPSS output for two regression analyses predicting weight

Regression 1: Single Predictor

R	R Squared	Adjusted R Squared	Std. Error of Estimate
.59	.35	.34	17.30

ANOVA Results

	Sum of Squares	df	Mean Square	F Value	p Value
Regression	9392.41	1	9392.41	31.39	.000
Residual	17355.77	58	299.24		
Total	26748.18	59			

	Unstandardized Coefficients		Standardized Coefficient		
	B	Std. Error	Beta	t	p Value
Intercept	90.14	4.53		19.88	.000
Drinks per Month	2.09	.36	.59	5.60	.000

Regression 2: Multiple Predictors

R	R Squared	Adjusted R Squared	Std. Error of Estimate
.67	.45	.43	16.05

ANOVA Results

	Sum of Squares	df	Mean Square	F Value	p Value
Regression	12057.31	2	6028.66	23.39	.000
Residual	14690.87	57	257.74		
Total	26748.18	59			

	Unstandardized Coefficients		Standardized Coefficient		
	B	Std. Error	Beta	t	p Value
Intercept	41.45	15.68		2.64	.011
Drinks per Month	1.50	.38	.44	3.99	.001
Age	4.35	1.35	.35	3.22	.002

First, the R and R Squared values increased, compared to the output for the first regression in Table 13.9. Adding a second predictor to the regression model, age, increased the percentage of variance explained in weight from 35 percent to 45 percent. Second, notice that the regression coefficients for "Drinks per Month," both standardized and unstandardized, became smaller in the second regression. That is because when we added the second variable, age, to the model, it overlapped (i.e., was correlated with) the first predictor variable, and therefore cut into the percentage of variance that first predictor variable explained in the dependent variable, weight.

Wrapping Up and Looking Forward

The overlap between correlation (Chapter 12) and regression are plain. In fact, simple linear regression provides a statistic, the regression coefficient, that is simply the unstandardized version of the Pearson correlation coefficient. What may be less clear, but equally important, is that regression is also a close relative of ANOVA. As you saw in the discussion of Table 13.6, regression *is* a form of analysis of variance. Once again, we are interested in dividing up the variance of a dependent variable and explaining it with our independent variables. The major difference between ANOVA and regression generally involves the types of variables that are analyzed, with ANOVA using categorical independent variables and regression using continuous independent variables. As you learn more about regression on your own, you will learn that even this simple distinction is a false one, as categorical independent variables can be analyzed in regression.

In the next chapter, we turn our attention to nonparametric statistics, particularly the chi-square test of independence. Unlike the inferential statistics we have discussed in most of the previous chapters of the book, nonparametric tests are not based on the assumption that dependent variables are normally distributed or measured using an interval scale. In the last chapter of the book we will return to a consideration of statistical techniques—factor analysis and reliability analysis—that are based on correlation among variables.

Work Problems

Suppose I want to know something about the study habits of undergraduate college students. I collect a random sample of 200 students and find that they spend 12 hours per week studying, on average, with a standard deviation of 5 hours. I am curious how their social lives might be associated with their studying behavior, so I ask the students in my sample how many other students at their university they consider "close friends." The sample produces an average of 6 close friends with a standard deviation of 2. Please use this information to answer the following questions. The correlation between these two variables is −.40.

1. Assume that "hours spent studying" is the Y variable and "close friends" is the X variable. Calculate the regression coefficient (i.e., the slope) and wrap words around your results. What, exactly, does this regression coefficient tell you?
2. What would the value of the standardized regression coefficient be in this problem? How do you know?
3. Calculate the intercept and wrap words around your result.
4. If you know that somebody studied had 10 close friends, how many hours per week would you expect them to study?
5. What, exactly, is a residual (when talking about regression)?
6. Regression is essentially a matter of drawing a straight line through a set of data, and the line has a slope and an intercept. In regression, how is it decided where the line should be drawn? In other words, explain the concept of least squares.
7. Now suppose that I add a second predictor variable to the regression model: hours per week spent working for money. And suppose that the correlation between hours spent working and hours spent studying is −.50. The correlation between the two predictor variables (number of close friends and hours spent working for money) is −.30.
   a. What effect do you think the addition of this second predictor variable will have on the overall amount of variance explained (R^2) in the dependent variable? Why?
   b. What effect do you think the addition of this second predictor variable will have on the strength of the regression coefficient for the first predictor variable, compared to when only the first predictor variable was in the regression model? Why?

 For answers to these work problems, and for additional work problems, please refer to the website that accompanies this book.

Notes

1 It is also possible to use categorical predictor variables with more than two categories in a multiple regression, but these variables must first be transformed into multiple dichotomous predictor variables and entered into the regression model as separate predictor variables.
2 I have modified the SPSS output to make it easier to read and rounded values to the nearest hundredth.

CHAPTER **14**

The Chi-Square Test of Independence

All of the inferential statistics discussed in this book share a set of assumptions. Regression, ANOVA, correlation, and *t* tests all assume that the data involved are scores on some measure (e.g., IQ scores, height, income, scores on a measure of depression) calculated from samples drawn from populations that are normally distributed, and everything is fine in the world of research. Of course, as discussed in Chapter 1, these conditions are often not met in social science research. Populations are sometimes skewed rather than normal. Sometimes researchers want to know about things besides those that can be measured. Research is often messy and unpredictable rather than clean and easy.

The violation of these assumptions represents a sort of good news, bad news situation. The bad news is that if the assumptions are violated to an alarming degree, the results of these statistics can be difficult to interpret, even meaningless. The good news is that "to an alarming degree" is an imprecise phrase and is open to interpretation. In many situations, violating assumptions of normally distributed data do not make the results invalid, or even alter them very much. Another piece of good news is that even when the assumptions of these statistics are horrifically violated, there is a whole batch of statistics that researchers can use that do not have the same assumptions of normality and random selection: **nonparametric statistics.**

There are a number of nonparametric tests available. The **Mann–Whitney U** test is a sort of nonparametric equivalent of the independent *t* test. The **Wilcoxon signed-rank** test can be used in place of the paired or dependent samples *t* test when a nonparametric test is needed. The **Kruskal–Wallis** analysis of variance for ranked data can be roughly substituted for the one-way ANOVA for continuously scaled variables. These nonparametric statistics can be extremely useful, and descriptions of their uses and characteristics can be found in most standard-length statistics textbooks. In this chapter, I limit my attention to one of the most commonly used nonparametric tests: the **chi-square (χ^2)** test of independence. This test is appropriate for use when you have data from two categorical, or nominally scaled, variables (see Chapter 1 for a description of these variable types). With categorical variables, the cases in your sample are divided among the different categories of your categorical variables. For example, gender is a categorical variable, and the cases in a sample of human beings can be divided into male and female, the two categories of the gender variable. When you have two categorical variables, you may want to know whether the division of cases in one variable is *independent of* the other categorical variable. For example, suppose you have a sample of boys and girls from the fifth, eighth, and twelfth grades of school. You may want to know whether your representation of boys and girls *depends on* their grade level, or if the division of boys and girls is about what you would expect *independent of* grade level. That is the type of question that the chi-square test of independence was designed to answer.

A more precise way of stating the purpose of the chi-square test of independence is this: It allows you to determine whether cases in a sample fall into categories in proportions equal to what one would expect by chance. For example, suppose that you work in a liberal arts college. You want to know whether the men and women in your college differ in their selection of majors. So you randomly select 100 men and 100 women and ask them to tell you their major. You get the data presented in Table 14.1.

TABLE 14.1   Gender and major data for chi-square test of independence

	Psychology	English	Biology
Men	35	50	15
Women	30	25	45

Does this distribution of data represent a statistically significant gender difference in majors? Before you can answer this question, you need to know more information. Specifically, you need to determine how many men and women you *expect* to major in these three areas just based on the numbers of each gender and each major in the sample. This is the type of question that the chi-square test of independence allows you to answer.

Chi-Square Test of Independence in Depth

The chi-square test of independence works by comparing the categorically coded data that you have collected (known as the **observed frequencies**) with the frequencies that you would expect to get in each cell of a table by chance alone (known as the **expected frequencies**). What the test allows you to determine is whether the observed frequencies are *significantly* different from the expected frequencies. When conducting *t* tests (Chapter 8), you calculated an observed *t* value and compared that to a critical *t* value that you found by looking at the values in Appendix B. These critical values were based on a family of theoretical distributions, and you had to use the degrees of freedom to determine which *t* distribution you should use. You used a similar process to compare your observed and critical *F* values in ANOVA (Chapter 9). As luck would have it, there happens to be a family of distributions for the chi-square statistic as well, and the critical values from this family of distributions are presented in Appendix E. Just as with *t* values and *F* values, you will need to use degrees of freedom to find the appropriate chi-square value as well.

But first things first: How do you calculate the observed χ^2 value? Well, we need to add a little bit of information to Table 14.1. Namely, we need to add the column totals, the row totals, and the overall total number of cases. Table 14.2 provides the revised table. With these totals, we can calculate the expected values for each cell. Note that the table of values to be analyzed in a chi-square test of independence is known as a **contingency table**. That is because, in this type of analysis, we are testing whether the number of cases in one category of one variable is *contingent upon* (i.e., dependent on or independent of) the other variable. For example, does the proportion of Biology majors depend on the gender of the student?

Using the observed frequencies in each cell of the table (i.e., 35 male Psychology majors, 30 female Psychology majors, 50 male English majors, etc.) and the total frequencies for the rows, columns, and total sample, a set of expected frequencies can be calculated for each of the six cells in Table 14.2. To find the expected frequency for a cell, you just need to do a little arithmetic. The first (i.e., top-left) cell of Table 14.2 includes 35 male Psychology majors. Given the numbers of men and Psychology majors in the total sample, how many male Psychology majors would we expect to have in our sample *by chance*? To answer this question, we divide the total number of men in our sample (100) by the total sample size (200), then we divide the total number of Psychology majors (65) by the total sample (200), multiply these two fractions together, and multiply that number by the total sample. The result looks like this:

TABLE 14.2   Revised gender and major data for chi-square test of independence with column and row totals

	Psychology	English	Biology	*Row Totals*
Men	35	50	15	100
Women	30	25	45	100
Column Totals	65	75	60	200

$$\left(\frac{100}{200}\right)\left(\frac{65}{200}\right)(200)$$

$$= \frac{(100)(65)}{200}$$

$$= 32.5$$

Therefore, based on the total number of men and the total number of Psychology majors in my sample, I would expect (based on probability alone) that 32.5 members of my sample would be male Psychology majors.

I can follow the same procedure to calculate expected values for each of the other five cells in the table as well. If I did so, I would get the expected values that are summarized in Table 14.3.

Notice that the expected values for men and women are equal for the two columns in each cell. That is because there are equal numbers of men and women in the sample. With equal numbers of men and women in the sample, we would expect there to be (based on probability alone) an equal number of male and female Psychology majors, an equal number of male and female English majors, and an equal number of male and female Biology majors. Of course, the selection of a major is not based solely on probability, so our expected values differ from our observed values. But do they differ *significantly*? To answer this question we must calculate the χ^2 statistic. For this, I will need to compare the observed and expected values. When comparing these values, it helps to have all of the expected and observed values in one place, so I have combined the values from Table 14.1 with the values from Table 14.3 together in Table 14.4.

To compare the observed and expected frequencies, and in the process produce a χ^2 value, I use the formula presented in Table 14.5.

When I apply the formula from Table 14.5 to the values in Table 14.4, I get the values for calculating the χ^2 statistics presented in Table 14.6. The final step in the process is to add up, or sum,

TABLE 14.3 Expected values for gender and major data

	Psychology	English	Biology
Men	$\frac{(100)(65)}{200} = 32.5$	$\frac{(100)(75)}{200} = 37.5$	$\frac{(100)(60)}{200} = 30$
Women	$\frac{(100)(65)}{200} = 32.5$	$\frac{(100)(75)}{200} = 37.5$	$\frac{(100)(60)}{200} = 30$

TABLE 14.4 Combined observed and expected frequencies

	Psychology		English		Biology	
	Observed	Expected	Observed	Expected	Observed	Expected
Men	35	32.5	50	37.5	15	30
Women	30	32.5	25	37.5	45	30

TABLE 14.5 Formula for calculating χ^2

$$\chi^2 = \Sigma\left(\frac{(O-E)^2}{E}\right)$$

where **O** is the observed value in each cell,
E is the expected value in each cell.

TABLE 14.6 Calculations for the χ^2 statistic

	Psychology	English	Biology
Men	$\dfrac{(35-32.5)^2}{32.5}=.19$	$\dfrac{(50-37.5)^2}{37.5}=4.17$	$\dfrac{(15-30)^2}{30}=7.5$
Women	$\dfrac{(30-32.5)^2}{32.5}=.19$	$\dfrac{(25-37.5)^2}{37.5}=4.17$	$\dfrac{(45-30)^2}{30}=7.5$

the values produced in each of the six cells in Table 14.6. Summing the six squared differences between observed and expected values from Table 14.6 produces the χ^2 value:

$$.19 + .19 + 4.17 + 4.17 + 7.5 + 7.5 = 23.72$$

$$\chi^2 = 23.72$$

Notice that the relatively large differences between men and women choosing English or Biology as majors were the primary contributors to the large χ^2 value. Because the differences between the observed and expected values among the Psychology majors were fairly small, they contributed less to the overall χ^2.

Now that we have produced an observed χ^2 value, we must compare it to a critical χ^2 value from Appendix E to determine whether the differences between men and women in their choice of major is statistically significant. You read this table similarly to the *t* value table presented in Appendix B. First, you need to determine the degrees of freedom (*df*) for the problem. In a chi-square test of independence, $df = (R - 1)(C - 1)$ where **R** is the number of rows and **C** is the number of columns in the contingency table.

 To see a brief video describing how to read Appendix E, please refer to the website that accompanies this book.

In our example, $R = 2$ and $C = 3$, so $df = (2 - 1)(3 - 1) = 2$. Next, we need to determine our alpha level for this test. If we adopt an alpha level of .05, we can look in Appendix E (with 2 degrees of freedom) and find a critical χ^2 value of 5.99. Because our observed χ^2 value is 23.72, we conclude that there is a statistically significant difference in choice of major between men and women. In fact, our observed χ^2 value is large enough to be statistically significant at the .001 level (i.e., $p < .001$).

What did we just do there? If you read Chapter 7, you may recognize what we did as hypothesis testing. In the preceding example, our null hypothesis was that choice of major was independent of (or unrelated to) gender. Our alternative hypothesis was that the major students selected in college depended on whether the students were men or women. We then calculated an observed value of χ^2, selected an alpha level (.05), found the critical value of χ^2, and determined that our observed χ^2 was larger than our critical χ^2 value. Therefore, we rejected the null hypothesis and concluded that choice of major did depend on gender. In fact, the probability of getting an observed χ^2 as large as the one we found, by chance, was less than .001 ($p < .001$). Written in hypothesis-testing form, we did the following:

H_0: Gender and choice of major are independent, or unrelated.
H_A: Choice of major depends on, or is contingent upon, gender.

$$\alpha = .05$$

$$df = 2$$

$$\chi^2{}_{critical} = 5.99$$

$$\chi^2{}_{observed} = 23.72$$

Decision: Reject H_0 and conclude that choice of major depends on the gender of the student.

Example: Generational Status and Grade Level

Researchers often use chi-square tests of independence to examine whether members of a sample are evenly distributed among different groups. If some students are "overrepresented" in one group and "underrepresented" in another, it can be difficult to interpret the results of analyses. For example, suppose I want to know whether boys or girls in a high school perform better on a standardized math test. This is a typical question among high school principals. They must often report to parents and the larger community on how their students are doing, and whether they are serving their male and female students equally well. So I conduct an independent samples *t* test and find that, on average, the boys score significantly higher than the girls on the standardized math test. Is that the end of the story? Maybe not.

Before I can comfortably conclude that boys and girls scored differently on the test, I need to see whether the groups of boys and girls differ in ways that might be related to performance on the math test. For example, suppose that this sample has a large number of students from families that immigrated to the United States fairly recently. In this example, suppose that we compare first-generation students (who were born outside of the United States and then moved here), second-generation students (who were born in the United States to mothers born outside of the United States), and third-generation students (students and their mothers both born in the United States). When we compare these three groups' scores on the math test using a one-way ANOVA, we find that the third-generation students did *worse* on the test, on average, than either the first- or second-generation groups.

So here is the big question: What if more of the low-scoring, third-generation students in the sample were girls than boys? If this is true, then the cause of the girls scoring lower than the boys on the math test may be due to their generational status (i.e., girls are more likely than boys to be third-generation) rather than their gender. So before reaching any conclusions about gender differences in math abilities, we need to do a chi-square test of independence to see if gender and generational status are independent groups.

With the help of data that I collected from 913 high school students and the SPSS statistical software, I am able to conduct this test in seconds. The results are presented in Table 14.7. Each cell in the table includes the observed frequency ("Count") on the top row and the expected frequency below it ("Expected Count"). Notice that in most cells, the differences between the observed and expected frequencies are quite small. The largest disparities appear in the column for the second generation ("2nd Gen."). The observed χ^2 value, with $df = 2$, is 5.19. As we learned earlier in this chapter, the critical χ^2 value, with $df = 2$ and $\alpha = .05$, is 5.99. Therefore, the test of independence is not statistically significant, and we can conclude that generational status is independent of gender. Neither boys nor girls are significantly overrepresented in any of the three generational groups.

So what are we to make of this result? Well, it appears that the difference between boys and girls in their scores on the math test is not due to unequal numbers of boys and girls in the different generational groups. Of course, there may be other factors to rule out before concluding that the gender differences in math scores are real and not just the by-product of differences on other

TABLE 14.7   SPSS contingency table for gender by generational status

			Generational Group			
			3+ Gen.	2nd Gen.	1st Gen.	Total
Gender	Girl	Count	156	215	125	496
		Expected Count	152.7	230.3	113.0	496.0
	Boy	Count	125	209	83	417
		Expected Count	128.3	193.7	95.0	417.0
Total		Count	281	424	208	913
		Expected Count	281.0	424.0	208.0	913.0

categorical variables (e.g., ethnicity) or continuous variables (e.g., socioeconomic status). But we can conclude that unequal numbers of girls and boys in each generational group is not the cause of the gender difference in math scores.

Writing it Up

The write-up for the chi-square analysis is very brief and straightforward: "A chi-square analysis was performed to determine whether girls and boys were represented across all three generational groups proportionally to their numbers in the sample. The analysis produced a non-significant χ^2 value ($\chi^2_{(2)} = 5.19, p = .08$), indicating that neither girls nor boys were overrepresented in any of the three generational categories."

Worked Example

In this section I provide another example of how to calculate a chi-square test of independence. Recently, there has been a lot of attention given to possible differences in how children are punished in school. Specifically, there is a concern that African-American students are more likely than White students to be suspended from school. Because school suspensions are predictive of other problems (e.g., dropping out of school, engaging in delinquent behavior), any disciplinary action by the school that may be racially biased is troubling. Although a chi-square test cannot prove whether a disciplinary process is racially biased (because it is not a test of cause and effect), the first step in the evidence process would be to determine whether students are suspended disproportionately by ethnicity.

Suppose that in a high school there are 600 African-American students, representing 33 percent of the student body. Of these 600 students, 200 (33 percent) have been suspended from school for at least one day during the academic year. The school also contains 1,200 White students (67 percent of the total student population at the school). In this group, 290 (24.16 percent) have been suspended for at least one day. Is the difference in the suspension rates of African-American and White students at this school statistically significant?

These data are summarized in Table 14.8. We can use these numbers to calculated the number of students we would *expect* to have in each cell of Table 14.8 (e.g., number of White students who have been suspended, number of African-American students who have been suspended, etc.) by chance. I will use the formula presented earlier in this chapter to calculate the *expected* values for each cell. These calculations and resulting expected values are presented in Table 14.9.

TABLE 14.8 Observed values for school suspensions by ethnicity

	African-American	White	*Row Total*
Suspended	200	290	490
Not Suspended	400	910	1310
Column Total	600	1200	1800

TABLE 14.9 Expected values for school suspensions by ethnicity

	African-American	White
Suspended	$\dfrac{(600)(490)}{1800} = 163.33$	$\dfrac{(1200)(490)}{1800} = 326.67$
Not Suspended	$\dfrac{(600)(1310)}{1800} = 436.67$	$\dfrac{(1200)(1310)}{1800} = 873.33$

TABLE 14.10 Squared differences between observed and expected values, divided by expected values, for school suspensions by ethnicity

	African-American	White
Suspended	$\dfrac{(200-163.33)^2}{163.33} = 8.23$	$\dfrac{(290-326.67)^2}{326.67} = 4.12$
Not Suspended	$\dfrac{(400-436.67)^2}{436.67} = 3.08$	$\dfrac{(910-873.33)^2}{873.33} = 1.54$

By comparing the numbers in Table 14.8 with those in Table 14.9, you can see that there are more African-American students being suspended than we would expect, and fewer White students being suspended than we would expect. These differences are presented graphically in Figure 14.1. To determine whether the differences between the observed and expected values are statistically significant, we need to calculate the chi-square statistic. To do this, we use the formula presented in Table 14.5. For each cell in the table, we calculate the difference between the observed value and the expected value, square that difference, and then divide it by the expected value for that cell. For our example, the results are summarized in Table 14.10. Once this step is completed, the next step is to add these squared differences between the observed and expected values together:

$$8.23 + 3.08 + 4.12 + 1.54 = 16.97$$

So 16.97 is our observed chi-square value. The final step in the process is to compare our observed value to our critical chi-square value. We look in Appendix E to find the critical value. The number of degrees of freedom for this problem is $(R-1) + (C-1)$ where R is the number of rows in our contingency table and C is the number of columns. Our table has two rows and two columns, so our number of degrees of freedom (*df*) is 2. In Appendix E, we find a critical value of 5.99 using an alpha level of .05 and 2 degrees of freedom. Our observed value is larger than our critical value (i.e., 16.97 > 5.99), so we can conclude that our results were not due to chance. African-American students are being suspended *significantly* more than we would expect them to be based on chance alone, and White students are being suspended significantly less. We do not know why this is happening, but we now have a statistical justification for investigating the issue further.

 To see a video demonstration of how to interpret the output from a chi-square analysis conducted using SPSS, please refer to the website that accompanies this book.

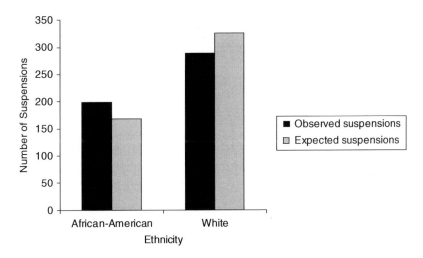

FIGURE 14.1 Comparison of observed and expected suspensions by ethnic group.

Wrapping Up and Looking Forward

The chi-square test of independence is only one of many nonparametric tests used by social science researchers. Because social scientists often use data that violate one or more of the assumptions required for the valid use of parametric statistics, it is important that you become familiar with several nonparametric techniques. The limited scope of this book precludes me from describing most of these techniques. Do not let their exclusion lull you into a false sense of security with parametric statistics—they are not always the adequate tools for the job.

In the final chapter of the book, we will examine two statistical techniques that social science researchers often use to organize and make sense of their data: factor analysis and Cronbach's alpha reliability analysis.

Work Problems

Suppose I want to know whether there are differences in the likelihood of being diagnosed with depression for people who live in different types of communities (urban, suburban, rural). I collect data from people from these three different types of communities and get the data summarized in Table 14.11. Use this data to answer the following set of questions.

1. Calculate the expected values for each of the six cells in the table.
2. Calculate the sum of squared differences between the observed and expected values to find the observed chi-square value.
3. Report the degrees of freedom (*df*) for this problem.
4. Using the *df* you just calculated, and an alpha level of .05, find the critical value for the chi-square statistic in Appendix E.
5. Compare the critical value from Appendix E with the observed chi-square value that you calculated in Question 2 and decide whether your observed value is statistically significant.
6. What does the chi-square statistic that you calculated tell you? What doesn't it tell you?

Here are two more questions that are not based on the data presented above.

7. Explain when you would use a nonparametric test rather than a parametric test.
8. Suppose that in a large company, there is an allegation of gender bias in relation to who receives promotions and who does not. Explain how the chi-square test of independence compares observed and expected frequencies to determine whether this allegation is true.

TABLE 14.11 Raw data of depressed and not depressed people living in urban, rural, and suburban areas

	Urban	Rural	Suburban	Row Total
Depressed	120	90	100	310
Not Depressed	600	300	400	1300
Column Total	720	390	500	1610

For answers to these work problems, and for additional work problems, please refer to the website that accompanies this book.

CHAPTER **15**

Factor Analysis and Reliability Analysis: Data Reduction Techniques

In social science research, it is quite common for researchers to measure a single construct using more than one item. This is especially common in survey research. For example, in my own research examining student motivation, I have often given students surveys that asked them about their interests, values, and goals. And I have used several survey **items** to measure each of these **constructs**. To measure how much students value what they are learning in school, I have often used a commonly used measure developed by Eccles and her colleagues (Eccles et al., 2004) that includes three statements, and students indicate how much they agree or disagree with each statement: (1) The information we learn in this class is interesting; (2) The information we learn in this class is important; (3) The information we learn in this class will be useful to me.

Although these three items on the survey are all separate questions, they are assumed to all be parts of a larger, underlying construct called Value. The three survey items are called **observed variables** because they have actually been measured (i.e., observed) with the survey items. The underlying construct these items are supposed to represent, Value, is called an **unobserved variable** or a **latent variable** because it is not measured directly. Rather, it is inferred, or **indicated**, by the three observed variables. When researchers use multiple measures to represent a single underlying construct, they must perform some statistical analyses to determine how well the items in one construct go together, and how well the items that are supposed to represent one construct separate from the items that are supposed to represent a different construct. The way that we do this is with **factor analysis** and **reliability analysis**. In this chapter, I present a very brief overview of these two types of statistical analyses. These analyses are complicated and have many variations (especially factor analysis), so my goal in this chapter is not to teach you how to calculate these analyses. Rather, I want this chapter to introduce you to these important concepts and help you understand them better when you encounter them in your reading of social science research.

Factor Analysis in Depth

There are many different kinds of factor analysis, and we do not have enough space in this chapter to talk about all of them in depth. So I will focus on one of the forms of factor analysis that is used often in the social sciences, **principal components analysis (PCA)**. To perform a principal components factor analysis, all of the variables in the analysis must be measured **continuously** (i.e., intervally scaled; see Chapter 1), and have normal distributions. It is also important to have a large enough sample size. A general rule of thumb is that you need 30 cases for the first observed variable and 10 cases for each additional observed variable in a factor analysis. So if you have 10 observed variables in the analysis, you should have at least 30 + 90 cases in your sample, for a total of 120.

I think factor analysis is a confusing subject to discuss in abstract form, so I will rely heavily on examples for this discussion. First, a hypothetical example. Suppose that you were conducting a study to examine how satisfied American adults were with their work. As anyone who has ever worked knows, satisfaction with work is a multifaceted construct. So you decide to ask several questions on a survey to measure the single construct of work satisfaction. You ask a question about whether people are happy with their pay. You ask another question about whether people feel they have a good relationship with their boss. You ask a third question about whether people are happy with the amount of responsibility they are given at work, and a fourth question about whether they like the physical space in which they work.

There are two reasons you might ask so many questions about a single underlying construct like work satisfaction. First, you want to cover several aspects of work satisfaction because you want your measure to be a good representation of the construct. Second, you want to have some confidence that the participants in your study are interpreting your questions as you mean them. If you just asked a single question like "How happy are you with your work?" it would be difficult for you to know what your participants mean by their responses. One participant may say that he is very happy with his work because he thought you were asking whether he thinks he is producing work of high quality. Another participant may say she is very happy because she thought you were asking whether she feels that she is paid enough, and she just received a large bonus. So if you only measure your construct with a single question, it may be difficult for you determine if the same answers on your question mean the same things for different participants. Using several questions to measure the same construct helps researchers feel confident that participants are interpreting the questions in similar ways.

If the four items that you asked about work satisfaction really do measure the same underlying construct, then most participants will answer all four questions in similar ways. In other words, people with high work satisfaction will generally say that they are paid well, like their boss, have an appropriate level of responsibility, and are comfortable in their work space. Similarly, most people with low work satisfaction will respond to all four of your questions by indicating low levels of satisfaction. To use statistical language, the responses on all of the questions that you use to measure a single construct should be **strongly correlated**.

Now suppose that you were interested in more than just work satisfaction. As a smart researcher who is unafraid of examining the messiness of human life, suppose that you also want to know whether work satisfaction is related to other aspects of workers' lives, such as their marital satisfaction. Perhaps people who are happy at work bring less stress home, and their marital relationships are more harmonious as a result. On the other hand, people who love their work may spend long hours at the office, causing resentment in their marital relationships. Ever curious, you want to know. So, in addition to questions about work satisfaction, your survey includes a set of questions about marital satisfaction. Again, marital satisfaction is a multifaceted construct, so you ask several questions about it: (1) My spouse and I communicate with each other well; (2) I am satisfied with the way my spouse and I share responsibilities around the house; (3) My wife/husband and I have a good sex life. Again, there should be strong correlations in the answers to all three of these questions if all three really represent the underlying construct of marital satisfaction.

So what does all of this have to do with factor analysis? What a factor analysis does, in a nutshell, is find out which items are most strongly correlated with each other, and then group them together. As a researcher, you hope and expect that the items you use to measure one construct (e.g., work satisfaction) are all highly correlated with each other, and can be grouped together. Naturally, you hope this is also true for your three marital satisfaction items. In addition, you hope that your marital satisfaction questions are correlated with each other *more strongly* than they are correlated with the work satisfaction items. In factor analysis parlance, you hope that your survey questions group into separate **factors**, as illustrated in Figure 15.1. Factor analysis can tell you whether your hopes and expectations have been realized.

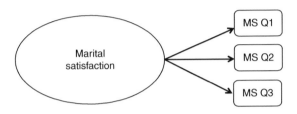

FIGURE 15.1 Hypothetical factor model for work satisfaction and marital satisfaction.

Here's how it works. In an **exploratory factor analysis (EFA)** you put a set of items, such as the seven questions for work satisfaction and marital satisfaction above, into the analysis. The EFA then looks for which items are most strongly correlated with each other. When it finds them, it groups them together into a factor and then looks for the next strongest batch of correlated items and puts those together into another factor. What the EFA is trying to do is to create factors that are able to explain the most variance possible in all of the items that you put into the analysis. The more strongly the items are correlated with each other, the more variance these items explain in each other. So the factor analysis will first create a factor that explains the most variance in all of the items, the second factor will explain the second-most variance, and so on. When new factors would not explain very much additional variance, the EFA stops, and you are left to interpret your results. This process is known as **extraction**. In essence, the factor analysis process involves extracting factors from a set of items until there are no more meaningful factors to be extracted.[1]

Each item in your analysis will have what is called a **factor loading**. The stronger an item loads onto a factor, the more that item defines the factor. Generally speaking, factor loadings are analogous to correlation coefficients and typically range from −1.0 to 1.0 (although it is possible, and not all that uncommon, for an item to have a factor loading greater than 1.0 or less than −1.0). Going back to our example, satisfaction with pay may have the strongest factor loading on our work satisfaction factor, something like .90, because most people are happy at work if they feel that they are being well paid. Another item, such as having an appropriate level of responsibility, may have a factor loading of .60. If we had a negatively worded item, such as "I am usually bored at work," this item may have a negative factor loading of −.70 with our work satisfaction factor. This is still a strong factor loading, just in the negative direction.

One of the coolest features of factor analysis, but also the most difficult to understand, is **factor rotation**. In the process of identifying and creating factors from a set of items, the factor analysis works to make the factors distinct from each other. In the most common method of factor rotation, orthogonal, the factor analysis rotates the factors to maximize the distinction between them. So the factor analysis will create the first factor (i.e., work satisfaction), then it will try to create a second factor that is as different from the first factor as possible. This will result in the creation of the marital satisfaction factor, assuming that the work satisfaction items are more strongly correlated with each other than they are with the marital satisfaction items. If the factor analysis did not employ this kind of rotation, it would produce several factors that were all some variation of the most highly correlated items before ever getting around to the next, more weakly, correlated items. So, using rotation, the factor analysis works to create factors that are as separate from each other, or unique, as possible.

TIME OUT FOR TECHNICALITY: ORTHOGONAL VS. OBLIQUE FACTOR ROTATION

Most social science researchers use **orthogonal** factor rotation in their exploratory or principal components factor analyses. One meaning of orthogonal is that it involves 90 degree angles. Another meaning is that variables in statistics are unrelated to each other. The strategy behind an orthogonal factor rotation is to create factors that are as independent, or separate, from each other as possible. This is the factor rotation method that produces the maximum distinctions between the factors. But there are other methods of factor rotation, most notably **oblique**. Oblique factor rotation does not assume that all of the factors will be orthogonal to one another, and allows the factors that are created to be correlated. In a lot of social science research, the factors will be moderately correlated, so it makes sense to use an oblique factor rotation method. For example, although work satisfaction is most likely a separate factor from marital satisfaction, these two factors will probably be moderately correlated with each other. In fact, they may well represent a larger factor: life satisfaction. If I were to conduct an EFA with items representing work and marital satisfaction, I would probably use oblique factor rotation rather than orthogonal rotation.

A More Concrete Example of Exploratory Factor Analysis

To further illustrate how EFA works, I will demonstrate it with my own survey data using the SPSS software package. I was interested in examining the motivation of high school students, so I gave surveys to a sample of 857 students. The surveys included questions asking about "Mastery" goals, "Performance" goals, and "Family"-related concerns regarding education. (The goals and family-related concerns are the "constructs" and each survey question that is supposed to measure a construct is an "item.") Mastery goals represent a desire to learn, improve, and understand new concepts. Performance goals represent a desire to appear smart and to do better than others. And the family questions were about whether parents help with homework, whether parents expect the student to attend college, and whether the student wants to succeed for the sake of pleasing family members. I selected three items from each construct and have listed the items, along with their means and standard deviations, in Table 15.1. Each of these items was measured on a 5-point scale with 1 indicating less agreement with the statement and 5 indicating total agreement with the statement.

Often, when researchers use surveys to collect data, they expect respondents to answer questions that are supposed to be measuring the same construct in similar ways. But it is important to test this expectation using factor analysis, because respondents often do not interpret items as we expect them to, and researchers sometimes do not create clearly articulated items. I fully expect the three Mastery items in Table 15.1 to be more strongly correlated with each other than with either the Performance or Family items, but I need to test my assumption using factor analysis.

When I entered these nine items into my principal components factor analysis in SPSS using varimax rotation (i.e., one of the SPSS versions of orthogonal factor rotation), the program first produced the descriptive statistics in Table 15.1. Next, it produced a table of bivariate correlations which I present in Table 15.2. As you can see, the three Mastery items are all correlated with each

TABLE 15.1   Descriptive statistics for survey items in the factor analysis

	Mean	Std. Deviation	Analysis *N*
Mastery 1: I do class work because I like to learn new things.	3.37	1.034	857
Mastery 2: I do work in class because I want to get better at it.	3.68	1.024	857
Mastery 3: It is important for me to understand the work in this class.	3.86	.947	857
Performance 1: It is important for me to appear smarter than others.	2.45	1.168	857
Performance 2: I would feel successful if I did better than other students in this class.	3.19	1.225	857
Performance 3: I want to do better than other students in this class.	3.33	1.222	857
Family 1: My parents help me with my school work.	2.31	1.249	857
Family 2: My parents expect me to go to college.	4.66	.764	857
Family 3: I want to do well in school to please my parents.	3.82	1.169	857

TABLE 15.2   Correlation matrix for survey items in the principal components factor analysis

	Mast. 1	Mast. 2	Mast. 3	Perf. 1	Perf. 2	Perf. 3	Family 1	Family 2
Mastery 1: I do class work because I like to learn new things.	–							
Mastery 2: I do work in class because I want to get better at it.	.48	–						
Mastery 3: It is important for me to understand the work in this class.	.42	.42	–					
Performance 1: It is important for me to appear smarter than others.	.05	.06	.07	–				
Performance 2: I would feel successful if I did better than other students in this class.	–.01	.04	.05	.43	–			
Performance 3: I want to do better than other students in this class.	.08	.15	.17	.42	.57	–		
Family 1: My parents help me with my school work.	.13	.12	.08	–.04	–.08	–.01	–	
Family 2: My parents expect me to go to college.	.14	.16	.20	.03	.05	.13	–.02	–
Family 3: I want to do well to please my parents.	–.02	.12	.13	.16	.18	.22	.13	.25

other above the $r = .40$ level and are correlated with the Performance and Family items at the $r < .25$ level. Similarly, all of the Performance items are correlated with each other above $r = .40$ and are correlated with the other six items below $r < .25$. In contrast, the three Family items are not very strongly correlated with each other (r's < .30), and in some cases are more strongly correlated with a Mastery or Performance item than with other Family items. These correlations suggest that the Mastery and Performance items will separate into nice, clean, separate factors in our factor analysis, but the Family items may not. Let's see.

The next bit of information we get from our SPSS analysis is the table of **eigenvalues** and variance explained. When SPSS (or any other statistics program) performs a factor analysis, it keeps reorganizing all of the items in the analysis into new factors and then rotating these factors away from each other to create as many meaningful, separate factors as it can. The first factor starts by combining the most strongly correlated items because it is these items that explain the most variance in the full collection of all nine items. Then it creates a second factor based on the items with the second-strongest set of correlations, and this new factor will explain the second-most variance in the total collection of items. If you look at the values in Table 15.3 under the heading "Initial Eigenvalues," you will see that each time the program creates a new factor, the new factors will explain less and less of the total variance. Pretty soon, the new factors being created hardly explain any additional variance, and they are therefore not very useful.

TABLE 15.3 Table of eigenvalues and variance explained from principal components factor analysis

Factor	Initial Eigenvalues			Rotation Sums of Squared Loadings		
	Total	% of Variance	Cumulative %	Total	% of Variance	Cumulative %
1	2.332	25.910	25.910	1.983	22.038	22.038
2	1.770	19.672	45.583	1.913	21.250	43.288
3	1.096	12.180	57.763	1.258	13.979	57.267
4	1.009	11.206	68.969	1.053	11.701	68.969
5	.681	7.564	76.532			
6	.623	6.921	83.453			
7	.589	6.546	89.999			
8	.488	5.418	95.416			
9	.413	4.584	100.000			

One of the jobs of the researcher is to interpret the results of the factor analysis to decide how many factors are needed to make sense of the data. Typically, researchers use several pieces of information to help them decide, including some of the information in Table 15.3. For example, many researchers will only consider a factor meaningful if it has an **eigenvalue**[2] of at least 1.0. Similarly, some researchers believe that factors that explain less than 10 percent of the total variance in the full set of items are too weak to be considered. In addition, conceptual and theoretical considerations are important. I may have a factor that has an eigenvalue greater than 1.0, but the items that load most strongly on the factor do not make sense together and it is difficult to understand the factor using the theory that is guiding the research, so I may not keep this factor in my subsequent analyses.

The values in Table 15.3 suggest that my nine items form four meaningful factors. The statistics in the three columns on the right of Table 15.3 come from the rotated factor solution. These show that there are four factors with eigenvalues greater than 1.0 (under the column heading "Total" within the "Rotation Sums of Squared Loadings" section of Table 15.3), each explaining more than 10 percent of the variance in the total set of items. Next, I need to take a look at the **rotated factor matrix** to see how the SPSS program grouped the items. The rotated factor matrix shows me how the items are related to each factor after the program has rotated the factors. To make this table easier to interpret, I told the SPSS program not to print any factor loadings that were less than .30. Generally speaking, if an item has a factor loading below .30, it is not really a strong indicator of that factor. The results of the rotated factor matrix are presented in Table 15.4.

As you can see by looking at Tables 15.3 and 15.4, the first factor, which explained about 22 percent of the total variance and had a rotated eigenvalue of 1.98 (this information is in Table 15.3), was dominated by the three Performance items (this information is in Table 15.4). Each of these items was strongly correlated with the first factor (factor loadings greater than .70) and weakly related to the other three factors (factor loadings less than .30, and therefore

TABLE 15.4 Rotated factor matrix for the four-factor solution

Survey Items	Factors			
	1	2	3	4
Performance 2: successful if I did better than other students	.836			
Performance 3: want to do better than other students in class	.801			
Performance 1: important to appear smarter than others	.754			
Mastery 1: do class work because I like to learn new things		.826		
Mastery 2: do work in class because I want to get better		.779		
Mastery 3: important that I understand the work		.735		
Family 2: parents expect me to go to college			.805	
Family 3: do well to please parents			.734	.344
Family 1: parents help with school work				.931

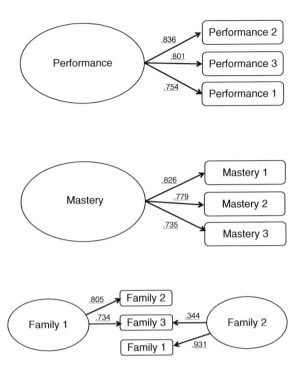

FIGURE 15.2 Four-factor solution with factor loadings for Performance, Mastery, and Family factors.

invisible). Similarly, the second factor in Table 15.4 was dominated by the three Mastery items. This factor explained almost as much variance as the first factor (21 percent) and had a similar rotated eigenvalue (1.91). The third and fourth factors were comprised of the three Family items. These two factors explained considerably less variance (13.979 percent and 11.701 percent, respectively) than each of the first two factors, and had substantially smaller eigenvalues. In addition, one of the Family items, wanting to "do well to please parents," had factor loadings greater than .30 on each of the two Family factors, indicating overlap among these two factors rather than a clean separation. A graphic illustration of these factor loadings is presented in Figure 15.2.

Because my initial factor analysis produced two nice, clean factors and two sort of messy, overlapping factors, I decided to play around a little. First, I told the SPSS program to force my nine items into only three factors. The results of this analysis are summarized in Table 15.5 and Figure 15.3. When I did this, the first two factors remained the same: one clear Performance factor and one clear Mastery factor. The three Family items went together to produce the third factor, as I expected. What is interesting about this third factor is that the strongest factor loading, the one that sort of defines the factor, was the "I want to do well to please my parents" item. This is the item

TABLE 15.5 **Rotated factor matrix for the three-factor solution**

	Factors		
Survey Items	1	2	3
Performance 2: successful if I did better than other students	.839		
Performance 3: want to do better than other students in class	.801		
Performance 1: important to appear smarter than others	.745		
Mastery 1: do class work because I like to learn new things		.830	
Mastery 2: do work in class because I want to get better		.777	
Mastery 3: important that I understand the work		.723	
Family 3: do well to please parents			.669
Family 2: parents expect me to go to college			.805
Family 1: parents help with school work			.353

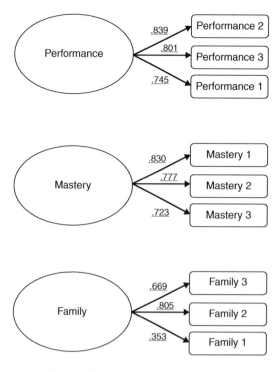

FIGURE 15.3 Three-factor solution with factor loadings for Performance, Mastery, and Family items.

that **cross-loaded** on the two Family factors in my previous analysis. In this new, unitary Family factor, "My parents help me with my school work" is the item with the weakest factor loading. Just looking at the three Family items, it seems clear that this parental help item is conceptually distinct from the other two. Whereas the first two items on the Family factor are both about beliefs and future-oriented goals, the parental help item is about specific behavior. The factor analysis is telling us that this question about parental behavior is distinct from the other two Family items, and the students in my study answered this item differently than they answered the other two.

To summarize, I performed an exploratory factor analysis on these nine survey items, using a principal components extraction method and orthogonal factor rotation. This initially produced a four-factor solution with one clear Performance factor, one clear Mastery factor, and two over-lapping Family factors. When I re-ran the analysis and forced the items into three factors, the Performance and Mastery factors remained unchanged, and a unitary Family factor emerged with strong loadings for the parental expectations and desire to please parents items but a rela-tively weak loading for the parents helping with school work item. These results suggest that the Performance, Mastery, and Family items are distinct from each other and that the parental help with school work item is conceptually distinct from the other two Family items.

 To see a video in which I describe how to interpret SPSS output from a principal com-ponents factor analysis, please refer to the website that accompanies this book.

Confirmatory Factor Analysis: A Brief Introduction

As described above, exploratory factor analysis (EFA) is a good tool for finding the structure in a set of variables. Another form of factor analysis, **confirmatory factor analysis (CFA)** is often used by researchers to test how well a hypothesized organizational structure fits a set of data. This is a complicated procedure that is part of a larger set of statistical techniques known collectively as **structural equation modeling**, and a detailed description of CFA is beyond the scope of this book. I will spend just a couple of paragraphs here introducing the concept so that it is not com-pletely foreign when you encounter it in articles that you might read.

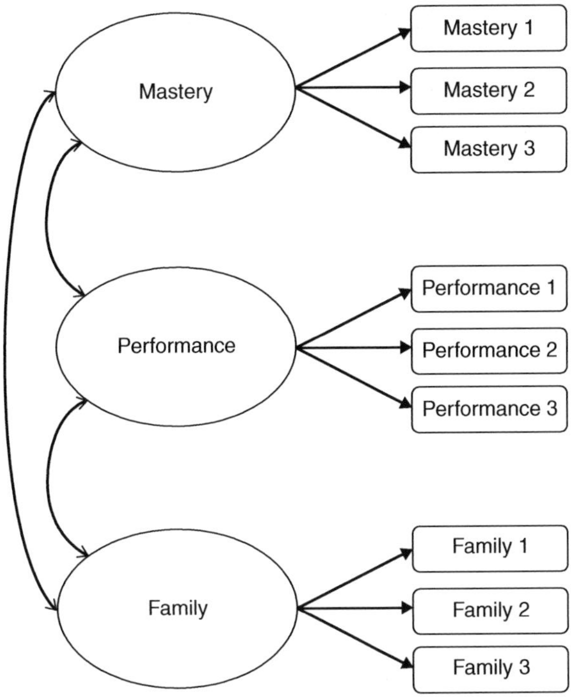

FIGURE 15.4 Theoretical model for confirmatory factor analysis.

The idea behind a CFA is that the researcher may already have had a good guess about how the variables in the study, such as a set of survey items, should go together, but needs to test this guess with some statistics. Unlike the EFA, which takes a set of items and organizes them according to the strength of the correlations among them, the CFA begins with the researcher organizing the items according to a strong theoretical rationale. For example, using the Performance, Mastery, and Family items we have become familiar with, I might let prior research and theory guide me to a reasonable hypothesis. Namely, I will expect all of the questions about doing better than others to form one factor (i.e., Performance), all of the items about learning and improving to form another factor (Mastery), and all of the items about family concerns to form a distinct third factor (Family). This hypothesized three-factor structure is presented in Figure 15.4.

Once I have developed my hypothesis about which items should indicate (i.e., load on) which factors, I can run my CFA to test my hypothesis. The CFA analysis will produce a set of **fit statistics**. There are several of these, and they all provide information about how well my proposed factor model fits the actual data that I have collected. In my model, I am proposing that all three of the Performance items will load on the Performance factor, but will not load strongly on either of the other two factors. The same is true for the Mastery and Family items: I expect them all to load strongly on their respective factors and weakly on the other factors. If this is actually the case in my data, my CFA will produce strong fit statistics. But if it is not the case, then my CFA will produce weak fit statistics, and I will need to modify my model to improve the model fit. Given what we know about the weak factor loadings of some of the items on the Family factor, I suspect that my hypothesized factor model in Figure 15.4 will not produce strong fit statistics in my CFA, and modifications to my model will be needed.

Reliability Analysis in Depth

Once the factor analysis has done its job of organizing items into groups, it is time to see how well the groups of items hold together. This is the job of reliability analysis. Although there are many different reliability statistics, the most commonly used is the **Cronbach's alpha.** The

Cronbach's alpha (with a Greek symbol of α) uses the associations among a set of items to indicate how well the items, as a group, hold together. Conceptually, the idea is that all of the survey items that are supposed to measure a single underlying construct should be answered in a similar way by respondents. This similarity of responses indicates that the construct is being measured **reliably**[3] by all of the items. On the other hand, if a person gives very different answers to items that are supposed to be measuring the same underlying construct, it is difficult to argue that these items offer a reliable measure of the construct.

In a sense, the Cronbach's alpha (more commonly referred to as the alpha) indicates the *average* correlations among a set of items.[4] Generally speaking, the more items there are in a reliability analysis, the higher the Cronbach's alpha will be. After all, if two items have a correlation of $r = .50$, that is some evidence that the two items may represent an underlying construct. But if eight or ten items are all correlated with r's of .50 or greater, then we can have a lot of confidence that these items measure one underlying construct. Similarly, if there are only three items, and one of them is not strongly correlated with the other two, the overall average correlation will be quite weak. But if there are eight items and only one does not correlate strongly with the others, the overall average correlation will not be greatly reduced. So the strength of the alpha depends both on the number of items and on the strength of the correlations among the items. The strongest a Cronbach's alpha can be is 1.0. A common rule of thumb is that when a set of items has an alpha level of .70 or higher, it is considered acceptably reliable.

Returning to our example of the Mastery, Performance, and Family items, we can already predict from the factor analysis that the Performance items will have the highest Cronbach's alpha because the first factor to emerge in an exploratory factor analysis is always the one with the strongest correlations among the items. Similarly, because all three of the Performance items had strong factor loadings on the first factor, and all of the Mastery items had strong loadings on the second factor, we can predict that the alpha levels for both the Performance items and the Mastery items will be pretty high. Finally, based on the results of the factor analysis, we can predict that the Cronbach's alpha for the Family items may not be very strong. Recall that the three Family items originally split into two factors, and when they were forced into a single factor one of the items had quite a weak loading on the factor. So our factor analysis would lead us to suspect that the Performance and Mastery items may have acceptable alpha levels (i.e., $\alpha > .70$), but the Family items probably will not. Let's take a look.

Using SPSS to run the analyses, I first examined the set of Performance items. The program produced a few tables, and I present the most relevant of these in Table 15.6. First, I can see that the three Performance items produce an alpha of .729 (see the box labeled "Cronbach's Alpha"). Next, SPSS produces a table that is full of interesting information. The first column shows all of the items in the analysis. The second column shows the "Corrected Item–Total

TABLE 15.6 Reliability statistics for the Performance items

Cronbach's Alpha	N of Items
.729	3

	Corrected Item–Total Correlation	Squared Multiple Correlation	Cronbach's Alpha if Item Deleted
Performance 1: important to appear smarter than others	.479	.230	.723
Performance 2: successful if I did better than other students	.598	.370	.583
Performance 3: want to do better than other students in class	.579	.354	.607

TABLE 15.7   Reliability analysis for the Mastery items

Cronbach's Alpha	N of Items
.700	3

	Scale Mean if Item Deleted	Scale Variance if Item Deleted	Corrected Item–Total Correlation	Cronbach's Alpha if Item Deleted
Mastery 1: do class work because I like to learn new things	7.54	2.770	.531	.592
Mastery 2: do work in class because I want to get better	7.23	2.780	.534	.587
Mastery 3: important that I understand the work	7.05	3.123	.488	.645

Correlation" which indicates how strongly each item is correlated with the overall group of items, often referred to as a **scale**. The third column shows the "Squared Multiple Correlation," which is simply the item–total correlation squared. Finally, the last column in Table 15.6 reveals what the Cronbach's alpha would be if a specific item were deleted from the group. These numbers reveal that the overall alpha would be about the same without the first Performance item as it is with it. This suggests that this first item, "It is important to appear smarter than others," is perhaps a little different from the other two, which both ask about wanting to do better than other students.

The analysis of the Mastery items followed a pretty similar pattern as the Performance items. The summary of this analysis is presented in Table 15.7 and indicates that the three Mastery items produced a Cronbach's alpha of .700, and all of the items contribute to the overall alpha. Notice that the alpha is reduced if any of the items are deleted.

As expected, the analysis of the three Family items produced a very different picture (see Table 15.8). The overall alpha for the three Family items is a paltry .265, and it would not rise above .36 if any single item were deleted. In other words, it is not as though two of the items were strongly correlated and the alpha was messed up by a single rogue item. Rather, the reliability analysis reveals that none of the three Family items are strongly related to each other. Even though the factor analysis did produce a factor with these three items, and the factor had an eigenvalue greater than one, the reliability analysis shows that these three items do not form a reliable scale, and these items cannot be said to reliably indicate a single underlying factor.

 To see a video in which I describe how to interpret SPSS output from a reliability analysis, please refer to the website that accompanies this book.

TABLE 15.8   Reliability analysis for the Family items

Cronbach's Alpha	N of Items
.265	3

	Scale Mean if Item Deleted	Scale Variance if Item Deleted	Corrected Item–Total Correlation	Cronbach's Alpha if Item Deleted
Family 1: parents help with school work	8.47	2.384	.085	.356
Family 2: parents expect me to go to college	6.13	3.293	.138	.224
Family 3: do well to please parents	6.97	2.111	.234	−.038

Writing it Up

If I were to write up the results of this study for a journal, it would look something like this:

"I conducted a factor analysis on a set of nine items from the survey: three Performance items, three Mastery items, and three Family items. The initial factor analysis, using principal components extraction and orthogonal factor rotation, produced four factors with eigenvalues greater than 1.0. The first factor was distinguished by strong factor loadings for all three of the Performance items and none of the other items. This factor explained 22 percent of the total variance in the items. The second factor had strong factor loadings for all three of the Mastery items and none of the other items, and explained an additional 21 percent of the variance. The third and fourth factors revealed a split among the three Family items with the third factor indicated by high parental expectations and a desire to make parents proud. The fourth factor also was indicated by the "make parents proud" item, as well as the item about parents helping with school work. These two factors explained 14 percent and 12 percent of the variance, respectively.

A subsequent factor analysis was performed, forcing the items into three factors. The Performance and Mastery factors remained unchanged, but the Family items all merged into a single factor with a strong factor loading for the desire to please parents item, a moderate loading for the parental expectations item, and a weak loading for the parental help with school work item.

Next, a reliability analysis was performed to examine the internal consistency of the three factors produced by the second factor analysis. This reliability analysis revealed that the Performance items formed a reliable scale (Cronbach's α = .73) and the alpha would not be improved with the removal of any of the items. Interestingly, the alpha would not be lowered substantially (.01) if the item about wanting to appear smart were removed from this scale. The Mastery items also produced a scale with an acceptable level of internal consistency (Cronbach's α = .70). All of these items had item–total correlations greater than .45 and the alpha would not be improved with the removal of any single item. Finally, the Family items failed to produce an internally consistent scale (Cronbach's α = .27). Although removing the "Parents help with school work" item would improve the alpha to .36, this is still unacceptably low. It appears that the three Family items simply do not belong together."

Work Problems

Suppose that I wanted to examine the attitudes of college students regarding their concerns for the future. I asked a sample of college students to complete a survey that contained four questions about the environment (e.g., "I am worried about climate change"), four questions about their own economic security (e.g., "I hope I am able to find a good job after graduation"), and four questions about their social relationships (e.g., "I am worried I will lose touch with my friends from college after I graduate").[5] I suspect that students will respond similarly to all of the items within each particular category. In other words, I believe that students who are very concerned about one aspect of the environment will be concerned about all aspects of the environment, and will therefore answer all four of the survey items about the environment similarly. To see whether students' responses to my survey items grouped together, I conducted an exploratory principal components factor analysis and the reliability analysis. Some of the results of these analyses are summarized in Tables 15.9 and 15.10. Please answer the following questions, some of them based on the information provided in these tables.

1. What is the purpose of conducting a factor analysis?
2. What does a reliability analysis tell you?

TABLE 15.9 Eigenvalues, percentage of variance explained, and rotated factor matrix for work problems

| | Rotation Sums of Squared Loadings | | | Rotated Factor Matrix | | | |
Factor	Total (Eigenvalue)	% of Variance	Survey Items	1	2	3	4
1	1.92	23.8	Enviro 1	.88			
2	1.54	19.2	Enviro 2	.86			
3	.83	8.4	Enviro 4	.81			
4	.71	6.3	Enviro 3	.53			.36
			Money 4		.92		
			Money 2		.84		
			Money 3		.74		
			Money 1		.32	.76	
			Social 1			.62	
			Social 2			.42	
			Social 3				.64
			Social 4				.57

3. Using the information about eigenvalues and percentage of variance explained in Table 15.9, how many solid factors do you think emerged from the factor analysis of the survey items? Why do you think so?

4. Using the information from the Rotated Factor Matrix in Table 15.9, which items are cross-loading on more than one factor? What does this tell you about these items?

5. Looking at the factor loadings from the Rotated Factor Matrix in Table 15.9, what would you predict the Cronbach's alpha to be for the four Social items? Why?

6. What does the information provided in Table 15.10 suggest regarding which item, if any, might be eliminated from the Environmental items to create a good scale?

7. From a conceptual standpoint, how is the Environmental survey item with the weakest contribution to the Cronbach's alpha different from the other three Environmental items? And how is this difference reflected in the cross-loading of this item on two factors?

 For answers to these work problems and for additional work problems, please refer to the website that accompanies this book.

TABLE 15.10 Reliability statistics for environmental items for work problems

Cronbach's Alpha	N of Items
.68	4

	Corrected Item–Total Correlation	Squared Multiple Correlation	Cronbach's Alpha if Item Deleted
Enviro 1: "I am worried about climate change."	.61	.37	.58
Enviro 2: "Rising sea levels are a serious problem."	.58	.34	.60
Enviro 3: "My friends and I volunteer to clean up the environment."	.41	.17	.76
Enviro 4: "I am concerned about how humans are harming the planet."	.55	.30	.62

Wrapping Up

Factor and reliability analyses are powerful statistical techniques that are frequently employed by social science researchers. Both allow researchers to organize large sets of variables into smaller, more meaningful groups. The purpose of this chapter was to provide a brief introduction to these methods. Keep in mind that each technique, but especially factor analysis, has a wide range of variations depending on the types of data that are being examined and the precise research question of the researcher. As you read about, and perhaps engage in, research that requires the use of factor and reliability analysis, I encourage you to read more about the topic and learn about all of the benefits that these techniques have to offer.

The purpose of this book was to provide plain English explanations of the most commonly used statistical techniques. Because this book is short, and because there is only so much about statistics that can be explained in plain English, I hope that you will consider this the beginning of your journey into the realm of statistics rather than the end. Although sometimes intimidating and daunting, the world of statistics is also rewarding and worth the effort. Whether we like it or not, all of our lives are touched and, at times, strongly affected by statistics. It is important that we make the effort to understand how statistics work and what they mean. If you have made it to the end of this book, you have already made substantial strides toward achieving that understanding. I'm sure that with continued effort, you will be able to take advantage of the many insights that an understanding of statistics can provide.

Notes

1 There are several methods for extracting factors. The most commonly used is **principal components analysis**, often called **PCA**. **Maximum likelihood** is another useful extraction method but it is used less frequently than PCA in social science research.

2 An eigenvalue is a measure of variance explained in the vector space created by the factors. This is confusing, I know. But you do not need to fully grasp the "factors in space" idea to get the basic idea of factor analysis. To get a more complete explanation of eigenvalues and factor analysis in general, I suggest you read one of the readings on factor analysis that are provided in the bibliography.

3 The type of reliability assessed in a Cronbach's alpha is known as the internal consistency of a set of variables. It is different from test–retest reliability, where the goal is to see when two identical measures given at different time points yield similar results.

4 Other measures of reliability use different methods to calculate the reliability statistics. For example, the omega statistic is based on the hierarchical structure of the items in the analysis. For more information about this method of reliability analysis, I suggest you read the articles by McDonald (1999) and by Zinbarg et al. (2006) that appear in the bibliography.

5 These data are not real. I just made them up for the sake of these work problems.

Appendices

Appendix A

AREA UNDER THE NORMAL CURVE BEYOND Z

Z	\multicolumn{10}{c}{Probability Content from $-\infty$ to Z}
	.00	.01	.02	.03	.04	.05	.06	.07	.08	.09
.0	.5000	.5040	.5080	.5120	.5160	.5199	.5239	.5279	.5319	.5359
.1	.5398	.5438	.5478	.5517	.5557	.5596	.5636	.5675	.5714	.5753
.2	.5793	.5832	.5871	.5910	.5948	.5987	.6026	.6064	.6103	.6141
.3	.6179	.6217	.6255	.6293	.6331	.6368	.6406	.6443	.6480	.6517
.4	.6554	.6591	.6628	.6664	.6700	.6736	.6772	.6808	.6844	.6879
.5	.6915	.6950	.6985	.7019	.7054	.7088	.7123	.7157	.7190	.7224
.6	.7257	.7291	.7324	.7357	.7389	.7422	.7454	.7486	.7517	.7549
.7	.7580	.7611	.7642	.7673	.7704	.7734	.7764	.7794	.7823	.7852
.8	.7881	.7910	.7939	.7967	.7995	.8023	.8051	.8078	.8106	.8133
.9	.8159	.8186	.8212	.8238	.8264	.8289	.8315	.8340	.8365	.8389
1.0	.8413	.8438	.8461	.8485	.8508	.8531	.8554	.8577	.8599	.8621
1.1	.8643	.8665	.8686	.8708	.8729	.8749	.8770	.8790	.8810	.8830
1.2	.8849	.8869	.8888	.8907	.8925	.8944	.8962	.8980	.8997	.9015
1.3	.9032	.9049	.9066	.9082	.9099	.9115	.9131	.9147	.9162	.9177
1.4	.9192	.9207	.9222	.9236	.9251	.9265	.9279	.9292	.9306	.9319
1.5	.9332	.9345	.9357	.9370	.9382	.9394	.9406	.9418	.9429	.9441
1.6	.9452	.9463	.9474	.9484	.9495	.9505	.9515	.9525	.9535	.9545
1.7	.9554	.9564	.9573	.9582	.9591	.9599	.9608	.9616	.9625	.9633
1.8	.9641	.9649	.9656	.9664	.9671	.9678	.9686	.9693	.9699	.9706
1.9	.9713	.9719	.9726	.9732	.9738	.9744	.9750	.9756	.9761	.9767
2.0	.9772	.9778	.9783	.9788	.9793	.9798	.9803	.9808	.9812	.9817
2.1	.9821	.9826	.9830	.9834	.9838	.9842	.9846	.9850	.9854	.9857
2.2	.9861	.9864	.9868	.9871	.9875	.9878	.9881	.9884	.9887	.9890
2.3	.9893	.9896	.9898	.9901	.9904	.9906	.9909	.9911	.9913	.9916
2.4	.9918	.9920	.9922	.9925	.9927	.9929	.9931	.9932	.9934	.9936
2.5	.9938	.9940	.9941	.9943	.9945	.9946	.9948	.9949	.9951	.9952
2.6	.9953	.9955	.9956	.9957	.9959	.9960	.9961	.9962	.9963	.9964
2.7	.9965	.9966	.9967	.9968	.9969	.9970	.9971	.9972	.9973	.9974
2.8	.9974	.9975	.9976	.9977	.9977	.9978	.9979	.9979	.9980	.9981
2.9	.9981	.9982	.9982	.9983	.9984	.9984	.9985	.9985	.9986	.9986
3.0	.9987	.9987	.9987	.9988	.9988	.9989	.9989	.9989	.9990	.9990

Source: http://isites.harvard.edu/fs/docs/icb.topic1499785.files/Public%20Domain%20Normal%20 Distribution%20Table.pdf. Public domain. Reprinted with permission of William Knight.

Far-Right Tail Probabilities

Z	p{Z to ∞}	Z	p{Z to ∞}	Z	p{Z to ∞}	Z	p{Z to ∞}
2.0	.02275	3.0	.001350	4.0	.00003167	5.0	2.867 E–7
2.1	.01786	3.1	.0009676	4.1	.00002066	5.5	1.899 E–8
2.2	.01390	3.2	.0006871	4.2	.00001335	6.0	9.866 E–10
2.3	.01072	3.3	.0004834	4.3	.00000854	6.5	4.016 E–11
2.4	.00820	3.4	.0003369	4.4	.000005413	7.0	1.280 E–12
2.5	.00621	3.5	.0002326	4.5	.000003398	7.5	3.191 E–14
2.6	.004661	3.6	.0001591	4.6	.000002112	8.0	6.221 E–16
2.7	.003467	3.7	.0001078	4.7	.000001300	8.5	9.480 E–18
2.8	.002555	3.8	.00007235	4.8	7.933 E–7	9.0	1.129 E–19
2.9	0.001866	3.9	0.00004810	4.9	4.792 E–7	9.5	1.049 E–20

Source: http://isites.harvard.edu/fs/docs/icb.topic1499785.files/Public%20Domain%20Normal%20 Distribution%20Table.pdf. Public domain. Reprinted with permission of William Knight.

Appendix B

CRITICAL VALUES OF THE *t* DISTRIBUTIONS

	α level for two-tailed test					
	.20	.10	.05	.02	.01	.001
	α level for one-tailed test					
df	.10	.05	.025	.01	.005	.0005
1	3.078	6.314	12.706	31.821	63.657	636.619
2	1.886	2.920	4.303	6.965	9.925	31.598
3	1.638	2.353	3.182	4.541	5.841	12.924
4	1.533	2.132	2.776	3.747	4.604	8.610
5	1.476	2.015	2.571	3.365	4.032	6.869
6	1.440	1.943	2.447	3.143	3.707	5.959
7	1.415	1.895	2.365	2.998	3.499	5.408
8	1.397	1.860	2.306	2.896	3.355	5.041
9	1.383	1.833	2.262	2.821	3.250	4.781
10	1.372	1.812	2.228	2.764	3.169	4.587
11	1.363	1.796	2.201	2.718	3.106	4.437
12	1.356	1.782	2.179	2.681	3.055	4.318
13	1.350	1.771	2.160	2.650	3.012	4.221
14	1.345	1.761	2.145	2.624	2.977	4.140
15	1.341	1.753	2.131	2.602	2.947	4.073
16	1.337	1.746	2.120	2.583	2.921	4.015
17	1.333	1.740	2.110	2.567	2.898	3.965
18	1.330	1.734	2.101	2.552	2.878	3.922
19	1.328	1.729	2.093	2.539	2.861	3.883
20	1.325	1.725	2.086	2.528	2.845	3.850
21	1.323	1.721	2.080	2.518	2.831	3.819
22	1.321	1.717	2.074	2.508	2.819	3.792
23	1.319	1.714	2.069	2.500	2.807	3.767
24	1.318	1.711	2.064	2.492	2.797	3.745
25	1.316	1.708	2.060	2.485	2.787	3.725
26	1.315	1.706	2.056	2.479	2.779	3.707
27	1.314	1.703	2.052	2.474	2.771	3.690
28	1.313	1.701	2.048	2.467	2.763	3.674
29	1.311	1.699	2.045	2.462	2.756	3.659
30	1.310	1.697	2.042	2.457	2.750	3.646
40	1.303	1.684	2.021	2.423	2.704	3.551
60	1.296	1.671	2.000	2.390	2.660	3.460
120	1.289	1.658	1.980	2.358	2.617	3.373
∞	1.282	1.645	1.960	2.326	2.576	3.291

Note: To be significant, the *t* value obtained from the data must be equal to or greater than the value shown in the table.
Source: Fisher, R. A., & Yates, F. (1963). *Statistical Tables for Biological, Agricultural, and Medical Research* (6th ed.). Boston, MA: Addison-Wesley. Reprinted with permission of Addison-Wesley, Longman, and Pearson Education.

Appendix C

CRITICAL VALUES OF THE *F* DISTRIBUTIONS

CRITICAL VALUES OF THE F DISTRIBUTIONS

α levels of .05 (lightface) and .01 (boldface) for the distribution of F

Degrees of Freedom (for the numerator of F ratio)

Degrees of freedom (for the denominator of the F ratio) — each cell: lightface (.05) / boldface (.01)

df	1	2	3	4	5	6	7	8	9	10	11	12	14	16	20	24	30	40	50	75	100	200	500	∞
1	161 / 4,052	200 / 4,999	216 / 5,403	225 / 5,625	230 / 5,764	34 / 5,859	237 / 5,928	239 / 5,981	241 / 6,022	242 / 6,056	243 / 6,082	244 / 6,106	245 / 6,142	246 / 6,169	248 / 6,208	249 / 6,234	250 / 6,258	251 / 6,286	252 / 6,302	253 / 6,323	253 / 6,334	254 / 6,352	254 / 6,361	254 / 6,366
2	18.51 / 98.49	19.00 / 99.00	19.16 / 99.17	19.25 / 99.25	19.30 / 99.30	19.33 / 99.33	19.36 / 99.34	19.37 / 99.36	19.38 / 99.39	19.39 / 99.40	19.40 / 99.41	19.41 / 99.42	19.42 / 99.43	19.43 / 99.44	19.44 / 99.45	19.45 / 99.46	19.46 / 99.47	19.47 / 99.48	19.47 / 99.49	19.48 / 99.49	19.49 / 99.49	19.49 / 99.49	19.50 / 99.50	19.50 / 99.50
3	10.13 / 34.12	9.55 / 30.82	9.28 / 29.46	9.12 / 28.71	9.01 / 28.24	8.94 / 27.91	8.88 / 27.67	8.84 / 27.49	8.81 / 27.34	8.78 / 27.23	8.76 / 27.13	8.74 / 27.05	8.71 / 26.92	8.69 / 26.83	8.66 / 26.69	8.64 / 26.60	8.62 / 26.50	8.60 / 26.41	8.58 / 26.35	8.57 / 26.27	8.56 / 26.23	8.54 / 26.18	8.54 / 26.14	8.53 / 26.12
4	7.71 / 21.20	6.94 / 18.00	6.59 / 16.69	6.39 / 15.98	6.26 / 15.52	6.16 / 15.21	6.09 / 14.98	6.04 / 14.80	6.00 / 14.66	5.96 / 14.54	5.93 / 14.45	5.91 / 14.37	5.87 / 14.24	5.84 / 14.15	5.80 / 14.02	5.77 / 13.93	5.74 / 13.83	5.71 / 13.74	5.70 / 13.69	5.68 / 13.61	5.66 / 13.57	5.65 / 13.52	5.64 / 13.48	5.63 / 13.46
5	6.61 / 16.26	5.79 / 13.27	5.41 / 12.06	5.19 / 11.39	5.05 / 10.97	4.95 / 10.67	4.88 / 10.45	4.82 / 10.27	4.78 / 10.15	4.74 / 10.05	4.70 / 9.96	4.68 / 9.89	4.64 / 9.77	4.60 / 9.68	4.56 / 9.55	4.53 / 9.47	4.50 / 9.38	4.46 / 9.29	4.44 / 9.24	4.42 / 9.17	4.40 / 9.13	4.38 / 9.07	4.37 / 9.04	4.36 / 9.02
6	5.99 / 13.74	5.14 / 10.92	4.76 / 9.78	4.53 / 9.15	4.39 / 8.75	4.28 / 8.47	4.21 / 8.26	4.15 / 8.10	4.10 / 7.98	4.06 / 7.87	4.03 / 7.79	4.00 / 7.72	3.96 / 7.60	3.92 / 7.52	3.87 / 7.39	3.84 / 7.31	3.81 / 7.23	3.77 / 7.14	3.75 / 7.09	3.72 / 7.02	3.71 / 6.99	3.69 / 6.94	3.68 / 6.90	3.67 / 6.88
7	5.59 / 12.25	4.74 / 9.55	4.35 / 8.45	4.12 / 7.85	3.97 / 7.46	3.87 / 7.19	3.79 / 7.00	3.73 / 6.84	3.68 / 6.71	3.63 / 6.62	3.60 / 6.54	3.57 / 6.47	3.52 / 6.35	3.49 / 6.27	3.44 / 6.15	3.41 / 6.07	3.38 / 5.98	3.34 / 5.90	3.32 / 5.85	3.29 / 5.78	3.28 / 5.75	3.25 / 5.70	3.24 / 5.67	3.23 / 5.65
8	5.32 / 11.26	4.46 / 8.65	4.07 / 7.59	3.84 / 7.01	3.69 / 6.63	3.58 / 6.37	3.50 / 6.19	3.44 / 6.03	3.39 / 5.91	3.34 / 5.82	3.31 / 5.74	3.28 / 5.67	3.23 / 5.56	3.20 / 5.48	3.15 / 5.36	3.12 / 5.28	3.08 / 5.20	3.05 / 5.11	3.03 / 5.06	3.00 / 5.00	2.98 / 4.96	2.96 / 4.91	2.94 / 4.88	2.93 / 4.86
9	5.12 / 10.56	4.26 / 8.02	3.86 / 6.99	3.63 / 6.42	3.48 / 6.06	3.37 / 5.80	3.29 / 5.62	3.23 / 5.47	3.18 / 5.35	3.13 / 5.26	3.10 / 5.18	3.07 / 5.11	3.02 / 5.00	2.98 / 4.92	2.93 / 4.80	2.90 / 4.73	2.86 / 4.64	2.82 / 4.56	2.80 / 4.51	2.77 / 4.45	2.76 / 4.41	2.73 / 4.36	2.72 / 4.33	2.71 / 4.31
10	4.96 / 10.04	4.10 / 7.56	3.71 / 6.55	3.48 / 5.99	3.33 / 5.64	3.22 / 5.39	3.14 / 5.21	3.07 / 5.06	3.02 / 4.95	2.97 / 4.85	2.94 / 4.78	2.91 / 4.71	2.86 / 4.60	2.82 / 4.52	2.77 / 4.41	2.74 / 4.33	2.70 / 4.25	2.67 / 4.17	2.64 / 4.12	2.61 / 4.05	2.59 / 4.01	2.56 / 3.96	2.55 / 3.93	2.54 / 3.91
11	4.84 / 9.65	3.98 / 7.20	3.59 / 6.22	3.36 / 5.67	3.20 / 5.32	3.09 / 5.07	3.01 / 4.88	2.95 / 4.74	2.90 / 4.63	2.86 / 4.54	2.82 / 4.46	2.79 / 4.40	2.74 / 4.29	2.70 / 4.21	2.65 / 4.10	2.61 / 4.02	2.57 / 3.94	2.53 / 3.86	2.50 / 3.80	2.47 / 3.74	2.45 / 3.70	2.42 / 3.66	2.41 / 3.62	2.40 / 3.60
12	4.75 / 9.33	3.88 / 6.93	3.49 / 5.95	3.26 / 5.41	3.11 / 5.06	3.00 / 4.82	2.92 / 4.65	2.85 / 4.50	2.80 / 4.39	2.76 / 4.30	2.72 / 4.22	2.69 / 4.16	2.64 / 4.05	2.60 / 3.98	2.54 / 3.86	2.50 / 3.78	2.46 / 3.70	2.42 / 3.61	2.40 / 3.56	2.36 / 3.49	2.35 / 3.46	2.32 / 3.41	2.31 / 3.38	2.30 / 3.36
13	4.67 / 9.07	3.80 / 6.70	3.41 / 5.74	3.18 / 5.20	3.02 / 4.86	2.92 / 4.62	2.84 / 4.44	2.77 / 4.30	2.72 / 4.19	2.67 / 4.10	2.63 / 4.02	2.60 / 3.96	2.55 / 3.85	2.51 / 3.78	2.46 / 3.67	2.42 / 3.59	2.38 / 3.51	2.34 / 3.42	2.32 / 3.37	2.28 / 3.30	2.26 / 3.27	2.24 / 3.28	2.22 / 3.18	2.21 / 3.16

Degrees of Freedom (for the numerator of F ratio)

df	1	2	3	4	5	6	7	8	9	10	11	12	14	16	20	24	30	40	50	75	100	200	500	∞
14	4.60 **8.86**	3.74 **6.51**	3.34 **5.56**	3.11 **5.03**	2.96 **4.69**	2.85 **4.46**	2.77 **4.28**	2.70 **4.14**	2.65 **4.03**	2.60 **3.94**	2.56 **3.86**	2.53 **3.80**	2.48 **3.70**	2.44 **3.62**	2.39 **3.51**	2.35 **3.43**	2.31 **3.34**	2.27 **3.26**	2.24 **3.21**	2.21 **3.14**	2.19 **3.11**	2.16 **3.06**	2.14 **3.02**	2.13 **3.00**
15	4.54 **8.68**	3.68 **6.36**	3.29 **5.52**	3.06 **4.89**	2.90 **4.56**	2.79 **4.32**	2.70 **4.14**	2.64 **4.00**	2.59 **3.89**	2.55 **3.80**	2.51 **3.73**	2.48 **3.67**	2.43 **3.56**	2.39 **3.48**	2.33 **3.36**	2.29 **3.29**	2.25 **3.20**	2.21 **3.12**	2.18 **3.07**	2.15 **3.00**	2.12 **2.97**	2.10 **2.92**	2.08 **2.89**	2.07 **2.87**
16	4.49 **8.53**	3.63 **6.23**	3.24 **5.29**	3.01 **4.77**	2.85 **4.44**	2.74 **4.20**	2.66 **4.03**	2.59 **3.89**	2.54 **3.78**	2.49 **3.69**	2.45 **3.61**	2.42 **3.55**	2.37 **3.45**	2.33 **3.37**	2.28 **3.25**	2.24 **3.18**	2.20 **3.10**	2.16 **3.01**	2.13 **2.96**	2.09 **2.89**	2.07 **2.86**	2.04 **2.80**	2.02 **2.77**	2.01 **2.75**
17	4.45 **8.40**	3.59 **6.11**	3.20 **5.18**	2.96 **4.67**	2.81 **4.34**	2.70 **4.10**	2.62 **3.93**	2.55 **3.79**	2.50 **3.68**	2.45 **3.59**	2.41 **3.52**	2.38 **3.45**	2.33 **3.35**	2.29 **3.27**	2.23 **3.16**	2.19 **3.08**	2.15 **3.00**	2.11 **2.92**	2.08 **2.86**	2.04 **2.79**	2.02 **2.76**	1.99 **2.70**	1.97 **2.67**	1.96 **2.65**
18	4.41 **8.28**	3.55 **6.01**	3.16 **5.09**	2.93 **4.58**	2.77 **4.25**	2.66 **4.01**	2.58 **3.85**	2.51 **3.71**	2.46 **3.60**	2.41 **3.51**	2.37 **3.44**	2.34 **3.37**	2.29 **3.27**	2.25 **3.19**	2.19 **3.07**	2.15 **3.00**	2.11 **2.91**	2.07 **2.83**	2.04 **2.78**	2.00 **2.71**	1.98 **2.68**	1.95 **2.62**	1.93 **2.59**	1.92 **2.57**
19	4.38 **8.18**	3.52 **5.93**	3.13 **5.01**	2.90 **4.50**	2.74 **4.17**	2.63 **3.94**	2.55 **3.77**	2.48 **3.63**	2.43 **3.52**	2.38 **3.43**	2.34 **3.36**	2.31 **3.30**	2.26 **3.19**	2.21 **3.12**	2.15 **3.00**	2.11 **2.92**	2.07 **2.84**	2.02 **2.76**	2.00 **2.70**	1.96 **2.63**	1.94 **2.60**	1.91 **2.54**	1.90 **2.51**	1.88 **2.49**
20	4.35 **8.10**	3.49 **5.85**	3.10 **4.94**	2.87 **4.43**	2.71 **4.10**	2.60 **3.87**	2.52 **3.71**	2.45 **3.56**	2.40 **3.45**	2.35 **3.37**	2.31 **3.30**	2.28 **3.23**	2.23 **3.13**	2.18 **3.05**	2.12 **2.94**	2.08 **2.86**	2.04 **2.77**	1.99 **2.69**	1.96 **2.63**	1.92 **2.56**	1.90 **2.53**	1.87 **2.47**	1.85 **2.44**	1.84 **2.42**
21	4.32 **8.02**	3.47 **5.78**	3.07 **4.87**	2.84 **4.37**	2.68 **4.04**	2.57 **3.81**	2.49 **3.65**	2.42 **3.51**	2.37 **3.40**	2.32 **3.31**	2.28 **3.24**	2.25 **3.17**	2.20 **3.07**	2.15 **2.99**	2.09 **2.88**	2.05 **2.80**	2.00 **2.72**	1.96 **2.63**	1.93 **2.58**	1.89 **2.51**	1.87 **2.47**	1.84 **2.42**	1.82 **2.38**	1.81 **2.36**
22	4.30 **7.94**	3.44 **5.72**	3.05 **4.82**	2.82 **4.31**	2.66 **3.99**	2.55 **3.76**	2.47 **3.59**	2.40 **3.45**	2.35 **3.35**	2.30 **3.26**	2.26 **3.18**	2.23 **3.12**	2.18 **3.02**	2.13 **2.94**	2.07 **2.83**	2.03 **2.75**	1.98 **2.67**	1.93 **2.58**	1.91 **2.53**	1.87 **2.46**	1.84 **2.42**	1.81 **2.37**	1.80 **2.33**	1.78 **2.31**
23	4.28 **7.88**	3.42 **5.66**	3.03 **4.76**	2.80 **4.26**	2.64 **3.94**	2.53 **3.71**	2.45 **3.54**	2.38 **3.41**	2.32 **3.30**	2.28 **3.21**	2.24 **3.14**	2.20 **3.07**	2.14 **2.97**	2.10 **2.89**	2.04 **2.78**	2.00 **2.70**	1.96 **2.62**	1.91 **2.53**	1.88 **2.48**	1.84 **2.41**	1.82 **2.37**	1.79 **2.32**	1.77 **2.28**	1.76 **2.26**
24	4.26 **7.82**	3.40 **5.61**	3.01 **4.72**	2.78 **4.22**	2.62 **3.90**	2.51 **3.67**	2.43 **3.50**	2.36 **3.36**	2.30 **3.25**	2.26 **3.17**	2.22 **3.09**	2.18 **3.03**	2.13 **2.93**	2.09 **2.85**	2.02 **2.74**	1.98 **2.66**	1.94 **2.58**	1.89 **2.49**	1.86 **2.44**	1.82 **2.36**	1.80 **2.33**	1.76 **2.27**	1.74 **2.23**	1.73 **2.21**
25	4.24 **7.77**	3.38 **5.57**	2.99 **4.68**	2.76 **4.18**	2.60 **3.86**	2.49 **3.63**	2.41 **3.46**	2.34 **3.32**	2.28 **3.21**	2.24 **3.13**	2.20 **3.05**	2.16 **2.99**	2.11 **2.89**	2.06 **2.81**	2.00 **2.70**	1.96 **2.62**	1.92 **2.54**	1.87 **2.45**	1.84 **2.40**	1.80 **2.32**	1.77 **2.29**	1.74 **2.23**	1.72 **2.19**	1.71 **2.17**
26	4.22 **7.72**	3.37 **5.53**	2.98 **4.64**	2.74 **4.14**	2.59 **3.82**	2.47 **3.59**	2.39 **3.42**	2.32 **3.29**	2.27 **3.17**	2.22 **3.09**	2.18 **3.02**	2.15 **2.96**	2.10 **2.86**	2.05 **2.77**	1.99 **2.66**	1.95 **2.58**	1.90 **2.50**	1.85 **2.41**	1.82 **2.36**	1.78 **2.28**	1.76 **2.25**	1.72 **2.19**	1.70 **2.15**	1.69 **2.13**

Degrees of freedom (for the denominator of the F ratio)

(continued on next page)

CRITICAL VALUES OF THE F DISTRIBUTIONS (continued)

α levels of .05 (lightface) and .01 (**boldface**) for the distribution of F

Degrees of Freedom (for the numerator of F ratio)

Degrees of freedom (for the denominator of the F ratio) shown in leftmost and rightmost columns. Each cell: .05 (lightface) / **.01 (boldface)**.

df	1	2	3	4	5	6	7	8	9	10	11	12	14	16	20	24	30	40	50	75	100	200	500	∞
27	4.21 / **7.68**	3.35 / **5.49**	2.96 / **4.60**	2.73 / **4.11**	2.57 / **3.79**	2.46 / **3.56**	2.37 / **3.39**	2.30 / **3.26**	2.25 / **3.14**	2.20 / **3.06**	2.16 / **2.98**	2.13 / **2.93**	2.08 / **2.83**	2.03 / **2.74**	1.97 / **2.63**	1.93 / **2.55**	1.88 / **2.47**	1.84 / **2.38**	1.80 / **2.33**	1.76 / **2.25**	1.74 / **2.21**	1.71 / **2.16**	1.68 / **2.12**	1.67 / **2.10**
28	4.20 / **7.64**	3.34 / **5.45**	2.95 / **4.57**	2.71 / **4.07**	2.56 / **3.76**	2.44 / **3.53**	2.36 / **3.36**	2.29 / **3.23**	2.24 / **3.11**	2.19 / **3.03**	2.15 / **2.95**	2.12 / **2.90**	2.06 / **2.80**	2.02 / **2.71**	1.96 / **2.60**	1.91 / **2.52**	1.87 / **2.44**	1.81 / **2.35**	1.78 / **2.30**	1.75 / **2.22**	1.72 / **2.18**	1.69 / **2.13**	1.67 / **2.09**	1.65 / **2.06**
29	4.18 / **7.60**	3.33 / **5.42**	2.93 / **4.54**	2.70 / **4.04**	2.54 / **3.73**	2.43 / **3.50**	2.35 / **3.33**	2.28 / **3.20**	2.22 / **3.08**	2.18 / **3.00**	2.14 / **2.92**	2.10 / **2.87**	2.05 / **2.77**	2.00 / **2.68**	1.94 / **2.57**	1.90 / **2.49**	1.85 / **2.41**	1.80 / **2.32**	1.77 / **2.27**	1.73 / **2.19**	1.71 / **2.15**	1.68 / **2.10**	1.65 / **2.06**	1.64 / **2.03**
30	4.17 / **7.56**	3.32 / **5.39**	2.92 / **4.51**	2.69 / **4.02**	2.53 / **3.70**	2.42 / **3.47**	2.34 / **3.30**	2.27 / **3.17**	2.21 / **3.06**	2.16 / **2.98**	2.12 / **2.90**	2.09 / **2.84**	2.04 / **2.74**	1.99 / **2.66**	1.93 / **2.55**	1.89 / **2.47**	1.84 / **2.38**	1.79 / **2.29**	1.76 / **2.24**	1.72 / **2.16**	1.69 / **2.13**	1.66 / **2.07**	1.64 / **2.03**	1.62 / **2.01**
32	4.15 / **7.50**	3.30 / **5.34**	2.90 / **4.46**	2.67 / **3.97**	2.51 / **3.66**	2.40 / **3.42**	2.32 / **3.25**	2.25 / **3.12**	2.19 / **3.01**	2.14 / **2.94**	2.10 / **2.86**	2.07 / **2.80**	2.02 / **2.70**	1.97 / **2.62**	1.91 / **2.51**	1.86 / **2.42**	1.82 / **2.34**	1.76 / **2.25**	1.74 / **2.20**	1.69 / **2.12**	1.67 / **2.08**	1.64 / **2.02**	1.61 / **1.98**	1.59 / **1.96**
34	4.13 / **7.44**	3.28 / **5.29**	2.88 / **4.42**	2.65 / **3.93**	2.49 / **3.61**	2.38 / **3.38**	2.30 / **3.21**	2.23 / **3.08**	2.17 / **2.97**	2.12 / **2.89**	2.08 / **2.82**	2.05 / **2.76**	2.00 / **2.66**	1.95 / **2.58**	1.89 / **2.47**	1.84 / **2.38**	1.80 / **2.30**	1.74 / **2.21**	1.71 / **2.15**	1.67 / **2.08**	1.64 / **2.04**	1.61 / **1.98**	1.59 / **1.94**	1.57 / **1.91**
36	4.11 / **7.39**	3.26 / **5.24**	2.86 / **4.38**	2.63 / **3.89**	2.48 / **3.58**	2.36 / **3.35**	2.28 / **3.18**	2.21 / **3.04**	2.15 / **2.94**	2.10 / **2.86**	2.06 / **2.78**	2.03 / **2.72**	1.98 / **2.62**	1.93 / **2.54**	1.87 / **2.43**	1.82 / **2.35**	1.78 / **2.26**	1.72 / **2.17**	1.69 / **2.12**	1.65 / **2.04**	1.62 / **2.00**	1.59 / **1.94**	1.56 / **1.90**	1.55 / **1.87**
38	4.10 / **7.35**	3.25 / **5.21**	2.85 / **4.34**	2.62 / **3.86**	2.46 / **3.54**	2.35 / **3.32**	2.26 / **3.15**	2.19 / **3.02**	2.14 / **2.91**	2.09 / **2.82**	2.05 / **2.75**	2.02 / **2.69**	1.96 / **2.59**	1.92 / **2.51**	1.85 / **2.40**	1.80 / **2.32**	1.76 / **2.22**	1.71 / **2.14**	1.67 / **2.08**	1.63 / **2.00**	1.60 / **1.97**	1.57 / **1.90**	1.54 / **1.86**	1.53 / **1.84**
40	4.08 / **7.31**	3.23 / **5.18**	2.84 / **4.31**	2.61 / **3.83**	2.45 / **3.51**	2.34 / **3.29**	2.25 / **3.12**	2.18 / **2.99**	2.12 / **2.88**	2.07 / **2.80**	2.04 / **2.73**	2.00 / **2.66**	1.95 / **2.56**	1.90 / **2.49**	1.84 / **2.37**	1.79 / **2.29**	1.74 / **2.20**	1.69 / **2.11**	1.66 / **2.05**	1.61 / **1.97**	1.59 / **1.94**	1.55 / **1.88**	1.53 / **1.84**	1.51 / **1.81**
42	4.07 / **7.27**	3.22 / **5.15**	2.83 / **4.29**	2.59 / **3.80**	2.44 / **3.49**	2.32 / **3.26**	2.24 / **3.10**	2.17 / **2.96**	2.11 / **2.86**	2.06 / **2.77**	2.02 / **2.70**	1.99 / **2.64**	1.94 / **2.54**	1.89 / **2.46**	1.82 / **2.35**	1.78 / **2.26**	1.73 / **2.17**	1.68 / **2.08**	1.64 / **2.02**	1.60 / **1.94**	1.57 / **1.91**	1.54 / **1.85**	1.51 / **1.80**	1.49 / **1.78**
44	4.06 / **7.25**	3.21 / **5.12**	2.82 / **4.26**	2.58 / **3.78**	2.43 / **3.46**	2.31 / **3.24**	2.23 / **3.07**	2.16 / **2.94**	2.10 / **2.84**	2.05 / **2.75**	2.01 / **2.68**	1.98 / **2.62**	1.92 / **2.52**	1.88 / **2.44**	1.81 / **2.32**	1.76 / **2.24**	1.72 / **2.15**	1.66 / **2.06**	1.63 / **2.00**	1.58 / **1.92**	1.56 / **1.88**	1.52 / **1.82**	1.50 / **1.78**	1.48 / **1.75**
46	4.05 / **7.21**	3.20 / **5.10**	2.81 / **4.24**	2.57 / **3.76**	2.42 / **3.44**	2.30 / **3.22**	2.22 / **3.05**	2.14 / **2.92**	2.09 / **2.82**	2.04 / **2.73**	2.00 / **2.66**	1.97 / **2.60**	1.91 / **2.50**	1.87 / **2.42**	1.80 / **2.30**	1.75 / **2.22**	1.71 / **2.13**	1.65 / **2.04**	1.62 / **1.98**	1.57 / **1.90**	1.54 / **1.86**	1.51 / **1.80**	1.48 / **1.76**	1.46 / **1.72**
48	4.04 / **7.19**	3.19 / **5.08**	2.80 / **4.22**	2.56 / **3.74**	2.41 / **3.42**	2.30 / **3.20**	2.21 / **3.04**	2.14 / **2.90**	2.08 / **2.80**	2.03 / **2.71**	1.99 / **2.64**	1.96 / **2.58**	1.90 / **2.48**	1.86 / **2.40**	1.79 / **2.28**	1.74 / **2.20**	1.70 / **2.11**	1.64 / **2.02**	1.61 / **1.96**	1.56 / **1.88**	1.53 / **1.84**	1.50 / **1.78**	1.47 / **1.73**	1.45 / **1.70**

Degrees of Freedom (for the numerator of F ratio)

(denom)	1	2	3	4	5	6	7	8	9	10	11	12	14	16	20	24	30	40	50	75	100	200	500	∞
50	4.03 / **7.17**	3.18 / **5.06**	2.79 / **4.20**	2.56 / **3.72**	2.40 / **3.41**	2.29 / **3.18**	2.20 / **3.02**	2.13 / **2.88**	2.07 / **2.78**	2.02 / **2.70**	1.98 / **2.62**	1.95 / **2.56**	1.90 / **2.46**	1.85 / **2.39**	1.78 / **2.26**	1.74 / **2.18**	1.69 / **2.10**	1.63 / **2.00**	1.60 / **1.94**	1.55 / **1.86**	1.52 / **1.82**	1.48 / **1.76**	1.46 / **1.71**	1.44 / **1.68**
55	4.02 / **7.12**	3.17 / **5.01**	2.78 / **4.16**	2.54 / **3.68**	2.38 / **3.37**	2.27 / **3.15**	2.18 / **2.98**	2.11 / **2.85**	2.05 / **2.75**	2.00 / **2.66**	1.97 / **2.59**	1.93 / **2.53**	1.88 / **2.43**	1.83 / **2.35**	1.76 / **2.23**	1.72 / **2.15**	1.67 / **2.06**	1.61 / **1.96**	1.58 / **1.90**	1.52 / **1.82**	1.50 / **1.78**	1.46 / **1.71**	1.43 / **1.66**	1.41 / **1.64**
60	4.00 / **7.08**	3.15 / **4.98**	2.76 / **4.13**	2.52 / **3.65**	2.37 / **3.34**	2.25 / **3.12**	2.17 / **2.95**	2.10 / **2.82**	2.04 / **2.72**	1.99 / **2.63**	1.95 / **2.56**	1.92 / **2.50**	1.86 / **2.40**	1.81 / **2.32**	1.75 / **2.20**	1.70 / **2.12**	1.65 / **2.03**	1.59 / **1.93**	1.56 / **1.87**	1.50 / **1.79**	1.48 / **1.74**	1.44 / **1.68**	1.41 / **1.63**	1.39 / **1.60**
65	3.99 / **7.04**	3.14 / **4.95**	2.75 / **4.10**	2.51 / **3.62**	2.36 / **3.31**	2.24 / **3.09**	2.15 / **2.93**	2.08 / **2.79**	2.02 / **2.70**	1.98 / **2.61**	1.94 / **2.54**	1.90 / **2.47**	1.85 / **2.37**	1.80 / **2.30**	1.73 / **2.18**	1.68 / **2.09**	1.63 / **2.00**	1.57 / **1.90**	1.54 / **1.84**	1.49 / **1.76**	1.46 / **1.71**	1.42 / **1.64**	1.39 / **1.60**	1.37 / **1.56**
70	3.98 / **7.01**	3.13 / **4.92**	2.74 / **4.08**	2.50 / **3.60**	2.35 / **3.29**	2.23 / **3.07**	2.14 / **2.91**	2.07 / **2.77**	2.01 / **2.67**	1.97 / **2.59**	1.93 / **2.51**	1.89 / **2.45**	1.84 / **2.35**	1.79 / **2.28**	1.72 / **2.15**	1.67 / **2.07**	1.62 / **1.98**	1.56 / **1.88**	1.53 / **1.82**	1.47 / **1.74**	1.45 / **1.69**	1.40 / **1.62**	1.37 / **1.56**	1.35 / **1.53**
80	3.96 / **6.96**	3.11 / **4.88**	2.72 / **4.04**	2.48 / **3.56**	2.33 / **3.25**	2.21 / **3.04**	2.12 / **2.87**	2.05 / **2.74**	1.99 / **2.64**	1.95 / **2.55**	1.91 / **2.48**	1.88 / **2.41**	1.82 / **2.32**	1.77 / **2.24**	1.70 / **2.11**	1.65 / **2.03**	1.60 / **1.94**	1.54 / **1.84**	1.51 / **1.78**	1.45 / **1.70**	1.42 / **1.65**	1.38 / **1.57**	1.35 / **1.52**	1.32 / **1.49**
100	3.94 / **6.90**	3.09 / **4.82**	2.70 / **3.98**	2.46 / **3.51**	2.30 / **3.20**	2.19 / **2.99**	2.10 / **2.82**	2.03 / **2.69**	1.97 / **2.59**	1.92 / **2.51**	1.88 / **2.43**	1.85 / **2.36**	1.79 / **2.26**	1.75 / **2.19**	1.68 / **2.06**	1.63 / **1.98**	1.57 / **1.89**	1.51 / **1.79**	1.48 / **1.73**	1.42 / **1.64**	1.39 / **1.59**	1.34 / **1.51**	1.30 / **1.46**	1.28 / **1.43**
125	3.92 / **6.84**	3.07 / **4.78**	2.68 / **3.94**	2.44 / **3.47**	2.29 / **3.17**	2.17 / **2.95**	2.08 / **2.79**	2.01 / **2.65**	1.95 / **2.56**	1.90 / **2.47**	1.86 / **2.40**	1.83 / **2.33**	1.77 / **2.23**	1.72 / **2.15**	1.65 / **2.03**	1.60 / **1.94**	1.55 / **1.85**	1.49 / **1.75**	1.45 / **1.68**	1.39 / **1.59**	1.36 / **1.54**	1.31 / **1.46**	1.27 / **1.40**	1.25 / **1.37**
150	3.91 / **6.81**	3.06 / **4.75**	2.67 / **3.91**	2.43 / **3.44**	2.27 / **3.14**	2.16 / **2.92**	2.07 / **2.76**	2.00 / **2.62**	1.94 / **2.53**	1.89 / **2.44**	1.85 / **2.37**	1.82 / **2.30**	1.76 / **2.20**	1.71 / **2.12**	1.64 / **2.00**	1.59 / **1.91**	1.54 / **1.83**	1.47 / **1.72**	1.44 / **1.66**	1.37 / **1.56**	1.34 / **1.51**	1.29 / **1.43**	1.25 / **1.37**	1.22 / **1.33**
200	3.89 / **6.76**	3.04 / **4.71**	2.65 / **3.88**	2.41 / **3.41**	2.26 / **3.11**	2.14 / **2.90**	2.05 / **2.73**	1.98 / **2.60**	1.92 / **2.50**	1.87 / **2.41**	1.83 / **2.34**	1.80 / **2.28**	1.74 / **2.17**	1.69 / **2.09**	1.62 / **1.97**	1.57 / **1.88**	1.52 / **1.79**	1.45 / **1.69**	1.42 / **1.62**	1.35 / **1.53**	1.32 / **1.48**	1.26 / **1.39**	1.22 / **1.33**	1.19 / **1.28**
400	3.86 / **6.70**	3.02 / **4.66**	2.62 / **3.83**	2.39 / **3.36**	2.23 / **3.06**	2.12 / **2.85**	2.03 / **2.69**	1.96 / **2.55**	1.90 / **2.46**	1.85 / **2.37**	1.81 / **2.29**	1.78 / **2.23**	1.72 / **2.12**	1.67 / **2.04**	1.60 / **1.92**	1.54 / **1.84**	1.49 / **1.74**	1.42 / **1.64**	1.38 / **1.57**	1.32 / **1.47**	1.28 / **1.42**	1.22 / **1.32**	1.16 / **1.24**	1.13 / **1.19**
1000	3.85 / **6.66**	3.00 / **4.62**	2.61 / **3.80**	2.38 / **3.34**	2.22 / **3.04**	2.10 / **2.82**	2.02 / **2.66**	1.95 / **2.53**	1.89 / **2.43**	1.84 / **2.34**	1.80 / **2.26**	1.76 / **2.20**	1.70 / **2.09**	1.65 / **2.01**	1.58 / **1.89**	1.53 / **1.81**	1.47 / **1.71**	1.41 / **1.61**	1.36 / **1.54**	1.30 / **1.44**	1.26 / **1.38**	1.19 / **1.28**	1.13 / **1.19**	1.08 / **1.11**
∞	3.84 / **6.63**	2.99 / **4.60**	2.60 / **3.78**	2.37 / **3.32**	2.21 / **3.02**	2.09 / **2.80**	2.01 / **2.64**	1.94 / **2.51**	1.88 / **2.41**	1.83 / **2.32**	1.79 / **2.24**	1.75 / **2.18**	1.69 / **2.07**	1.64 / **1.99**	1.57 / **1.87**	1.52 / **1.79**	1.46 / **1.69**	1.40 / **1.59**	1.35 / **1.52**	1.28 / **1.41**	1.24 / **1.36**	1.17 / **1.25**	1.11 / **1.15**	1.00 / **1.00**

Degrees of freedom (for the denominator of the F ratio)

Note: To be statistically significant the F obtained from the data must be equal to or greater than the value shown in the table.

Source: From Statistical Methods, by G. W. Snedecor and W. W. Cochran, (7th ed.). Copyright © 1980 Iowa State University Press. Reprinted with permission.

Appendix D

CRITICAL VALUES OF THE STUDENTIZED RANGE STATISTIC (FOR TUKEY HSD TESTS)

CRITICAL VALUES OF THE STUDENTIZED RANGE STATISTIC (FOR TUKEY HSD TESTS)

$\alpha = .05$

| df error | \multicolumn{14}{c}{Number of levels of the independent variable} | | | | | | | | | | | | | |
	2	3	4	5	6	7	8	9	10	11	12	13	14	15
1	17.97	26.98	32.82	37.07	40.41	43.12	45.40	47.36	49.07	50.59	51.96	53.20	54.33	55.36
2	6.08	8.33	9.80	10.88	11.74	12.44	13.03	13.54	13.99	14.39	14.75	15.08	15.38	15.65
3	4.50	5.91	6.82	7.50	8.04	8.48	8.85	9.18	9.46	9.72	9.95	10.15	10.35	10.53
4	3.93	5.04	5.76	6.29	6.71	7.05	7.35	7.60	7.83	8.03	8.21	8.37	8.52	8.66
5	3.64	4.60	5.22	5.67	6.03	6.33	6.58	6.80	7.00	7.17	7.32	7.47	7.60	7.72
6	3.46	4.34	4.90	5.31	5.63	5.90	6.12	6.32	6.49	6.65	6.79	6.92	7.03	7.14
7	3.34	4.16	4.68	5.06	5.36	5.61	5.82	6.00	6.16	6.30	6.43	6.55	6.66	6.76
8	3.26	4.04	4.53	4.89	5.17	5.40	5.60	5.77	5.92	6.05	6.18	6.29	6.39	6.48
9	3.20	3.95	4.42	4.76	5.02	5.24	5.43	5.60	5.74	5.87	5.98	6.09	6.19	6.28
10	3.15	3.88	4.33	4.65	4.91	5.12	5.30	5.46	5.60	5.72	5.83	5.94	6.03	6.11
11	3.11	3.82	4.26	4.57	4.82	5.03	5.20	5.35	5.49	5.60	5.71	5.81	5.90	5.98
12	3.08	3.77	4.20	4.51	4.75	4.95	5.12	5.26	5.40	5.51	5.62	5.71	5.79	5.88
13	3.06	3.74	4.15	4.45	4.69	4.88	5.05	5.19	5.32	5.43	5.53	5.63	5.71	5.79
14	3.03	3.70	4.11	4.41	4.64	4.83	4.99	5.13	5.25	5.36	5.46	5.55	5.64	5.71
15	3.01	3.67	4.08	4.37	4.60	4.78	4.94	5.08	5.20	5.31	5.40	5.49	5.57	5.65
16	3.00	3.65	4.05	4.33	4.56	4.74	4.90	5.03	5.15	5.26	5.35	5.44	5.52	5.59
17	2.98	3.63	4.02	4.30	4.52	4.70	4.86	4.99	5.11	5.21	5.31	5.39	5.47	5.54
18	2.97	3.61	4.00	4.28	4.50	4.67	4.82	4.96	5.07	5.17	5.27	5.35	5.43	5.50
19	2.96	3.59	3.98	4.25	4.47	4.64	4.79	4.92	5.04	5.14	5.23	5.32	5.39	5.46
20	2.95	3.58	3.96	4.23	4.44	4.62	4.77	4.90	5.01	5.11	5.20	5.28	5.36	5.43
24	2.92	3.53	3.90	4.17	4.37	4.54	4.68	4.81	4.92	5.01	5.10	5.18	5.25	5.32
30	2.89	3.49	3.84	4.10	4.30	4.46	4.60	4.72	4.82	4.92	5.00	5.08	5.15	5.21
40	2.86	3.44	3.79	4.04	4.23	4.39	4.52	4.64	4.74	4.82	4.90	4.98	5.04	5.11
60	2.83	3.40	3.74	3.98	4.16	4.31	4.44	4.55	4.65	4.73	4.81	4.88	4.94	5.00
120	2.80	3.36	3.69	3.92	4.10	4.24	4.36	4.47	4.56	4.64	4.71	4.78	4.84	4.90
∞	2.77	3.31	3.63	3.86	4.03	4.17	4.29	4.39	4.47	4.55	4.62	4.68	4.74	4.80

$\alpha = .01$

Number of levels of the independent variable

df error	2	3	4	5	6	7	8	9	10	11	12	13	14	15
1	90.03	135.00	164.30	185.60	202.20	215.80	227.20	237.00	245.60	253.20	260.00	266.20	271.80	277.00
2	14.04	19.02	22.29	24.72	26.63	28.20	29.53	30.68	31.69	32.59	33.40	34.13	34.81	35.43
3	8.26	10.62	12.17	13.33	14.24	15.00	15.64	16.20	16.69	17.13	17.53	17.89	18.22	18.52
4	6.51	8.12	9.17	9.96	10.58	11.10	11.55	11.93	12.27	12.57	12.84	13.09	13.32	13.53
5	5.70	6.98	7.80	8.42	8.91	9.32	9.67	9.97	10.24	10.48	10.70	10.89	11.08	11.24
6	5.24	6.33	7.03	7.56	7.97	8.32	8.62	8.87	9.10	9.30	9.48	9.65	9.81	9.95
7	4.95	5.92	6.54	7.00	7.37	7.68	7.94	8.17	8.37	8.55	8.71	8.86	9.00	9.12
8	4.75	5.64	6.20	6.62	6.96	7.24	7.47	7.68	7.86	8.03	8.18	8.31	8.44	8.55
9	4.60	5.43	5.96	6.35	6.66	6.92	7.13	7.32	7.50	7.65	7.78	7.91	8.02	8.13
10	4.48	5.27	5.77	6.14	6.43	6.67	6.88	7.06	7.21	7.36	7.48	7.60	7.71	7.81
11	4.39	5.15	5.62	5.97	6.25	6.48	6.67	6.84	6.99	7.13	7.25	7.36	7.46	7.56
12	4.32	5.05	5.50	5.84	6.10	6.32	6.51	6.67	6.81	6.94	7.06	7.17	7.26	7.36
13	4.26	4.96	5.40	5.73	5.98	6.19	6.37	6.53	6.67	6.79	6.90	7.01	7.10	7.19
14	4.21	4.90	5.32	5.63	5.88	6.08	6.26	6.41	6.54	6.66	6.77	6.87	6.96	7.05
15	4.17	4.84	5.25	5.56	5.80	5.99	6.16	6.31	6.44	6.56	6.66	6.76	6.84	6.93
16	4.13	4.79	5.19	5.49	5.72	5.92	6.08	6.22	6.35	6.46	6.56	6.66	6.74	6.82
17	4.10	4.74	5.14	5.43	5.66	5.85	6.01	6.15	6.27	6.38	6.48	6.57	6.66	6.73
18	4.07	4.70	5.09	5.38	5.60	5.79	5.94	6.08	6.20	6.31	6.41	6.50	6.58	6.66
19	4.05	4.67	5.05	5.33	5.55	5.74	5.89	6.02	6.14	6.25	6.34	6.43	6.51	6.58
20	4.02	4.64	5.02	5.29	5.51	5.69	5.84	5.97	6.09	6.19	6.28	6.37	6.45	6.52
24	3.96	4.55	4.91	5.17	5.37	5.54	5.69	5.81	5.92	6.02	6.11	6.19	6.26	6.33
30	3.89	4.46	4.80	5.05	5.24	5.40	5.54	5.65	5.76	5.85	5.93	6.01	6.08	6.14
40	3.82	4.37	4.70	4.93	5.11	5.26	5.39	5.50	5.60	5.69	5.76	5.84	5.90	5.96
60	3.76	4.28	4.60	4.82	4.99	5.13	5.25	5.36	5.45	5.53	5.60	5.67	5.73	5.78
120	3.70	4.20	4.50	4.71	4.87	5.01	5.12	5.21	5.30	5.38	5.44	5.51	5.56	5.61
∞	3.64	4.12	4.40	4.60	4.76	4.88	4.99	5.08	5.16	5.23	5.29	5.35	5.40	5.45

Source: Harter, M. L. (1960). Tables of range and studentized range. *Annals of Mathematical Statistics, 31,* 1122–1147. Reprinted with permission.

Appendix E

CRITICAL VALUES OF THE χ^2 DISTRIBUTIONS

	α LEVELS				
df	.10	.05	.02	.01	.001
1	2.71	3.84	5.41	6.64	10.83
2	4.60	5.99	7.82	9.21	13.82
3	6.25	7.82	9.84	11.34	16.27
4	7.78	9.49	11.67	13.28	18.46
5	9.24	11.07	13.39	15.09	20.52
6	10.64	12.59	15.03	16.81	22.46
7	12.02	14.07	16.62	18.48	24.32
8	13.36	15.51	18.17	20.09	26.12
9	14.68	16.92	19.68	21.67	27.88
10	15.99	18.31	21.16	23.21	29.59
11	17.28	19.68	22.62	24.72	31.26
12	18.55	21.03	24.05	26.22	32.91
13	19.81	22.36	25.47	27.69	34.53
14	21.06	23.68	26.87	29.14	36.12
15	22.31	25.00	28.26	30.58	37.70
16	23.54	26.30	29.63	32.00	39.25
17	24.77	27.59	31.00	33.41	40.79
18	25.99	28.87	32.35	34.80	42.31
19	27.20	30.14	33.69	36.19	43.82
20	28.41	31.41	35.02	37.57	45.32
21	29.62	32.67	36.34	38.93	46.80
22	30.81	33.92	37.66	40.29	48.27
23	32.01	35.17	38.97	41.64	49.73
24	33.20	36.42	40.27	42.98	51.18
25	34.38	37.65	41.57	44.31	52.62
26	35.56	38.88	42.86	45.64	54.05
27	36.74	40.11	44.14	46.96	55.48
28	37.92	41.34	45.42	48.28	56.89
29	39.09	42.56	46.69	49.59	58.30
30	40.26	43.77	47.96	50.89	59.70

Note: To be significant, the χ^2 obtained from the data must be equal to or larger than the value shown in the table

Source: Fisher, R. A., & Yates, F. (1963). *Statistical Tables for Biological, Agricultural, and Medical Research* (6th ed.). Boston, MA: Addison-Wesley. Table IV. Reprinted with permission of Addison-Wesley, Longman, and Pearson Education.

Bibliography

Aiken, L. S., & West, S. G. (1991). *Multiple Regression: Testing and Interpreting Interactions.* Newbury Park, CA: Sage.

American Chemical Society. (2002, August 16). Flawed Sampling, Not Just Pollution, May Be Responsible For Beach Closings. *ScienceDaily.* Retrieved December 2, 2015 from www.sciencedaily.com/releases/2002/08/020816072327.htm

Berry, W. D., & Feldman, S. (1985). *Multiple Regression in Practice.* Beverly Hills, CA: Sage.

Burger, J. (1987). Increased performance with increased personal control: A self-presentation interpretation. *Journal of Experimental Social Psychology*, 23, 350–360.

Cohen, J., & Cohen, P. (1975). *Applied Multiple Regression/Correlation Analysis for the Behavioral Sciences.* Hillsdale, NJ: Lawrence Erlbaum.

Cohen, J. (1988). *Statistical Power Analysis for the Behavioral Sciences* (2nd ed.). Hillsdale, NJ: Lawrence Erlbaum.

Cumming, G., & Finch, S. (2001). A primer on the understanding, use, and calculation of confidence intervals that are based on central and noncentral distributions. *Educational and Psychological Measurement*, 61, 633–649.

Doshi, V. (2015, October). Why doctors still misunderstand heart disease in women: Reconsidering the "typical" heart attack symptoms. *The Atlantic.* Retrieved December 2, 2015 from www.theatlantic.com/health/archive/2015/10/heart-disease-women/412495/

Eccles, J. S., Vida, M. N., & Barber, B. (2004). The relation of early adolescents' college plans and both academic ability and task value beliefs to subsequent college enrollment. *Journal of Early Adolescence*, 24, 63–77.

Elliot, A. J., & McGregor, H. A. (2001). A 2 × 2 achievement goal framework. *Journal of Personality and Social Psychology*, 80, 501–519.

Goldbach, J. T., Berger Cardoso, J., Cervantes, R. C., & Duan, L. (2015). The relation between stress and alcohol use among Hispanic adolescents. *Psychology of Addictive Behaviors*, 29, 960–968.

Glass, G. V., & Hopkins, K. D. (1996). *Statistical Methods in Education and Psychology* (3rd ed.). Harlow, UK: Pearson.

Hinkle, D. E., Wiersma, W., & Jurs, S. G. (1998). *Applied Statistics for the Behavioral Sciences* (4th ed.). Boston, MA: Houghton Mifflin Harcourt.

Howell, D. C. (2010). *Confidence intervals on effect size.* University of Vermont. Retrieved August 5, 2015 from https://www.uvm.edu/~dhowell/methods7/Supplements/Confidence%20Intervals%20on%20Effect%20Size.pdf

Iverson, G. R., & Norpoth, H. (1987). *Analysis of Variance* (2nd ed.) Newbury Park, CA: Sage.

Jaccard, J., Turrisi, R., & Wan, C. K. (1990). *Interaction Effects in Multiple Regression.* Newbury Park, CA: Sage.

Kim, J. O., & Mueller, C. W. (1978). *Factor Analysis: Statistical Methods and Practical Issues.* Newbury Park, CA: Sage.

Levitt, S. D., & Dubner, S. J. (2009). *Freakonomics: A Rogue Economist Explores the Hidden Side of Everything.* New York, NY: HarperCollins.

McDonald, R. P. (1999). *Test Theory: A Unified Treatment.* Mahwah, NJ: Lawrence Erlbaum.

Midgley, C., Kaplan, A., Middleton, M., Maehr, M. L., Urdan, T., Anderman, L. H., Anderman, E., & Roeser, R. (1998). The development and validation of scales assessing students' achievement goal orientations. *Contemporary Educational Psychology*, 23, 113–131.

Miyake, A., Kost-Smith, L. E., Finkelstein, N. D., Pollock, S. J., Cohen, G. L., & Ito, T. A. (2010). Reducing the gender achievement gap in college science: A classroom study of values affirmation. *Science*, 330, 1234–1237.

Naglieri, J. A. (1996). *The Naglieri Nonverbal Ability Test.* San Antonio, TX: Harcourt Brace.

Neuschwander, T., Macias, B., & Hargens, A. (2008, April). *Backpack straps decrease upper extremity blood flow.* Presented at the 121st Annual Meeting of the American Physiological Society, San Diego, CA.

Pedhazur, E. J. (1982). *Multiple Regression in Behavioral Research: Explanation and Prediction* (2nd ed.). New York, NY: Harcourt Brace.

Spatz, C. (2010). *Basic Statistics: Tales of Distributions* (10th ed.). Belmont, CA: Cengage Learning.

Steiger, J. H., & Fouladi, R. T. (1997). Noncentral interval estimation and the evaluation of statistical models. In L. L. Harlow, S. A. Mulaik, & J. H. Steiger (Eds). *What If There Were No Significance Tests?* Mahwah, NJ: Lawrence Erlbaum.

Walton, G. M., & Cohen, G. L. (2011). A brief social-belonging intervention improves academic and health outcomes of minority students. *Science*, 331, 1447–1451.

Wildt, A. R., & Ahtola, O. T. (1978). *Analysis of Covariance.* Beverly Hills, CA: Sage.

Zinbarg, R. E., Yovel, I., Revelle, W., & McDonald, R. P. (2006). Estimating generalizability to a latent variable common to all of a scale's indicators: A comparison of estimators for ω_h. *Applied Psychological Measurement*, 30, 121–144.

Glossary of Terms

Alpha: Shorthand for Cronbach's alpha.

Alpha level: The *a priori* probability of falsely rejecting the null hypothesis that the researcher is willing to accept. It is used, in conjunction with the p value, to determine whether a sample statistic is statistically significant.

Alternative hypothesis: The alternative to the null hypothesis. Usually, it is the hypothesis that there is some effect present in the population (e.g., two population means are not equal, two variables are correlated, a sample mean is different from a population mean, etc.).

Analysis of covariance (ANCOVA): An analysis of variance conducted with a covariate. It is an analysis conducted to test for differences between group means after partialing out the variance attributable to a covariate.

Asymptotic: When the ends, or "tails," of a distribution never intersect with the X axis; they extend indefinitely.

Bell curve: The common term for the normal distribution. It is called the bell curve because of its bell-like shape.

Between-groups: Refers to effects (e.g., variance, differences) that occur between the members of different groups in an ANOVA.

Between-groups effect: Differences in the average scores for different groups in the ANOVA model.

Between-subjects effect: Differences attributable to variance among the scores on the dependent variable for individual cases in the ANOVA model.

Biased sample: When a sample is not selected randomly, it *may* be a biased sample. A sample is biased when the members are selected in a way that systematically overrepresents some segment of the population and underrepresents other segments.

Bimodal: A distribution that has two values that have the highest frequency of scores.

Boxplot: A graphic representation of the distribution of scores on a variable that includes the range, the median, and the interquartile range.

Categorical, nominal: When variables are measured using categories, or names.

Causation: The concept that variation in one variable *causes* variation in another variable.

Cell size: The number of cases in each subgroup of the analysis.

Central limit theorem: The fact that as sample size increases, the sampling distribution of the mean becomes increasingly normal, regardless of the shape of the distribution of the population.

Chi-square: A statistic used to compare observed and expected frequencies in sample data.

Coefficient of determination: A statistic found by squaring the Pearson correlation coefficient, which reveals the percentage of variance explained in each of the two correlated variables by the other variable.

Communalities: A measure of the amount of variance in each of the observed variables in an exploratory factor analysis that is explained by the set of factors.

Confidence interval: An interval calculated using sample statistics to contain the population parameter, within a certain degree of confidence (e.g., 95 percent confidence).

Confirmatory factor analysis (CFA): A type of factor analysis in which the researcher specifies, *a priori*, how the observed variables should be grouped together into factors and then tests how well the specified model fits the observed data.

Constant: A construct that has only one value (e.g., if every member of a sample was 10 years old, the "age" construct would be a constant).

Constructs: Latent variables that are not directly measured but may be indicated by a set of observed variables.

Contingency table: A table that shows the intersection of two categorical (nominal) variables. This table produces the cells in which expected and observed frequencies can be compared.

Continuous, intervally scaled: When variables are measured using numbers along a continuum with equal distances, or values, between each number along the continuum.

Continuous variables: Variables that are measured using an interval or ratio scale.

Convenience sampling: Selecting a sample based on ease of access or availability rather than because it is random.

Correlation coefficient: A statistic that reveals the strength and direction of the relationship between two variables.

Correlational research design: A style of research used to examine the associations among variables. Variables are not manipulated by the researcher in this type of research design.

Covariance: The average of the cross products of a distribution.

Covariate(s): A variable, or group of variables, used to control, or account for, a portion of the variance in the dependent variable, thus allowing the researcher to test for group differences while controlling for the effects of the covariate.

Cronbach's alpha: A statistic that indicates the internal consistence of a set of observed variables.

Cross-loaded: Items that are loaded fairly strongly (i.e., a factor loading greater than an absolute value of .30) on more than one factor.

Cross product: The product of multiplying each individual's scores on two variables.

Curvilinear: A relationship between two variables that is positive at some values but negative at other values.

Degrees of freedom: Roughly, the minimum amount of data needed to calculate a statistic. More practically, it is a number, or numbers, used to approximate the number of observations in the dataset for the purpose of determining statistical significance.

Dependent, or paired, samples *t* test: A test of the statistical similarity between the means of two paired, or dependent, samples.

Dependent, outcome, criterion variable: Different terms for the dependent variable. This is the variable that is being predicted in a regression analysis.

Dependent variable: A variable for which the values may depend on, or differ by, the value of the independent variable. (For example, height depends, in part, on gender.) When the dependent variable is statistically related to the independent variable, the value of the dependent variable "depends" on, or is predicted by, the value of the independent variable.

Descriptive statistics: Statistics that describe the characteristics of a given sample or population. These statistics are only meant to describe the characteristics of those from whom data were collected.

Dichotomous: Divided into two categories.

Dichotomous variable: A variable that has only two discrete values (e.g., a pregnancy variable can have a value of 0 for "not pregnant" and 1 for "pregnant.")

Direction: A characteristic of a correlation that describes whether two variables are positively or negatively related to each other.

Dispersion: The spread of the scores in a distribution.

Distribution: A collection, or group, of scores from a sample on a single variable that indicates how frequently each value occurs. Often, but not always, these scores are arranged in order from smallest to largest.

Effect size: A measure of the size of the effect observed in some statistic. It is a way of determining the practical significance of a statistic by reducing the impact of sample size.

Eigenvalue: A measure of the strength of a factor produced in an exploratory factor analysis. It is one measure of the percentage of variance in all of the observed variables in an EFA that is explained by a particular factor.

Error: Amount of difference between the predicted value and the observed value of the dependent variable. It is also the amount of unexplained variance in the dependent variable.

Error (a.k.a. random sampling error): Variation among individual scores in a distribution or among statistics derived from samples that is due solely to random sampling.

Eta squared: The statistic that reveals the percentage of variance in the dependent variable that is explained by an independent variable; it is the most common measure of effect size.

Expected frequencies: The number of cases that one would expect to appear in the cell, row totals, or column totals based on probability alone.

Expected value of the mean: One would expect to get the value of the mean from a random sample selected from a population with a known mean. For example, if one knows the population has a mean of 5 on some variable, one would expect a random sample selected from the population to also have a mean of 5.

Experimental research design: A type of research in which the experimenter, or researcher, manipulates certain aspects of the research. These usually include manipulation of the independent variable and assignment of cases to groups.

Explained variance: The percentage of variance in one variable that we can account for, or understand, by knowing the value of the second variable in the correlation.

Exploratory factor analysis (EFA): A method of analyzing a set of observed variables to determine which variables are most strongly associated with each other and perhaps indicative of an underlying latent construct.

Extraction: A procedure in exploratory factor analysis whereby factors are produced, or extracted, from a set of observed variables.

F value: The statistic used to indicate the average amount of difference between group means relative to the average amount of variance within each group.

Factor analysis: A statistical procedure used to organize and group a set of observed variables.

Factor loading: A statistic that indicates how strongly a particular observed variable is associated with a particular factor.

Factor rotation: The part of the exploratory factor analysis procedure in which factors are formed and separated from each other.

Factors: The combinations of observed variables that are produced in a factor analysis.

Factorial ANOVA: An analysis of variance with at least two categorical independent variables.

Fit statistics: The statistics produced in any structural equation modeling analysis, including confirmatory factor analysis, that indicate how well the specified model fits with the observed data.

Frequency: How often a score occurs in a distribution.

Generalize (or Generalizability): The ability to use the results of data collected from a sample to reach conclusions about the characteristics of the population, or any other cases not included in the sample.

Grand mean: The statistical average for all of the cases in all of the groups on the dependent variable.

Graph: A pictorial or visual representation of data.

Group variable(s): Categorical independent variable(s) in the ANOVA model.

Homogeneity of variance: An assumption of all ANOVA models that there are not statistically significant differences in the within-group variances on the dependent variable between the groups being compared.

Independent samples *t* test: A test of the statistical similarity between the means of two independent samples on a single variable.

Independent, predictor variable: Different terms for the independent variable.

Independent variable: A variable that may predict or produce variation in the dependent variable. The independent variable may be nominal or continuous and is sometimes manipulated by the researcher (e.g., when the researcher assigns participants to an experimental or control group, thereby creating a two-category independent variable).

Indicated: The representation of a latent, unobserved variable by one or more observed variables, as in "This survey item was an indicator for the latent variable of work satisfaction."

Inferential statistics: Statistics generated from sample data that are used to make inferences about the characteristics of the population the sample is alleged to represent.

Interaction (effect): When the relationship between the dependent variable and one independent variable is moderated by a second independent variable. In other words, when the effect of one independent variable on the dependent variable differs at various levels of a second independent variable.

Intercept: The point at which the regression line intersects the Y axis. Also the value of Y when $X = 0$.

Interquartile range (IQR): The difference between the 75th percentile and 25th percentile scores in a distribution.

Interval or Ratio variable: Variables measured with numerical values with equal distance, or space, between each number (e.g., 2 is twice as much as 1, 4 is twice as much as 2, the distance between 1 and 2 is the same as the distance between 2 and 3).

Item–total correlation: How strongly, and in what direction, individual items in a construct are correlated with the full set of items in the construct. It is used in the calculation of the Cronbach's alpha.

Kruskal–Wallis: A nonparametric statistic, using ranked data, that is roughly analogous to a one-way ANOVA.

Kurtosis: The shape of a distribution of scores in terms of its flatness or peakedness.

Latent variable: An unobserved variable that is represented by a set of observed (i.e., measured) variables.

Leptokurtic: A term regarding the shape of a distribution. A leptokurtic distribution is one with a higher peak and thinner tails.

Main effects: These are the effects for each independent variable on the dependent variable. In other words, differences between the group means for *each* independent variable on the dependent variable.

Mann–Whitney U: A nonparametric statistic, using ranked data, that is roughly analogous to an independent samples t test.

Matched, paired, dependent samples: When each score of one sample is matched to one score from a second sample. Or, in the case of a single sample measured at two times, when each score at Time 1 is matched with the score for the same individual at Time 2.

Matched, paired, dependent samples t test: Test comparing the means of paired, matched, or dependent samples on a single variable.

Maximum likelihood: A method of extraction used in exploratory factor analysis. In this method, unit covariances are used on the diagonal of the matrix that is being analyzed in the factor analysis. This is the preferred method of factor extraction when one cannot assume that each observed variable in the analysis contributes equally to the shared variance among the set of items.

Mean: The mathematical average of a distribution of sample or population data.

Mean square between: The average squared deviation between the group means and the grand mean.

Mean square error: The average squared deviation between each individual and their respective group means.

Mean square within: The average squared deviation between each group mean and the individual scores within each group.

Mean square for the differences between the trials: The average squared deviation between the participants' average across all trials and their scores on each trial.

Mean square for the subject by trial interaction: The average squared deviation between each individual's change in scores across trials and the average change in scores across trials.

Median: The score in a distribution that marks the 50th percentile. It is the score at which 50 percent of the distribution falls below and 50 percent falls above.

Median split: Dividing a distribution of scores into two equal groups by using the median score as the divider. Those scores above the median are the "high" group, whereas those below the median are the "low" group.

Mode: The score in the distribution that occurs most frequently.

Moderator: When the relationship between the dependent variable and one independent variable differs according to the level of a second independent variable, the second independent variable acts as a moderator variable. It is a variable that moderates, or influences, the relationship between a dependent variable and an independent variable.

Mu: Population mean.

Multicollinearity: The degree of overlap among predictor variables in a multiple regression. High multicollinearity among predictor variables can cause difficulties in finding unique relations among predictors and the dependent variable.

Multimodal: When a distribution of scores has two or more values that have the highest frequency of scores.

Multiple correlation coefficient: A statistic measuring the strength of the association between multiple independent variables, as a group, and the dependent variable.

Multiple regression: A regression model with more than one independent, or predictor, variable.

Negative correlation: A descriptive feature of a correlation indicating that as scores on one of the correlated variables increase, scores on the other variable decrease, and vice versa.

Negative skew: In a skewed distribution, when most of the scores are clustered at the higher end of the distribution with a few scores creating a tail at the lower end of the distribution.

Negatively skewed: When a tail of a distribution of scores extends toward the lower end of the distribution.

Nominally scaled variable: A variable in which the numerical values assigned to each category are simply labels rather than meaningful numbers.

Nonparametric statistics: A group of statistics that are not tied to assumptions common to parametric statistics, including normally distributed data and homogeneity of variance.

Normal distribution: A bell-shaped distribution of scores that has the mean, median, and mode in the middle of the distribution and is symmetrical and asymptotic.

Null hypothesis: The hypothesis that there is no effect in the population (e.g., that two population means are not different from each other, that two variables are not correlated in the population).

Oblique rotation: The name in SPSS of one method of rotating factors in a factor analysis that does not try to maximize the distinction between the factors (i.e., oblique rotation). It is the appropriate method of factor rotation when the factors are assumed to be correlated with each other.

Observed frequencies: The actual, or observed, number of cases in the cells, rows, or columns of a contingency table.

Observed value: The actual, measured value of the *Y* variable at a given value of *X*.

Observed variable: A variable that is directly measured in some way (i.e., with a survey, an observation, a scale, a test, etc.).

One-tailed: A test of statistical significance that is conducted just for one tail of the distribution (e.g., that the sample mean will be *larger* than the population mean).

One-way ANOVA: Analysis of variance conducted to test whether two or more group means differ significantly on a single dependent variable.

Ordinal variable: Variables measured with numerical values where the numbers are meaningful (e.g., 2 is larger than 1) but the distance between the numbers is not constant.

Ordinary least squares regression (OLS): A common form of regression that uses the smallest sum of squared deviations to generate the regression line.

Outliers: Extreme scores that are more than two standard deviations above or below the mean. (See Chapter 3 for an explanation of standard deviations.)

Overpredicted: Observed values of Y at given values of X that are *below* the predicted values of Y (i.e., the values predicted by the regression equation).

p **value:** The probability of obtaining a statistic of a given size from a sample of a given size by chance, or due to random error.

Parameter: A value, or values, derived from the data collected from a population, or the value inferred to the population from a sample statistic.

Partial and controlled effects: When the shared, or explained variance between a dependent variable and an independent variable (or a covariate) is held constant, thereby allowing the researcher to examine group differences *net of* the controlled effects.

Pearson product-moment correlation coefficient: A statistic indicating the strength and direction of the relation between two continuous variables.

Percentile scores: Scores that indicate the point in a distribution below which a particular percentage of the scores in the distribution falls. For example, the score that marks the 35th percentile in a distribution indicates that 35 percent of the scores in that distribution fall below that score and 65 percent fall above it.

Perfect negative correlation: A correlation coefficient of $r = -1.0$. Occurs when the increasing scores of a given size on one of the variables in a correlation are associated with the decreasing scores of a related size on the second variable in the correlation (e.g., for each 1-unit increase in the score on variable X there is a corresponding 2-unit decrease in the scores on variable Y).

Perfect positive correlation: A correlation coefficient of $r = +1.0$. Occurs when the increasing scores of a given size on one of the variables in a correlation are associated with increasing scores of a related size on the second variable in the correlation (e.g., for each 1-unit increase in the score on variable X there is a corresponding 2-unit increase in the scores on variable Y).

Phi coefficient: The coefficient describing the correlation between two dichotomous variables.

Platykurtic: A term regarding the shape of a distribution. A platykurtic distribution is one with a lower peak and thicker tails.

Point-biserial coefficient: The coefficient describing the relationship between one interval or ratio scaled (i.e., continuous) variable and one dichotomous variable.

Population: The group from which data are collected or a sample is selected. The population encompasses the entire group for which the data are alleged to apply.

Positive correlation: A characteristic of a correlation, when the scores on the two correlated variables move in the same direction, in general. As the scores on one variable rise, scores on the other variable rise, and vice versa.

Positive skew: In a skewed distribution, when most of the scores are clustered at the lower end of the distribution with a few scores creating a tail at the higher end of the distribution.

Positively skewed: When a tail of a distribution of scores extends toward the upper end of the distribution.

Post-hoc tests: Statistical tests conducted after obtaining the overall F value from the ANOVA to examine whether each group mean differs significantly from each other group mean.

Practical significance: A judgment about whether a statistic is relevant, or of any importance, in the real world.

Prediction: The ability, allowed by correlation statistics, to make predictions about the scores on one variable based on the scores from a second variable.

Predicted values: Estimates of the value of Y at given values of X that are generated by the regression equation.

Predictor (i.e., independent) variable: This is the variable, or set of variables, that are used to predict and explain variance in the dependent variable in a regression analysis.

Principal components analysis (PCA): A common method of extracting factors in an exploratory factor analysis. In this method, unit correlation coefficients (i.e., values of 1.0) are used on the diagonal of the matrix that is being analyzed in the factor analysis. This is the preferred method of factor extraction when one assumes that each observed variable in the analysis contributes equally to the shared variance among the set of items.

Probability: The likelihood of obtaining a statistic by chance (i.e., random sampling error).

Qualitative (or categorical) variable: A variable that has discrete categories. If the categories are given numerical values, the values have meaning as nominal references but not as numerical values (e.g., in 1 = "male" and 2 = "female," 1 is not more or less than 2).

Quantitative (or continuous) variable: A variable that has assigned values and the values are ordered and meaningful, such that 1 is less than 2, 2 is less than 3, and so on.

Quasi-experimental research design: A type of research in which the experimenter, or researcher, manipulates certain aspects of the research, such as the independent variable, but conducts the research within naturally occurring settings.

Random assignment: Assignment of members of a sample to different groups (e.g., experimental and control) randomly, or without considering any sample members' characteristics.

Random chance: The probability of a statistical event occurring due simply to random variations in the characteristics of samples of a given size selected randomly from a population.

Random error: Refers to differences between individual scores and sample means that are presumed to occur simply because of the random effects inherent in selecting cases for the sample. (Note that random error, more broadly, refers to differences between sample data or statistics and population data or parameters caused by random selection procedures.)

Random sample (or Random sampling): Selecting cases from a population in a manner that ensures each member of the population has an equal chance of being selected into the sample.

Random sampling error: The error, or variation, associated with randomly selecting samples of a given size from a population.

Randomized controlled trial or randomized controlled study (RCT or RCS): A research design in which study participants are randomly assigned to groups that either receive some sort of treatment or do not.

Range: The difference between the largest score and the smallest score of a distribution.

Raw scores: These are the individual observed scores on measured variables.

Regression coefficient: A measure of the relationship between each predictor variable and the dependent variable. In simple linear regression, this is also the slope of the regression line. In multiple regression, the various regression coefficients combine to create the slope of the regression line.

Regression equation: The components, including the regression coefficients, intercept, error term, and X and Y values that are used to generate predicted values for Y and the regression line.

Regression line: The line that can be drawn through a scatterplot of the data that best "fits" the data (i.e., minimizes the squared deviations between observed values and the regression line).

Reliability: In the context of a Cronbach's alpha analysis, it refers to the internal consistency of a set of items.

Reliability analysis: A statistical analysis that reveals how strongly a group of items are related to each other.

Repeated-measures analysis of variance (ANOVA): A statistical technique used to examine whether the average scores on a dependent variable change over time or trials (i.e., when measured repeatedly).

Representative sampling: A method of selecting a sample in which members are purposely selected to create a sample that represents the population on some characteristic(s) of interest (e.g., when a sample is selected to have the same percentages of various ethnic groups as the larger population).

Residuals: Errors in prediction. The difference between observed and predicted values of *Y*.

Rotated factor matrix: A display of the factor loadings for each item on each factor after the factors have been rotated.

Sample: An individual or group, selected from a larger population, from whom or which data are collected.

Sampling distribution: A theoretical distribution of any statistic that one would get by repeatedly drawing random samples of a given size from the population and calculating the statistic of interest for each sample.

Sampling distribution of the differences between the means: The distribution of scores that would be generated if one were to repeatedly draw two random samples of a given size from two populations and calculate the difference between the sample means.

Sampling distribution of the mean: The distribution of scores that would be generated if one were to repeatedly draw random samples of a given size from a population and calculate the mean for each sample drawn.

Scale: A set of observed variables that has been combined for use as a single variable.

Scattergram or Scatterplot: A graphical depiction of each member of a distribution's score on two variables simultaneously.

Shared variance: The concept of two variables overlapping such that some of the variance in each variable is shared. The stronger the correlation between the two variables, the greater the amount of shared variance between them.

Significant: Shortened form of the expression "statistically significant."

Simple effects: The differences between the means of each subgroup in a factorial ANOVA. (A subgroup involves the division of an independent variable into smaller groups. For example, if ethnicity is one independent variable, e.g., African-American, Asian-American, and Hispanic-Latino, and gender is another variable, then each ethnic group has two subgroups, e.g., African-American females and African-American males.)

Simple linear regression: The regression model employed when there is a single dependent and a single independent variable.

Skew: When a distribution of scores has a high number of scores clustered at one end of the distribution with relatively few scores spread out toward the other end of the distribution, forming a tail.

Slope: The average amount of change in the *Y* variable for each one unit of change in the *X* variable.

Spearman rho coefficient: The correlation coefficient used to measure the association between two variables measured on an ordinal scale (e.g., ranked data).

Spurious correlation: A correlation between two variables that is coincidental or caused by some third variable, not the result of any causal association between the two correlated variables.

Squared deviation: The difference between an individual score in a distribution and the mean for the distribution, squared.

Standard error: The standard deviation of the sampling distribution.

Standard error of the difference between the means: A statistic indicating the standard deviation of the sampling distribution of the difference between the means.

Standard score: A raw score that has been converted to a z score by subtracting it from the mean and dividing by the standard deviation of the distribution. It is an individual score expressed as a deviation from the mean in standard deviation units.

Standardization: The process of converting a raw score into a standard score.

Standardized regression coefficient (i.e., "beta"): The regression coefficient converted into standardized values.

Statistic: A characteristic, or value, derived from sample data.

Statistical significance: When the probability of obtaining a statistic of a given size due strictly to random sampling error, or chance, is less than the selected alpha level, the result is said to be statistically significant. It also represents a rejection of the null hypothesis.

Statistically significant: A term indicating that a phenomenon observed in a sample (or samples) is very unlikely to have occurred by chance (i.e., random sampling error) alone. Therefore, the result found in the sample (or samples) has implications for the population (e.g., that the difference between a sample mean and a population mean is *statistically significant* or that a relationship observed between two variables in a sample is strong enough, relative to the standard error, to indicate a relationship between the two variables in the population from which the sample was selected).

Strength, magnitude: A characteristic of the correlation with a focus on how strongly two variables are related.

Strongly correlated: Mathematically related to each other strongly.

Structural equation modeling: A method of statistical analysis in which the researcher specifies *a priori* how a set of variables should be organized and then tests to see how well this specified model fits with the observed data.

Studentized range statistic: Distributions used to determine the statistical significance of post-hoc tests.

Sum of squared deviations, sum of squares: The sum of each squared deviation for all of the cases in the sample.

Sum of squares between: Sum of the squared deviations between the group means and the grand mean.

Sum of squares error: Sum of the squared deviations between individual scores and group means on the dependent variable.

Sum of squares total: Sum of the squared deviations between individual scores and the grand mean on the dependent variable. This is also the sum of the SS_b and the SS_e.

Symmetrical: When a distribution has the same shape on either side of the median.

Theoretical distribution: A distribution based on statistical probabilities rather than empirical data.

Time, trial: Each time for which data are collected on the dependent variable.

Truncated range: When the responses on a variable are clustered near the top or the bottom of the possible range of scores, thereby limiting the range of scores and possibly limiting the strength of the correlation.

Tukey HSD: Name of a common post-hoc test.

Two-tailed: A test of statistical significance that is conducted for both tails of the distribution (e.g., the sample mean will be *different from* the population mean).

Type I error: Rejecting the null hypothesis when in fact the null hypothesis is true.

Type II error: Retaining (i.e., failing to reject) the null hypothesis when in fact it is false.

Underpredicted: Observed values of Y at given values of X that are above the predicted values of Y (i.e., the values predicted by the regression equation).

Unimodal: A distribution that has a single mode.

Unique variance: The proportion of variance in the dependent variable explained by an independent variable when controlling for all other independent variables in the model.

Unobserved variable: A variable that is inferred, or indicated, by one or more measured, or observed, variables, but that is never directly measured itself.

Variable: Any construct with more than one value that is examined in research.

Variance: The sum of the squared deviations divided by the number of cases in the population, or by the number of cases minus one in the sample.

Varimax: The name of one method in SPSS of rotating the factors such that the factors are as distinct from each other (i.e., orthogonal) as possible.

Wilcoxon signed-rank: A nonparametric test, using ranked data, that is roughly analogous to a paired, or dependent samples, *t* test.

Within-group: Refers to effects (e.g., variance, differences) that occur between the members of the same groups in an ANOVA.

Within-subject variance: Differences within each individual case on scores on the dependent variable across trials.

Within-subjects design: A repeated-measures ANOVA design in which intra-individual changes across trials are tested. This technique allows the researcher to test whether, on average, individuals score differently at one time than another.

X-bar: Sample mean.

z score: Another term for a standard score.

Glossary of Symbols

Σ	The sum of; to sum.
X	An individual, or raw, score in a distribution.
ΣX	The sum of X; adding up all of the scores in a distribution.
$\bar{X}$	The mean of a sample.
μ	The mean of a population.
n	The number of cases, or scores, in a sample.
N	The number of cases, or scores, in a population.
P_{50}, Mdn	The median.
s^2	The sample variance.
s	The sample standard deviation.
σ^2	The population variance.
σ	The population standard deviation.
SS	The sum of squares, or sum of squared deviations.
z	A standard score.
$s_{\bar{x}}$	The standard error of the mean estimated from the sample standard deviation.
$\sigma_{\bar{x}}$	The standard error of the mean when the population standard deviation is known.
p	p value, or probability.
α	Alpha level.
d	Effect size.
S	The standard deviation used in the effect size formula.
∞	Infinity.
H_0	The null hypothesis.
H_A or H_1	The alternative hypothesis.
r	The sample Pearson correlation coefficient.
ρ	Rho, the population correlation coefficient.
s_r	The standard error of the correlation coefficient.
r^2	The coefficient of determination.
df	Degrees of freedom.
Φ	The phi coefficient, which is the correlation between two dichotomous variables.
$s_{\bar{x}1-\bar{x}2}$	The standard error of difference between two independent sample means.
$s_{\bar{D}}$	The standard error of the difference between two dependent, matched, or paired samples.
s_D	The standard deviation of the difference between two dependent, or paired sample means.
t	The t value.
MS_w	The mean square within groups.

MS_e	The mean square error (which is the same as the mean square within groups).
MS_b	The mean square between groups.
SS_e	The sum of squares error (or within groups).
SS_b	The sum of squares between groups.
SS_T	The sum of squares total.
$\bar{X}_T$	The grand mean.
F	The F value.
K	The number of groups.
N	The number of cases in all of the groups combined.
n	The number of cases in a given group (for calculating SS_b).
n_g	The number of cases in each group (for a Tukey HSD test).
$MS_{s \times T}$	The mean square for the interaction of subject by trial.
MS_T	The mean square for the differences between the trials.
$\hat{Y}$	The predicted value of Y, the dependent variable.
Y	The observed value of Y, the dependent variable.
b	The unstandardized regression coefficient.
a	The intercept.
e	The error term.
R	The multiple correlation coefficient.
R^2	The percentage of variance explained by the regression model.
χ^2	The chi-square statistic.
O	The observed frequency.
E	The expected frequency.
R	Symbol representing the number of rows in the contingency table.
C	Symbol representing the number of columns in the contingency table.

Index